Lloyd George
and the
Challenge of Labour

BY THE SAME AUTHOR

David Lloyd George and the British Labour Movement (1976)
A. J. P. Taylor: A Complete Bibliography (1980)
A History of British Industrial Relations vols I and II (editor, 1982 and 1986)
William Barnes the Dorset Poet (editor, 1984)
Warfare, Diplomacy and Politics (editor, 1986)
Arthur Henderson (1990)

Lloyd George and the Challenge of Labour

The Post War Coalition 1918–1922

Chris Wrigley

Emeritus Professor of History, University of Nottingham and former President of the Historical Association, UK

New Edition with a new Introduction

EER
Edward Edward Root, Publishers, Brighton, 2018.

EER

Edward Everett Root, Publishers, Co. Ltd.,
30 New Road, Brighton, Sussex, BN1 1BN, England.
www.eerpublishing.com
(Details of our overseas agencies are on our website)

edwardeverettroot@yahoo.co.uk

David Lloyd George And The Challenge of Labour
C.J. Wrigley

First published in England 1990.

© C.J. Wrigley 1990; 2018.

This edition © Edward Everett Root Publishers 2018.

ISBN: 978-1-912224-28-9 Hardback
ISBN: 978-1-912224-29-6 Paperback

C.J. Wrigley has asserted his right to be identified as the author of this Work in accordance with the Copyright, Designs and Patents Act 1988 as the owner of this Work.

All rights reserved. No part of this publication may be reproduced, stored in a retrieval system or transmitted in any form or by any means, electronic, mechanical, photocopying, recording or otherwise, without the prior permission of the copyright owner.

Contents

	Acknowledgments	vii
	New Introduction to 2018 edition	ix
1	At the top of the greasy pole	1
2	The spectre haunting Europe	13
3	Unrest in the armed forces	24
4	Unrest in the police force	53
5	Holding on through the period of economic transition: From Armistice to February 1919	80
6	Holding on through the period of economic transition: appealing to public opinion February to March 1919	126
7	Adopting a tougher stance towards Labour: April to October 1919	174
8	The road to 'Black Friday', April 1921	233
9	Lloyd George and the challenges of Labour	291
	Primary sources	319
	Index	321

Acknowledgements

This book has been a part of my life for a long time, nearly as long as I have enjoyed researching into the political career of David Lloyd George. The research began in the Beaverbrook Library in 1968. Most of the research for this book which involved the former Beaverbrook collections was carried out before they were transferred to the House of Lords Record Office. I have very warm memories of working in the Beaverbrook Library, and I remain grateful to A. J. P. Taylor, Katharine Bligh and Della Hilton (who ran it in its last phase) for their help and encouragement.

Many people have kindly helped me over the years. These include Eric Hobsbawm, Michael Dockrill, Michael Fry, Peter Lowe, Philip Williamson, Kathleen Burk, Keith Hamilton, Jean Raymond, Mike Shuker and Steve Tennison. In the book's later stages I am greatly indebted to Maggie Walsh, who read and commented on the whole manuscript, Su Spencer, who typed it and Farrell Burnett of Harvester Wheatsheaf who drove me on to completion. I am also grateful to the numerous research seminars and Historical Association branches which have listened to papers on the subject of this book. My research for the book benefited from my being a Visiting Research Fellow at the Institute for Advanced Studies, Edinburgh University in the summer term of 1982 and at both the Borthwick Institute and the Institute for Social and Economic Research, York University in the summer term of 1986.

I am also indebted to the copyright holders for permission to use material in this book. I am especially grateful to A. J. P. Taylor and the First Beaverbrook Foundation, Mrs K. Idwal Jones, Mrs J. Simon, Lord Mottistone, Mrs P. Dower, the Hon. G. Samuel, Lord Gainford, Mr R. Farquhar-Oliver, the Dowager Lady Addison, Lady White, the House of Lords Record Office, the Warden and Fellows of New College, Oxford, Birmingham University Library, Newcastle University Library, the British Library, the Master, Fellows and scholars of Churchill College, Cambridge, the London School of Economics and Political Science and the Labour Party. Transcripts from Crown copyright records in the Public Record Office appear by permission of the Controller of HM Stationery Office. If I have failed to contact any copyright holders I sincerely apologise to them.

In writing such a book as this I have benefited from the work of many other writers, many of whom feature in the Notes at the back of the book. For those wishing to read more on this period, I warmly commend Kenneth Morgan's wide ranging and excellent study *Consensus and Disunity: The Lloyd George coalition government 1918–1922* (Oxford: Clarendon Press, 1979) and Maurice Cowling's *The Impact of Labour 1920–1924* (Cambridge: Cambridge University Press, 1971). I am grateful to them for permission to quote from these books. For those interested in Lloyd George the best starting place is John Grigg's shrewd and lively multi-volume biography, *Lloyd George* (London: Methuen, 1973, 1978, 1985 and 2002) and for his career after 1922 there is John Campbell's splendid *Lloyd George: The goat in the wilderness 1922–1931* (London: Cape, 1977).

I am sorry that John Angus, Diane Freeman and Viola Keat, who read my *David Lloyd George and the British Labour Movement* (Hassocks, Harvester, 1976) will not see this volume. I dedicate this book to their memory.

New Introduction to 2018 edition

Lloyd George emerged from the First World War victorious both in war and in the 1918 general election, which he called in the euphoria of victory. His coalition government won by a landslide. It proved to be too big an electoral victory for Lloyd George as the coalition Conservatives plus the independent Conservatives had a majority in the House of Commons without him or his coalition Liberals. This situation placed limitations on what policies Lloyd George could get through the House of Commons.

Lloyd George faced postwar turmoil in the UK. This was not unexpected. There was awareness of the serious social unrest that had followed the Napoleonic Wars, and the lesser economic dislocation that had followed the Crimean and the South African wars. However, in 1919 there were fears that revolution could spread in to the UK from eastern and central Europe. Lloyd George was aware of occasional major risks of disorder at home, but he was sufficiently politically astute to play up to the fears of some Conservative politicians to secure, or try to secure, their acquiescence in social reform and some moderation in the terms given to the defeated countries at the peace conferences.

He was at the peak of his career during the Paris Peace Conference which began on 18 January 1919 and resulted in the Treaty of Versailles in June 1919.[1] Even during this period backbench Conservatives threatened revolt against his leadership when he argued there should be a more generous settlement with Germany in a memorandum composed at Fontainebleau in late March 1919. He saw this challenge off.[2] After the Treaty of Versailles, signed on 28 June 1919, Lloyd George's position seemed increasingly precarious, and the surprise was that he lasted as Prime Minister until October 1922 and did not fall from office sooner.

Lloyd George had crossed his political Rubicon with his khaki election in December 1918. This ensured bad feelings on the part of Asquith's followers, especially when most lost their seats. However, it was exceedingly unlikely that a victorious David Lloyd George would leave his main wartime coalition partners for an icy reception from those he had broken with in December 1916. The December 1918 election also marked a decisive break with the Labour Party, which had been reinvigorated by its new socialist constitution, its more ambitious programme and its organisational overhaul in 1917–18. Lloyd George had been a key player in the pre-war progressive alliance of Liberals and Labour, but from the end of 1918 he headed a predominantly reactionary alliance of Coalition Conservatives and a minority of Coalition Liberals and a handful of Coalition Labour MPs. Lloyd George's hopes of fusion between Coalition Liberals and Coalition Conservatives finally died in January 1922.

The nearly four years from the Armistice to Lloyd George's departure from office on 23 October 1922 were eventful and challenging years for Lloyd George and his government. This book examines the challenge from the Labour Movement. Alongside conflict with trade unions and the Labour Party, Lloyd George's government faced crises in Ireland, India and Egypt, had to resolve peace terms with defeated nations up to the Treaty of Sevres in 1920, and needed to determine its relations with the Middle East, Bolshevik Russia, Germany as well as dealing with social reconstruction and the problem of large-scale unemployment from 1921.

Lloyd George's relationship with Labour remained very important after October 1922.[3] When Stanley Baldwin called a general election in 1923 to justify bringing in tariffs, Lloyd George reunited with H.H. Asquith and the non-coalition Liberals, becoming again Asquith's deputy leader (in name, not just in reality as he had been before the war).

Lloyd George had the energy, political imagination and overall flair that was no longer apparent in Asquith, who was 71 in late 1923, although Asquith's health did not crumble until June 1926. Such qualities were not overabundant in the Parliamentary Labour Party. MacDonald, who had charisma and skills in oratory, alienated major trade unionists such as Ernest Bevin, by his cautious policies and failure to consult the Labour Movement when Prime Minister in 1924 and in 1929–31. As a result, a few Labour politicians envisaged Lloyd George joining the Labour Party and even becoming its leader.

In 1924–9 Lloyd George Lloyd George injected fresh ideas in to the Left of British politics. As David Marquand has observed, under

Asquith 'the Liberal Party could easily be portrayed as the bankrupt survivor of a vanished epoch. Lloyd George made nonsense of this portrait.' The new Liberal policies inspired by Lloyd George 'were at least as radical as anything produced by the Labour Party.'[4]

However, many of Asquith's followers loathed Lloyd George for his actions between December 1916 and the 1923 general election, and resented his return as Deputy Leader. The differences between Asquith and much of the Liberal leadership and Lloyd George over the General Strike in May 1926 provided the occasion for Lloyd George to be dismissed from the Liberal Shadow Cabinet. In the ensuing uproar, it was claimed that Lloyd George was going to defect to the Labour Party, a claim most virulently made by W.M.R. Pringle, an avid supporter of Asquith. Lloyd George took care to emphasise that he remained a Liberal. In a speech in Manchester on 5 June 1926, Lloyd George said that although he could be 'driven out of the Shadow Cabinet', he 'would not alter his course as long as the constituency that has stuck to me for 36 years and knows me best, because I am one of them – as long as they return me to Parliament and there is breath in my body, I will be a Liberal member of the House of Commons …'[5]

With Lloyd George's public sympathy for the coal miners and hostility to the Baldwin Government's part in bringing about the General Strike Thomas Johnson, an Independent Labour Party MP and the editor of *Forward*, wrote in the issue of 29 May 1926, 'Lloyd George is apparently to be fired from the Liberal Party for siding too much with the working classes.' In contrast, Ramsay MacDonald had made public his differences with the ILP and its 'Socialism in Our Time' policy a month earlier. Emrys Hughes, the sub-editor of *Forward,* wrote in it on 17 April an article entitled, 'A Lost Leader' on MacDonald. There was also speculation on the Left that Lloyd George might join Labour and even take over as leader.

Joseph Burgess published on 2 July 1926, *Will Lloyd George Supplant Ramsay MacDonald?*[6] Burgess's book was criticised very reasonably as 'a hotch-potch', but it contained a detailed analysis of MacDonald and Snowden's pre-war desires for an understanding with the Liberals. Reviewing MacDonald's and Snowden's past and present desires to link up with the Liberals, Burgess predicted that they would seek a coalition after the next general election. Burgess, who had been a pioneer of Independent Labour Party politics and editor of *Workmen's Times*, had no time for MacDonald, who had succeeded him as ILP candidate for Leicester and won and held the seat through understandings with the Liberals. In his book, he gave the argument of an imaginary socialist about Lloyd George,

> which of us would believe one promise, even one statement of fact that, that he made? And yet – is there another man with his flair, his vitality, his imagination? Can you see him acting as our leaders acted during the strike? Give him six months to feel the pulse of the movement, and his temperament would force him to evolve a tactic for getting Socialism. He has a welcoming mind. Fancy having a leader whose mind is not hermetically sealed against new ideas![7]

Yet Lloyd George was highly unlikely to work to achieve socialism. He was, as he repeatedly said, a Liberal, not a socialist. His friend, Lord Riddell, noted in his diary in 1919 that Lloyd George had commented:

> I am convinced that the world cannot be carried on without the aid of the skilled managerial class. You must have leaders and captains of industry if you are to have any progress. You cannot have adequate production unless you invoke the aid of the clever manufacturers and businessmen working for their own profit. But you must see they do not grind the other classes under their heel.[8]

Earlier, Riddell had written, that while Lloyd George 'has a genuine desire to improve the position of the poorer classes… he cannot bring himself to attack the capitalist for whom, when all is said, he has lawyer-like respect.'[9]

It was also highly unlikely that Lloyd George could work in the Labour Party with MacDonald. Before the war they had been friends. With the war and the wartime hostility shown to MacDonald, MacDonald had come to hate Lloyd George. According to Joseph Burgess, MacDonald's response to the rumour that Lloyd George might seek to join the Labour Party had been that it was 'the Communist Party to which Lloyd George was most sympathetic in temperament.'[10]

Lloyd George was interested in forming a new Progressive Alliance in Parliament, even if an informal one. He offered Labour co-operation in the House of Commons, 'the only condition', MacDonald noted in his diary, was that 'we should take up his land scheme in the original form and not as amended by the Liberal

Conference.' This was the subject of a speech by the Liberal former MP, W.M. Pringle.[11] Lloyd George's moves in this direction seem to be more about influencing Liberal policy and electoral opportunities than linking with Labour. He wrote to Frances Stevenson of the need for 'a strenuous land campaign', adding, 'Whatever happens we must strengthen our grasp on the rural districts and the capture of a few of the towns where Liberalism is still a force.'[12] Land did not prove to be the big idea to revive the Liberal Party. Lloyd George's land campaign of 1925–29 fizzled out. His old Liberal colleague, Frank Edwards, warned him in January 1927 that in Brecon and Radnor 'there is much apathy among our farmers about it – they need to have it clearly explained to them.'[13] The new land campaign did not have the appeal of the 1912–4 campaign and it did not greatly distinguish Liberal policy on the land from that which Labour offered.[14]

After the General Strike Lloyd George had moved well away from his 1922–3 hopes of a new coalition government along the lines of 1918–22. Frances Stevenson noted in her diary on 15 May 1926,

> D's idea is to go definitely towards the *Left*, and gradually to co-ordinate and consolidate all the progressive forces in the country, against the Conservative and reactionary forces. Thus, he will get all sane Labour as well as Liberalism behind him. ... D. will not leave the Liberal Party.[15]

However, there were ideological obstacles to Lloyd George going far in this direction. The Liberal policy statement for coal mining, *Coal and Power* (1924), had been close to the Minority Report to the Sankey Commission by Sir Arthur Duckham. (See page 208 of this volume). This had been used to evade the main Sankey recommendation, and certainly did not appeal to the Miners' Federation then. It would not appeal to them in the 1920s. More generally, Lloyd George was unsympathetic to big powerful trade unions. This was a feature of many Liberals after the First World War. Michael Freeden, in his study of post First World War Liberalism, delivered the verdict that 'there was a growing preoccupation of liberals with monopolies of labour rather than capital.'[16]

Yet Lloyd George and the Liberals moved towards greater acceptance of state intervention, influenced in part by the experiences of state controls of large sectors of the wartime economy. In 1928, it was stated in the introduction to *Britain's Industrial Future,*

> We have no love for state intervention in itself ... The Theory that private competition, unregulated and unaided, will work out, with certainty, to the greatest advantage of the community is found by experience to be far from the truth. The scope of useful intervention by the whole Society, whether by constructive action of its own or by regulating or assisting private action, is seen to be much larger than was formerly supposed.[17]

Under Lloyd George's leadership the Liberals again promoted conciliation in British industrial relations. The fifth section of *Britain's Industrial Future* was on industrial relations with a version of Whitley Councils favoured as well as other joint committees in industry. Joint committees had been fostered by Liberals since the second half of the nineteenth century. They were supported by moderate trade unionists in the Labour Party, such as J.R. Clynes and Arthur Henderson. While the Liberal Industrial Inquiry did not call for the resurrection of the National Industrial Conference of 1919 (see this book, especially 130–42), it did call for 'a representative Council of Industry', made up of nine representatives each of both sides of industry plus six persons nominated by the head of a new Ministry of Industry.[18] After the General Strike, the Liberals sought to position themselves in the centre of British politics regarding industrial relations. Leading figures of other parties made similar calls. Most notably, there was Arthur Henderson who in October 1928 publicly called for the resurrection of the National Industrial Conference as a new National Industrial Council. In the Conservative Party, Arthur Steel-Maitland was eager to emphasise similarities in outlook on both sides of industry, and was favourable to some modest schemes of profit sharing and for some trade union involvement in setting workshop conditions. 'The settlement of workshop conditions,' he commented, 'is quite different from the executive management of a company.' He was also attracted to some form of Whitley Councils.[19] Steel-Maitland cautiously welcomed the Mond-Turner Talks between a group of industrialists and leaders of the TUC. He suggested a possible topic to consider was 'a permanent group which may form something like the German economic council.'[20]

Lloyd George had steadily gained respect from Labour MPs during the later 1920s, both for his stance during the General Strike and for his promotion of positive social and industrial policies in opposition. Even before the General Strike, Labour MPs had moved from howling him down, as they had after 1922, to cheering him when he got up to speak in the Commons. Frances Stevenson proudly noted in her diary, 'Now he speaks almost as Leader of the Opposition, with the Labour and Liberal benches around him, the former hanging on his words and loud in their praises.' While she was obviously a very biased commentator, she was right about the Labour MPs changed view of him in the mid to late 1920s over 1918–22, the subject of this book.[21]

The 1929 general election saw the number of Liberal MPs rise from 40 to 59, well below the 159 of 1923. Labour went from151 MPs to 288, becoming for the first time the largest party in the House of Commons. The Liberals again held the balance of power, but Lloyd George's ability to influence policy making was undercut by serious divisions in the Parliamentary Liberal Party, with Sir John Simon and his followers moving increasingly closer to the Conservative Party. Also, Lloyd George found, as the Labour Party had found in 1910–14, that holding the bance of power made the smaller party more a captive of the situation than its controller. Lloyd George no more wanted an early general election than did Ramsay MacDonald.

Lloyd George pressed hard to influence unemployment and agriculture policies, but his negotiations got nowhere. Lloyd George complained in a lengthy letter to Ramsay MacDonald of a lack of co-operation and called for a major programme of road building. He followed it up with a 160 page 'Memorandum on Liberal Proposals on Unemployment and Agriculture', which was published as *How to Tackle Unemployment* (1930).[22] Lloyd George did secure in February 1931 the Labour's support for a motion calling for a programme of national development. Otherwise, he fruitlessly sought to get the electoral system altered to some form of proportional representation through a deal with either Labour or the Conservatives.

Lloyd George was more radical than Philip Snowden, the Chancellor of the Exchequer, or MacDonald in his approach to funding measures to reduce unemployment. He urged them, 'You must make allowances for the political bias of the City. They have always been against a progressive government – always'. He recalled his budget struggles of 1909–10 and commented, 'Neither Mr. Asquith or I took any notice of them.' George Lansbury was impressed by this and earlier speeches and on 11 February 1931, Lansbury wrote to Lloyd George, 'Why don't you join the Labour Party?', adding 'Your help would be invaluable, *as one of us.*' Lloyd George replied,

> 'Coming over' is not the best way to help. It would antagonise millions of Liberals with hereditary party loyalties who otherwise would support any government from any party provided it carried through a bold programme for the reconditioning of Britain. ...
>
> Like yourself I am now merely concerned with spending the remainder of my life and strength in advancing ideas and causes which I was brought up to believe in. Despite the 'opportunism' which is one of the necessities of office and now and again deflects every man from his course, I have always sincerely striven to do my best for the class from which I sprang.[23]

Lloyd George and the Labour Government came closer in its last months. There was talk of Lloyd George and other Liberals joining it. After its fall, Lloyd George wrote to his old friend Herbert Lewis on 31 December 1931, 'When I was stricken down in the late summer we had complete control of the Parliamentary situation, and the Labour Government was getting more and more into our hands.'[24] Herbert Lewis wrote to him in early 1932 that 'the older and younger Conservatives' would rather have 'a bigger figure to pelt than Lansbury', Labour's leader in the Commons. But Lloyd George did not play a leading role in the Commons, though he remained an influential figure until 1940.

Lloyd George's career began in the era of Gladstone and shortly before the election of independent Labour MPs. He was well aware of how the SPD had displaced Liberals in Germany and was largely successful in making a radical appeal to British voters before the First World War. The war boosted the British Labour Movement and undercut the Liberal Party, with Lloyd George playing a central role in the party's division. Lloyd George became adroit in dealing with industrial disputes. At the time of the General Strike, he observed, 'The settlement of a strike is a very difficult business. I have had more experience probably than any politician in trying to accommodate industrial differences.'[25] This was true. He had also had much experience as prime minister in dealing often in a firm, or even tough manner, with organised labour, as analysed in this book.

Labour was one major theme of his career, and the rapid decline of the Liberal Party, especially from 1924, resulted in his ministerial career ending at the age of 59. This was a young age compared to Gladstone, who was only one year into his first of four premierships at that age.

Notes and references

1. For a detailed analysis of Lloyd George's foreign policy when Prime Minister, see Michael G. Fry, *And Fortune Fled: Lloyd George, the First Democratic Statesman, 1916–1922*, Bern, Peter Lang, 2011.
2. See this book, pp. 174–80. For a recent analysis, see Fry, *And Fortune Fled*, pp. 228–46.
3. The major study is by John Campbell, *Lloyd George: The Goat in the Wilderness*, Cape, 1977. See also Chris Wrigley, 'Lloyd George and the Labour Party after 1922' in J. Loades, ed., *The Life and Times of David Lloyd George*. Bangor, 1991, pp.49–69. For a good, recent biography see Travis L. Crosby, *The Unknown Lloyd George: A Statesman in Conflict*, IB Tauris, 2014.
4. David Marquand, *Ramsay MacDonald*, Cape, 1977, p. 464.
5. 'Liberal Split', *Times*, 7 June 1926.
6. It was published by Burgess and printed in Leicester. Its reviews included *Aberdeen Press and Journal*, 3 July 1926 and *Journal*, 9 July 1926.
7. Burgess, *Will Lloyd George*, p.47.
8. Riddell's diary, 20 September 1919. Lord Riddell, *Intimate Diary*, p.128.
9. Riddell's diary, 2 March 1919. Riddell Papers, British Library, Add. Ms. 629083, f.63.
10. Burgess, *Will Lloyd George*, p.44.
11. Ramsay MacDonald's diary, 14 May 1926; Ramsay MacDonald Papers, National Archives, 39/1753. Pringle, in a speech, 5 July 1926. 'Lloyd George and Labour', *Times*, 7 July 1926.
12. Lloyd George to Stevenson, 20 August 1925; printed in A.J.P. Taylor, *My Darling Pussy: The letters of Lloyd George and Frances Stevenson 1913–41*, Weidenfeld and Nicolson, 1975, p. 97.
13. Sir Francis Edwards to Lloyd George, 15 January 1927; Lloyd George Papers, G/6/11/17. Edwards had been one of the rebels who resigned the Liberal Whip over Welsh Disestablishment in 1894. Labour won the Brecon and Radnor seat in 1929.
14. Ian Packer, *Lloyd George, Liberalism and the Land: The Land Issue and Party Politics in England, 1906–1914*, Woodbridge, Boydell Press, 2001, pp.182–9.
15. A.J.P. Taylor, ed., *Lloyd George: A Diary by Frances Stevenson*, Hutchinson, 1971, p.246.
16. Michael Freeden, *Liberalism Divided*, Oxford University Press,1986, p.200.
17. *Britain's Industrial Future*, Ernest Benn, 1928, p. xix.

18. *Britain's Industrial Future*, pp. 172–5, 211–3 and 222–5. On political support for Whitleyism, see Chris Wrigley, 'Trade Unionists, Employers and the Cause of Industrial Unity and Peace 1916–21' in C. Wrigley and J. Shepherd, ed., *On The Move*, Hambledon Press, 1991, pp.155–84.
19. Henderson's speech at Todmorden, *Times*, 24 October 1928. Arthur Steel-Maitland, memorandum, 'Industrial peace after the coal dispute', sent with comments to Lord Weir, December 1926; Weir Papers, Archives of the University of Glasgow, 4/14/6–13. Steel-Maitland to Lord Robert Cecil,25 May 1927; Ceil Papers, British Library Add. Ms 51071, f. 143
20. Memorandum of discussions with Mr. Richmond and others, 25 January,1928. Steel-Maitland Papers, National Archives of Scotland, GD 193/94/2/115–7.
21. Diary entry, 1 April 1926.Taylor, ed., *Lloyd George: A Diary*, pp 244–5.
22. Lloyd George to MacDonald, 22 August 1930; National Archives, PREM 1/198 and Lloyd George Papers, G/13/2/6
23. Raymond Postgate, *The Life of George Lansbury*, Longmans, Green, 1951, pp.265–6. John Shepherd, *George Lansbury: At the Heart of Old Labour*, Oxford University Press, 2002, p.267. Peter Rowland, *Lloyd George*, Barrie and Jenkins, 1975, pp 677–8.
24. Rowland, *Lloyd George*, pp.694–5.
25. *Times*, 7 July 1926.

1
At the top of the greasy pole

Lloyd George was at the peak of his political career in 1919. His Coalition government had been returned with a massive majority in the general election of 1918 which had been called soon after the Armistice of 11 November. He himself was lauded as 'The Man Who Won The War', a title succeeding the popular press's earlier wartime one of Minister of 'What-Most-Needs-Doing'. As one of the victors he went to Paris for the peacemaking, succeeding to the role taken in 1815 by kings and aristocrats. At 56, he was still relatively young for the premiership.[1]

Like most politicians who have reached the top, Lloyd George was physically resilient. He could work long hours for long periods. Nevertheless, physically the war had been very wearing. In its later stages he had ignored medical advice to rest. This took its toll. He was unwell in February and September 1918.[2] Failure to take proper breaks from work was to cause him problems again during his post-war government. Thus, in June and August 1921, he was forced to cancel all engagements and to rest. A little earlier, Bonar Law observed, 'LG must be having just about the hardest time he has ever had' and added, 'LG with his temperament would be utterly miserable if he were to drop out of everything as I have done, but even his buoyancy will not last indefinitely under the terrific strain he is always undergoing.'[3] Generally, though, his resilience was strong.

This was not just a physical matter. Like Winston Churchill, he was fully absorbed in politics. Politics were central to his being. Lloyd George enjoyed being at the top of the greasy pole. In January 1919, he commented with satisfaction 'that the position he had reached was beyond all his youthful expectations, and youthful expectations are very wild and hopeful'.[4]

Lloyd George's position at the top was somewhat precarious, especially from 1920. He was to be a victim of the success of his 1918 election campaign. This had ended up as 'a full blooded khaki election of the 1900 type'.[5] Lloyd George had started the campaign promising to provide 'a fit country for heroes to live in' but had ended it appealing to those already clamouring for revenge on Germany. His reward was 526 supporters in the new House of Commons, including 333 Conservative and Unionists, 127 Liberals and 14 Labour and National Democratic MPs who had received the 'coupons' of endorsement from the Coalition leadership.[6] However, the combined number of Unionists (those who had received the 'coupon' and some 52 or 53 who had not) was more than a majority, without counting Lloyd George and his Coalition Liberals, in a House of Commons of 707 seats.[7]

It would be wrong to make too much of this point for the first year to eighteen months of Lloyd George's post-war government. For this period Conservative and Unionist supporters appear to have approved of the Coalition and of Lloyd George at its head. Moreover, most of the Coalition Unionist MPs remained very conscious during these months that the electorate had returned them on manifestos pledging support for this arrangement. Where there were Liberal Coalition MPs, the Conservative and Unionists had secured very clear pledges of support for the Coalition. Thus in the Colne Valley constituency in the 1918 election they issued a leaflet which included:

> The whole Unionist party believe that such a Coalition led by Mr. Lloyd George and Mr. Bonar Law should have every possible support in the new Parliament....
> Mr. F. W. Mallalieu [Liberal] is the accepted Coalition candidate for the Division, and has, during his term of office, consistently supported the Coalition Government, and pledges himself to give the same support if elected.
> Mr. Mallalieu having pledged himself to resign in case he finds himself unable to continue his adherence to the Government, we most strongly advise all Conservatives and Unionists in the Division to use every endeavour . . . to return Mr. Mallalieu at the head of the Poll.[8]

In such circumstances it would have been hard for them to have reneged quickly on the Coalition.

While rank-and-file Tory enthusiasm for the Coalition was waning from 1920, nearly all the Tory leadership supported Lloyd George and the Coalition until its fall in October 1922; and some stayed loyal to it even after that. The certainties of pre-First World War party politics had been shaken, in some cases obliterated, by the war. This was true for many Tories as well as for the Liberal Coalitionists. In these circumstances the claim of approaching new conditions pragmatically could disguise political expediency. The constraints on

Lloyd George's pragmatism during the Coalition are well illustrated in a memorandum by Arthur Balfour of a discussion he had with Bonar Law in December 1922:

> In the course of our conversation I incidentally observed that the feeling of the Conservative Party in the House of Commons and throughout the country against Lloyd George was singular in view of the fact, that so far as my knowledge went, Lloyd George had never shown the smallest party bias. Bonar Law agreed with this; and we were at one in thinking that Lloyd George's character and habit of mind made him approach any new problem in a spirit of complete detachment from traditional prejudices or principles. This made him absolutely impartial as between parties, which, for the head of a coalition government was a great advantage. He, however, added that this impartiality by no means prevented him from occasionally making suggestions which, if carried out, would have justly excited much Conservative resentment. One of these was to accept one of the proposals of the miners during the coal strike – namely the nationalisation of the mines; the other he declared to have been thrown out at a dinner party at Lloyd George's own table, where he (Bonar Law) and Carson were, if not the only, at all events the chief guests. On that occasion and to this audience Lloyd George appears to have advocated the coercion of Ulster. When Bonar Law pointed out that this would certainly break up the Unionist Party, Lloyd George appears to have replied that, on the contrary, both Austen and F. E. Smith were agreed to agree.[9]

As for Lloyd George, wartime needs had been the justification for power-sharing with the Tories. In this, of course, he was following Asquith. Power-sharing with political opponents was one thing in the midst of a grave national crisis, as in late 1916, after the introduction of conscription, the failure on the Somme and the increasing impact of the U-boat campaign; it was another in peacetime, even with the excuse of peace-making.

If the Liberal Party had not split during the war, it is quite possible that after the war Lloyd George and the Liberals would have disengaged from the Tories and vigorously opposed them in the post-war politics. It is also quite possible, that given the wartime labour market would have strengthened organised labour, the Liberals would have competed with a stronger Labour Party – though, perhaps, in a hung Parliament, some Progressive Alliance of the pre-1914 kind might have been arranged. Of course it is easy and dangerous for the historian to speculate on 'might-have-beens'. Yet it is hard – given the Liberal split, the eight years since the previous general election, the fairly sudden ending of the war, and Lloyd

George's leadership of a government which had just emerged victorious in the greatest war the world had known – to see, realistically, a way Lloyd George could have emerged to fight a general election on Liberal versus Tory lines even if he had wished to.

All periods of history are coloured by our knowledge of what happened next. Hindsight gives past life certainties that are lacking from our lives today. With the distance of time the options facing past politicians are likely to appear simpler and less complex. There were numerous issues in the years 1917 to 1921 where later developments have affected our understanding and led us to forget the uncertainty that existed at that time of 1917–21. These include the decline of the Liberal Party; the exclusion from office of Lloyd George after 1922; the return to familiar party politics from 1922 onwards; the existence of a fairly lengthy post-war boom followed by long-term unemployment in the areas of the old staple industries instead of the expected post-war unemployment and then recovery; the 'settling' of Ireland as far as the English were concerned for several decades (accompanied, historically, by the segregating of Irish issues from British ones); and the nature of Stalinist Russia being read back into 1917–21.

Perhaps there has not been sufficient emphasis on the extent to which politics were in a state of flux in 1917–18. This went much further than the well-known division in the Liberal Party. The possibilities this gave for new political alignments affected both Lloyd George's attitude to continuing the alliance with Bonar Law and his attitude to the Labour movement.

The Labour Party had divided at the start of the war, between those who supported the war effort and those who opposed it or, like Ramsay MacDonald, took up an ambiguous position of not actively supporting it whilst vigorously condemning the causes of the war. As the war lengthened and the economic commitment intensified, further strains took place within the Labour Party as well as within the wider Labour movement. Henderson broke with Lloyd George's government in August 1917 over the proposed Stockholm Conference, but other Labour ministers stayed in office. Organised labour stretched across a range of views from those wanting to 'follow Russia' after the October Revolution of 1917 to those of the super patriots involved in Milner's British Workers' League.[10]

The militaristic and 'patriotic' issues of wartime gave the Conservatives and Unionists less problems. But even here there were threats of divisions. With employers organising, and the Federation of

British Industries (FBI) emerging in 1916, there was some talk of a Businessman's Party. Right-wing impatience even with Lloyd George's government led to an actual breakaway party from the Tories: the National Party, launched in August 1917. While this was of little importance as a political party, it was a significant ginger group on the Right which propagated Milnerite and Tariff Reform League values.[11] In this it was but one example of the challenge to traditional Toryism which advocates of social imperialism made during such a struggle.[12]

Lloyd George's pre-war attitudes towards 'national efficiency' meant that little readjustment was needed on his part to work with the Milnerite Right. With them, there was no basic clash of outlook, as there was between Lloyd George and the old squirearchy element of the Tory Party.[13] Lloyd George's commitment to equality of opportunity always remained strong. Sir Wilfrid Eady, reflecting after Lloyd George's death on his political philosophy, placed first:

> A fierce anger that ability should have its rewards even if it did not belong to the right Family Name. The political aristocrats – including the Whigs – were no doubt pretty cruel to this Welsh attorney who was gate-crashing their parties.[14]

This was a characteristic outlook of the various strands of Edwardian politics which sought 'national efficiency'. As Robert Scally has observed, 'Combining the ethic of the civil servant, the imperial bureaucrat, and the self-made man with the ambition of talent without means, the doctrine of efficiency became the hallmark of what H. G. Wells aptly called "the revolt of the competent".'[15]

For the Milnerite Right during the war Lloyd George was the outstanding politician fully committed to a 'thorough' policy of winning. As Milner's protégé, F. S. Oliver put it to General Sir Hubert Gough in March 1917 (when Gough was very antagonistic to Lloyd George):

> Honestly speaking, I think *the Goat has one thought in regard to this war – how to win it.* I hold no brief for him; but I do believe, that if by being hanged tomorrow he could win it he would elect to be hanged. That being so we must put up with his vagaries as best we can, and thank God that we have someone who wants to win – and will do anything, even to the losing of his soul, in order to win – rather than someone who was drifting easily into losing it on gentlemanly principles![16]

Like the Milnerites, Lloyd George aimed to appeal to unorganised labour. He could sympathise with 'the poor', with unorganised and unskilled labour. He gave the impression that he never understood the skilled worker, as T. J. MacNamara put it, 'he had only seen them from the outside'.[17] During the war Lloyd George was dismissive of Labour being able to take a dominant role in, let alone complete control of, government. Thus in discussion with Lord Buckmaster and C. P. Scott in December 1917, Lloyd George responded to Buckmaster's suggestion that in the next government 'Labour will be strong enough to dicate policy and they will insist that wealth shall pay'.

> 'I am not so sure', said G, 'about Labour dictating. "Labour" means skilled Labour, and there is quite as great a gulf between skilled and unskilled Labour as between the propertied class and Labour generally. Besides Labour has shown itself in Parliament to be ineffective'.
> I remarked that the new Labour Party would be a transformed party, that it would not consist, as at the present, of the hand workers only, but would contain a very large proportion of the head workers, the so called 'intellectuals'. 'These' said G, 'would only be the Radicals over again'. I said, 'Yes, but Radicals with a difference'. G. had evidently not quite waked up to what is before him.[18]

Lloyd George was readily drawn into Milner's attempts to set up a rival Labour Party for the post-war period. Before the First World War there had been previous attempts to harness non-socialist Labour to the Unionist and tariff reform cause.[19] The war provided new opportunities. Within a few days of the end of the serious May 1917 engineering strikes, Milner wrote to Lloyd George, praising the setting up of Industrial Commissions but also raising the possibilities of 'patriotic labour' and urging him to see its leading light, Victor Fisher. Milner wrote,

> there remains the problem of counter-acting the deliberate agitation of mischief-makers, who sow discontent among the workmen, which will not be stopped, though it will no doubt lose some of its opportunities, by the removal of real grounds of complaint.

Milner observed that he did not believe in prosecuting individuals.

> What I do believe in [he continued] is systematic work by Labour men who are on our side, to counteract the very systematic and active propaganda of the Pacifists, and to prevent their capturing the Trades

Councils and other bodies, who profess to represent, though they often misrepresent, the working classes. This process of countermining has been carried on for some little time past, to my own knowledge by a comparatively new organisation, called the 'British Workers' League'. . . .

This League is not, like some previous organisations of the kind, a bogus thing. It consists of genuine Labour men, having Labour objects, but being at the same time patriotic and national.[20]

Milner and the Unionists needed Lloyd George's blessing for their attempts to boost 'patriotic labour'. To do much they needed to be able to give it a free run in some seats not winnable by straight Tory candidates. For this they needed to move towards some electoral understanding with Lloyd George and Coalition Liberals.[21] The British Workers' League was very much the Unionists' creature, with Bonar Law giving it a public blessing at a Special Unionist Conference on 30 November 1917. Bonar Law declared it as a duty to get working with the Unionists 'the section of Labour which is national and imperialistic . . . the section of Labour which recognises that for all classes, employers and employed, production is the one thing to be aimed at'.[22]

In the 1918 general election 'patriotic labour' reached its height. Now under the name National Democratic Party, it won ten seats. In addition there were four former Labour Party MPs, George Barnes, George Roberts, George Wardle and James Parker, who refused to leave the Coalition and as a result were expelled from the Labour Party. Barnes and Roberts were kept in ministerial office when the post-war Coalition government was formed. However the significance of this element in the Coalition government was to evaporate quickly. All the National Democratic Party MPs were beaten by Labour candidates in the 1922 general election. Parker also was defeated then and Roberts was in the 1923 general election, the other two retiring without facing the electorate again.[23] However this could not be foreseen in late 1918.

Nor could the decline in influence of the interventionist Unionism associated with Milner. This decline was not as rapid as that of 'patriotic labour': but being politically far more important, the waning of 'social imperialism' as an influence in the Coalition government was very significant. In the aftermath of world war, 'Home Rule for Industry' was to be a more powerful notion than state intervention to restructure industry along the lines advocated by the Milnerite and Tariff Reform League enthusiasts before the war. Similarly, notions of 'sound finance', 'anti-waste' and 'realistic' wage levels were to prove more potent among middle-class voters than providing 'Homes Fit For Heroes' or other social reform.

Lloyd George, allied with most of the Unionist Party, with his Coalitionist section of the Liberal Party and with the small forces of 'patriotic labour', turned on both the Asquithian Liberals and the Labour Party as the 1918 general election campaign developed. The Asquithian Liberals generally were not in outright opposition to the Liberal Coalitionists. Nor did they explicitly offer an alternative government or have a clear attitude to Labour. In contrast, Labour had withdrawn from the Coalition and opposed continued rule by the Lloyd George Coalition government.[24]

At the end of the 1918 election campaign Lloyd George focused his attack on the Labour Party. By then he appears to have realised that Labour would be the real opposition. He wrote to his wife on 13 December, 'I hope the Labourites will get more than the Asquithians. There would then be a clear issue for the future.'[25] That night, at an eve-of-poll meeting in Camberwell, Lloyd George vigorously attacked the Labour Party saying that it was not run by the Labour men who had supported him in the war ('there have been no more patriotic men in this country') but 'by the extreme pacifist, Bolshevist group', and named Ramsay MacDonald, Snowden and Smillie. He warned 'the moderate patriotic workmen' that if they voted Labour then they would find that it was the extremists who 'really believed in . . . Bolshevism' who would run the government. 'That is exactly what happened in Russia.'[26]

This was simply dishonest electioneering. Lloyd George knew better of Ramsay MacDonald, Snowden and Smillie. In March he was speaking at the Peace Conference of how his policy of meeting the legitimate grievances that were generating Bolshevism was causing such powerful Labour leaders as Smillie to help the government prevent social conflict.[27] Even if his attitude towards Smillie changed over three months, he certainly knew better of MacDonald. Lloyd George fully knew MacDonald's position, and had even discussed it with him over lunch in October 1914.[28] In December 1915 MacDonald had observed, when smarting at comments made about him by Lloyd George,

> Months ago I offered to do anything I could which, whilst not implicating me in any way as to the origin of the war or tying me in the action which I propose to take when it is over, would nevertheless influence workmen in

doing eident [good Scottish word] service whilst the war lasts, but in a round about way I was given to understand that no-one who was not prepared to swallow the whole poisonous bolus of government policy would be sanctified by being allowed to do anything.[29]

The war completely broke up what had been a good personal relationship between the two men, and Lloyd George appears to have been largely responsible for this. It also pushed MacDonald into a more anti-Establishment position than he might otherwise have adopted. Elibank, who knew MacDonald well, felt that the government had made a big mistake in rebuffing MacDonald, who earlier had co-operated with the India Office when he visited India and had kept the Labour Party in hand during the troubles in Bengal when there was a good deal of encouragement to do otherwise. Elibank reflected, 'we shall never do anything in England until we learn how to employ men like Ramsay MacDonald; otherwise they will end up in employing us unless we are careful'.[30]

Lloyd George's conscious decision to ally himself with the Conservatives after the Armistice ensured a gulf between himself and the Labour movement. The venomous nature of his attack at Camberwell in December 1918 and his constant playing of the 'Red Peril' card thereafter created a chasm. An embittered Ramsay MacDonald, who lost his parliamentary seat in the election, was left complaining,

> I a Bolshevist! I a pro-German! I am truly sorry that George condescended to that kind of thing. It was not quite the game.... I stood by him as you know in bad times, and though he and I profoundly disagree with each other now, he might have criticised severely without joining in a howl which he knows quite well is one of ignorance.[31]

Lloyd George's activities as Minister of Munitions, his espousal of conscription, his illiberal attitude to conscientious objectors, and much else in the war worried or alienated many of his nonconformist and working-class supporters. The breach with Arthur Henderson in 1917 was important in dividing Lloyd George and the Labour Movement. Nevertheless it is quite probable that Lloyd George's relationship with radical forces in British politics could have been mended, at least with many, after the end of the war. The 'coupon election' and the post-war Coalition government's treatment of organised labour ensured that did not happen. The events of 1918 to 1922 also ensured that after Lloyd George's fall from office in

October 1922 he remained an isolated and much distrusted figure on the Left of British politics.

Notes and references

1. For an example of such journalism see 'The peacemaker: Mr. Lloyd George's great services to the nation', *News of the World*, 28 May 1916. Lloyd George was born on 7 January 1863.
2. See, for example, Hankey to Esher, 18 September 1918. Hankey Papers, HNKY 4/10. Watkins Davies, a Criccieth man, has suggested that he was at the height of his powers in the first year of the war. Typescript of unpublished second volume of Lloyd George biography, p. 20. Watkins Davies Papers.
3. Bonar Law to Tom Jones, 4 May 1921. Tom Jones Papers, A5/6.
4. Megan Lloyd George's diary, January 1919. NLW 20476C/ 3184.
5. To use Beatrice Webb's words in her accurate prediction. Diary entry, 2 July 1918. Passfield Papers, 1, 34.
6. K. O. Morgan, *Consensus and Disunity* (Oxford: Clarendon Press, 1979), p. 42. The 'coupons' were letters of endorsement; the term was Asquith's, referring to wartime rationing coupons.
7. F. W. S. Craig, *British Parliamentary Election Statistics 1918–1970* (Glasgow: Political Reference Press, 1971), p. 2. One of the ten NDP MPs soon joined the Labour Party.
8. Colne Valley Conservative and Unionist Association, 1918 election leaflet; copy in Whiteley Papers, UL6/1.
9. Memorandum, 22 December 1922. Balfour Papers, Add. Ms. 49693, ff. 303–5.
10. On the latter see R. Douglas, 'The National Democratic Party and British Workers' League', *Historical Journal*, 15, 3 (1972), pp. 533–52, and J. O. Stubbs, 'Lord Milner and patriotic Labour 1914–1918', *English Historical Review*, 87, 4 (1972), pp. 717–54.
11. For a recent survey of this see C. Wrigley, '"In the excess of their patriotism": the National Party and threats of subversion' in C. Wrigley (ed.), *Warfare, Diplomacy and Politics* (London: Hamilton, 1986), pp. 93–119. For the British Commonwealth Union, an intended 'Industrial Party', see J. Turner, 'The British Commonwealth Union and the general election of 1918', *English Historical Review*, 93 (1978), pp. 528–59.
12. For a discussion of this see R. J. Scally, *The Origins of the Lloyd George Coalition* (Princeton, NJ: Princeton University Press, 1975), chapters 9–12.
13. On 'national efficiency' see G. R. Searle, *The Quest for National Efficiency* (Oxford: Blackwell, 1971) and Scally, *op. cit.* For Lloyd George's attitude to the landed interest, entrepreneurs and organised labour see C. Wrigley, *David Lloyd George and the British Labour Movement* (Hassocks: Harvester, 1976).
14. Eady to Tom Jones, 23 June 1948; Thomas Jones Papers, A2/46. Eady

was a leading civil servant at the Treasury, 1942–52, and had worked earlier at other ministries including the Ministry of Labour 1921–38.
15. Scally, *op. cit.*, p. 10.
16. Oliver to Gough, 16 March 1917; F. S. Oliver Papers 7726/97. Gough was Commander of the Fifth Army in France. At the end of the war, apart from the fighting forces, Oliver felt those to whom Britain owed most were Lloyd George, Milner, Henry Wilson and Hankey. Oliver to Hankey, 11 November 1918; Hankey Papers, 4/10/30.
17. In conversation with Lord Riddell, the owner of *The News of the World*, 3 October 1920, *Lord Riddell's Intimate Diary of the Peace Conference and After 1918–1923* (London: Gollancz, 1933), p. 240. Macnamara was Minister of Labour, 1920–2.
18. C. P. Scott's diary, 28 December 1917; unpublished extract, C. P. Scott Papers 50,904, ff. 221–3. Buckmaster had been Lord Chancellor in Asquith's Coalition Government. C. P. Scott was editor of the *Manchester Guardian*.
19. For a recent survey see C. Wrigley, 'Labour and the trade unions' in K. D. Brown (ed.), *The First Labour Party 1906–1914* (London: Croom Helm, 1985), pp. 129–57. On 'patriotic labour' see reference 10, above.
20. Milner to Lloyd George, 26 May 1917; Lloyd George Papers, F/38/2/5.
21. Thus a month before Milner's letter, Fisher had written to Arthur Steel-Maitland of 'difficulties which are enhanced by the uncertainty of the possible future claims of the L.G. organisation which is yet to be brought into existence'. Steel-Maitland Papers, GD 193/99/2/6. Steel-Maitland was Unionist MP for Birmingham, Erdington, and had been chairman of the Conservative and Unionist Party 1911–16.
22. Cited in J. Ramsden, *The Age of Balfour and Baldwin 1902–1940* (London: Longman, 1978), pp. 112–14. For the expected electoral benefits see R. A. Sanders (of Conservative Central Office) to Bonar Law, 18 March 1918. Bonar Law Papers, 83/1/15.
23. G. D. H. Cole, *A History of the Labour Party From 1914* (London: Routledge and Kegan Paul, 1948), pp. 87–8.
24. T. Wilson, *The Downfall of the Liberal Party 1914–1935* (London: Collins, 1966), pp. 164–74.
25. K. O. Morgan (ed.), *Lloyd George Family Letters 1885–1936* (Cardiff: University of Wales Press and Oxford University Press, 1973), p. 189. In the event there were sixty-one Labour MPs (including one Co-op and two unendorsed) and twenty-seven Independent Liberals. On Asquith's performance, see S. R. Ball, 'Asquith's decline and the general election of 1918', *Scottish Historical Review*, 61 (1982), pp. 44–61.
26. *The Times*, 14 December 1918.
27. A. J. Mayer, *Politics and Diplomacy of Peacemaking* (New Haven, CT: Yale University Press, 1967), p. 595.
28. D. Marquand, *Ramsay MacDonald* (London: Cape, 1977), p. 176.
29. Ramsay MacDonald to Arthur Murray, 31 December 1915; Elibank Papers 8803, ff. 275–76. Murray, a Liberal MP, had arranged for MacDonald to help with a volunteer ambulance corps in Belgium in

December 1914, but this had been thwarted by the authorities. MacDonald was writing shortly after Lloyd George had used his name on the Clyde to try to gain a hearing from militant workers.
30. Arthur Murray's diary, 18 January 1918; Elibank Papers, 8804, f. 138.
31. Ramsay MacDonald to Elibank, 14 January 1919; Elibank Papers, 8808, f. 3.

2
The spectre haunting Europe

In 1919 the word 'revolution' was on every lip, as it was in 1793, 1830 and 1848: in 1922 you will hear that the British working man is too staid and sensible a person ever to think of revolution except through the ballot box.[1]
(So wrote Basil Thomson, former head of Special Branch, in 1922.)

There was a special mood in 1919, especially in the first four or five months, which is hard now for the historian to recapture. It was a mood which had disappeared largely by late 1920 if not earlier. That it was so strong in early 1919 is partially obscured both by hindsight and by some unduly alarmist writing of the time. Yet there was a feeling, widespread in Britain, of fear, or of expectation, that major social change was imminent. Like a vehicle on a long, heavily rutted route, British society had been severely shaken by the war. Some of the old social norms were displaced, many stabilisers were broken and fears had been generated that worse was ahead.

As the First World War dragged on, the old ruling classes of Europe felt that they faced a precipice. Whether they were on the winning or losing side, many began to feel that their old social systems would be engulfed by the economic and social forces stirred up by the war. Shortly after the Armistice, Orlando, the Italian Prime Minister observed, 'The war is at the same time the greatest political and social revolution history records, exceeding even the French Revolution'.[2] There had been attempts to halt the war before it should spell ruin for the civilised world (to use Lord Lansdowne's phraseology of November 1917).[3] After talking with Tom Jones, Assistant Secretary to the Cabinet, Beatrice Webb noted in her diary for 15 May 1917,

> Milner and the British Junker party are seriously alarmed at the revolutionary tendencies in the UK and in the Empire, heightened by the Russian revolution. They would gladly have peace with the Hohenzollerns if they could get good terms for Great Britain, France and Belgium, leaving the Slavs to stew in their own juice, as mixed for them by Germany.[4]

This was before the Bolshevik Revolution. Of course such anxieties were greatly increased after that.

The collapse of old regimes in Europe and continuing labour unrest at home did nothing to lessen the alarm of the propertied classes in Britain after the Armistice. Pre-war fears of 'savagery' threatening 'civilised Western values', epitomised by the Boxer uprising in China in 1900, were raised again with the upheavals in Eastern and Central Europe. Those who had been outraged by Lloyd George's 'socialistic' finance before the war were faced with the outright expropriation of bondholders in Russia. Added to these concerns, racist fears were fostered yet again by the Right on the basis that several leading Bolsheviks in Russia and elsewhere were Jewish.

In the latter part of 1918 and early 1919 several prominent members of the government feared revolution in Britain. In late December Milner, who on Armistice Day had not been unduly worried about the spread of revolutionary ideas in Britain, was feeling that 'the Bolshevist position' was 'very menacing'. In January Curzon expressed concern in the War Cabinet that no concerted action was being taken by government departments to combat the spread of Bolshevism in Britain.[5] Walter Long, who had been growing especially anxious about co-ordinating intelligence on subversion at home from 1917, initially because of his ministerial involvement with Ireland, sent Lloyd George several alarmist memoranda. In one of these there were claims that there were more Bolsheviks per head of population in the UK than there had been in Russia in 1917 and a warning that if the government failed to take firm steps 'there will be some sort of revolution in this country . . . before twelve months are past.' Long endorsed it with the comment, 'I am confident the danger is real.'[6]

At times Lloyd George himself feared serious disturbances in Britain. Thus in early February 1919 he was sufficiently concerned that when his elder daughter spoke of bringing her baby to London, he objected saying that there might be riots and that the child had better stay where she was.[7] But it is unlikely that Lloyd George felt actual revolution was ever imminent in post-war Britain. He had a strong belief in British Parliamentary democracy being an adequate channel for expressing widely held grievances. For him the only real threat was the mishandling of unrest – either by blind reaction or by a weak Labour government which would lack the will to deal with any uprising.[8] He took a traditional Liberal view of not being surprised at revolutions in continental countries where popular feelings had been suppressed by reactionary governments, thereby enabling extremists to lead justifiable discontent.

Part of the mood of early 1919 was to do with the fact that discontent appeared to be everywhere. At home the propertied classes were faced with a marked lack of deference from much of the working class. There was full employment and considerable mobility of labour. There were widespread strikes, accompanied by much militant talk. There were changed attitudes to social discipline among the disillusioned hundreds of thousands returning from the Western Front. And there was unrest among the forces of law and order – mutinies in the army, grumblings in the navy, and a threat of further strikes in the police force.

Yet, to understand the degree of concern it is necessary to put domestic anxieties in the context of wider ones. On the continent Ministers were confronted with the example of the Bolshevik Revolution in Russia, and collapse of much of Eastern Europe, with Soviet governments springing up in Bavaria and Hungary, and revolution being predicted for Germany and Austria. The integrity of the Empire was called into question by the growth of non-co-operation and serious unrest fostered by the war among the peoples of India, Egypt, Ireland and elsewhere. The determined challenge of Sinn Fein and the Irish Volunteers seemed to many to be a threat comparable to that posed by adherents of 'direct action' among organised labour in Britain. Of the former, Long observed on 31 December 1918 that it was 'the most difficult and dangerous' movement in Ireland in at least forty years:

> Their leaders are brave and fanatical and do not fear imprisonment or death; they are not to be influenced by private negotiations with Bishops or Priests or captured by getting the patronage of appointments, which has been the favourite instrument of the Irish Government since 1905. Neither do they care a straw for the press.[9]

Links between advocates of Direct Action in British industrial relations, Sinn Fein and Russian Bolshevism were perceived time and time again in the post-war period. This was a threat felt by members of the government not just in 1919, but as late as the 1921 coal dispute. Then Edward Shortt, the Home Secretary warned the Cabinet. 'In my opinion [the] country [is] in great danger indeed.' He spoke of gelignite and bombs found after a raid on a Sinn Fein unit's house in Manchester, and added, 'Same thing everywhere. Communists can have riots all about'. Five days later, on 9 April 1921, the Solicitor-General for Scotland told the Cabinet of 'wrecking by a peripatetic body' in the Scottish coalfields which he deemed to be the work of 'Bolsheviks, Sinn Fein, mining and local people'.[10] The major industrial challenges were taken to be one part of a wider challenge to the existing social and imperial order.

One of the several roles which the post-war Lloyd George Coalition government took on was that of being a strong government with the will to deal with social disorder. The British upper and middle classes needed reassurance with so many signs of the disintegration of the old social order at home and abroad. Between 1917 and 1919 a whole host of political rallying points sprang up, each stressing the need for a restoration of order and the rights of property. Bodies such as the National Party, the Duty and Discipline Movement, the Middle Class Union, the British Commonwealth Union and the British Empire Union (which incorporated the Anti-German Union) all tried to mobilise against labour 'extremism', by which they referred to all, or nearly all, members of the Labour Party.[11]

Such fears, combined with the enhanced position of labour and the trade unions in the wartime economy, led to more businessmen becoming involved in politics. Dudley Docker and his associates gave backing to both the National Party and to 'patriotic labour' in 1918 and 1919.[12] Major companies donated large sums. Sir Vincent Caillard, for example, wrote to a senior colleague in Vickers in May 1918,

> We are subscribing a substantial amount in support of the Women's Party, which is doing such admirable work all over the kingdom in combating Labour Unrest, Bolshevism etc. and we are going to pass a debit-note for £500 as our share of the subscription. When you get this debit-note you will therefore know of what reason it is passed to you.[13]

Caillard also dealt direct with Lloyd George, both speaking to him and writing to him about 'the revolutionary movement which is going on underhand in the country'.[14]

None of the anti-socialist pressure groups which mushroomed up in the latter part of the war and in 1919 were individually important, but collectively they did reveal widespread apprehensions among the propertied classes of losing social control. Such fears were played on to convince 'true blue' Tories that it was desirable to maintain the

Coalition after the Armistice. Apparently, in October 1918, Bonar Law was even telling supporters that if Lloyd George was not kept in a Coalition 'he would probably go in with the extreme socialists and be very dangerous'.[15] More usually Lloyd George was portrayed as the political leader who could appeal successfully to a wide spectrum of democratic opinion in the country and who could guide the country through the painful readjustment to peace.

For Lloyd George's part the threat of revolution was a valuable card he could play to keep Unionist support for the Coalition government and also to go further in social reform than the Unionists would have agreed to in more normal times. However, in some respects their excessive fears of Bolshevism constrained Lloyd George, most notably with regard to policies towards Russia both during the Paris Peace Conference and afterwards.

The Paris Peace Conference took place whilst unrest was simmering in Britain and on the boil in other parts of Europe. The participants were very much aware of unrest elsewhere.[16] There was also a certain amount of looking over shoulders for the ghosts of the past, the men who had tried to stabilise Europe against revolution at the Congress of Vienna in 1815. On the day of the Armistice Lord Esher even advised Sir Maurice Hankey, Secretary of the Cabinet and to be secretary to the British delegation at the Peace Conference, against Paris as a venue. He warned,

> if you settle upon Paris, you will have scandals that will damage LG, and you will be outmanoeuvred by the Quai d'Orsay.
> Nothing will give a greater fillip to Bolshevism than an *orgy* such as there was in Vienna 100 years ago.
> If you go to Paris, in big houses and hotels, with motors and dinners and lawn tennis, you will return to a revolutionary England.[17]

During much of the period of most acute post-war social tension in Britain Lloyd George was away at the Paris Peace Conference. He arrived in Paris on 11 January 1919 and finally left France on 29 June, the day after he signed the Treaty of Versailles. He did return to London twice, the longest visit being between 8 February and 6 March, and the length of that visit was largely a response to industrial unrest in Britain. His other return to London, between 14 and 17 April, was to deal with Tory backbench concern, stimulated by Lord Northcliffe's newspapers, that he was not being tough enough with Germany.

Russia was a major concern of Lloyd George and the other peacemakers in Paris. But its importance at the conference should not be overstated. Lloyd George was deeply involved in a wide range of issues from asserting the right of naval blockade and trying to gain control of former German colonies for the Empire through the redrawing Europe's boundaries and assessing the scale of reparations to be squeezed from Germany.

Nevertheless Russia was an issue which often overshadowed relationships within the governing Coalition as well as Lloyd George's relationship with the British Labour movement, especially in 1919 and 1920. In essence, those who had lost money in Russia and those who were fearful of Bolshevism spreading from Russia to Britain demanded vigorous British intervention in Russia to overthrow Lenin's government. Such views were pushed hard by the Tory Right and in the cabinet by Winston Churchill, still a Coalition Liberal MP.

Lloyd George had no liking for Bolshevik ideas. However he was less impressed with notions of the sanctity of property or the rights of vested interests than his Tory colleagues or Churchill. Hankey, in early 1918, apprehensively noted, 'LG, who is half a Bolshevist himself, wants to get into closer relations with them.' In private conversation Lloyd George, in jest, could tell well-heeled company, 'I am not sure that twelve months of Bolshevism would not be a good thing for this country, so as to clear away a lot of the vested interests which are always stopping progress.'[18] His own view, often expressed, was that communism was impractical, and if it was well for it to be tried and shown to be a failure, then it was best that the experiment be in Russia, not Britain. Shortly before the Armistice, at one of his working breakfasts, Lloyd George observed to those present that he 'had no solution for the Russian problem, and said the only thing was that the revolution must burn itself out'.[19]

In the immediate post-war period Lloyd George was clear that it would be politically impractical to make a major military campaign in Russia, especially when President Wilson made it clear that he would not countenance it. Britain was war weary after the slaughter of the previous four years. Unrest in the army appeared menacing. In January the War Cabinet was informed that many soldiers were unwilling to serve in Russia.[20] In campaigning against intervention the Labour movement was in line with the popular mood. In April Basil Thomson warned the War Cabinet that 'even mild trade unionists are said to be strongly moved over the matter'.[21]

Lloyd George could, and did, make the point to Churchill and others that large-scale intervention in Russia was more likely to foster Bolshevism elsewhere than to eliminate it. In early February, at the time of the Clyde and Belfast strikes, Lloyd George exclaimed to Riddell, 'Winston is in Paris. He wants to conduct a war against the Bolsheviks. That *would* cause a revolution! Our people would not permit it.'[22] Later in February, when a serious coal strike appeared to be imminent in Britain, Lloyd George was firm with Churchill, who was then at the Peace Conference. He telegrammed,

> If Russia is really anti-Bolshevik, then a supply of equipment would enable it to redeem itself. If Russia is pro-Bolshevik, not merely is it none of our business to interfere with its internal affairs, it would be positively mischievous: it would strengthen and consolidate Bolshevik opinion. An expensive war of aggression against Russia is a way to strengthen Bolshevism in Russia and create it at home. We cannot afford the burden. Chamberlain says we can hardly make both ends meet on a peace basis, even at the present crushing rate of taxation; and if we are committed to a war against a continent like Russia, it is the road to bankruptcy and Bolshevism in these islands.

After warning Churchill against being swayed by the French, whose opinion was 'largely biased by the enormous number of small investors who [had] put their money into Russian loans', he said,

> I also want you to bear in mind the very grave labour position in this country. Were it known that you had gone over to Paris to prepare a plan of war against the Bolsheviks it would do more to incense organised labour than anything I can think of; and what is still worse, it would throw into the ranks of the extremists a very large number of thinking people who now abhor their methods.[23]

Nevertheless Lloyd George was considerably annoyed at Russian Bolshevik activities in other countries. This was much discussed in the War Cabinet in 1918, and continued to be in 1919.[24] In early 1919 it was felt that their agents were contributing to the considerable unrest in Eastern and Central Europe and affecting Italy, France and, to a lesser extent, Britain. On 31 December 1918 the War Cabinet agreed to support any government menaced by Bolshevism 'in any manner which did not involve military intervention . . . and that our general policy should be that . . . of walling off a fire in a mine'.[25] Lloyd George was willing to contain or even defeat Bolshevism by supporting forces other than British. Bolshevism in

Russia was surrounded by a German army in the west, the Finnish army further north, and by White Russian armies in the south and north-east. The Cabinet gave £100 million to aid Denikin and Kolchak. Some of the materials (notably railway stock) sent to Russia could well have been used to help Britain's post-war recovery.[26] Similarly, surplus war material was sent to Romania, which helped Romania crush the Bela Kun government. This was in spite of Bonar Law making it clear in the Cabinet that Lloyd George had objections to surreptitiously building up an army anywhere to invade Russia.[27] Even so, there was a considerable British military presence in Russia until 1920; the troops took part in fighting and the Navy, in August 1919, made a daring raid on the Red fleet at Kronstadt.[28]

Yet even during this period Lloyd George was willing to make moves for an accommodation. He seems to have been willing to have Bolshevik representatives at the Peace Conference and was firmly against a meeting with the various emigré groups. He supported Borden's and Smut's plan to call the warring Russian groups to a Conference at Prinkipo to try and settle their differences. When this failed he supported Bullitt's mission to sound out Lenin as to peace terms, but dropped this when he learned the Bolshevik's terms and when the Tory backbenchers revolted at the possibility of an understanding with Bolshevism. He then supported the Nansen plan for supplying food via neutral auspices to Russia – on the understanding that the Bolsheviks would restrain their armies from further advances.[29]

Lloyd George basically hoped each country would solve its own Bolshevik problem. He hoped that Bolshevik regimes would be overthrown in favour of Liberal democratic institutions – but he felt this would take place if they lacked support in their own country. Thus in September 1919 after Bela Kun had been ousted he told the Council of Allied Powers in Paris, 'it was not the concern of the Allies what action was taken in Hungary to prevent Bolshevism. That was the task of the Hungarians themselves. Each nation ought to deal with its own problem in this respect.'[30] Lloyd George was sceptical of the effectiveness of outside intervention in Russia – and frequently drew comparisons with the French Revolution. On one occasion he advised the House of Commons that if they wished to understand the problem of intervention they should 'just . . . read up the story of the French Revolution'.[31] He soon doubted much faith should be put in the White Armies. As early as February 1919 he asserted in the War Cabinet that 'the Russian non-Bolshevik armies were inferior to the Bolsheviks neither in men nor guns, and if the Russian population had been behind them they would certainly have made headway. For months the Bolsheviks had had none of the essentials of a disciplined army, yet the [White] Russians had made no effective advance.'[32]

Overall chaos in Russia appeared to suit British policy as long as it did not extend outside. Balfour exclaimed in the Imperial War Cabinet in December 1918 that 'no one could wish that Russia's boundaries should be the same as before.'[33] When, in April 1919, Kolchak briefly appeared to be likely to overthrow Lenin, Lloyd George was concerned to put limitations on his power.[34] However the persistence of such unrest dislocated European trade. With growing unemployment in Britain, Lloyd George soon switched to the more positive policy of trying to bring Russia back into European trade and to make a trade treaty with her.

Notes and references

1. B. Thomson, *Queer People* (London: Hodder and Stoughton, n.d. [1922]), p. 273.
2. On 20 November 1918. Cited in C. S. Maier, *Recasting Bourgeois Europe* (Princeton, NJ: Princeton University Press, 1975), p. 62.
3. For Lansdowne's proposals see A. J. Mayer, *Political Origins of the New Diplomacy 1917–1918* (New Haven, CT: Yale University Press, 1959), pp. 282–6.
4. N. and J. MacKenzie (eds), *The Diary of Beatrice Webb*, Vol. 3 (London: Virago, 1984), p. 278. See also M. I. Cole (ed.), *Beatrice Webb's Diaries 1912–1924* (London: Longmans, Green, 1952), p. 97; D. Chapman-Huston, *The Lost Historian* (London: Murray, 1936), pp. 267–71 and 276–9; and A. M. Gollin, *Proconsul In Politics* (London: Blond, 1964), pp. 552–4.
5. Milner's diary, 27 December 1918; Milner Papers, vol. 89. A. J. Mayer, *Politics and Diplomacy of Peacemaking* (London: Weidenfeld and Nicolson, 1967), p. 71. War Cabinet Minutes (hereafter WC) 518, 22 January 1919; CAB 23–9–19. Curzon was Lord President and in charge of the Foreign Office whilst Balfour was at the Peace Conference. He was to be chairman of the Cabinet's Secret Service Committee of 1919 and 1920.
6. W. Long to Lloyd George, 9 January 1919; Lloyd George Papers (hereafter LG) F/33/2/3. C. Andrew, *Secret Service* (London: Heinemann, 1985), pp. 230–2.
7. *Lord Riddell's Intimate Diary of the Peace Conference and After 1918–1923* (London: Gollancz, 1933), p. 21.
8. For an example of the former fear, there is his speech made in Downing Street to Liberals on 12 November 1918 with its declaration,

'Revolution I am not afraid of. Bolshevism I am not afraid of. It is reaction I am afraid of.' T. Wilson, *The Downfall of the Liberal Party 1914–35* (London: Collins, 1966), p. 137.

9. Cited in C. Townshend, *The British Campaign in Ireland 1919–1921* (London: Oxford University Press, 1975), p. 14.
10. Cabinet notes by Tom Jones of 4 and 9 April 1921; Tom Jones Papers, C/1/6 and C/1/15.
11. For a survey of many of these see Independent Labour Party Information Committee, *Who Pays for the Attacks on Labour?* (1920) and also S. White, 'Ideological hegemony and political control: the sociology of anti-Bolshevism in Britain 1918–1920', *Scottish Labour History Society Journal*, 9 (1975), pp. 3–20. The British Empire Union apparently even obtained a concession from the income tax authorities that contributions should be tax free; *New Statesman*, 14, 352, 10 January 1920, p. 395.
12. R. Davenport-Hines, *Dudley Docker* (Cambridge: Cambridge University Press, 1984), pp. 127–30. See also J. Turner, 'The British Commonwealth Union and the general election of 1918', *English Historical Review*, 93 (1978), pp. 528–59 and his 'The politics of "organised business" in the First World War' in J. Turner (ed.), *Businessmen and Politics* (London: Heinemann, 1980).
13. Caillard to McKechnie, 30 May 1918. Sir James McKecknie Papers, 392; Vickers Historical Records, 119.
14. Caillard to Lloyd George, 12 October 1918; LG F/6/1/23. From the contents of the letter Caillard clearly had been shown secret service information. His list of 'Leading Rebels' included G. D. H. Cole, Margaret Bondfield, Mary Macarthur and Philip Snowden as well as more predictable names.
15. Lord Derby's diary entry, 16 October 1918, sent by him to Balfour, 20 October 1918; Balfour Papers, 49744, f. 74.
16. This is vividly described in Mayer, *Politics and Diplomacy* and D. Mitchell, *1919: Red Mirage* (London: Cape, 1970).
17. Esher to Hankey, 11 November 1918; Hankey Papers, HNKY 4/10/27–8. The Quai d'Orsay is the location of the French Foreign Office.
18. Diary, 8 February 1918; cited in S. Roskill, *Hankey: Man of Secrets*, vol. 1 (London: Collins, 1970), p. 493. Lord Riddell's diary entry on a dinner party, 27 July 1919; *Intimate Diary*, p. 107.
19. W. C. Bridgeman's diary, 7 November 1918; Bridgeman Papers.
20. WC (515), 10 January 1919; CAB 23–9–8.
21. Report of 30 April 1919; cited in Andrew, *op. cit.*, p. 229.
22. Diary entry, 8 February 1919; *Intimate Diary*, p. 21.
23. 16 February 1919. Text in Churchill papers, and printed in M. Gilbert, *Winston S. Churchill, Vol. 4: Companion* 1 (London: Heinemann, 1977), p. 539. There is a modified version in D. Lloyd George, *The Truth About the Peace Treaties*, vol. 1 (London: Gollancz 1938), pp. 371–2. Churchill's attitude to Russia is discussed in depth in Martin Gilbert's valuable fourth volume of his biography of Churchill (London: Heinemann, 1975).

24. The War Cabinet frequently discussed its policy towards this from January 1918. For that month see WC (322, 324 and 335), 15, 17 and 31 January 1918; CAB 23–5–40, 45 and 76.
25. WC (413); CAB 23–8–111.
26. WC (573), 29 May 1919; CAB 23–10–66.
27. WC (550), 24 March 1919; CAB 23–9–124.
28. For the details see R. H. Ullman, *Anglo-Soviet Relations, Vol. 2: Britain and the Russian Civil War* (Princeton, NJ: Princeton University Press, 1968).
29. *Ibid.* and Mayer, *Politics and Diplomacy*.
30. *Documents on British Foreign Policy 1919–1939*, Vol. 1 (London: HMSO, 1947), p. 687.
31. On 12 February 1919; 112, *HC Deb.* 5s. c. 133–8.
32. WC (531), 12 February 1919; CAB 23–9–66.
33. Imperial War Cabinet Minutes (41), 3 December 1918; CAB 23–42.
34. Mayer, *Politics and Diplomacy*, pp. 814–25.

3
Unrest in the armed forces

The fear of serious social unrest, even revolution, which was widespread among the propertied classes in early 1919 was accentuated by considerable unrest in the army, navy and police. Army mutinies over demobilisation arrangements in the first few days of the year were very embarrassing for the government. Lloyd George himself appears to have been especially alarmed by unrest in the police. Such unrest raised questions about the dependability of the forces of law and order should there be a major challenge to the government by organised labour.

Shortly after the Armistice Lord Milner, one of the ministers especially worried about social unrest, wrote to Lloyd George about the dilemma facing governments after the convulsions of the previous years. 'With the state of Europe and the revolutionary tendency, greater or less, in all countries', he warned, 'it is as dangerous to have no army as to have too big a one.'[1]

Anxiety of this kind combined with fears about the challenge of organised labour in the latter half of the war and in the subsequent three years led the government to pay considerable attention not only to trying to ensure the unquestioning loyalty of the forces of law and order but also to developing other options for dealing with organised social dissent. This involved moving further from pretences of an 'impartial state'. In practice, the government used the state apparatus to organise on behalf of the propertied classes against a very wide range of 'challenges', from possible revolution to workers attempting to defend the wage rates and conditions of work that they had secured during the First World War and the post-war boom. In the mouths of some ministers and on the pages of many right-wing newspapers and journals 'Bolshevism' could cover a surprisingly wide range of matters, from lack of deference to those who deemed themselves to be social betters, to high taxation and to the 'nationalisation of women'.

The unrest in the army over demobilisation was not in essence a serious challenge to the government. It was an eruption of discontent at ill-conceived administrative arrangements. The sluggish and poorly explained programme of demobilisation was one which aroused the opposition of newspapers such as the *Daily Express* and the *Daily Mail*, as well as businessmen and moderate municipal bodies; though there was a more radical side to the issue. Complete and rapid demobilisation would leave Britain with a very small army, making it difficult to deploy adequate forces in Europe and the Empire let alone to maintain intervention in Russia.

After the Armistice Lloyd George was anxious that the British Army should maintain Britain's role as a victorious Power. Hence he regretted a War Cabinet decision that British troops should not take part in the occupations of Vienna and Budapest.[2] However, he was also very concerned about the slowness in demobilising miners and other key men from the armed forces.

Lloyd George was well aware that coal output had been seriously dislocated by the removal of miners following the manpower emergency which had arisen from the German offensive of March 1918. In mid-October Sir Albert Stanley, the President of the Board of Trade, had advocated that the public should be warned that 'there would be a grave shortage of coal, that many people would be thrown out of employment, and that there would be grave difficulties and hardships'. However, Lloyd George had favoured the return only of men from divisions which were resting and would not be engaged in active operations again in 1918.[3]

After the Armistice Lloyd George took an active role in pressing for action by the War Office on this issue. Hankey recorded in his diary for 24 November 1918,

> No War Cabinet, but at noon I was sent for by Ll.G, who had summoned an impromptu conference of the President of the Board of Trade, Coal Controller [Sir Guy Calthrop], Milner, and the Adjutant-General [Lt-Gen. Sir G. Macdonogh] to insist on the rapid return of coal miners from the front. It was arranged that Lord Milner should go at once to G.H.Q. and speed things up.[4]

Failure to secure their speedy return would hamper post-war industrial growth. Moreover, as Lloyd George commented to Milner on 25 November,

> Unless the supplies of coal . . . were increased, it was not impossible that there might be a revolution. . . . The spirit of lawlessness was apparent,

and none could say what might happen if . . . there was no coal in the East End in December.[5]

In spite of his urgings, demobilisation of miners and other key workers did not begin until 9 December. Lloyd George vented his wrath on Milner on 6 December, in front of a crowd of ministers and officials. Milner noted in his diary that Lloyd George had been 'in his most explosive mood and rather more than offensive in his complaints of the slowness with which the miners were being released'. Milner offered his resignation, but Lloyd George successfully pressed Milner to stay for the time being.[6]

By this time demobilisation had become a major issue in the press. Lloyd George wrote on 10 December to Balfour, who was in Paris, that he could not possibly leave London as he was devoting a week 'to the problems connected with demobilisation. They are becoming very pressing, and might become menacing if not attended to.' On 19 December, in a move to get order from chronic administrative overlapping on demobilisation (fourteen separate departments were involved), Lloyd George appointed Sir Eric Geddes to co-ordinate demobilisation. Geddes was First Lord of the Admiralty and had been a member of the War Priorities Committee from its establishment in the autumn of 1917. Soon Geddes was confirming Lloyd George's belief that the existing plans for demobilisation would have to be altered. He informed Lloyd George on 29 December that 'something will have to be done at a very early date to radically alter the surety and speed of extraction of men from the Army'. His best estimate then was that of a war effort of roughly ten million men and women, only three-quarters of a million had been released by that date (made up of 270,000 from the armed forces, 115,000 prisoners of war, including civilians, and 390,000 discharged munitions workers).[7]

Unrest erupted at various army camps in Britain from Friday 3 January, beginning at Folkestone with men due to return to France. Similar demonstrations soon took place in Dover and other parts of Kent, and thereafter spread to London, and other parts of Great Britain. The prime issue was demobilisation, with fears of being drafted to serve in Russia as a concern. Other matters such as poor quality food, low pay and unpleasant work contributed to crumbling discipline. There was also unrest among British troops in France after the Armistice, most notably at Calais, where an incident began on 2 January and where there was disquiet for the rest of the month.[8]

On 4 January Milner expressed concern in his diary about the demonstrations at Folkestone, observing that the giving of concessions to the men was 'the best way out of a bad business'.[9] On 7 January he wrote to Lloyd George to warn that 'this military insubordination is becoming very grave. . . . I am firmly convinced . . . drastic action will be necessary if we are to prevent a state of general disorder. But before taking drastic action we must have public opinion on our side.'[10]

On the 6, 7 and 8 January deputations of soldiers from camps in the London area travelled to Whitehall to present their grievances. On 6 January 150 travelled in three lorries from Osterley Park to Whitehall, where they were joined by other soldiers, and eventually were seen by a staff officer of the quartermaster-general's department. The next day a group of soldiers from Uxbridge travelled to Whitehall and tried to see Lloyd George. He did not see them personally but passed on to Milner the information that the men were annoyed about their food 'which they say is insufficient in quantity and of very poor quality'. That afternoon over 500 soldiers in 13 lorries went to Horse Guards Parade and sent a deputation to the War Office.[11]

Most dramatic of all, on 8 January, was a mass demonstration of some 1,500 soldiers from Park Royal outside a War Cabinet meeting. Sir Henry Wilson, Chief of the Imperial General Staff, indignantly noted that on his way to the meeting he had 'found a soldiers' demonstration outside Downing Street, and had to work my way through the soldiers to the door. The men were quite respectful and quiet, but not much saluting.'[12] Lloyd George told his colleagues that he was quite willing to see the soldiers, and sympathetically observed that after the years of strain during the war 'a violent reaction was natural, especially as nine-tenths of the men knew that they would not serve as soldiers again, and saw around them civilians drawing very high rates of pay'. He also argued that 'they must be quite sure that any steps they decided on with a view to suppressing the demonstrations . . . were certain to be successful.' Milner and the various representatives of the War Office argued strongly against him seeing the soldiers (who moved to Horse Guards Parade during the course of the meeting); Wilson warned that the soldiers' delegation 'bore a dangerous resemblance to a soviet'. The War Cabinet agreed that Sir William Robertson (who appeared sympathetic to them) should address the soldiers and inform them that an investigation would be made into their grievances and that Lloyd George was preparing a statement on demobilisation which would be issued shortly. This Robertson did, having first listened to the men's complaints.[13]

The previous day Wilson had told Lloyd George that there must be a firm line taken with the unrest. He had been amazed to find Lloyd George consulting Horatio Bottomley, who, in his journal *John Bull*, had adopted the role of the ordinary soldiers' champion. According to Wilson's diary, after Bottomley left,

> I told Lloyd George plainly what I thought – viz. he must come out in the open at once and back the War Office and the officers. He must crush out the poisonous part of the Press. He must say the War is not over. He must prepare the public mind for armies of occupation in India, Gibraltar, Malta, France etc. I spoke very plainly and frightened him. He agreed to all my proposals.

Wilson's views were shared by his fellow military members on the Army Council, who felt that if a firm statement was not made to the country then 'the whole army will be turned into a rabble'.[14]

So on the evening of 8 January, after the further troop demonstrations in Whitehall, Lloyd George issued such a statement. It began:

> The Prime Minister has been giving careful personal attention to the speed at which the process of demobilising the Army is being maintained. He considers that the first duty is to make sure that the fruits of victory which have been won by the sacrifice of so many lives, and by so many brave deeds, are not jeopardised by any apparent weakness on the part of Britain during the critical months of peace negotiations. For this purpose it is imperative that we should maintain a strong Army on the Rhine, and, of course the necessary services behind the front, both in France and at home.

It ended with the warning:

> One thing is certain, the work of demobilisation is not going to be quickened – on the contrary it is bound to be delayed – by the men trying to take the law into their own hands. It is not by these irregular assemblies or marches that anything can be put right. The reason why public opinion has been tolerant of these demonstrations is because the country knows that all ranks would have cheerfully done their duty if actual fighting had been going on. But a point has now been reached where real harm is being

done to the national cause and to the reputation of the British Army, and it is therefore essential that discipline should be maintained.[15]

Whilst being firm, the statement also had a tone of reasonableness not unlike Lloyd George's observations in the War Cabinet. It was an appeal to public opinion as well as to discontented troops. It appears to have been effective in helping to reduce unrest among troops stationed within Britain.

Lloyd George then replaced Milner with Winston Churchill with effect from 10 January. He had suggested this office to Churchill in late December, when discussing the reconstruction of the government after the general election. Before taking over, Churchill secured an undertaking 'that the Secretary of State for War should have the final word against all civilian departments in matters affecting the discipline of the troops'.[16] Churchill soon pleased Wilson and other hardliners in the War Office, not only by his handling of demobilisation but also by the extremity of his hostility to Bolshevik Russia. Churchill scrapped the existing demobilisation plans and replaced them in late January with a scheme based on length of service, war wounds and age, aimed at satisfying the soldiers' sense of fair play. Men who had enlisted before 1916 or who were over 40 were to be released quickly, and thereafter men who had been wounded would receive priority treatment. However, alongside this Churchill followed the War Office line that Britain needed to maintain a large army of well over a million men, and that involved maintaining conscription. This pill was to be sugared by a substantial pay rise. Churchill summed up his scheme as consisting in 'releasing two men out of three and paying the third man double to finish the job'.

By late January Churchill and the War Office could make a strong case for the need of a large army, given Britain's overseas commitment as well as potential unrest in the British Isles. On 28 January Churchill told his colleagues that of 1,200,000 men needed by the War Office, 250,000 were needed at home. Of the home forces, 35,000 were earmarked to maintain order in England, Wales and Scotland, 45,000 were to be based in Ireland with a further 30,000 in England as a reinforcement for the Irish garrisons.

Churchill secured this policy in spite of the initial opposition of Lloyd George (who was in Paris) and many of his senior colleagues in the government.[17] During the 1918 general election Lloyd George had explicitly rebutted charges made by J. H. Thomas, the railwaymen's leader and leading Labour Party politician, that 'a vote for Coalition is a vote for conscription'. On 11 December 1918 Lloyd George declared early on in a major speech at Bristol that it was being said 'that the government mean to keep up a great conscript army in this country. It is not true.'[18] When Churchill had first aired the maintenance of a large army, Lloyd George had reacted angrily, observing on 18 and 20 January that with the demobilisation of the German army it was unnecessary and that it could lead to trouble in the British army. Lloyd George had been sufficiently anxious about the mood of soldiers and newly demobilised soldiers a few days earlier to criticise Bonar Law for choosing to join him in Paris when 'we might have 50,000 demobilised soldiers . . . marching up Whitehall'.[19]

Once Lloyd George had accepted Churchill's case for maintaining a large army the government set about winning press support. After the Cabinet approved the scheme on 28 January Churchill saw representatives of the press at the War Office. He could inform Lloyd George, 'The newspaper men took it all like lambs . . . they are naturally keeping Germany to the front in their very helpful articles.'[20] Churchill also wrote personally to Lord Northcliffe to secure the support of his newspapers. Among the leading army figures there was still concern as to the response of the men who, as a result of this policy, would have their demobilisation considerably delayed. Sir Henry Wilson noted in his diary that after the press had brought out their 'puffs' and the Army Order had been issued,

> then the great adventure of 'compulsing' a million men in time of peace, to serve abroad, will have begun. There is not a moment to lose, as all power over the army is slipping away. We shall get about a million men, who will be compelled to serve for 12 months. Of course, if these men really refuse to serve, we are done; but I have no fear of this if the case is properly put to the men, and if Winston and I can get the support of the Press.

Having simplified the plans for demobilisation to appeal to the soldiers' sense of fairness and having improved pay, the army leadership was determined to reassert authority within the army. After a long conversation with Haig on 27 January, Wilson noted that he was 'clearly of opinion that our proposals for a clean cut and extra pay will produce a force that can be disciplined'.[21]

That very day serious unrest began among British troops at Calais. Two groups mutinied. A strike began on 27 January among skilled trade unionists in the Royal Army Ordnance Corps, whose work was essential to maintain the army's main supply lines. Their action soon spread, and stopped the movement of supplies on the railways, with French railway workers refusing to handle their work. Their grievances were a mixed bag. They wanted quicker demobilisation, better pay, and a thirty-six-hour week. They also called for recognition of their soldiers' council and permission to attend the 'Hands Off Russia' rally to be held in the Albert Hall on 8 February which was being organised by the British Socialist Party. The next day troops at nearby leave camp also went on strike, refusing to return inland and instead demanding to go back to Britain to seek employment. They formed a strike committee which took over their camp and negotiated with General Sir Julian Byng of the Third Army.

Byng took a firm line with the strikers in the leave camp on 30 January. Two brigades with machine guns were sent to surround the camp, and one with fixed bayonets was sent in to end the strike. Three leaders were arrested. Before they were tried by court martial, Haig wrote to Churchill informing him that it was essential that these men should be executed otherwise 'the discipline of the whole Army will suffer, both immediately and for many years to come.' Churchill wisely urged that death sentences should not be passed on them. Instead they received lengthy prison sentences.[22]

In the case of the Royal Army Ordnance Corps and the other supply and service troops the authorities took milder action. Their strike ended with an unconditional return to work after a five-hour conference between their delegates and officers. Their negotiating position was much stronger than that of the infantry men. As Gloden Dallas and Douglas Gill have concluded, the army's leadership had to be more cautious with these men:

> Had it turned to force, had it arrested every ordnance soldier in Calais, the troops at Dunkirk and the other British bases might simply have downed tools. With neither stores nor transport, and cut-off from the sea, the British army could not fight, it could scarcely eat or move.[23]

For the government the unrest in Calais was especially alarming as it came at the same time as the major strikes in Belfast and on the Clyde. The army strikers may also have had their eyes on these developments. One participant later recalled that 'the collapse of the expected general strike which had begun on the Clyde on the same day as our own' was one reason why the strike in the supply organisation was abandoned.[24] However, the announcements of changes in the plans of demobilisation and the big increases in pay are likely to have had an especially big impact in ending such hazardous action. In the War Cabinet meeting on 28 January Sir Laming Worthington-Evans, the Minister of Pensions, had bluntly observed, 'The reason for the increase was frankly to allay unrest, and the present unrest would only be increased unless an adequate increase was made.'[25]

After the serious incidents at Calais and the introduction of clearer demobilisation plans and better pay, there was still worrying, but less serious, disaffection. For some months the authorities remained nervous about the mood of the conscripted soldiers. There were further incidents; but none as serious as those of January 1919. In February the War Office was still facing periodic trouble from men at home on leave who were due to go back to France or Germany. On 7 February there was a major incident arising from 3,000 troops being stranded in London with no money, when awaiting transport to take them to the continent. After attempting to wreck Victoria Station, they marched with their arms to Whitehall. Churchill later recalled that he learnt that the men were 'filling the Horse Guards' Parade armed and in a state of complete disorder'. He was informed that a Battalion of Grenadier Guards was available.

> I asked whether the Battalion would obey orders, and was answered 'The officers believe so'. On this I requested the general to surround and make prisoners of the disorderly mass. . . .
>
> I remained in my room a prey to anxiety. A very grave issue had arisen at the physical heart of the State.
>
> . . . .back came the generals in a much more cheerful mood. . . . . The Grenadiers with fixed bayonets had closed in upon the armed crowd; the Household Cavalry had executed an enveloping movement on the other flank; and the whole 3,000 men had been shepherded and escorted under arrest to Wellington Barracks, where they were all going to have breakfast before resuming their journey to France.

There was a more serious incident in North Wales in early March, involving mostly Canadian troops at Kinmel Park Camp. On 4 and 5 March, after repeated postponements of sailings, there were riots which resulted in five men killed, forty injured and much damage to property. At one point a large number of men attempted to march on Abergele, but were turned back by loyal troops from Chester. The *Morning Post* reported, a crowd was seen to be advancing with a man who, it is alleged, was a Russian Jew at their head, carrying a red flag and shouting 'Come on you Bolsheviks!'. They were armed with rifles, bayonets and revolvers. . . . . The man who carried the red flag was shot dead, and this was the signal for the serious fighting. Rifles were discharged and bayonets were used, and in the rioting that followed other casualties . . . occurred.

Given the various serious problems with conscripted men most members of the government were worried when, in late February 1919, Churchill proposed to insert a clause in the Naval, Military and Air Force Bill to enable the call up of young men if this proved necessary in order to maintain the size of the army at over a million. Bonar Law, Austen Chamberlain and other ministers predicted political trouble if this were done. Seely, the Under Secretary of State for Air, warned that the Labour movement 'would say that the government was trying to obtain men at a low rate of wages'. Lloyd George observed that 'the Labour Party would certainly prefer a volunteer army to any conscripts'. He went on to argue that

> with the men of eighteen years of age already in the Army and volunteers it ought to be possible to maintain a sufficiently large army for all proximate purposes without any form of compulsion. . . . It was very desirable not to do anything now which would intensify the suspicion which . . . was at the bottom of our labour troubles.

As a result a clause to renew the wartime conscription clauses was omitted from the Bill. In early August 1919 Churchill agreed to bring conscription quickly to an end, and, later in the month, largely as an economic measure, the War Cabinet agreed to restrict armed services' expenditure by working on the assumption that 'the British Empire will not be engaged in any great war during the next ten years, and that no Expeditionary Force is required for this purpose.'[26]

The government also became concerned about attempts to get service men to demobilise themselves on 11 May 1919. Under the recruitment scheme organised by Lord Derby in October 1915 men had stated their willingness to serve in the army, and they had signed a form which stated, 'You may be retained after the termination of hostilities until your service can be spared, but in no case shall this retention exceed six months.' The belief among many of the Derby men that they should be released within six months of the signing of the Armistice was taken up by the Soldiers', Sailors' and Airmen's

Union (SSAU) which had been formed some time at the end of 1918 or early in 1919, and by the *Daily Herald* under George Lansbury.[27]

The SSAU's advocacy of a potentially very disruptive issue gave the government the opportunity to take firm action against it. Whilst it had not developed into a major body within the armed forces as the Police Union had within the police, it could nevertheless be seen as a focal point for dissent. The SSAU's aims were not very dramatic. It advocated more rapid demobilisation and the abolition of conscription. Its other aims were to

> improve the status of serving men; to increase pay; to bring about shorter hours of duty; adequate pensions and maintenance for all dependants; prevent victimisation; secure recognition of the Union by the government and prevent servicemen from being employed as strike-breakers.[28]

The War Office apparently watched the SSAU's progress, at first without great concern. A report in *The Times*, which purportedly came from 'a news agency' but presumably came from the War Office or Scotland Yard, commented that, 'The union appears to have originated for a perfectly legitimate purpose ... the improvement of the conditions of demobilised men, and at first officers and serving soldiers were invited to become hon. members, the active membership being then confined to the discharged men.' However the report contrasted this with later developments, when the appeal was made to serving men to become trade unionists, and this was allegedly 'developed and enthused by civilians of extreme socialistic, not to say, revolutionary tendencies'. To Special Branch the SSAU had 'now become definitely a branch of the Herald League'.

Whether or not there was such a change in the nature and policies of the SSAU, clearly the story given to the press was intended to warn soldiers from either attending demonstrations or attempting to discharge themselves on 11 May. The report in *The Times* predicted, 'It is extremely doubtful whether these demonstrations will take place in view of the steps taken by the authorities.' It also gave a clear warning:

> Even if the organised demonstration fails, there is reason for saying that the union leaders are still urging men to take 'French leave' tomorrow. A news agency states that it is in a position to announce that any man who acts on this advice will be arrested and dealt with as a deserter.[29]

After the 11 and 12 May passed, Basil Thomson, head of Scotland Yard's Special Branch and newly appointed Director of Intelligence under the Home Office, made the most of what had been planned. He reported to the War Cabinet,

> Evidence is in the hands of the police, showing that the plot was widespread, that Mr. George Lansbury had subscribed £80 to the union funds, and that H. T. MacDonald, a *Herald* reporter, intended to go with Eden Paul, the notorious revolutionary speaker, to Grove Park and other centres, and bring a disorderly demonstration to Whitehall. Owing to the effective steps taken by the military authorities and to publicity given to the movement in the press, as well as the action of the police in searching premises and putting the two ringleaders under observation, the movement collapsed.[30]

It seems that the authorities were concerned about the mood of the soldiers, but not unduly fearful of the SSAU. Before 11 May there appears to have been real concern that large numbers of soldiers might try to discharge themselves. Military intelligence first heard of this from 'a coffee shop rumour among British soldiers in Paris' in late April. Churchill, whilst stating that he thought that 'nothing untowards would happen', nevertheless warned the War Cabinet on 8 May:

> It was possible that on this day [11] soldiers might march out of camp and discard their uniforms. He had received information from the Adjutant General as to conditions in France, at Kempton Park, Winchester and other centres, to the effect that the men might possibly demobilise themselves. *The Daily Herald* had fostered this campaign amongst the men, and the leaders who had been working the affair up had been to see General Childs and confessed to him that they were frightened at the turn events had taken. . . . . The commands had been notified and steps taken to meet any great outbreak that might occur.

In the event Thomson could only report threatened action by just under 1,000 men – about 800 at Battersea and 150 at Osterley – which ended after peaceful persuasion by officers.[31]

The encouragement of soldiers to discharge on 11 May gave the authorities the opportunity to discredit and to 'disorganise' the SSAU, a body which was not felt to be strong but which was deemed to contain a 'Bolshevik element'. Earlier action against the SSAU had been difficult, as it had grown by using the loophole of giving 'honorary membership' to serving soldiers and sailors. The authorities had condoned this ploy when encouraging the growth of a 'patriotic' ex-servicemen's organisation, the Comrades of the Great War, as a counter to others more worrying to them.

Unrest over the slowness of demobilisation co-existed with concern over pay and the level of allowances granted to dependants. The very unsatisfactory provision for dependants had caused discontent on and off throughout the First World War. In early 1918 troops in France had been angered by news of food shortages at home. One Ministry of Food memorandum reported that the effect of this 'is very serious and . . . their morale has suffered considerably in consequence'. J. R. Clynes, the Food Controller and a Labour member of the government, recalled in his autobiography,

> Serious outbreaks occurred in France among the troops behind the lines. Rumours had reached them, very much exaggerated, of starvation in England; and things began to look ugly when they held mass meetings to know why, while they risked their lives for their country, she could not even manage to feed their wives and children at home.[32]

Given the appalling conditions facing the troops on the Western Front it is surprising that there was not more collective discontent than appears to have taken place. Individual dissent or failure was dealt with extremely harshly.[33] But probably for most soldiers a belief in Britain's cause and the thought that good would come of a decisive conclusion to the war was both a justification for being in the trenches and a means to keep going. As one sergeant in the Royal Marines put it, when explaining why he was willing to put up with the war going on for another year,

> of course I should like it to finish tomorrow but I should like it to finish properly, that is that Germany gets such a smashing that she won't be able to try the experiment again for a good many years, not during our lifetime or our Boy's lifetime, you see its no use to indulge in selfish thoughts, that is thinking of your own happiness, we are not only fighting for our present happiness, but fighting for the generation that is to come into the world.[34]

Such sentiments, reflecting the national justification put forward by Lloyd George and other political leaders, were very widespread. Many soldiers could hold and express such views to loved ones at home and yet simultaneously share the live-and-let live philosophy that was equally common among many soldiers enduring the conditions on the Western Front.

While the majority of troops did not support calls for a compromise early peace, they did want improvements in their pay and conditions, which were dramatically inferior to those of Dominion troops often in nearby lines or rest camps. They also wanted better separation allowances and pensions paid to their wives and children. Such concerns were the major features of the ex-servicemen's organisations – and they exerted pressure on these as well as over demobilisation. For most of the soldiers who had seen it through on the Western Front or elsewhere the achievement of a better deal on pay, allowances and pensions was paramount. There was less interest in linking up with socialist groups which had been pacifist during the war. Britain did not suffer defeat – so there was less questioning among the British ex-servicemen's organisations generally of the whole political and social structure than was the case in many other countries.

During the First World War the government had been slow and reluctant to improve the terms given to soldiers and sailors and their dependants. By late 1916 the real value of separation allowances and pensions had fallen by 33 per cent. This decline caused hardship and discontent, especially in urban areas. In rural areas there was often less concern as farm labourers' families had experienced very low wages before the war. In Loughborough one soldier's wife, who had three children, made the appeal:

> Give us a fair allowance, or it will be found necessary to add an extra wing to the workhouse, for the day of miracles is past, and we come to the final conclusion that we cannot compete with the constant 'going up' of food prices.[35]

Many servicemen's families avoided destitution because of the enhanced opportunities for women to work in relatively well paid jobs. Early on in the war, when many families were excluded from allowances and when the payment to others was slow, there would have been hardship for many other families had it not been for the help from the various wartime charities. The War Office long resisted accepting responsibility for soldiers' families. In 1916 Kitchener was still asserting that 'a pension or gratuity for dependants . . . should not be granted as a right.' In July 1916 a large number of municipal authorities revolted at the government's plans to leave them to raise and administer supplementary money for the dependants of serving men.[36]

The reluctance of the authorities to pay reasonable sums as pensions to discharged men or as separation allowances to dependants became a political issue during the war and gave rise to several ex-servicemen's organisations. There were public meetings of protest. In early September 1915 the Labour MP Will Thorne called on the Home Secretary to stop the police breaking up such meetings 'because all of us are absolutely dissatisfied with the pay allowed to the wives and children'. Another leading trade unionist of the New Unionism period, Ben Tillett, won a notable by-election victory against a Coalition candidate in North Salford on 2 November 1917, as an Independent (though in reality a 'patriotic labour' candidate) calling for vigorous prosecution of the war, action against war profiteers and, following a TUC resolution, a 200 per cent increase in pay for soldiers and sailors.[37]

There was a radical edge to the campaigns of the National Association of Discharged Sailors and Soldiers and of later left-wing ex-servicemen's organisations. In late 1916 contrasts could and were made between the extravagance of wealthy people going out to eat dinners at 7s 6d a head at a time when the newspapers of the North were carrying complaints of married men being discharged from the army and having to live on 4s 8d to 6s 8d per week. The formation of the National Association (initially the Blackburn and District) in September 1916 arose from cases such as these and from the success of the Blackburn Trades and Labour Council in getting two men's allowances increased from 5s 3d to 16s 3d a week.[38]

With the introduction of conscription from 1916 there was a feeling among those conscripted that the state had an obligation to provide welfare and pensions for those disabled. The Liberal MP James Hogge championed servicemen's issues and in January 1917 formed an organisation, the Naval and Military War Pensions League, to further the case for statutory pensions. His campaign widened with the passing of the Military Service (Review of Exceptions) Act on 5 April 1917, whereby discharged ex-servicemen, some disabled, could be recalled to the armed forces. Hogge campaigned for the repeal of this Act. From his and others' efforts, a new organisation called the National Federation of Discharged and Demobilised Sailors and Soldiers emerged, replacing Hogge's League.[39] This body soon challenged the son of Lord Derby, the Secretary of State for War, in a by-election in the Abercromby constituency of Liverpool in June 1917. This was a stronghold of Liverpool Toryism – but Derby was embarrassed when the campaign centred on repeal of the recent Act and better pensions, training and employment for ex-servicemen. Whilst the Federation's candidate was soundly beaten, the War

Cabinet was concerned about the outcome, and two days before polling Bonar Law promised an enquiry into the way that review tribunals operated.[40]

In response to the pressure from these ex-servicemen's organisations Lord Derby, backed by his colleagues in the War Cabinet, set about creating an ex-servicemen's organisation (the Comrades) of an ostensibly non-political nature, unlike the other two which tended towards Labour or Radicalism. In reality, the Comrades was of a Conservative complexion. It received considerable financial support from many figures in commerce and industry, including £500 from Stanley Baldwin and £1,000 from David Davies, Chairman of Ocean Coal and Cambrian Railways. The Army Council welcomed the new organisation, observing in August 1917 that 'the formation of an organisation of this character would serve the useful secondary purpose of countering the activities of the promoters of other associations amongst soldiers and ex-soldiers which avowedly have for their object an organised opposition to authority.'[41]

In mid-1917, following the February Revolution in Russia and the major engineering strikes in Britain in May, the authorities were anxious about revolutionary activities involving soldiers and sailors and ex-servicemen. After the Leeds Convention of June 1917 called for the establishment of Workers' and Soldiers' Councils, the War Cabinet determined to enforce firmly Army regulation 451 which forbade soldiers to 'take part in any meetings, demonstrations or processions for party or political purposes, in barracks, quarters, camps or their vicinity. Under no circumstances whatever will he attend such meetings, wherever held, in uniform.' A representative of the War Office informed the War Cabinet on 31 July that

> largely under the influence of what had taken place in Russia, efforts were being made to induce soldiers to interest themselves actively in political agitation of a character likely to weaken the discipline of the Army. Cases had already occurred where meetings had been convened and addressed by soldiers, but, as there were grounds for thinking that the instigators were not fully cognisant of the King's Regulations, the offenders have been dealt with leniently.

These cases were presumably at Tonbridge Wells and Birmingham, where soldiers had already been involved in forming Workers' and Soldiers' Councils. The War Cabinet decided that soldiers could not be permitted to join such bodies, that the Army regulations would be enforced 'regardless of whether the meetings were likely to be for or against the government's war policy', and that these decisions would have to be enforced 'in all circumstances'. At the same meeting, after learning that at Barrow and Liverpool attempts had been made to get soldiers loaned to munitions works to join strikes, the War Cabinet decided that where a strike was authorised by a trade union all soldiers lent to munitions works in the area would be withdrawn, and where it was unofficial 'soldiers joining with the strikers should be recalled to the colours'.[42]

The War Cabinet heard more of Workers' and Soldiers' Councils just over a week later when it received a request from the authorities in Glasgow to prohibit such a body representing the whole of Scotland from meeting in Glasgow on 11 August. The Glasgow authorities called for a ban on the grounds of potential disorder, counter-demonstrations being threatened. The Cabinet decided that this and future meetings held there or elsewhere should be banned and that an announcement should be made making it clear that it regarded 'the objects of such meetings as illegal and would not permit them to be held'. The Cabinet ordered that the announcement of the prohibition of the Glasgow meeting should not be made until 4 p.m. on the Friday, presumably to prevent support for the meeting being organised in the factories.[43]

By mid-September 1917 Brigadier Childs told the War Cabinet that 'the efforts to create a Workers' and Soldiers' Council in this country had been a complete failure so far as the army was concerned.'[44] This failure was due not only to the government's firmness but, in contrast to other countries, to the relative lack of disaffection in the army and to the weakness of the revolutionary movement. This weakness was accentuated by their martyrdom as conscientious objectors. One recent verdict has been, 'The failure of soviets in Britain, if they can be so dignified, was inevitable given that the organisers were sheep dressed in wolves' clothing.'[45]

Even if the spread of soviets among British troops did not occur, the government nevertheless was faced with sufficient discontent among servicemen in the later stages of the war and its immediate aftermath to feel that the periodic granting of substantial improvements in pay and conditions was necessary. A major move to do this took place after the May 1917 engineering strikes, and was prompted by pressure from the General Federation of Trade Unions.[46] Sir Edward Carson chaired a committee to review the pay and other conditions of the army and navy, which made five reports between September 1917 and May 1918, all of which were carried out after War Cabinet consideration. Further reviews were carried out under the Labour Party minister George Barnes during the remainder of 1918 and in mid-October, not long before the war ended, separation allowances were revised to take account of the considerable rise in the cost of living. Lloyd George urged his colleagues in the War Cabinet to grant a generous settlement as he felt the troops had a very real grievance, and observed,

> it was not right that the government should make concessions reluctantly in the case of the soldiers when they had conceded large concessions to every other class. ... The government had provided for all those who were working at home in security, and it was only right that they should adequately provide for the wives of the fighting forces of the Crown.[47]

Whilst discontent in the army was often at the forefront of ministerial concern, there was similar unrest in the navy. By mid-1917 sailors were airing their resentment at low levels of pay, and in October the men of the Grand Fleet were circulating a petition calling for a 50 per cent pay rise and an increase in allowances. Whilst the government conceded pay rises that autumn, the authorities court martialled two men from HMS *Resolution* for organising the petition.[48]

There was further unrest in the navy and on merchant shipping in 1918. In May the War Cabinet was informed of a mutiny on a transport ship. The crew, which 'had refused duty and were demanding a 50 per cent increase of wages', had been arrested.[49] In naval bases from the spring of that year there were again calls for large pay rises and in May the Workers' Union proposed formal links with lower-deck organisations. At Devonport the men were looking to the Labour Party to put forward their grievances.

Lloyd George took up the particular problems of the sailors in September 1918 after receiving a copy of a pamphlet by Lionel Yexley (the pen name of James Woods) and being assured by Admiral Fisher that Yexley, who had been campaigning for better conditions for sailors since the 1890s, was well informed and reliable. Lloyd George considered seeing Yexley, but decided to refer the issues raised in Yexley's pamphlet to the Board of the Admiralty. Sir Eric Geddes, First Lord of the Admiralty, reassured him that the Board felt that 'although there is a certain amount of dissatisfaction on the Lower Deck there is no probability of this assuming proportions that would impair the discipline of the Navy or lead to any serious incident.' Nevertheless Geddes acted quickly on most of the causes of unrest that Yexley had raised.[50]

Unrest in the navy continued long after the end of the war, for much the same reasons as in the army. Sailors' families were still being squeezed by inflation. Walter Long, who had succeeded Geddes as First Lord of the Admiralty, told the War Cabinet in late January 1919 that in some cases sailors were 'actually compelled to return to the fleet before the expiration of their leave . . . because their means were not sufficient to maintain them without making inroads upon the supplies for their women and children'. Lloyd George received numerous warnings that month about the inadequacy of naval pay. Early in January, following serious unrest among crews of minesweepers, Admiral Wemyss, the First Sea Lord, advised Lloyd George that the trouble would not be resolved 'unless both officers and men are put on such a financial basis as to enable them to cope with the higher prices and higher standard of living now prevalent'.[51] Basil Thomson forwarded to Lloyd George a more alarming, indeed alarmist, appraisal of the situation which warned that 'the whole of the Lower Deck is in deadly earnest' over the pay demands drawn up 'by sub-committees representing the whole of the Lower Deck Societies', and that there was a very real danger of a general strike in the navy and perhaps even attempts to blow up certain ships.[52]

The unrest in the army and navy, combined with major industrial disturbances and tension, pushed the War Cabinet into agreeing the sizeable increases in pay for the armed forces on 28 January 1919. Long, the First Lord of the Admiralty, vigorously argued that any pay rise should be permanent, not given as a temporary adjustment, otherwise 'the Board of the Admiralty could not be responsible for the consequences'.[53]

By the time that the Jerram Committee, which had been set up in December 1918 to look into pay and conditions in the navy, reported to the Admiralty unrest was becoming very serious. The Admiralty received the report on 27 March, but it was not until 29 April that it was discussed by the War Cabinet. Austen Chamberlain, as Chancellor of the Exchequer, was shocked to find that to carry out the report's recommendations would cost an additional £25 million if pre-war manpower levels were maintained. Churchill was alarmed that acceptance of the report's findings would set off demands for comparable treatment in the army and air force. The representatives of the Admiralty, however, were emphatic that a decision was urgently required. Long reported that the sailors had been loyal during their Christmas leave:

> all attempts to work on their grievances in order to sap their loyalty had proved ineffective. Then, like a bombshell, had come the miners' demands, and the men would have been more than human if they had not felt how badly they were paid, and had not experienced bitterness when they saw the results obtained by collective bargaining. It was impossible to exaggerate the seriousness of the position. Unless the Jerram Report were adopted there would be a feeling of intense bitterness among the men, and a great opportunity would be given to the agitators to foment unrest and insubordination.

In spite of Long's dire warnings the War Cabinet postponed making a decision until 8 May 1919. Long told his colleagues that he had received 'such serious reports regarding the Fleet' two days earlier that he had telephoned Lloyd George in Paris. The War Cabinet was warned,

> There was no doubt that the lower deck was in a serious condition and trouble occurred on some ships, and it would be said that the War Cabinet, before whom the matter had been brought during December, would be breaking their word if the concessions now asked were not granted to them. The immediate settlement of the question was now of the greatest importance, and he thought that if this settlement was delayed over the weekend it would be at the gravest possible risk. The First Sea Lord said that he gave this warning because, in the event of trouble and nothing having been settled, he was afraid that he would have to state in public that he had warned the War Cabinet of the consequences of delayed action.

Substantial concessions were agreed the next day, after Bonar Law had returned from Lloyd George in Paris with full powers to act.[54]

In the first half of 1919 the giving of substantial pay rises and other benefits was not just a matter of allaying unrest. It was also a preliminary, or even a prerequisite, to restoring order and discipline. In both the army and navy the authorities continued to fear that there might be trade unionisation or politicisation of the men if such grievances were not remedied. While the emergence of the Sailors', Soldiers' and Airmen's Union was the most dramatic manifestation of this in early 1919, the naval authorities were anxious to limit the role of the lower-deck organisations which were rapidly growing in membership and threatening to develop well beyond their tolerated role as benefit societies. Some of the activists were promoting links with the trade union movement, especially with the Workers' Union, and with the Labour Party. During 1919 the Admiralty was willing not only to make concessions on pay and other benefits but also to allow the men limited democratic involvement in discussing welfare provisions; at least as long as there was turbulence among men based in home waters and in the Baltic as well as in British society generally. As Anthony Carew has observed in his study of the lower deck,

> The Admiralty's strategy was to ride out the period of militancy and then later to re-establish a firm grip on the lower deck. Indeed, the welfare system was specifically designed to remove any justification for men to approach members of Parliament or to have any contact with naval trade unionism.[55]

Whilst the best known incidents of unrest in the armed forces took place early in 1919, in fact there were major problems for the authorities at intervals later, especially in the autumn of 1919. Some were to do with general conditions of service. However, many were to do with opposition to the British role in Russia or Ireland or unease at the use of troops or sailors during industrial disputes.

The celebrations on the weekend of 19 and 20 July 1919 to mark the signing of the peace were accompanied by boycotts and, in some places, disorder, by groups of ex-servicemen and their supporters. The most dramatic instance of rioting was at Luton, where the Town Hall was burnt down, following the local council's refusal to permit ex-servicemen's organisations to hold their own commemoration meeting in a municipal park. Three ex-servicemen's organisations boycotted the celebrations: the National Federation and two splinter groups from it, the National Union of Ex-Servicemen (NUX) and the International Ex-Service's Union (IUX). The NUX and IUX had broken away in May to adopt more political stances: the former, which was to form over 100 branches, aligned with the Labour Party (formally so doing in December) and the latter, much smaller (attracting some 7,000 members) and centred on Glasgow was, according to its organiser, intended to be 'an out and out revolutionary socialist organisation'.[56]

The boycotts of the peace celebrations were designed to contrast the readiness to spend money on festivities with the failure to spend adequately on pensions for the disabled former servicemen or to provide work for those unemployed. Such demonstrations of discontent by ex-servicemen were electorally worrying for Lloyd George and his colleagues. It was not difficult to arouse popular support for the plight of the disabled former soldiers, sailors and airmen by contrasting their rewards with the greed and excessive life styles of the war profiteers. In Britain, as across Europe in 1919, there was a feeling of camaraderie among discharged soldiers – and the Coalition government, like so many others, was faced with 'the almost mystical rights of the veterans'.[57]

The National Federation organised national and local demonstrations during 1919. In late May some 10,000–20,000 turned out to one in London, with the police using batons against some who tried to move away from it to the House of Commons. There were further London demonstrations in September 1919 and in the spring of 1920. In Sheffield 20,000 men and 5,000 widows attended one huge demonstration. Other places which held demonstrations included Edinburgh, Durham, Nottingham, Portsmouth, Brighton and Eastbourne. Overall the activities of the ex-servicemen frequently alarmed the government and ensured that it extended the timespan of the unemployment donation. When the War Cabinet was considering such an extension in May 1919, Horne warned,

> The discharged soldiers' societies were in a dangerous mood and tainted with Bolshevism. The Glasgow society had converted itself to something like a soviet, and had changed its name to 'The International Discharged Soldiers' Society', and he understood that they were now in touch with Russian Bolsheviks. The police and the Triple Alliance were active, and ... considering the disturbed state of these organisations ... the government could not afford to run any risks.[58]

Major concessions by the government on pensions and other ex-servicemen's issues in the second half of 1919 and early 1920 reduced the degree of animosity surrounding these issues. After much pressure by the National Federation, and months of resistance by Worthington-Evans and other ministers, the government allowed pensions for those maimed in the war to be taken 'out of the realm of grace or good nature' and to be given as a statutory right with the passing of the War Pensions (Administrative Provisions) Act of August 1919. When the issue of statutory right to a pension had come up in discussion in the War Cabinet on 26 July Lloyd George had declared that the principle 'was a good one, but it was too early to do so at present: we were too near the end of the war'. Yet following the debate in the House of Commons the principle was conceded. The Act was also seen as a means of getting soldiers' children out of the workhouses, thereby resolving another source of embarrassment for the government. Ex-servicemen's groups were officially recognised and consulted, and were given places on a new central committee set up to advise the Minister of Pensions.[59] In 1921 the National Federation, the National Association and the Comrades amalgamated into the British Legion, and, with the Earl Haig of Bemersyde as its president and the Prince of Wales as its patron, the ex-servicemen's main organisation became ostensibly non-political.

Discontent over rates of pay and conditions, whether of servicemen or ex-servicemen, could be remedied by major concessions. Unrest over state policy was a more serious matter for the authorities. Troops exhausted by the war against Germany were not eager in the autumn of 1918 to volunteer for service in Russia. Attempts to draft men hoping for speedy demobilisation or rumours that such action was being planned were among the causes of the mutinies in the army of January 1919. Frequently during 1919 there was serious unrest among troops sent to fight the Bolsheviks, including those at Reval and Archangel. In February there was disaffection among the 13th Yorkshires at Seletskoye, some 100 miles south of Archangel. Eight ringleaders were sent for court martial. Two sergeants were given death sentences, but these were commuted to life imprisonment.[60] In the navy there were numerous mutinies among men involved in operations against the Bolsheviks. These included the crew of a gunboat, the *Cicala*, refusing to sail up the River Dvina in June and widespread unrest among destroyer crews at Sheerness and Rosyth in October. The disaffection in October was sufficiently widespread for delegations of sailors to set off from Rosyth and Devonport to protest at the Admiralty. In both cases the men were arrested in London. In Plymouth in October 150 troops who had returned from Russia started a riot.

The most serious incident of mutiny occurred in north Russia, where two companies of Royal Marines refused an order to advance and some threw down their weapons. This followed a series of lesser incidents spread over six months. The authorities took a firm line, court martialling eighty-seven men. Thirteen received death sentences, others prison sentences. Whilst the death sentences were commuted and the prison sentences reduced, the authorities showed their intention to take a firm line against dissent towards an undeclared war, and, as such, one in which the dependants of those killed were deemed not to be entitled to pensions.[61]

British operations in Ireland also created concern among British troops. The most dramatic incidents were in the Punjab at Jullandur and Solon at the end of June and in early July 1920. There men of a battalion of the Connaught Rangers mutinied as a protest against Black and Tan atrocities in Ireland. Other matters contributed to the unrest. The men at Julandur were mobilised on a 'frontier basis' with their comforts stopped, yet, as they were not put into action, they still had to parade in great heat and put up with insensitive officers. But the fundamental cause was the news, via mail and new recruits, of the brutal policies of the government in their home areas. Hence they put up such slogans as 'We will fight against the Black and Tans' and 'Stop the murder-gang in Ireland', they raised the green-white-and-gold tricolour, and wore nationalist rosettes.

As with the Royal Marines, large numbers of men were court martialled. Sixty-nine men were brought before the court and sixty-one sentenced. Fourteen received death sentences while the others were given prison sentences ranging from one to twenty years. When thirteen of the fourteen death sentences were commuted, the one man of whom an example was made by being executed by a firing squad, was James Daly, a 22-year-old private who was an articulate nationalist. He had been the leader of a group of men at Solon who had tried to reclaim the rifles that they had voluntarily handed in after making their protest. In this attempt to recover guns, guards had opened fire and two men had been killed.[62]

While the refusals to carry out normal duties at Jullandur and Solon had implications for maintaining British rule in the north-west of India, not least in the local population seeing Irish tricolours replacing Union Jacks on flag poles, the incidents were very much intended to be peaceful gestures for Ireland. Thus at Jullandur the men promised to return to duty should the Indians pose a threat. As T. P. Kilfeather has observed, 'in giving such a guarantee the Connaught Rangers were prepared to keep Pax Britannica in India, although they themselves were protesting against use of the same force in Ireland.'[63]

In Egypt and elsewhere, where there was unrest in the British army it appears to have centred primarily on the men's own concerns, notably a speedy return home and early demobilisation; though, as in India, such unrest did challenge the execution of imperial policies in those places. Thus in April 1919 Allenby in Cairo, faced with a nationalist strike of government employees, complained to Sir Henry Wilson.

> I'm sorry to say that some 3,000 men at the Demobilisation Camp at Kantara have refused to allow men to come on as helpers on the railways ... some trade union microbe has got into them; and they are obstinate, though polite, in their refusal. I can't shoot them all for mutiny; so I must carry on as best as I can, and I must resume demobilisation. ... The reasons given by the men was that to work on the railways would be 'strike breaking'. However the real reason is homesickness, and distrust of the War Office and their promises.

He added, 'Demobilisation must go on, or my troops will mutiny.'[64]

Infection of the armed services by 'some trade union microbe' was a major worry for Lloyd George and his government in the aftermath of the First World War. In both the army and navy there were hopes that a return to normality after the titanic upheavals of the Great War would bring a return to the old discipline. 'Temporary men', some from trade unionised occupations and most eager to return to civilian life, would be gone. The British navy would be dispersed around the world's oceans not concentrated in British waters where they would be in contact with domestic unrest and more open to subversive ideas. Haig was quite explicit as to his attitude to conscripts in the army:

> The influence of these men and their antecedents generally are [sic] not such as to foster any spirit but that of unrest and discontent; they come forward under compulsion and they will depart the Army with relief. Men of this stamp are not satisfied with remaining quiet, they come from a class which like [sic] to air real or fancied grievances, and their teaching in this respect is a regrettable antidote to the spirit of devotion and duty of earlier troops.[65]

In the aftermath of the war concern about the reliability of soldiers, sailors and airmen to obey orders if instructed to maintain services during strikes was to lead Lloyd George and his government to look to civilian volunteers to help operate strike-breaking organisations.

While the unrest in the British armed forces in the two years after the Armistice never reached anything like the proportions of dissent in the Russian Imperial Army in Petrograd or on Russia's western front by February 1917, nevertheless it did contribute to the considerable social tension that existed in Britain in the first half of 1919 and at times afterwards.[66] To a ruling class the example of Russia made clear the dangers of a combination of serious industrial unrest and forces of law and order which were themselves disaffected.

Winston Churchill, writing a decade after the Armistice, captured the uncertainties of the times after the sudden ending of the Great War. He commented on the initial appeal of the Bolshevik Revolution and observed,

> So many frightful things had happened, and such tremendous collapses of established structures had been witnessed, the nations had suffered so long, that a tremor, and indeed a spasm, shook the foundations of every State. . . .
> Certainly there were factors which nobody could measure and which no one had ever before seen at work. Armies of nearly four million men had been suddenly and consciously released from the iron discipline of war, from the inexorable compulsions of what they believed to be a righteous cause. All these vast numbers had been taught for years how to kill. . . . If these armies formed a united resolve, if they were seduced from the standards and duty of patriotism, there was no power which could even have attempted to withstand them.[67]

Notes and references

1. Milner to Lloyd George, 13 November 1918; Milner Papers, vol. 35.
2. War Cabinet draft minutes, 25 November 1918; CAB 23–27–132.
3. WC (486), 15 October 1918; CAB 23–8–30.
4. S. Roskill, *Hankey: Man of Secrets, Vol. 2: 1919–1931* (London: Collins, 1972), pp. 24–5.
5. C. Wrigley, *David Lloyd George and the Labour Movement* (Hassocks: Harvester, 1976), pp. 226–7. Cabinet Paper, GT 6374; CAB 24–70. P. B. Johnson, *Land Fit for Heroes* (Chicago: Chicago University Press, 1968), p. 301.
6. Milner diary, 6 December 1918; Milner Papers, vol. 89. See also J. E. Wrench, *Alfred Lord Milner* (London: Eyre and Spottiswoode, 1958), pp. 353–4. Lloyd George was also angered by the administrative failures surrounding soldiers' ability to vote in the 1918 general election.
7. Lloyd George to Balfour, 10 December 1918; LG F/3/3/49. Eric Geddes to Lloyd George, 29 December 1918; LG F/18/2/36. For the original plans and the changing government policies see S. Graubard, 'Military demobilisation in Great Britain following the First World War', *Journal of Contemporary History*, 19, 3 (1947), pp. 297–311.
8. The best surveys of the unrest in the army are A. Rothstein, *The Soldiers' Strikes of 1919* (London: Macmillan, 1980), which draws on

a wide range of local press reports, and G. Dallas and D. Gill, *The Unknown Army* (London: Verso, 1985), pp. 89–125. See also T. H. Wintringham, *Mutiny* (London: Drummond, 1936), pp. 312–16.
9. Milner Papers, vol. 90.
10. Milner to Lloyd George, 7 January 1919; LG F/39/1/5.
11. Rothstein, *op. cit*, pp. 43–7. Dallas and Gill, *op. cit*, pp. 106–7. Lloyd George to Milner, 7 January 1919; LG F/39/1/4.
12. C. E. Callwell, *The Life of Sir Henry Wilson* (London: Cassell, 1927), p. 162.
13. WC (514), 8 January 1919; CAB 23–9–5/6.
14. Diary entries 7 and 6 January 1919; Callwell, *op. cit.*, p. 161.
15. *The Times*, 9 January 1919.
16. W. S. Churchill, *The Aftermath* (London: Thornton Butterworth, 1929), p. 54.
17. WC (521), 28 January 1919; CAB 23–9–27. M. Gilbert, *Winston S. Churchill, Vol. 4: Companion* (London: Heinemann, 1975), pp. 181–91.
18. *The Times*, 12 December 1918. Graubard, *op. cit.*, p. 306.
19. Gilbert, *op. cit.*, pp. 186–7. Lloyd George in conversation with Lord Robert Cecil; Cecil's diary, 13 January 1919. Cecil Papers, 51131, f. 13.
20. Churchill to Lloyd George, 29 January 1919; cited Gilbert, *op. cit.*, p. 191.
21. Callwell, *op. cit.*, p. 166.
22. Dallas and Gill, *op. cit.*, pp. 94–9 and 113–20. Rothstein, *op. cit.*, pp. 69–70. Wintringham, *op. cit.*, pp. 311–24. Gilbert, *op. cit.*, pp. 192–3. R. Blake (ed.), *The Private Papers of Douglas Haig 1914–1919* (London: Eyre and Spottiswoode, 1952), p. 353.
23. Dallas and Gill, *op. cit.*, p. 120.
24. *ibid*, pp. 119–20. Wintringham *op. cit.*, pp. 321–2.
25. WC (520), 28 January 1919; CAB 23–9–24.
26. Churchill, *op. cit.*, p. 63. Rothstein, *op. cit.*, pp. 96–7. WC (537), 26 February 1919; CAB 23–9–86/7. WC (606A and 616A) 5 and 15 August 1919; CAB 23–15–164/7 and 270. *Morning Post*, 7 and 10 March 1919.
27. For surveys of the SSAU's history see S. R. Ward, 'Intelligence surveillance of British ex-servicemen, 1918–1920', *Historical Journal*, 16, 1 (1973), pp. 179–188, especially pp. 183–5, and D. Englander, 'Troops and trade unions, 1919', *History Today*, 37, 3 (1987), pp. 8–13.
28. A SSAU handbill; cited in Englander, *op. cit.*, p. 10.
29. *The Times*, 10 May 1919. Report on revolutionary organisations in the United Kingdom (GT 7196), 30 April 1919; CAB 24–78–391.
30. Report on revolutionary organisations in the United Kingdom (GT 7254); CAB 24–79–175. He also wrote of this in his memoirs, *Queer People* (London: Hodder and Stoughton, 1922), pp. 277–8.
31. Reports on revolutionary organisations, 7 and 14 March 1919 (GT 7218 and 7254); CAB 24–79–64 and 175. WC (564), 8 May 1919; CAB 23–10–37.

32. B. Waites, *A Class Society At War: England 1914–1918* (Leamington Spa: Berg, 1987), pp. 230–1. J. R. Clynes, *Memoirs 1869–1924* (London: Hutchinson, 1937), pp. 235–6.
33. For the savage response to individual dissent, misbehaviour or failure to carry out orders through shell shock as well as desertion see A. Babington, *For the Sake of Example* (London: Cooper, 1983). For collective unrest see D. Gill and G. Dallas, 'Mutiny at Etaples base in 1917', *Past and Present*, 66 (1975), pp. 88–112 and Dallas and Gill, *op. cit.*, especially chapters 6 and 7.
34. Bert Feilder to his wife, Nell, 8 November 1915. Printed in M. Moynihan, *A Place Called Armageddon* (Newton Abbot: David and Charles, 1975), p. 51.
35. *Loughborough Echo*, 1 December 1916.
36. E. S. Pankhurst, *The Home Front* (London: Hutchinson, 1932), pp. 78–84. *The Times*, 20 July 1916.
37. J. Schneer, *Ben Tillett* (London: Croom Helm, 1982), pp. 192–3.
38. G. Wootton, *The Politics of Influence* (London: Routledge and Kegan Paul, 1963), pp. 45 and 78–9.
39. S. R. Ward, 'Great Britain: land fit for heroes lost', pp. 10–37 in Ward (ed.), *The War Generation: Veterans of the First World War* (Port Washington, NY: Kennikat Press, 1975) and also Ward, 'Intelligence surveillance', pp. 180–1.
40. Ward, 'Great Britain', pp. 15–16. P. Waller, *Democracy and Sectarianism* (Liverpool: Liverpool University Press, 1981), p. 280.
41. Wootton, *op. cit.*, pp. 67 and 103. Ward, *War Generation*, p. 17.
42. WC (200), 31 July 1917; CAB 23–3–146. Memorandum (GT 1522) by Lord Derby, 26 July 1917; CAB 24–21–74/5.
43. WC (207), 8 August 1917; CAB 23–3–165. Memorandum (GT 1625) by Munro, 6 August 1917; CAB 24–22–135/8.
44. WC (231), 12 September 1917; CAB 23–4–39.
45. D. Englander and J. Osborne, 'Jack, Tommy and Henry Dubb: the armed forces and the working class', *Historical Journal*, 21, 3 (1978), pp. 593–621.
46. WC (196), 26 July 1917; CAB 23–3–134/5.
47. WC (486), 15 October 1918; CAB 23–8–29.
48. A. Carew, *The Lower Deck of the Royal Navy 1900–1939* (Manchester: Manchester University Press, 1981), pp. 72–7.
49. WC (411), 14 May 1918; CAB 23–6–14.
50. E. Geddes to Lloyd George, 26 September 1918; L6 F/18/2/21. Carew, *op. cit.*, pp. 88–92. See also W. Kendall, *The Revolutionary Movement in Britain 1900–1921* (London: Weidenfeld and Nicolson, 1969), pp. 190–2. Yexley was a radical in politics, and eager to divide the lower deck from the Labour Party.
51. WC (520), 28 January 1919; CAB 23–9–24. Wemyss to Lloyd George, 4 January 1919; LG F/47/4/10. Waldorf Astor also made this point to him in an undated letter; LG F/2/7/3.
52. B. Thomson to J. T. Davies, 20 January 1919; L6 F/46/9/3.
53. WC (520) 28 January 1919; CAB 23–9–24.

54. WC (560, 564 and 565), 29 April, 8 and 9 May 1919; CAB 23–10–20/2 and 37/40.
55. Carew, *op. cit.*, pp. 105–15.
56. Churchill, *op. cit.*, p. 61. Rothstein, *op. cit.*, p. 60. Ward, 'Intelligence surveillance', pp. 186–7. Ward, *War Generation*, pp. 25–6.
57. C. S. Maier, *Recasting Bourgeois Europe* (Princeton, NJ: Princeton University Press, 1975), p. 5.
58. Wootton, *op. cit.*, p. 125. WC (574), 30 May 1919; CAB 23–10–70.
59. *ibid.*, pp. 108–9 and 203–10. WC (600), 26 July 1919; CAB 23-11-68/70. Addison to Worthington-Evans, 12 August 1919; Addison Papers, Box 43.
60. Rothstein, *op. cit.*, pp. 44, 47, 55–8 and 78–81. For the courageous opposition of a diplomat to the British invasion at Archangel, and for his loss of career and pension, see Rothstein's *When Britain Invaded Soviet Russia: The Consul who Rebelled* (London: Journeyman Press, 1979), especially pp. 81–6 and 110–11.
61. I am indebted for these and more details of naval mutinies to Carew, *op. cit.*, pp. 110–13 and 212–13.
62. T. P. Kilfeather, *The Connaught Rangers* (Dublin: Anvil, 1969), pp. 1–9 and 128–95. K. Jeffery, 'The post-war army', pp. 210–37; especially pp. 227–28 in I. F. Beckett and K. Simpson (eds), *A Nation in Arms* (Manchester: Manchester University Press, 1985). M. Hay, 'The Indian mutiny that made an Irish martyr', *Observer Magazine*, 4 November 1979, pp. 103–4.
63. Kilfeather, *op. cit.*, p. 146.
64. Allenby to Wilson, 21–3 April 1919. Printed in K. Jeffery (ed.), *The Military Correspondence of Field Marshal Sir Henry Wilson 1918–1922* (London: Bodley Head, 1985), pp. 98–9. For similar comments in a letter of 17 May 1919, see also pp. 101–3.
65. War Cabinet Memorandum GT 6874, 3 October 1917; quoted in Ward, *War Generation*, p. 28.
66. On the importance of the disaffection of the army in Petrograd in February 1917, in contrast to its role in 1905, see T. Hasegawa, *The February Revolution: Petrograd, 1917* (Seattle: University of Washington Press, 1981) and A. K. Wildman, *The End of the Russian Imperial Army* (Princeton, NJ: Princeton University Press, 1980).
67. Churchill, *op. cit.*, p. 60.

4
Unrest in the police force

The reliability of much of the police force was in doubt when the government needed the forces of law and order most. Between August 1918 and August 1919 there was much disaffection among police officers over pay and working conditions. Even more worrying for the government, this discontent led to an upsurge in support for trade unionism.

One of the most notable features of this period is the ruthless determination of the government to stamp out trade unionism in the police force, following the considerable concessions of August 1918. The plans to eradicate trade unionism came from the top. Lloyd George had been embarrassed that the London police strike of August 1918 had caught the government by surprise. Thereafter, he was personally much involved in the plans to deal with further trade union action by policemen.

As with the armed forces, unrest in the police was centred on the way their real standard of living had been dropping in the face of soaring prices. This had been exacerbated by knowledge of the scale of pay rises and war bonuses that many groups of industrial workers had extracted from the government. At the time of the 1918 strike a dock labourer's basic pay was £3 4s 11d and a policeman's £2 2s. The policemen also had many particular grievances. These included severe and often arbitrary discipline, involving heavy fines which could be deducted from their wage packets over many weeks, working long hours that were frequently badly arranged, and the loss of their rest days due to wartime manpower shortages. In 1916 discontent had been sufficiently severe among the Birkenhead police force for eighty-five men to resign and so be called up for the army.[1]

In late August 1918 Lloyd George and the War Cabinet were taken by surprise when the National Union of Police and Prison Officers (NUPPO) warned that it would suspend its no-strike rule at midnight on 29 August unless a series of demands were met. Its ultimatum, issued on 27 August 1918, called for the reinstatement of PC Thomas Thiel, its provincial organiser, who, on 25 August, had been dismissed from the force for his union activities; the current 12s war bonus to be increased to £1, to be converted into permanent wages and made pensionable; for the police to be given the 12.5 per cent bonus that many other groups of workers had received; and for union recognition. Although the Commissioner of the Metropolitan Police was in the process of preparing a package of wage concessions and was fully aware of the case for them, nothing had been intimated to the men, and the senior officers at Scotland Yard were quite oblivious that a crisis was imminent in London's police force.[2] As a result no precautions had been made to meet a strike.

The big issue as far as the government was concerned was union recognition. Brief strikes in 1872 and 1890 had been seen as mutinies; and while concessions had been made on each occasion, the ringleaders were dismissed from the force. When the predecessor of NUPPO had been formed in secret in 1913, the Home Office soon made it very clear that any policeman joining it would be dismissed. In February 1917 detectives even raided a house in London where a union meeting was being held, and twenty-four members of the Metropolitan Police who were among those present were subsequently suspended.[3] So there had been consistent and very firm resistance to unionisation in the police in the past. In the turbulent conditions of 1918 many in authority saw recognition as likely to have serious and wider repercussions. Sir Nevil Macready, then Adjutant-General of the Army, later recalled that on 31 August he warned Lord Milner

> that the Metropolitans being an organised force directly under the government any concessions made to them in the direction of union recognition would be more than a stepping-stone towards a similar state of affairs in the Army, an opportunity which would not be neglected by those who were already making insidious efforts to undermine the discipline of the troops.[4]

The strike began on 30 August, and was strongly supported. All the Metropolitan force struck, followed the same evening by most of the City of London force. On the morning of 30 August Lloyd George presided over an emergency meeting of the War Cabinet to which Smuts reported the outcome of a meeting he had held with the superintendents of the Metropolitan Police districts. They had been unanimous in the view that the men's pay demands were reasonable 'and that, unless this claim was conceded *in toto* there was no chance of a settlement of the dispute'. The superintendents were also unanimous in their opposition to recognising the union, but they were divided as to whether Thiel should be reinstated. The majority, however, felt 'that such reinstatement would practically amount to the recognition of the union', and so they opposed reinstatement. Smuts warned the War Cabinet, 'Undoubtedly the situation was very serious, as the union was affiliated to other trade unions, and there was a possibility of the strike extending to other trades.'

The gravity of the strike was also emphasised by the Assistant Commissioner for Police and by Macready. The Assistant Commissioner reported that all districts were affected and he predicted that there would be no police on night duty that night. As to special constables, he stated that 'those who belonged to the working classes were all union men and not to be depended on', but that others were already covering in place of those on strike. Macready informed the War Cabinet that he could arrange for military substitutes to be available if necessary. He also told them 'that most of the telephone wires to the police stations had been cut'.

The War Cabinet quickly agreed to concede the police pay demand. Indeed, there was anger among ministers (beyond the War Cabinet) that the police pay had not been increased sooner. Walter Long, the Colonial Secretary and a man who has been deemed to be 'an excellent example of the country squire in politics', expressed the feelings of many Conservatives when he observed to Bonar Law, 'The police are entitled to extra pay – why ag[ricultural] labourers now, under Prothero's ridiculous Act, get 30s to 38s.'[5] The War Cabinet delegated the task of arranging a settlement of the strike to General Smuts, one of its members, and to Sir George Cave, the Home Secretary. Smuts offered to see two policemen from each division but not the union leadership. His offer was rejected.[6]

The next morning, 31 August, Lloyd George took the matter into his own hands. He summoned Milner urgently to Downing Street at 11 a.m. to join an emergency War Cabinet meeting with Bonar Law, Cave, Macready and Sir Henry Wilson. The previous day, Milner had recorded in his diary that the police strike 'looks ugly'. At the meeting on 31 August Cave warned of 'the risk that if the question of the police strike was not settled at once it would be raised at the Trades Union Congress next week, and might lead to sympathetic strikes in many quarters'.

The military men present were willing to take tough action against the strikers. Wilson urged that if the policemen declined the government's offer to settle the dispute then 'they should be put in the trenches'. According to Wilson, Macready felt that if the offer of increased pay and the reinstatement of Thiel was not enough, then the policemen 'ought to be conscripted and made to carry out their police duties as soldiers'.

This line of argument begged the question of how indispensible the police were. Hence most of the discussion focused on whether the strikers could be replaced by special constables. Wilson, in urging his tough line, recognised it would 'raise difficulties of policing London' but was optimistic that 'by enlisting special constables and making some use of the military' they would cope. The Conservative politicians expressed confidence in the willingness of the middle classes to meet the needs of law and order. Bonar Law observed that 'the important thing was to get the country behind the government and then they would have no difficulty in getting special constables.' Macready, however, 'expressed doubts as to whether there were enough individuals with leisure to act as special constables'.

Lloyd George, who clearly wanted the dispute settled very quickly, was more interested in making some move towards meeting the men's desire to be represented. Cave felt 'that it was essential to give the men some means of collective representation of their grievances'. Lloyd George was emphatic that the police had either no such means or very inadequate means. He skilfully ended the discussion at that point, observing 'that the decision as to the action to be taken should be postponed until he had seen the men's representatives who . . . were shortly coming to Downing Street'. He added that 'until he had ascertained the temper of the men it would be premature to reach a decision'.[7]

At noon, when Lloyd George met the policemen's representatives he displayed his considerable powers of achieving a settlement by flattering those present, by avoiding addressing directly many of the key issues and by studied ambiguity. PC James Marston, NUPPO's vice-president, left feeling that Lloyd George fully sympathised with the men and their union. As the delegation departed, Lloyd George shook hands with Marston and allegedly told him, 'Now don't forget if ever a similar situation should arise you must come and see me'. In seeing Marston and his colleagues Lloyd George appeared to be granting NUPPO *de facto* recognition. Moreover he skilfully sidestepped the issue during the negotiations by allegedly saying that 'he could not in war-time sanction the recognition of a Police Union'. The NUPPO leaders left him secure in the belief that union recognition would be granted once the war was over.[8]

It was not by chance that Lloyd George's statements could not be officially confirmed. No transcript was made of the proceedings. This was probably a deliberate decision for it was normal to take down a full record of such meetings with senior government figures during the war (and indeed, it had often been done before the war). Although this meeting with the policemen's representatives was called quickly, it had not been called at such short notice (being arranged the previous night). So it seems to be the case that this was one of the many occasions when Lloyd George wished to make a quick settlement by glossing over real difficulties. The lack of a written record avoided any commitment to details which could embarrass him later with either his Conservative colleagues or NUPPO. Similarly, he was adroit as to what was put in the official communiqué of the meeting. Lloyd George told his colleagues that he was seeing the representatives 'as policemen and not as members of the union'. But this was carefully omitted from the official statement, much to the annoyance of Macready and others.

While Lloyd George was very sympathetic to policeman having better channels of communication through which to express their grievances to their superiors, he was not favourable to independent trade unionism in the police force. Indeed, within a few months he was involved in plans to crush NUPPO.

The August 1918 crisis in the London police force pointed to the limitations of special constables. They could be used to help deal with specific strikes or major emergencies. During the 1911 rail strike 4,142 special constables had been enrolled in Liverpool. But often most volunteers were not where they were most needed. In working-class industrial areas the local authorities were often unwilling to recruit special constables and where they were called for, few people volunteered. This was to be the pattern in 1926 in the General Strike. To obtain full-time, day and night replacements for the regular police in August 1918, the government had to turn to the armed forces protection of government and other key buildings. Macready was reluctant to rely on conscripted troops either for dealing with strikes or public disorder. Earlier in 1918 he had commented that the officers 'are not what they were in the days when we used to have strikes before the war. . . . The same applies almost equally to the men – [they] will not put up with what the troops . . . formerly used to put up with at the hands of strikers.'⁹ Hence a disciplined, reliable regular police force was a high priority for the British government facing the industrial and social tensions of the First World War and its aftermath.

Having settled the police strike, albeit by making 'a rather ambiguous recognition of their right to combine for the redress of grievances' (as Cave's biographer has put it), Lloyd George sacked the Chief Commissioner of Police, Sir Edward Henry. In this Lloyd George showed that he was 'a good butcher'. At the emergency War Cabinet on 31 August Cave had asked Lloyd George to see Henry who was in 10 Downing Street. Lloyd George had refused, and had bluntly stated that he would 'discuss the question of Sir Edward Henry when the present crisis was over'. That very afternoon Lloyd George discussed a replacement for Henry with Milner and Sir Henry Wilson. In spite of Macready's reluctance to leave his senior army position, he was pressed into service. Lloyd George rejected Cave's offer to resign as Home Secretary.¹⁰

The appointment of Macready to the post of Commissioner of the Metropolitan Police at this time was, in effect, a statement of Lloyd George's intent to restore discipline of a military kind in the police force. Macready was very much the kind of figure who would meet with the approval of Lord Milner and Sir Henry Wilson, Lloyd George's advisers in the matter. He was a professional soldier who had served throughout the Empire, with active service during the Egyptian campaign of 1882 and the Boer War. Macready, as a servant of the state, saw his duty to be non-political. But, probably by 1919 and certainly by 1921, most of his private political views appear to have been of the impeccably die-hard variety. He was something of a trouble-shooter for authority. After dealing with strikers in South Wales during late 1910 in a firm, yet usually cautious manner, he had handled the military side of other industrial disputes from the War Office in 1911 and 1912. He was in Ulster in 1914 and would return to Ireland again in March 1920 as Commander-in-Chief to co-ordinate the activities of the army and the police until the final evacuation of British troops at the end of 1922.¹¹

In 1919 Macready worked ruthlessly and relentlessly to undermine the police union. He clearly saw this as essential to his 'efforts to place the force on a sound footing'. Macready was totally out of sympathy with trade unionism, let alone police trade unionism, and appears to have been unable to understand its nature and objectives. Thus in his autobiography he wrote of the miners' unofficial strike committee of the Rhondda of late 1910 that it

> consisted of half a dozen fanatical socialists, strongly impregnated with the theories of Karl Marx . . . Sparing of words as a rule, rigid teetotallers, unable to see beyond the narrow tenets of their creed, they undoubtedly exercised a strong hold over the strikers, and defied the authority of the miners' agents. . . . For my own information I made enquiries about the antecedents of the members of the strike committees, and found that as a rule they were indifferent workmen and generally without any stake in the locality. Their energies being exhausted in attending meetings and in organising their adherents, it is hardly to be wondered that they had little time or inclination to become efficient workmen.

Macready did, however, concede 'that when they gave their word to me to carry out any undertaking it was scrupulously adhered to, a line of conduct which the employers might well have imitated'.

When it came to the police union's officials Macready was no less unsympathetic. Though he acknowledged in his memoirs that he 'came across cases of men with families who before the pay was increased were in a pitiable condition', he could only see the leaders of the union as 'those who were propagating the doctrine of a union to a great extent for their personal ends and ambition'.

As for dealing with the union officials, or indeed dealing with all ranks in the police, Macready expected obedience along military lines. His memoirs make much of how he dressed down even the most senior for lack of deference. As for the leader of NUPPO, he recalled, in an extraordinary passage in his memoirs,

> Marston when in my presence invariably adopted a hectoring bullying manner, calculated to disturb the temper of the most placid. It did not, however, require many interviews with him to see that my game was at all costs to remain unruffled until through sheer desperation he and his executive should make a false step and deliver themselves into my hand. In the meantime as the man had not a spark of humour I derived constant amusement at our interviews by 'pulling his leg' before his brother deputationists and turning the laugh on him, which had the effect of shaking their faith in him as their chosen leader. To have suspended him from duty and taken disciplinary action, which his conduct towards me on many occasions more than fully justified, would only have caused an explosion before the time was ripe, and therefore the only alternative was to swallow my natural inclinations and bide my time. This self-restraint, and it was considerable, was fully rewarded in August 1919.

Through such tactics Macready had gained a reputation in South Wales of being able to 'bamboozle' strike leaders. From early on in his appointment with the Metropolitan Police he was determined to outwit what he felt to be 'the machinations of Police-constable Marston and his executive'.[12]

Lloyd George's reliance on such a man in dealing with the Police and in Ireland calls into question the depth of his radicalism at this stage of his career. He was now adopting the 'thorough' policy, the attitude of 'the knock-out blow', against various 'enemies within' both in the final phases of the war and in the period after it.

Lloyd George's settlement of 31 August 1918 is important in understanding just how unreasonable Macready's anti-union activities appeared to the NUPPO leaders and to much of the wider Labour Movement. As well as dealing with the pay rise, widows' pensions and reinstatement of men dismissed for union membership, the settlement stated,

> A body should be set up representing the members of the Force in matters connected with their conditions of service and general welfare, other than questions of discipline. In setting up this organisation, it was arranged that the Home Secretary should consult with the representatives of the Metropolitan Police.
>
> There would be no objection to members of the force joining the National Union of Police and Prison Officers, so long as the Union did not attempt to interfere with the discipline of the service or to induce members of the Force to withhold their services.[13]

In accordance with this settlement the NUPPO leaders saw Cave on 12 September 1918 and agreed rules for the creation of a Representative Board which was to be elected by secret ballot. In the memorandum then agreed were two clauses which were to give Macready a lever against NUPPO. One stated that the Representative Board 'shall be entirely within the Force and shall be entirely independent of and unassociated with any outside body'. The other restated that men could join NUPPO providing it did not interfere or call strikes, but added 'that, in the event of a breach of this condition, members of the Force may be called upon to sever their connection with such Union'.[14]

The first Board was elected on 2 October 1918, with most, or all, of those elected being members of NUPPO. Macready was outraged that Metropolitan Policemen canvassed for support for NUPPO in other areas of the country (where other Representative Boards were being elected). He issued an order forbidding such action. Macready appears to have been unable to grasp, let alone accept, what Lloyd George had conceded. He wrote in his memoirs,

> These incidents all pointed to the fact that in spite of what had passed between the Prime Minister and the strikers' deputation on 31 August, Marston and his friends had no intention of relinquishing the campaign to obtain recognition of their union, together with the resulting claim to interfere in the discipline and organisation of the force. As if to emphasise this fact, when the executive committee of the Representative Board came to be elected, the whole of the members of the committee were made *ex-officio* members of the executive committee of the union, thus ensuring the domination of the union over the force.[15]

During the autumn of 1918 Macready continued to prod at NUPPO, to gauge the quality of its leadership and the degree of support it still held. In October 1918 he readily offered to comb-out a thousand men from the Metropolitan Police when there appeared to be further need for hitherto exempt men to be conscripted into the army. Macready fully recognised that this would have included 'some of the more energetic strikers' and he observed in his memoirs that this would have been 'a consummation most devoutly to be wished'. But the war ended before this purge could take place. While sparring with the union Macready was astute enough also to remedy some of the other causes of the 1918 strike, such as the worst features of the system of fines.[16]

Macready bided his time, allowing friction to occur between himself and the Representative Board. In this he was determined to display that the compromise over the union's status that Lloyd George had made was unworkable. Macready firmly believed that there was no middle way between hierarchical control of the police, of the kind he knew throughout his career in the army, and what he saw as NUPPO control of the force. He expected, and indeed worked towards, a show-down with NUPPO. In this he was like Milner in South Africa before the Boer War, who had felt that conflict between the British Empire and the Boers was inevitable. Perhaps someone less abrasive than Macready might have been conciliatory when dealing with the Representative Board and could have delineated an appropriate sphere within which NUPPO might have worked.

However, worries about the occurrence of potentially serious industrial and social disorder after the war strengthened Macready's hand. The unrest of the period highlighted the issue of allegiance especially as NUPPO thrived and affiliated to the Labour Party, the TUC, the London Trades Council and the Manchester Trades Council. In the case of Birmingham, Birmingham Trades Council actually took the initiative in forming a branch of NUPPO. As soon after the 1918 strike as September 1918 the authorities were working on the assumption that the police might not act decisively against strikers. This was demonstrated in the early part of the month by a threatened London Fire Brigade strike and later by a brief rail strike. In both cases it was arranged that troops would be ready in reserve.

The leaders of NUPPO did not think through their position as a public service union of a particularly sensitive kind, so as to set out and stand by defendable positions which would hold the allegiance of their members and gain public support. Instead of developing their own tactics to deal with their situation after August 1918 they made the mistake of reacting, and often over-reacting, to Macready's provocations. But in the mood of late 1918 and early 1919 the union leadership did not need much pushing to come out with what were injudicious comments to be made by leaders of such a public service union. In the heady days of early 1919 there was a view present among the NUPPO leadership, as Macready later observed, 'that Labour was stronger than the government'. Trade union strength in time of war had won the concessions of August 1918, and had been followed by an increase in NUPPO membership from about 10,000 to 50,000 between August and November 1918.[17] It is not surprising that NUPPO's leadership felt strong amidst the rising tide of trade union strength in the four or five months after the Armistice. However, when Labour's strength began to recede, the NUPPO leaders found that they were stranded in untenable positions (as far as much of public opinion was concerned) with Macready ready and waiting to humiliate them or expel them from the police force.

Lloyd George's role in dealing with NUPPO was characteristically *ad hoc*. If the compromise status of NUPPO set out in August was workable, then it was a curious decision of the erstwhile Radical to put a man such as Macready in charge. If, on the other hand, it was unworkable, then the August 1918 settlement becomes a prime example of Lloyd George's willingness to negotiate brilliantly for the short term, but to leave the longer term for another day or to the hope that things would resolve themselves. Probably Lloyd George's conduct can be explained by two political needs. One was to get a quick settlement. The second was to ensure that the government was not again taken by surprise by the Metropolitan Police and to appoint at its head someone who would have the confidence of the military and Imperial figures on whose support Lloyd George's government in part rested. Whether or not the compromise position of NUPPO was viable was a lesser consideration in Lloyd George's mind in late August 1918.

Macready's opportunity to get Lloyd George to agree to undermine his concessions of August came in the latter part of December. Lloyd George was overwrought after the geneal election campaign and anxious about demobilisation. Given his concern about discontent in the armed forces, he was anxious that the police would be able to respond to any serious unrest. Macready was able to reassure him that he and several Chief Constables had discussed more central coordination of the police, and specifically that the Home Office was 'already at work on the scheme for the purpose of facilitating the drafting of police from one district to another in case of need'.[18]

After talking with Lloyd George later in December, Macready could assure Hankey, the Cabinet Secretary, that 'he [Lloyd George] realises to the full the importance of authority being maintained in the metropolis.' It is likely that Macready discussed with Lloyd George the actions of Marston and his colleagues in raising the issue of official recognition of NUPPO with Parliamentary candidates during the election campaign. But above all he warned Lloyd George of the dangers of another police strike.

Whether there was a real likelihood of another police strike in December 1918 is doubtful. But Macready took the opportunity to make contingency plans. He advised Hankey,

> The moment any sign of a strike shows itself to issue an order to all Divisions that any man who fails to turn up for duty, or to do his duty when called upon, will be summarily dismissed from the Force – that such men will never be reinstated in any Police Force, and that any time they have made for pension will not count, even if they obtain Government employment hereafter. I have also arranged with Sir William Robertson that, if necessary, 90 out of the 200 odd police Stations in the Metropolis shall be at once occupied by small detachments of troops in order to give protection and confidence to men who remain loyal. These 90 Stations are pivotal, and the remainder may be allowed to look after themslves for the moment. I have also arranged for the Military to find motor cycle and side-car men in case the telephones are cut, which would of course be the

case.... Of course there will be threats of other unions coming out in sympathy and all that kind of thing, but I believe a bold front will not only save the situation, but will steady the police throughout the country for a very long time to come, and indeed will give the Government an opportunity to get rid once and for all of this Police Union, on the grounds that they gave it every latitude, with the result that the existence of such an organisation was found to be incompatible with public security.

Macready's letter to Hankey (which was forwarded on to Lloyd George and Bonar Law) is interesting also in showing how Macready perceived the campaign for official recognition of NUPPO as being part of the struggle for a different social order. He wrote of the Metropolitan Police, 'A very small minority are out for recognition of the union at all costs, and for the acceptance of their ideas of governing the country; whilst about half the Force would sit on the fence, but become loyal if firm action was taken against agitators.'[19] This fear of the police becoming enmeshed with the Labour Movement was fundamental. Indeed Macready viewed trade unionism in the police as tantamount to 'a Soviet organisation in [a] disciplined force'.

Macready made his next move in mid-January 1919. He took the opportunity of the appointment of a new Home Secretary, Edward Shortt, a Coalition Liberal and a barrister, to push forward dramatic changes to the constitution of the Representative Board. Macready suggested on 17 January that after four months' trial of the existing Representative Board that the next one, due to be elected on 31 March 1919, should be divided into three, with separate boards for inspectors, sergeants and constables. He argued that it was 'very prejudicial to discipline' to have men of various ranks mixed up together. Macready's real motive, however, was to break the power of the union, either by reducing its influence on the Representative Board or provoking it into the strike action he himself had been predicting a few weeks earlier. After some consideration, Shortt and the government agreed to Macready's proposals, which were formally put forward to Shortt and to the Representative Board on 4 March.

After Macready had decided on this unilateral change in the constitution of the Representative Board, but before his proposals became publicly known, NUPPO held a meeting in the Albert Hall, London on 18 January 1919. Attended by over 5,000 this meeting passed resolutions calling on the Home Secretary to grant official recognition of the union, to increase pay, to fulfil Lloyd George's August pledge on pensions, and to secure the reinstatement of three Midland Railway policemen who had been victimised.[20] Macready wrote to Lloyd George in Paris, giving him an account of the Albert Hall meeting and reassuring him that he was ready should a strike be called. Macready commented.

> I am satisfied that if anything of the sort is attempted we can stamp it out at once, and in that case get rid once and for all of these fire brands together with the union. . . .
> Personally I do not think that the Metropolitan Police will go out on strike as a body, but I think it is possible that the fire brands may try to get them out, and that a few hundred may follow their lead, but, if we strike quickly without an hour's delay on the lines which I have laid before Lord Cave and since then Mr. Shortt and discussed with Mr. Churchill, I feel sure that 90 per cent of the Force will carry on. The whole matter will depend upon our moving the moment there is any indication of a strike, without further parley, as every hour's delay will mean the drifting of the weaker men towards the malcontents, because they will think that the Government will yield to their demands. . . .
> . . . the whole business is nothing more than an attempt on the part of about a dozen individuals to glorify themselves into fat billets at the expense of the union.

Four days later, on 27 January, Macready in a letter explaining why he had been taking extra precautions, urged that confrontation with the union should take place immediately. He informed Lloyd George,

> I am strongly of opinion that the time is now ripe for the Government to make a definite decision that under no circumstances will any police union be officially recognised, and the sooner it is done the better. The few extremists at the head of the union are losing their nerve, the men both in London and the Provinces are, I believe, up to 80 per cent to be relied upon, and a pronouncement against recognition of the union would, in my opinion, enormously strengthen authority and would encourage and support the majority of the men who are getting 'fed up' with the autocratic methods the union officials.[21]

Lloyd George, however, was not yet ready to break with the union. The serious strikes and widespread unrest made it an inopportune time for a confrontation. This was come in March, after Marston had made statements which could be used to alienate moderates who supported the union. At the War Cabinet meeting of 24 January the Home Secretary had reminded his colleagues that the police union 'had been tacitly recognised as an existing entity by allowing the police to join it'.[22]

Nevertheless, later on the 27 January Lloyd George had a message telephoned to Bonar Law making it quite clear he fully supported Macready in taking vigorous measures against a further police strike.

> If the strike comes off, it must be dealt with strongly and firmly. We cannot give way on the question of recognition. As to whether the Prime Minister's promise with reference to pensions is carried out or not the PM would very much like to be satisfied on it because it is quite clear that we must not be accused of breach of faith – if there is a serious struggle – and here he would give the benefit of the doubt to the Police (that as if there is a doubt). Whether Macready or Horne [the Minister of Labour] is right as to the gravity of the menace he is not in a position to judge, but of this he is clear – that it is better to be prepared on the assumption that Horne is right. Unless this mutiny of the Guardians of Order is quelled the whole fabric of law may disappear. The Prime Minister is prepared to support any steps you may take, however grave, to establish the authority of social order.[23]

On the 3 February the War Cabinet discussed a memorandum by the Home Secretary in which he recommended the setting up of an enquiry into police conditions. Shortt told the meeting that 'Sir Nevil Macready attached great importance to attracting a high class and loyal body of policemen; and the Commissioner of Police doubted whether this was possible under present conditions.' Macready himself told the War Cabinet that he felt the London police were 'fairly content' with their pay, and that the 'heated resolutions' they were passing were the work of 'extremists, who were out to capture the next Representative Board'. The War Cabinet agreed on 6 February to the setting up of what was to be the Desborough Committee with very wide terms of reference.[24] The earlier assurances of the government to help resolve the case of the three railway policemen together with the setting up of an inquiry into police conditions of work ensured that there was no strike in late January or February 1919, a period which would have been extremely worrying for the government. Macready later reflected that the policemen had missed their moment in not striking at the turn of the year, as later he could cope with a police strike 'without recourse to military'. As for his position, he wrote,

> If the country had been free from labour unrest the question of the police would not have been so difficult to solve; as things were I felt that the only

thing to do was to keep smiling, and trust to Marston and his supporters to make a false step either from nervousness or from over-confidence.[25]

The NUPPO leadership made a series of false steps which alienated government ministers, some of its own supporters and quite probably public opinion. They gave Macready good propaganda material by apparently condoning absenteeism and malingering by constables who should be on the beat. In fact, on the issue of absenteeism, their cries of 'Prussianism' were not at punishment but at the severity of Macready's retribution for this misconduct – outright dismissal from the force. Another misjudgement was to counter Macready's dramatic proposals for a reconstituted Board with their own. The 1924 Inquiry summed up their proposals:

> the exclusion of discipline from their jurisdiction should cease; that they should have the power to compel the attendance before them of any member of the Police Force, which would include the Commissioner himself; that they should have access to all papers; and that, if they were not satisfied with the rulings of the Commissioner, they should have the power to go beyond him to the Home Secretary. It appears to have been the view of the Authorities that these counter-proposals would in fact have handed over the real control of the Metropolitan Police to the Executive Committee of the Board.[26]

In addition ministers' anxieties about the claims of NUPPO, much fostered by Macready, were made worse by a series of rash statements by NUPPO figures in the union journal and on public platforms. For example, on 27 February 1919 at the National Industrial Conference, which was attended by Lloyd George, Marston spoke of previous 'deliberate and persistent misdirection of the police in times of labour troubles', and declared that, 'The day when the government can use the police forces of the nation as a tool against any other section of the nation is past.'[27] Later, after a demobilised soldiers' rally in London on 26 May 1919 ended up in disorder with fighting between police and demonstrators, J. H. Hayes, the Secretary of NUPPO, issued a statement in which he condemned 'the military system against which we are strenuously fighting', declared that the union 'looked upon our comrades in the workshops and from the army as comrades', and observed,

> The rule about no demonstration being allowed to approach within one mile of the House [of Commons] is typical of many foolish and dangerous

regulations that help to segregate the police from the rest of the workers. Further, we state emphatically that the only solution for occurrences of this kind is the democratisation of the police force, the full and complete recognition of the union, and the closer linking up of the police with organised labour.[28]

However, by the time of Hayes's statement NUPPO had little to lose against a government which was explicitly determined to crush it.

For NUPPO it was downhill all the way from early to mid-March 1919. Macready's scheme for reconstituting the Representative Board was formally put forward on 4 March 1919. When a deputation from the existing Representative Board saw Shortt three days later they refused to limit discussions to the proposed reconstitution of the Board, as Shortt wished, and left having discussed nothing. Shortt, who gave Macready consistent and unqualified support throughout, approved Macready's constitutional changes the next day.

Short informed the War Cabinet on 13 March that the new structure for the Representative Board had been put to the police. The inspectors were willing to use the new body but the sergeants and constables threatened to boycott it. He added that Macready 'proposed to deal with this situation by saying to the men that he was sorry they had refused to accept the new scheme but that if the sergeants and the constables at any time changed their mind, they could have their Board'. Shortt advised the War Cabinet that 'the real fight was for recognition of the union.' Robert Munro, Secretary of State for Scotland, urged that the question of recognition should not be shelved any longer. He cited a conflict over the union in Scotland:

> At Oban the other day, the Chief Constable had before him four men who had joined the union, and gave them the choice of resigning their membership of the union or leaving the Force. They were given five minutes to decide. Two of the men had refused to give up their membership of the union, and had left the Force; the other two had remained in the Force and had resigned their membership of the union. The men who left the Force had over twenty years' service in it. This incident had created a great sensation in police circles, and was bound to raise the question as to whether it was legal to join the union or not.

The War Cabinet then decided not to recognise the union. In so doing they were influenced by their concern as to possibility of the growth of unions in the armed forces. Walter Long reminded them that 'in the Navy they have a somewhat similar difficulty'; there was 'a movement on the lower deck which asked for a channel of communication through which their wants could be represented to the Admiralty'. The War Cabinet also reflected on the example of the Post Office. Albert Illingworth, the Postmaster-General, observed that in the Post Office 'he had found . . . it was advantageous to keep the men in as many separate sections as possible'. Shortt pointed to the negotiations over recognition of the Railway Clerks' Association.[29] The War Cabinet's decision not to recognise NUPPO was made public on 18 March.

The NUPPO leadership prepared to fight. In late March the union held a conference at which it was agreed to change its rules to allow for strike action should there be a two-thirds majority in a ballot. They also organised a demonstration in Trafalgar Square on 4 May, primarily to protest at the sacking of a police constable named Spackman, who had urged his fellows to boycott the elections to the new Representative Board. It was an orderly demonstration, attended by some 9,000 policemen. The report in *The Times* recorded, 'Many of the divisional contingents in the procession were headed by bands, and upon the banners which were carried such sentences as "Tyranny is not discipline", "Let the punishment fit the crime" and "Kill Prussianism at home" were displayed repeatedly.' Marston called for negotiations with the authorities. As for Spackman he observed, 'The men did not desire and would not condone any breach of discipline; but when any breach occurred they demanded that the punishment should be such as was fitting the offence.' Hayes complained 'that War Office methods were being introduced into the Police Force, and that the authorities were endeavouring to make the Metropolitan Police a militarised body similar to the Royal Irish Constabulary'. Macready and Shortt were among the crowd. The next day Macready went to Paris for a meeting, and according to his memoirs, spoke to Lloyd George about the situation in the police force.[30]

Later in the month the NUPPO leadership organised a strike ballot. They asked their members, 'Are you prepared to withdraw from duty in order to obtain complete recognition of your union, reinstatement of ex-Police Constable Spackman, the reviewing of all cases of known victimisation, an immediate increase of pay and pensions for police and prison officers . . . and total abolition of military control of the police and prison services?' Macready later claimed that the ballot results were faked. But before the result was announced there is every sign that the government expected the union to gain the necessary two-thirds majority for a strike.

With the agreement of the War Cabinet and Lloyd George, on 30 May Macready published an order to all chief constables and superintendents. This instructed them in the event of another strike that 'officers of the rank of sergeants and upwards must, if necessary, be on duty continuously and remain at their place of duty', that soldiers would occupy police stations 'merely for the protection of the buildings and to free every police officer for police duty', and superintendents personally would be responsible for compiling and forwarding to the Commissioner daily lists of 'officers and men who "knowingly and wilfully" withdraw their services.' The order also instructed them to warn all those under their command that any officer or man going on strike would be dismissed. Moreover,

> such officer or man will under no circumstances be permitted to rejoin the Metropolitan Police, and dismissal will result in the loss of all service counting towards pension. The Commissioner will be unable to accept excuses that men are unable to parade or carry on their work due to intimidation.
> Officers and men will, if necessary, defend themselves by all legitimate means if interfered with in the execution of their duty.
> Men who remain loyal may count on the fullest support of the government and of the Commissioner.[31]

Shortt repeated this warning to the press. Two days earlier, following careful consideration in the War Cabinet, he had also announced in the House of Commons that there would be a substantial increase in pay, with a basic minimum rate rising from £2 15s to £3 10s per week, backdated to 1 April 1919.

Shortt's statements were designed to pre-empt a NUPPO mass demonstration in Hyde Park on 1 June. At this meeting Hayes announced that the ballot revealed 44,539 members in favour of a strike and a 4,324 against. But he also announced that the strike would not take place, observing that NUPPO would call a strike when it suited them and not when it suited Macready. Most probably the NUPPO leadership rightly felt that Shortt's announcement of a specific substantial pay rise had upstaged their ballot and made the support of the public doubtful. Hayes claimed to have had a message from Lloyd George. He told the rally,

'He deeply regrets that he has not been able to meet us. He can add nothing to what he has already said, at present. He says "at present". You can take it from me that Lloyd George is going to clear up this mess when he returns, and when he does return we shall ask him what he intends to do to redeem this pledge.

Marston in his speech referred back to Lloyd George's request of the previous August that he should consult Lloyd George if there was further trouble, and warned: 'We will see, if he is very quick, what he can do in the future, but his future will have to be very quick. We are not pandering to the Wizard of Wales much longer.'[32]

Lloyd George denied that he had sent Hayes such a message. Macready deemed Hayes's statement to be just 'another lie which was told' by the union and he used it to discredit the union. Yet it would have been foolish, and very uncharacteristic, for Hayes to have invented such a message for such a major meeting. Equally, Lloyd George was highly unlikely to make such a statement when he was well aware of Macready's plans and had refused to see a deputation from NUPPO in Paris, observing that he was fully informed of the situation in London.[33] What appears to have happened is that Pemberton Billing, a maverick, Independent right-wing MP, had been trying to act as an intermediary between NUPPO and Lloyd George. He had telephoned Lloyd George's secretary in Downing Street and had been given a polite, diplomatic answer. Billing attached more significance to the reply than it warranted, and passed it on as a reply of significance to Hayes.[34]

Several ministers were keen to take firm action against NUPPO before 1 June. Long, for example, wrote to Lloyd George warning him that

> the men in the Navy are watching the action of the London police very closely, and that any mistake made here would have serious consequences among them. They are of course being told by agitators that if they had a union with a consequential power to bring pressure upon the government that they would get very much better terms.

On the other hand, Bonar Law told Lloyd George that it seemed unlikely that prison warders would join in a strike, and added, 'I am very hopeful that it will come to nothing.' At the War Cabinet on 27 May ministers had agreed that a fight with NUPPO was inevitable, but debated whether to condemn the union before, or only when, it issued an ultimatum or called a strike.

However, the size of the majority in the strike ballot may have caused some wavering in government circles. Some consideration was given to a suggestion that existing policemen could stay in the union, but new recruits should not be allowed to join. Bonar Law wrote to Lloyd George to say that he did not like any 'differentiation between the new men and the old'. While he felt that 'there will be no peace while this union exists', he still observed, 'I am a little doubtful about the wisdom of pressing a fight on an issue raised by us, namely that they must leave the union, and am going to talk to Horne about it.'[35] Lloyd George, in very striking contrast to his role on 31 August 1918, was very firm against any compromise. In a telephone message to Shortt he observed,

> I do not think it would be possible to draw a distinction between old members of the Police Force and new members, and to allow those who are already members of the union to remain members whilst recruits are forbidden to join. It seems to me to be contrary to the fundamental principles of discipline for a semi-military body like the police to join a trades union, and if it is allowed it will be quite impossible logically to resist the demand which will certainly be put forward sooner or later on behalf of the Navy and Army. I should be disposed to recommend for the consideration of my colleagues a statement that it is proposed to set up a 'democratic organisation', to use the Home Secretary's words, to enable the Police to present their grievances to the Authorities. But once that organisation has been set up no policeman should be allowed to join a trade union. The sooner the issue is challenged the better. We are now in a position to face a strike, later on it will be quite impossible to do so. However . . . I have given my views without hearing what is to be said on the other side. But the Police Force is so essential to the stability of social order that at all hazards we must take steps to secure that we have a body of men at the disposal of the State that can be relied upon. We cannot command this at the present moment – as long as we have thousands of men who are under contract to disobey the Authorities at the behest of an outside committee.[36]

Shortt made a policy statement on the police in the House of Commons on 6 June. This had been approved beforehand by the War Cabinet, and it followed the line of thinking that Lloyd George had expressed in his telephone message. Shortt condemned NUPPO for interfering with discipline and then complained of NUPPO's links with the Labour Movement. He observed that 'people who are concerned with the *Daily Herald* newspaper and its activities are extremists. They hold extreme views. They are out for the social revolution.' He added that 'the union is affiliated with the London Trades Council ... and I presume would be liable, as would any other associated union, to a sympathetic strike.' Pressed as to what his response would be if the policemen did not want the new association that he offered but preferred NUPPO, Short retorted

> if they insist upon belonging to the National Union they will then cease to be policemen. They cannot be both. This is a free country. They are not obliged to be policemen. If they like to be industrial unionists they can be; if they like to be policemen they can be; but they cannot possibly be both.[37]

With legislation on the way, Marston raised the plight of NUPPO at the Labour Party Conference on 27 June. His motion condemned the government's policy of repression, called for recognition, instructed the executive committee of the Labour Party to consult with the TUC 'in the event of the government attempting to put into effect any further repressive measure' against the union, and protested 'against the suggested introduction of legislation to make provision for a representative organisation within the police force as being a direct opposition to the fundamental principles of trade unionism'. In moving his motion Marston warned the conference that 'the police service was one of the most vital arteries by which militarism and secret diplomacy were forced upon the community, especially the Labour section of the community.' He affirmed that police and prison officers 'now stood in the ranks of the workers and declined to be torn from them', but that they also 'remained fully conscious of their duties to the public and the government, for they were looking forward ... to the day when a Labour government should stand in charge of this country'.[38] So were many of the Labour movement's leaders, and they were uneasy about another police strike. Indeed several prominent moderate Labour Party leaders were doubtful as to whether there should be an independent police union at all. Later, when he himself was Home Secretary, Arthur Henderson stated in May 1924,

> Those of us who are prepared to bring about changes, either political or industrial, on constitutional lines, cannot make too clear the difference between the position of the military, the position of the police force or the position ... of the fire brigade, so far as taking up a 'down tools' policy is concerned.[39]

Yet at the time there were aspects of the government's policy which were anathema to the Labour movement. With the introduction of the Police Bill in the House of Commons on 8 July, Labour was faced, as James O'Grady argued in the Commons, 'for the first time since trade unions were emancipated' with a government which was 'going to suppress a registered trade union by law'. Clynes and other MPs deplored the forcing of men into a new body, deeming that to be an action 'which is not consistent with the sense of liberty which these men are supposed to serve'. A Radical MP bluntly observed, 'this is setting up an employers' trade union, nothing more or less.'[40] Macready had earlier further aroused trade union hostility when, on 10 June, he had addressed a mass meeting of policemen and had made what he dubbed 'a sporting offer'. This was that he would re-enrol Spackman if he ripped up his union membership card and would reinstate him at his full salary at the end of a year if he had a good report.[41]

However while Labour condemned the legal suppression of a trade union and in Parliament moved the rejection of the Police Bill, it was done so in an apologetic manner by most Labour speakers, all of whom conceded that the police were in some way a special case. Thus Clynes, their ablest leading spokesman then in the Commons, observed, 'so that while I should like to give the policemen the same opportunities and the same assistance which all workers are entitled to get through associated effort, there ought to be in this case ... some arrangement tending to make discipline perfectly secure.'[42]

Hence, although Marston succeeded in getting support from the Labour Party Conference, several trade unions and other organisations, many leading Labour politicians and trade unionists were ambivalent in their attitudes. As for strike action, the Labour Party leadership advised NUPPO not to use it against a Bill before Parliament.

NUPPO's leaders found themselves in a rapidly deteriorating situation during July. The first three sections of the Police Bill which was going through Parliament contained provision for setting up a Police Federation, making membership of NUPPO or any other such body a matter for automatic dismissal, and making it an offence to cause disaffection in the police or to try to organise a strike. With any effective action soon to be illegal, a union delegation tried to see Lloyd George. But he declined to see them. On 31 July NUPPO called its members out on strike 'until the gross injustice imposed by the provisions of Sections I, II and III of the Police Bill are remedied, and full and frank recognition of our union is conceded.' The union had to be careful to specify which parts of the Bill it objected to, for the War Cabinet had agreed on 10 July to include in the bill proposals to standardise pay and conditions of service in line with the Desborough Report. Thus there was a carrot as well as a stick within the Bill.[43]

This time the government was fully prepared and had long-laid plans to crush a further strike. Lloyd George merely drew the War Cabinet's attention to the strike and informed it that all strikers would be dismissed. Though organised Labour had given the police union much verbal support, when the strike broke out only the Nine Elms branch of the NUR struck in sympathy in London; and this was soon stopped by the NUR leaders, in spite of NUR Conference resolutions in favour of NUPPO.[44] In Liverpool tramwaymen went on strike, and dockers and railwaymen protested at government policy. But sympathetic strikes by other unions were not likely when NUPPO succeeded in calling out only some 2,366 police officers, roughly 4 per cent of the total employed in the country, and just over 5 per cent of those who on 1 June had been reported to have voted for strike action.

However, the response to the strike call was regional in strength. Thus in London about 6 per cent of the men went on strike (1,056 of 18,200 men in the Metropolitan Police Force and 58 of 970 in the City of London). In Birmingham 9 per cent of the total (120 of a force of 1,320) came out. But in Merseyside the strike was substantial. The percentages of strikers out of the forces were 51 for Liverpool (954 of 1,874), 63 for Birkenhead (114 of 180) and 82 (63 of 77) for Bootle. In addition 1 policeman went on strike in Wallasey, as did 68 prison warders at Wormwood Scrubs and 6 at Winson Green, Birmingham, and a number of railway police in Liverpool and Birkenhead.

Merseyside witnessed the sort of social disorder that the government always feared. The War Cabinet had been warned on 10 July that there could be a lightning strike among the police there. When a large proportion of the police stopped work, many poor people who had suffered extreme squalor for years took advantage of the situation. Rioting and looting took place during the weekend, with mass battles taking place between the crowds and the army and those policemen still on duty. In Liverpool one rioter was shot dead by the army. In view of the poor morale in the navy the Admiralty was reluctant to send forces there. Nevertheless the situation was deemed potentially serious enough for the despatch of two cruisers, the *Venomous* and *Whitley*, and a battleship, the *Valiant*, up the Mersey. Excluding the cost of troops and special constables, the riots cost Liverpool £122,000, Birkenhead over £12,000 and Bootle about £800 in compensation.[45]

Lloyd George appears to have been very anxious as to whether disorder would spread more widely. Riddell recorded in his diary of that weekend, 'Much talk about the Liverpool police strike. LG very anxious for news and continually asking Hankey to go to the telephone to enquire of Downing Street.' Later Lloyd George told Sir Archibald Salvidge, the dominant figure of the Liverpool Conservatives that,

> He looked on the Liverpool police strike as perhaps the turning point in the Labour movement, deflecting it from Bolshevist and Direct Actionist courses to legitimate trade unionism once again. Had Liverpool been wrongly handled and had the strikers scored a success, the whole country might very soon have been on fire.[46]

While this was characteristic retrospective embellishment by Lloyd George, designed to impress on Conservative chieftains how reliable and how indispensable Lloyd George was in maintaining the existing social order, nevertheless the 1919 police strike was a moment of truth for the government in its effort to restabilise British society. Lloyd George, Shortt and their other colleagues were relieved to have won.

As for those who went on strike they lost not only their jobs but their pensions. The most prominent striker in Birmingham was Sergeant Edward Taylor, who with twenty-two years of service, lost a pension of £140 per year. By one of life's bitter ironies, he had been the policeman with whom Lloyd George had escaped a violent anti-Boer mob at Birmingham Town Hall in December 1901.[47] After the strike Churchill urged that the dismissed men should not be left unemployed but should be allowed to join the army, and then sent abroad. Lloyd George was inclined to agree, providing the strike was completely broken and Macready would give his consent.[48] Nothing came of this suggestion. The dismissed men were left to hope that pressure from the Labour movement would achieve their reinstatement and in the meantime found that many employers blacklisted them.

Notes and references

1. The best accounts of policemen's conditions are in V. L. Allen, 'The National Union of Police and Prison Officers', *Economic History Review*, 2 Series (1959), pp. 133–43; G. W. Reynolds and A. Judge, *The Day that the Police Went On Strike* (London: Weidenfeld and Nicolson, 1968); and, for Liverpool conditions, R. Bean, 'Police, unionisation and the 1919 strike in Liverpool', *Journal of Contemporary History*, 15 (1980), pp. 633–52.
2. Home Office statement issued after the 1918 strike; copy in LG F/6/4/14. General The Rt Hon. Sir Nevil Macready, *Annals of an Active Life* 2 vols (London: Hutchinson, 1924), pp. 307–10. Entry 'August 1918', *Lord Riddell's War Diary 1914–1918* (London: Nicholson and Watson, 1933), p. 347. B. Thomson, *Queer People* (London: Hodder and Stoughton, 1922), pp. 293–94.
3. Allen, *op. cit.*, pp. 133–4.
4. Macready, *op. cit.*, pp 301–2.
5. WC (467), 30 August 1918; CAB 23–7–92. The assessment of Long was by C. L. Mowat, *Britain Between the Wars 1918–1940* (London: Methuen, 1955), p. 13. Long to Bonar Law, 1 September 1918; Bonar Law Papers, 84/1/1.
6. Allen, *op. cit.*, p. 136. Reynolds and Judge, *op. cit.*, p. 53.
7. WC (X27), 31 August 1918; CAB 23–17–103/4. Milner's diary, 30 and 31 August 1918; Milner Papers, 89. Wilson's diary, 31 August 1918; Major-General Sir C. E. Callwell, *Field Marshal Sir Henry Wilson*, vol. 2 (London: Cassell, 1927), p. 123. Macready's memoirs deliberately give the wrong impression that he was not involved in any government policy-making until after the strike had been settled.
8. Macready, *op. cit.*, pp. 307–8.
9. J. Morgan, *Conflict and Order* (Oxford: Clarendon Press, 1987), especially pp. 57–9 and 69–70. B. Weinberger, 'Keeping the peace and policing strikes', *History Today*, 37 (1987), pp. 29–35. C. J. Wrigley, 'The General Strike in local history', part I, *The Local Historian*, February 1984, pp. 36–48.
10. Sir Charles Mallet, *Lord Cave: A Memoir* (London: Murray, 1931), p. 216. Milner diary, 31 August 1918; Milner Papers, 89. Macready, *op. cit.*, pp. 302–3. Sir Sam Fay, *The War Office at War* (London: Hutchinson, 1937), p. 212. Cave to Bonar Law, 2 September 1918; Bonar Law Papers 84/1/3. As well as wanting Macready for the police post, he was also eager to move him from the War Office: D. R. Woodwood, *Lloyd George and the Generals* (Newark: University of Delaware Press, 1983), p. 312.
11. Macready was the son of the great Victorian actor, William Charles Macready. His memoirs are very revealing, being very arrogant and usually very critical of all but the die-hard Right (a notable exception being Churchill's conduct during the South Wales mining disputes of 1910–11). However, he had begun with Liberal sympathies and had been an admirer of Lloyd George until 1920.

12. Macready, *op. cit.*, pp. 141–2 and 309–12. J. Vincent (ed.), *The Crawford Papers* (Manchester: Manchester University Press, 1984), p. 393.
13. *Report of the Committee appointed to Enquire into the Claims of the Men Dismissed from the Police and Prison Services on Account of the Strike of 1919* (Cmd. 2297), 1924 (hereafter cited as *Report . . . into the Claims of the men Dismissed*), p. 10.
14. *ibid.*, p. 11.
15. Macready, *op. cit.*, pp. 313–14.
16. *ibid.*, pp. 323–4 and 328. From his own memoirs Macready appears to have misled the Representative Board, telling it that the new draft for the army was under consideration before his appointment.
17. R. Shackleton. 'The 1919 police strike in Birmingham' in A. Wright and R. Shackleton (eds), *Worlds of Labour* (Birmingham: Birmingham University, 1983), pp. 65–7. J. Morgan, pp. 72 and 80. P. Bagwell, *The Railwaymen* (London: Allen & Unwin, 1963), pp. 355–65. Macready, *op. cit.*, pp. 321–22 and 364.
18. S. Roskill, *Hankey: Man of Secrets*, vol. 2 (London: Collins, 1972), pp. 34–5. Macready to J. T. Davies, 12 December 1918; LG F/36/2/4.
19. Macready to Hankey, 30 December 1918; Bonar Law Papers, 84/4/26.
20. Macready, *op. cit.*, pp. 345–6 and 356. *Morning Post*, 21 January 1919.
21. Macready to Lloyd George, 23 and 27 January 1919; LG F/36/ 2/5 and 6.
22. At the War Cabinet on 24 January it was agreed that the Home Secretary and the Scottish Secretary should confer as to measures to be taken 'in the event of serious trouble threatening', WC (519). CAB 23–9–22.
23. Copy of telephone message to Bonar Law, 27 January 1919; LG F/30/ 3/8.
24. Cabinet papers GT 6730. WC (524 and 528), 3 and 6 February 1919; CAB 23–9–40/1 and 5.
25. Macready, *op. cit.*, pp. 333 and 352.
26. *Report . . . into the Claims of the Men Dismissed*, p. 13.
27. Reynolds and Judge, *op. cit.*, p. 102. *The Times*, 28 January 1919.
28. Printed in Macready, *op. cit.*, pp. 362–3.
29. WC (544), 13 March 1919; CAB 23–9–107.
30. *The Times*, 5 May 1919. Macready, *op. cit.*, p. 360. However, I have seen no confirmation of this in other sources. Lloyd George was preoccupied with the climax of drawing up the Peace Treaty, 5–7 May 1919.
31. *Report . . . into the Claims of the Men Dismissed*, p. 16. The Cabinet agreed Macready's order and Shortt's statements, subject to Lloyd George's approval. T. Jones to J. T. Davies, 28 May 1919; LG F/23/4/ 73. (The letter is minuted 'Yes'.)
32. *The Times*, 2 June 1919.
33. *The Observer*, 1 June 1919. Macready, *op. cit.*, pp. 387–8.
34. 116 HC Deb. 5s, 1685. 2 June 1919.
35. Long to Lloyd George, 28 May 1919; LG F/33/2/46. Bonar Law to Lloyd George, 31 May 1919; F/30/3/70.

Unrest in the police force 79

36. Lloyd George to Shortt, 4 June 1919; LG F/45/6/16.
37. 116 *HC Deb. 5s*, 2487–2500. 6 June 1919.
38. The Labour Party, *Report of the Nineteenth Annual Conference, 1919*, pp. 165–6.
39. C. J. Wrigley, *Arthur Henderson* (Cardiff: University of Wales Press, 1990), p. 146.
40. Comments during Labour's opposition to the second and third readings of the Bill, 18 June and 1 August 1919. 118 *HC Deb. 5s*, 819–21 and 2444–50.
41. Much of Macready's speech of 10 June echoed Shortt's in the House of Commons on 6 June. Macready reprints his in his memoirs, pp. 367–403.
42. 118 *HC Deb. 5s*, 842. 18 July 1919.
43. *Report . . . into the Claims of the Men Dismissed*, p. 17. WC (591), 10 July 1919; CAB 23–11–24/5.
44. WC (605), 1 August 1919; CAB 23–11–97. Allen, *op. cit.*, p. 143. Reynolds and Judge, *op. cit.*, p. 132.
45. *Report . . . into the Claims of the Men Dismissed*, pp. 17–25. There are also accounts of Merseyside in Reynolds and Judge, pp. 152–73, A. V. Sellwood, *Police Strike 1919* (London: W. H. Allen, 1978), pp. 116–75 and P. J. Waller, *Democracy and Sectarianism* (Liverpool: Liverpool University Press, 1981), pp. 284–5. For Birmingham, see Shackleton, *op. cit.* pp. 63–84. WC (591), 10 July 1919; CAB 23–11–24/5.
46. *Lord Riddell's Intimate Diary of the Peace Conference and After 1918–1923* (London: Gollancz, 1933), p. 108. S. Salvidge, *Salvidge of Liverpool*, (London: Hodder and Stoughton, 1934), p. 177.
47. Shackleton, *op. cit.*, pp. 63 and 73.
48. WC (608), 7 August 1919; CAB 23–11–106. Macready made it clear that he would resign if any men were reinstated in the police.

5
Holding on through the period of economic transition: from Armistice to February 1919

After the end of the war there was a general desire on the part of government ministers and business interests to return from a controlled economy to a self-regulating, free market economy. The problem for policy was just how fast this could be done. For some months there was a strong body of opinion that this process should not be rushed, given the scale of domestic and international economic dislocation and also the threat of serious social instability arising from the grievances of organised labour.

The six months or so after the Armistice of 11 November 1918, which cover the main period of economic transition from war to peace production, were also a crucial period in the evolution of government policies towards the trade union movement. The government's attitude became much firmer after it won an overwhelming majority in the December 1918 general election. Yet throughout these six months there was considerable concern on the government's part at the scale of labour unrest and at the ability of labour to exert such considerable pressure during a *downturn* in the economy. This and the following chapter examine in detail the government's response to industrial unrest between the Armistice and the start of the post-war boom. The detail is especially desirable for these months given the coincidence of so many industrial disputes at this time and the need for ministers' comments to be considered in context rather than to be treated as if applicable to any point in 1919.

For much of the year or so after the Armistice there were two conflicting fears present among government ministers and the propertied classes. First, there was alarm at the growing power of organised labour. For a while Lloyd George and his colleagues, many industrialists and some of the middle classes saw industrial and social concessions as necessary, even inevitable, after the upheaval of war.

Yet, second, there was also a fear among many Conservative politicians, in Treasury and other financial circles, and also much of the middle classes that too much was being conceded, and that the real threat to the social structure was inflation. In the period of economic transition this fear of inflation took second place in determining government policies. Later it was to predominate in the politics of the Coalition government.

The rise in prices accelerated with the post-war boom which was underway from the spring of 1919. By March 1920 wholesale prices had trebled over their pre-war levels. The economist, J. M. Keynes, who had left the Treasury in mid-1919, advised in February 1920 that high interest rates were necessary to curb this inflation and warned Austen Chamberlain, the Chancellor of the Exchequer,

> A continuance of inflationism and high prices will not only depress the exchanges but by their effect on prices will strike at the whole basis of contract, of security, and of the capitalist system generally. The new state of affairs created by persistent inflation will only be tolerable under socialistic control and that is where the present policy, if persisted in, will necessarily lead us, before we are really ripe for such a development.[1]

The desire for a return to orthodox financial ways had been expressed while the war was still being fought by the Cunliffe Committee, in its report of August 1918. Lord Cunliffe, the Governor of the Bank of England, together with a team made up almost entirely of bankers, had urged – as part of the planning for reconstruction after the war – that priority should be given to the restoration of the gold standard as that was felt to be 'the only effective remedy for an adverse balance of trade and an undue growth of credit'. Yet, as Addison, the Minister of Reconstruction, realised at the time, the necessary economic policies to achieve such a restoration would conflict with the government's commitment to reconstruction.[2]

Indeed for orthodox financial people this was part of the attraction of a return to gold. Sir John Bradbury, the Joint Permanent Secretary of the Treasury and its representative on the Cunliffe Committee, viewed the gold standard as 'knave proof', by which he meant that it was something that 'could not be rigged for political or even more unworthy reasons'.[3] Orthodox financial circles saw a return to the gold standard as being not only beneficial to Britain in helping to restabilise international trade and financial relations but also as a regulator on domestic politics, preventing politicians from being profligate with public finances in order to provide lavish welfare measures.

The exigencies of the First World War had ensured that financial orthodoxy had been set aside for much of its duration. Thus, for example, some restrictions on the Bank of England laid down in the 1844 Banking Act had been lifted. These regulations had laid down that the Bank of England should only be allowed to issue notes (beyond a certain sum) when they had sufficient gold to cover their value, and one of their effects had been to guard against politicians meeting the cost of expensive policies by simply printing more money.[4] Lloyd George, as Chancellor of the Exchequer until May 1915, had urged from early on in the war that 'The first interest of the taxpayer is that supplies should be secured.'[5] Thus during the war Treasury control of public expenditure gave precedence to the needs of the War Office and other key wartime departments.

Lloyd George, in the first six months or so after the end of the war, was inclined to tackle social reconstruction as another national priority. In late February Tom Jones, the Assistant Secretary to the Cabinet, reported to Hankey that, at a conference ministers on unemployment and the state of trade held on 25 February, Lloyd George had been telling his colleagues when they were worried about estimates of £71 million for reconstruction, 'Suppose the war had lasted another month, could we not have raised somehow or other another £2,000 million. It was nonsense to talk of a bagatelle like £71 million, a cheap insurance against Bolshevism.' Lloyd George frequently expressed such views in the early months of 1919. In this, as so much else, he was in line with popular sentiment. Indeed he had had such attitudes passed on to him by Churchill, eight days after the Armistice. Then Churchill had written, 'Workmen say freely that if the government were ready to spend £8 million a day for an indefinite period to win the war, they ought not to grudge a much smaller sum to carry the country over the transition period.'[6]

Until July 1919 Lloyd George pressed the commitment of providing 'a fit land for heroes to live in' as an overriding priority when faced with demands for a policy of 'dear money' and deflation. In so doing his position was strengthened by Bonar Law's clear-cut support. However, the Treasury and the City had been somewhat reassured by the appointment of Austen Chamberlain as Chancellor of the Exchequer when the Coalition government was reconstructed in January 1919. He was deemed to be sounder on the interests of finance than such possible alternatives as Churchill, Sir Auckland Geddes or Worthington-Evans. Chamberlain argued the case for monetary restraint within the government in early 1919, and his budget of 30 April did reduce planned public expenditure from £2,972 million in 1918–19 to £1,435 million in 1919–20. But otherwise financial orthodoxy did not fare well until the mid-summer of 1919.

Lloyd George's talk of major social reconstruction as 'a cheap insurance against Bolshevism' needs to be judged with a degree of caution. Concern to remove conditions likely to foster Bolshevism in Britain was a part of his motivation in early 1919 in making concessions to organised labour and pushing ahead with social reform; but only a part. Lloyd George frequently played up the threat of organised labour to boost support for himself among the Conservatives. And social reconstruction, doing something for the 'underdogs' in society, was a real commitment on Lloyd George's part.

This commitment to social reconstruction was partly altruistic and partly a shrewd attempt to occupy the political middle ground by a politician who had seen his political party crumble. In justifying his political stance to his close associates Sir George Riddell and Philip Kerr in the spring of 1918, he had commented

> I should describe myself . . . as a Nationalist-Socialist. I was and I am a strong believer in nationality, and I believe in the intervention of the state to secure that everyone has a fair chance and that there is no unnecessary want and poverty. Of course there are wasters who must suffer the penalty of their own misconduct; but every member of the community who behaves properly and does his best should be secured a fair chance.

He added that he had grown more tolerant over the years. 'I have grown to recognise that Dissenters are not always in the right and Anglicans always in the wrong, and that all landlords are not scoundrels of the deepest dye.'[7]

After the massive general election victory of 1918 Lloyd George was keen to position himself in politics as the leader of a national party, embracing all but the far Right of the Tory Party and ideological socialists in the Labour Party. To achieve this he needed to carry out reconstruction and to act for Britain at the Paris Peace Conference and subsequent international gatherings. Moreover in the months after the Armistice there was a very widespread belief that ordinary people were going to share in the fruits of victory and that there would be some redistribution of the good things in life towards working people. Riddell noted in late January 1919 a good example of this viewpoint, expressed by Bernard Baruch, the head of the United States War Board,

> He is strongly impressed with the intention of the working classes of the world to have more say. He says, 'so far as I am concerned I am prepared to give up voluntarily, through the medium of taxation, a very large part of my income. I am convinced that, unless the wealthier classes take that course, they may have everything taken from them'.[8]

In resisting deflation and attempting to meet many of the social and industrial grievances of working people in the early part of 1919 Lloyd George was responding to a mood of the times, as well as to the pressure of organised labour and his own remaining Radical predilections.

In approaching organised labour at the end of the war Lloyd George was aware both of labour's increased strength and of the likely dislocation of the economy for some months as the readjustment to peace took place. Like many of his contemporaries Lloyd George was very aware of the economic problems at the end of the Napoleonic, Crimean and Boer Wars. Two days after the Armistice he was speaking of the problems arising from shipping being 'engaged in bringing men and material home, in taking men and material back to America' and getting food to the defeated people of central Europe, and he also noted the difficulties arising from the rapid closing down of munitions work. Lloyd George made the case for unorthodox measures being carried on into the unorthodox times of economic transition. Hence the importance he ascribed to the actual signing of a peace treaty. He claimed that the return to normality could be deemed to begin then, not with the Armistice and the actual end of hostilities.[9]

The continuation of some economic controls was also deemed necessary to help Britain's economy during the difficult period of transition when world shortages and dislocated markets were expected for many crucial commodities. Indeed Sir Edward Carson had warned when he left the War Cabinet in January 1918 that economic restrictions were essential – 'In no other way can the country hope to escape from the perils of hunger, unemployment, social disorganisation, industrial paralysis and financial chaos.' Thus the case for the continuation of economic controls became based on world economic shortages rather than on the earlier need for such controls to defeat a still economically powerful Germany in world markets.[10]

Lloyd George predicted that there would be markets at home and abroad for British goods as the losses of war and arrears of demand were met. But that would take time. In the interim there could be surplus production, as British industry had become more efficient with output greatly increased, and a rise in unemployment, as demobilised soldiers and sailors as well as the discharged munitions workers joined the labour market. Given this situation, the reconstruction programme could be seen in part as an economic pump-priming exercise and as an essential aid to social stability during the transitional period of economic dislocation. This viewpoint was repeatedly expressed by several Cabinet ministers in early 1919. Lloyd George advised Austen Chamberlain.

> I think you will have to consider this year as . . . almost a war-condition year. You are getting out of the war condition, and I would not be in too great a hurry to get [fiscally] on to the absolute peace basis until you find the nation is actually on that basis.

Similarly Sir Eric Geddes, the Minister of Transport, observed

> You must be prepared to spend money on after-the-war war problems as you did during-the-war problems. That must be found, and added to our war debt if necessary. It is the period of reconstruction, and money has to be spent generously. . . . If we get over that period I think the trade of the country will revive.[11]

Lloyd George, in highlighting reconstruction schemes, made much not only of housing and transport, but also his old favourite of 'back to the land'. In December 1918 he declared that the government had 'schemes for rural development which will take the population back to the land, increase the output of food, provide new markets for our town industries'. For Lloyd George, as he put it, 'The more vigorous and healthy men we have on the land the better for the community'.

From the outset Lloyd George was eager to gain the co-operation of both organised capital and organised labour in overcoming the problems of the period of economic dislocation. In part his aim was to carry through into peace the more productive industrial practices of the war and, if possible, to gain agreement not to carry out in full the pledges of a restoration of pre-war industrial practices. Hence in the period after the Armistice he commented on the wartime record in glowing terms:

> By improved organisation, by stopping waste, by improved machinery, by the suspension of the old restrictions on output, the output of the engineering shops was increased enormously. The men and women had much better wages than they had ever been paid, and the state benefited. The experience of the munitions shops has been the experience almost all round.[12]

In part his aim was to try to settle wage rates amicably at a time of continuing high prices.

Shortly before the Armistice, on 8 November 1918, Lloyd George and several ministers saw some of the trade unionists who had signed the Treasury Agreement of 1915 to discuss how to implement the pledges of the government to restore the pre-war trade union practices. Following on from that meeting Lloyd George called a major conference of representatives of employers' organisations and trade unionists at Caxton Hall, London, on 13 November, just two days after the Armistice.

Beforehand Lloyd George had come down on the side of Addison and other ministers in feeling that the government's pledges had to be honoured. Addison was willing to resign if the many promises were broken. Lloyd George was faced not only with the fact that very clear pledges, several made personally by him, had been made on at least a dozen occasions when he had been responsible for munitions either as Chancellor of the Exchequer or as Minister of Munitions but also with the likelihood that to renege on them would undermine moderate trade unionists' trust in the good faith of the government. The government was anxious for their co-operation. Otherwise, as Addison told the War Cabinet, 'They would insist they had agreed to dilution for war work only, and would refuse to work on material which was intended for use in the reconstruction period'. George Roberts, the Minister of Labour, warned that 'wherever he went he found the government's delay in this matter to be one of the most active causes of industrial unrest, and further delay would tend to rally the reasonable elements among the workmen to the support of extremists.'

Given the strength of such arguments, Lloyd George disregarded the pleas of Churchill, Austen Chamberlain and various representatives of big business that to carry out the promise would harm British industry's efficiency. Churchill condemned the enactment of a Restoration of Trade Union Practices Bill as 'absurd and vicious', being one which would 'entrench a number of small and close corporations in restraint of trade'. Instead he suggested something not unlike the National Industrial Conference. The War Cabinet minutes record him arguing,

> When hostilities ceased, the state would be faced with the enormous task of bringing the armies home and of transferring the labour of women, and during that period the government must retain control of industrial conditions. He should like to see an attempt made by the government to come to terms with Labour for a reconstruction period, of say, two years, during which special conditions of control would be in force. This might be done by a National Conference, at which problems of wages and conditions of production might be examined, and a charter for Labour drawn up. If such a charter were secured and given a trial, he was satisfied that the resulting material prosperity during the transition period would be so great that there would not be the slightest desire on the part of anyone to revert to pre-war conditions.

Churchill's idea of such a conference may well have appealed to Lloyd George, but he had to agree with Sir David Shackleton of the Ministry of Labour that 'the promises of the government were clear and definite, and should be fulfilled.'[13]

Hence at the Caxton Hall conference Lloyd George declared that 'there is absolutely no doubt about those pledges', and added for good measure (with reference to the Kaiser's disregard for Belgian neutrality in 1914, the popularly accepted cause of Britain's entry into the war), 'Believe me, there is no question of treating them as a scrap of paper. Having fought against the doctrine of a scrap of paper we are not at the end of the war going to adopt that policy.'

Yet Lloyd George himself had long been equivocal on this issue. On 6 March 1917 he had told Labour leaders that he hoped that the working class would not set the example for demanding a return to pre-war conditions or all reconstruction might be blocked. A year later, in March 1918, when he saw a deputation from the Triple Alliance unions his briefing notes expressed the hope that a 'strict restoration' could be avoided.[14] So, in spite of his opening categorical affirmations of upholding the pledges, Lloyd George's later remarks suggest that he adhered to the advice he had been given in March 1918. He made it clear that he hoped that the pledges would not be honoured in full, and certainly not immediately. Although Lloyd

George had accepted the argument of Addison and others that there was no half-way position between honouring or repudiating the pledges, he seems to have felt that there was a possibility that the government could announce its willingness to honour the pledges and yet the unions be persuaded not to press for 'strict restoration'. Indeed, one Cabinet Paper included the claim that 'the skilled workers do not desire . . . to insist on literal restoration, but [only as] a bargaining weapon to be used in obtaining new labour conditions.'[15]

Hence Lloyd George asked the Caxton Hall conference to set up a joint committee of employers and unions to advise on how to carry out the pledges. He asked them to be mindful that this needed to be done 'without a complete dislocation of industry' and suggested that the pledges would probably not be carried out for some months, until the peace treaty was signed and the war was unequivocally over. Lloyd George said that he wanted the joint committee to consider the government's draft Bill, and if it felt it was 'not the best way of doing it, it would be folly for us to stick to it'.[16] Thus Lloyd George was providing time and opportunity for both sides of industry to negotiate the extent of the restoration that should occur.

The conference set up a joint committee, with Arthur Henderson as its chairman. In his opening remarks Lloyd George had been careful to pay tribute to Henderson's 'very valuable assistance' during the war. Henderson, who had been chairman of the National Advisory Committee which had assisted the government in implementing workshop changes in the engineering industry after the Treasury Conference of 1915, now took on the task of helping to unwind his earlier work. Henderson had put his reputation on the line in guaranteeing that the wartime removal of trade union practices would be only temporary. Ministers had been aware that moderate trade unionists would be discredited if the government reneged on its pledges. Hence in the War Cabinet on 24 October 1918 Shackleton had observed,

> Failure to fulfil the pledges would be tantamount to throwing over the accredited leaders of the unions, who would be charged with having betrayed the men. The upshot would be the destruction of organised trade unionism, and a great stimulus to the extremists.

However, as in the war, the engineering unions were very suspicious of other trade unionists being involved in matters which primarily concerned them. As Roberts pointed out to Lloyd George, the engineering unions felt 'that skilled engineers were the parties mainly or entirely concerned in the redemption of pledges and ... the committee represented interests which would be quite opposed to theirs'.[17] So the engineering unions boycotted Henderson's committee, and negotiations between the engineering unions, the engineering employers and the government became very protracted before an agreed Bill finally went through Parliament in August 1919. The final version was fairly mild in its provisions, giving employers up to two months in which to restore pre-war practices, then requiring they be maintained 'for one year after such restoration is effected', and laying down a maximum fine of £25 per day that offences were permitted to occur. However, by the time that the Act came in, as Lloyd George had probably expected, much of the post-war readjustment had taken place. With the return to peacetime production many of the special wartime working practices were discontinued on different types of work undertaken in peace, and many employers shared the unions' prejudices against female labour and were happy to see women leave, voluntarily or involuntarily.[18]

The second issue that Lloyd George raised at Caxton Hall on 13 November was real wages. In view of the economic dislocations expected in the next four months, Lloyd George predicted that prices would remain high. 'In those circumstances,' he said, 'I think it is an obligation – and I put this as the deliberate opinion of the government for the moment – that wages shall be maintained at their present standard.' In proposing to stabilise wages during the period of post-war transition the government was also influenced by the imminent ending of the clauses of the Munitions of War Acts forbidding strikes and lock-outs, providing compulsory arbitration and procedures for approving wages in controlled establishments.

After the Caxton Hall conference the employers and unions soon agreed to what became, on 21 November 1918, the Wages (Temporary Regulation) Act which not only fixed minimum wages at Armistice levels for six months but also repealed parts of the Munitions Acts. The time span of the Act was extended twice, first to 21 November 1919 and then to 30 September 1920. The Act did not hinder employers or workers agreeing to higher rates of pay; but for new rates to be legally enforceable as minimum rates, and so enforceable on firms which had not been involved in the agreement, wage agreements had to be approved by the Minister of Labour. The

Minister of Labour could submit agreements to the Interim Court of Arbitration, which George Askwith, the Chief Industrial Commissioner, described as being 'in effect the Committee on Production with certain additional members to meet the altered circumstances'. In practice the area in which most agreements were submitted for approval under the Wages (Temporary Regulation) Acts was building. The building trade accounted for 166 out of 252 agreements approved because the Ministry of Health, responsible for the large post-war housing programme, would only recognise wage agreements which had been so approved.[19]

The Caxton Hall meeting early on showed some of the post-war dilemmas of government policy. At it Roberts declared that the government wanted industry to settle its own affairs as soon as possible. Yet most members of the government recognised that it could not wash its hands of all industrial problems during the transitional period after the Armistice and, indeed, it was still directly involved, as an interested party, in the industries that were still controlled and in housebuilding.

The meeting also marked a continuation of the advocacy of the ideals of Whitleyism. Lloyd George made an appeal which was very much in line with the thinking of moderates on both sides of British industry:

> I hope it is the beginning of a new era. . . . Instead of regarding each other as hostile bodies, I believe that the workmen of this country and the employers have got it into their minds that their interest is a common interest, and that they can work together, the one not taking advantage of a temporary prosperity which places employers at their mercy, and the other not taking advantage of a temporary depression to put workmen at their mercy, but on the contrary, working together through depression and prosperity, hand in hand, for their common country and for the whole of the people in the land. We worked together for four and a half years; I wonder whether we could not work together for a short time yet.

Lloyd George's appeal on 13 November was to be a dress rehearsal for his performance at the National Industrial Conference in February 1919.

The concern expressed at Caxton Hall to secure stability in the post-war transition period complemented the government's concern to provide for servicemen and munitions workers who remained unemployed after being discharged. A scheme for a military out-of-work donation was part of the demobilisation plans. Four days before the Caxton Hall conference, the government announced a noncontributory scheme to provide financial support for all civilians unemployed with the ending of the war. Initially intended to operate for six months from 25 November 1918, the scheme was extended until 24 November 1919, at a total cost of £23 million.[20] In covering all unemployed adults, with no insurance payments required, this out-of-work donation effectively met the Labour movement's old demand of 'work or maintenance'.

Lloyd George saw the immediate post-war period as being likely to be the most difficult for his government. Much of his policies towards organised labour in late 1918 and the first half of 1919 stemmed from his belief that all would be well if things could be held together until normal conditions were restored. In August 1918 he was predicting that after the war ended, 'The chances are that the world, including Great Britain and her colonies, will be crying out for goods'. Thus, after the Armistice, he was confident that international trade, along with the British economy and British society, would return to something like its pre-war equilibrium. By April 1919 he rightly felt that the economy was on the upturn. Then, commenting on industrial and other problems, he observed, 'I don't believe in meeting troubles half way. I have a sort of idea that we shall be able to scrape through with the revival of trade.'[21]

In this transitional period employers were eager to get industry quickly and smoothly back on a peacetime basis. Addison noted that 'every employers' organisation – indeed every joint council – is clamouring for information on what is to be done' to get machinery and material released from war work and to secure supplies of material and financial facilities to meet post-war orders.[22] Furthermore, employers were well aware of the increased strength of organised labour deriving from the war and were willing to make concessions to their workforce in order to get peacetime production underway.

A major area where concessions were made was working hours. Indeed one of the most marked and widespread drops ever in the length of the basic working day in British industry took place in the two years after the Armistice.[23] One estimate suggests that well over 6 million workers had their hours of work reduced by an average of six and a half hours a week in 1919, with over half a million workers gaining reductions of an average of 3 hours 40 minutes in 1920. Of the 1919–20 reductions it seems that over 90 per cent were gained in the first seven months of 1919, with over 35 per cent in January and

February and, cumulatively, over 60 per cent by the end of April. The length of the working week in British industry dropped by about 13 per cent in 1919–20.[24] As for earnings, the data for 1919 is poor. Professor Feinstein has estimated that on an index where 1913 = 100, average weekly wage rates rose from 179 in 1918 to 215 in 1919, average weekly earnings rose from 211 in 1918 to 241 in 1919 and retail prices rose from 199 in 1919 to 211 in 1919.[25] So it is highly likely that most workers experienced gains in their real incomes in 1919.

One of the least remarked features of organised labour's gains made in the five months after the Armistice is that they were achieved during a downturn in the business cycle. Thus the most remarkable reductions in hours of work were negotiated between the Armistice and April 1919. It was an unusual period as for once the trade unions were demanding shorter hours in order that the available work be shared when labour market conditions had not already undermined their negotiating strength. In this period regular trade unionists remained in work. Those who joined the ranks of the unemployed were mostly 'dilutees', women or males usually in other employment.

In late December 1918 Sir Eric Geddes wrote a confidential memorandum, marked 'Personal to PM', in which he observed 'I see nothing to be alarmed at, at the moment, in the unemployment figure, but its progressive increase if it continues as at present must cause great concern.' He provided Lloyd George with an analysis of the existing situation:

> Since the Armistice, when there was practically no uncmployment, the unemployment benefit figure has risen to five per cent of the insured workers, and is increasing now at the rate of 17 per 10,000 of the population per week. Today 65 of every 10,000 of the total population are receiving Unemployment Donation. This figure, growing as it is growing, is one which must be watched with the greatest care, and must be read at the present time in the knowledge that the date has not yet arrived when this Donation ceases. When that date does arrive, and the difficulty of obtaining employment at pre-Armistice wages is brought home to the workers, we may have to look for a possibility of trouble. Further, the figure does not include men discharged from the Army who are still working out their 28 days' leave and who will come on to out-of-work benefit for 26 weeks thereafter it unemployed.

But he observed that some unemployment had to be expected in the 'turn-over from war to peace'.

Unemployment levels continued to rise until early 1919. The Ministry of Labour's index, based on trade union returns, reached a peak of 2.8 per cent in February 1919. But that ignored the ex-servicemen and most female workers. The numbers of people receiving the out-of-work donation was greatest in the week ending 2 May 1919, when the total was 1,093,400, made up of over 619,000 men (380,000 of whom were ex-servicemen) and 474,000 women.[26] One can offer a 'guesstimate' of about 8 per cent unemployment in the labour force in the spring of 1919 before the re-stocking boom got underway. However, up to three-quarters of this could have been replacement labour or discharged service personnel, rather than people laid off from work geared to peacetime production.

Although the exact level of unemployment in early 1919 is open to dispute, what is quite clear is that post-Armistice unemployment had much less of a weakening effect on the unions than the 18 per cent unemployment of 1921. Nevertheless, at the time the unions, like the government, feared serious unemployment as a follow-on to a major war and pressed successfully for reductions in working hours.

The impact on industrial output of conceding a shorter working week is also an area very much open to debate. At the time many employers complained that weekly output fell. Yet later writers have often argued that, after an initial drop in output, the shorter hours were compensated for by management securing more intensified work by the labour force. Various worktime studies of the 1920s suggested that the 8-hour day, achieved in many industries in 1919, was the optimum length in industry in that period. Furthermore, the return of fit, experienced men from the services to the metal, chemical and some other industries in place of wartime substitutes is likely to have increased productivity.[27]

That the trade unions were not faced with a severely flooded labour market and a much weaker bargaining position – or the government faced with greater social tumult – was due in some measure to the phased nature of demobilisation (even after the revolts of early January 1919) and to the silent and sometimes self-sacrificing (albeit often enforced by unions) withdrawal of so many women from those industries which before the war had employed few women. By the end of January 1919 977,525 men had been demobilised – but it took until mid-October, at an averge rate of 10,000 men per day, for demobilisation to be completed. As for women, 797,000 extra had joined the industrial labour force during the war, and an additional 866,000 had joined non-industrial occupations. By July 1920 some 515,000 (65 per cent) of the additional women in industry and 322,000 (37 per cent) of the additional women in non-industrial occupations had left. Many of the 530,000 women drawing out-of-work donation in March 1919 must have come from those industries which before the war had employed few women (though the donation could be drawn by people not discharged from war work).[28]

While much post-war adjustment of industry took place without major incident, the government – in spite of its frequent statements of wishing to avoid continued involvement – often intervened in labour relations. A major reason for such interventions was that many industries pivotal for economic recovery were still under government control, and so the government was a party to any dispute. Another reason was that the wartime legislation and government economic policies had set the pattern of collective bargaining in many industries (in some cases where there had been no previous national collective bargaining). Both sides of industry had come to expect government involvement. Austen Chamberlain complained in the War Cabinet in early February 1919 that

> in recent years there has been an increasing reliance placed on the government as the ultimate arbiter in labour disputes, with the result that strikes were prolonged by the fact that neither side would say the last word as to what they were prepared to concede, as they expected the government to be called in.[29]

Government withdrawal from industry and industrial relations was complementary to the policy of deflation and a return to the imagined automatic regulator of the Gold Standard. Conversely, Lloyd George's willingness to contemplate nationalisation of the railways and possibly the mines as measures whose benefits would be likely to improve industrial harmony was complementary to his early strong support for reconstruction as a measure of social justice. Quite apart from nationalisation, continuing government controls over sectors of industry entailed continued government involvement in industrial relations. Lloyd George's often spectacular interventions, temporarily defusing strikes or threatened strikes, enhanced his reputation as a negotiator, or even as a Welsh Wizard, but the repeated raising of expectations of prime ministerial intervention brought more and more Conservative politicians and businessmen to the belief that the less the state intervened in such matters, the better.

The number of workpeople directly and indirectly involved in industrial disputes (2,591,000) in 1919 was only a little short of the combined total (2,712,000) for the four years 1915 to 1918. In the first half of 1919 the most affected workers were in three sectors – coal mining (39 per cent of the total), textiles (33 per cent) and engineering and shipbuilding (17 per cent).[30] While there were actual stoppages in these industries, the threat of a major strike on the railways loomed over at least the first three months of 1919.

The industrial disputes in the cotton industry in late 1918 and mid-1919 epitomised the type of unrest which the government expected after the war years. One official report observed,

> The settlement of grievances had often been postponed during the war, and now that the main business of winning the war had been accomplished, the workers wanted these grievances settled. . . . Moreover, with the removal of the patriotic motive for keeping at work and the withdrawal of restrictions such as the legal prohibition of strikes and lockouts, there was a tendency to go to the other extreme and to cease work readily, and this tendency was doubtless increased by the desire for a rest after the strenuous labour of the war years.[31]

In spite of the soaring cost of living cotton workers had accepted lower wages than they might have negotiated normally because the industry was regulated by the Cotton Control Board and because most of the workers felt there was need to make such sacrifices while fighting continued. However, as the workers knew, huge profits had been made, especially in the American cotton branch of the spinning industry up to September 1918. In November 1918 the weavers demanded a 50 per cent wage increase and a minimum wage to cover operatives unable to work owing to shortage of material. Their claim was followed by claims from the spinners and cardroom operatives, who were subject to a six-month agreement. The unions rejected the employers' protestations that they should accept a smaller wage increase as there had been a downturn in trade since the Armistice.

Lloyd George eventually intervened to settle the dispute. He had stepped in before, less than three months earlier, on 15 September 1918. Then, ill with a severe chill in Manchester, he had appealed successfully to the spinners in the name of 'our brave men who are engaged in deadly struggle with the enemy . . . to return to work, and leave the decision of the matters in dispute to the government after an inquiry by a tribunal to be at once appointed by the government'. That offer resulted in the week-long strike being called off but the inquiry did not result in any revision of the current six-month agreement.

Hence in December the spinners firmly rejected offers of arbitration when they demanded a wage advance of 125 per cent on their pre-war wages. Sir Albert Stanley, the President of the Board of Trade, made a public appeal to the owners and operatives to settle without a strike. He informed Lloyd George on 2 December, 'I am proposing while in Manchester to meet several of the owners and try to effect a settlement. I am not very hopeful.' He added that after talking with one of the union leaders he came away clear that the unions were 'determined to secure practically the whole of their demands'. Six days later, with 100,000 spinners and cardroom workers on strike he wrote to Lloyd George from his constituency, the Lancashire cotton town of Ashton, where he was campaigning,

> I am keeping in touch with Judson, the President of the Cotton Spinners' Union. He tells me that the feeling between the employers and the operatives' representatives is very bitter and he sees no hope of a settlement unless the employers are prepared to make further concessions. He feels that this is not just the moment for any attempt being made to re-open negotiations; but he is having a further talk with his colleagues and will let me know on Monday or Tuesday what steps he thinks might be taken with the hope of success.

Stanley pointed out that this was a matter for the Minister of Labour, but as he was on the spot he asked Lloyd George for permission to act. This permission was given by telephone.

Quite probably by the Tuesday Stanley had reached an understanding with both sides that they would call off the strike if Lloyd George made a public appeal to them to do so on the grounds of the national interest. On Wednesday, 11 December, three days before polling day, Lloyd George invited representatives of the employers and unions to Downing Street, and made it publicly known that he was setting aside one-and-a-half hours to see them. At this meeting the employers agreed to a 50 per cent increase in wages over 1914 levels for all categories of workers.[32] Lloyd George's eagerness for a settlement on this occasion owed much to the dispute occurring in the midst of the general election campaign, which – as Stanley put it – 'might have a very bad effect in Lancashire'.

The December 1918 cotton dispute accounted for most of the 1,174,000 working days lost that month. The industry also accounted for some 23 per cent of all working days lost through strikes and lockouts in 1919. The textile trades were the worst affected by unemployment in the spring of 1919. In the summer, when prices and profits in cotton were at record heights, the cotton workers took action; 450,000 cotton workers went on strike from 23 June to secure shorter working hours without loss of earnings. After eighteen days a settlement was reached which reduced working hours from 55.5 to 48 and increased wages by an additional 30 per cent over the 1914 levels to prevent a decrease of weekly earnings.[33]

A notable feature of these cotton disputes was that the government did not see them as a threat to the social order, nor did it depict them as such, in the way that it did with so many other industrial disputes of this period. One reason was that the cotton workers had a strong case on both occasions. Another was that the cotton union leaders did not pose a threat in the way that the Triple Alliance leaders did – neither in terms of power to disrupt the economy at large nor in being exponents of left-wing labour politics. Moreover their demands of increased wages and a shorter working week could hardly be dubbed 'political'. The cotton disputes were seen as being over traditional issues conducted by adversaries who kept within the traditional 'rules of the game'. Sir George Askwith commented of the negotiations of late 1918, 'The settlement was by no means easy, and would not have been effected but for the good-will shown by both parties, men well known to me in previous disputes.' After the Glasgow and Belfast strikes of early 1919, the Ministry of Labour contrasted favourably the 'fully representative action' of the strongly centralised cotton unions with the 'confusion and indecision' it felt to be characteristic of the more decentralised ASE. In short the cotton textile unions came near to fitting official notions of moderate trade unionism.[34]

The issue of the 8-hour day had been taken up strongly in August 1917 by the Associated Society of Locomotive Engineers and Firemen (ASLEF), the skilled union which was competing vigorously with the National Union of Railwaymen (NUR) for the allegiance of locomotivemen. ASLEF had threatened the government with an immediate strike if the 8-hour day was not accepted immediately in principle, with implementation to take place at the end of the war. Both the union's executives and the delegates at a special conference were very firm on the issue. Faced with a strike at midnight on 21 August, Stanley wrote to John Bromley, the union's secretary, confirming earlier verbal pledges that the government would continue the control of railways for some time after the war ended,

> so that there would be an opportunity afforded within one month to bring forward a request for a shorter working day while the railways were under control, and that any reasonable request for a short working day would have the immediate and sympathetic consideration of the government.

George Barnes went further when speaking to the executive of ASLEF and, as Stanley later informed Lloyd George, 'practically pledged the government to sympathetically consider an eight-hour day'.

The much larger NUR, with a membership of 416,000, was also pressing for the eight-hour day along with other improved working conditions. The NUR had agreed at its After-War Matters Conference held at Leicester on 20 November 1917 to end the wartime truce with the employers and the government and to call for the 8-hour day and the 48-hour week, the conversion of war wages into permanent wages, double pay for overtime and Sunday working, a guaranteed day and a guaranteed week as well as nationalisation and workers' participation in the management of the railways. Both unions were quick off the mark after the Armistice to press for their programmes of reform.[35]

The executive committee of ASLEF saw Stanley on 26 November and reminded him of the pledge of August 1917. Stanley attempted to evade the 8-hour issue, and merely suggested 'the appointment of a Commission or a Council to take this matter up, both in respect to bonus and wages, of various grades'.[36] Bromley rejected any further investigations or other time-wasting tactics, observing that 'all the information necessary was available, and that unless an immediate decision was given he would . . . bring about an immediate strike in the railways and put the spark to a big social upheaval.' In reporting this meeting to Lloyd George Stanley wrote that he had tried to secure a postponement of this matter until after the election, but without success, and complained that Bromley had been 'very violent, and used language which I resented at the time'.

Stanley had greater success with the Secretary of the NUR on 29 November. He reported to Lloyd George,

> I saw Mr. J.H. Thomas, and explained the situation to him, and officially told him that we desired to postpone considering this matter until after the

election. To this he agreed, and said that he would use his influence with Bromley to secure that end. He took the opportunity of saying to me that his union would not be satisfied with securing only an eight-hour day, but had other concessions with respect to wages and other matters which must be settled at the same time.[37]

Thomas repeated his acceptance of delay to Lloyd George, but he was soon under pressure from his members to get an immediate settlement.[38] This was just one of many occasions when Thomas was out of step with his members. Indeed Thomas had opposed the scale of demands in the NUR's 1917 programme. Beatrice Webb noted in her diary on 10 January 1919 that he was 'considerably alarmed at the insubordination and always increasing claims of the railwaymen'.[39]

By 5 December 1918 Stanley was warning of 'an immediate general strike on the railways' if the government did not 'at once concede the eight-hour day'. So a meeting of the War Cabinet was hastily convened for the next day. Lloyd George, having discussed the situation in depth with Stanley, was foremost in backing the men's claim. He urged the 8-hour day on humanitarian grounds,

> The public were coming to the conclusion that it was a question not whether the men could stand the physical strain of a longer day, but that the working classes were entitled to the same sort of leisure as the middle classes. The workmen said they were not going to be working machines but that they required time to enjoy life as well. The demand was one for more humane conditions for the working classes, and it was a demand which, in view of public opinion, would be very difficult to resist.

When Sir Herbert Walker, the chairman of the Railway Executive Committee and a leading general manager, and Stanley urged that the cost of the scheme, £20 to £25 million, would be too much for the railways and something that they would never have conceded under normal conditions, Lloyd George replied that 'They might have been forced by Act of Parliament to do so, as had happened in the case of granting terms to the miners before the war'. When Sir Eric Geddes urged that it was 'equivalent to an increase in wages of something like 150 per cent, and was in excess of concessions to any other class of workers' Lloyd George pointed out 'that the wages of agricultural labourers had trebled'. However, Lloyd George did suggest that exceptions to the principle might be made in the case of the one-fifth of railway workers in areas which dealt with little traffic. The War Cabinet agreed to accept the eight-hour principle, leaving it to

Stanley to try to exclude those workers in less busy areas and also on the Irish Railways. They also decided he should announce that after the election the government would investigate wages and conditions generally on the railways.[40]

Like the cotton workers, the railway workers exerted pressure at the right time. The government was nervous about the newly enfranchised electorate. There were 21.4 million electors, including some 6 to 8 million women in contrast to the 7.3 millions of the 1906 general election in which the Liberal Party had won a landslide victory. While Lloyd George was usually optimistic of winning the election by a good margin, indeed expressing the view the day after polling that he would feel badly treated with a majority of less than 120, his mercurial nature at times made him pessimistic of the outcome.[41] Hence, he and his colleagues were especially sensitive as to the claims of organised labour during the campaign. Thus on 8 December, after commenting on his 'hot fight' in his constituency, Stanley observed to Lloyd George that 'the railway settlement has had a good effect'.

After the election the new restructured Coalition government was less willing to make concessions to trade unions, even though the industrial unrest was much more severe. When condemning 'direct action' Arthur Henderson bluntly noted that the unions were in a weaker position politically. He informed the members of his union in July 1919,

> To many items in the government programme, Labour is opposed – it said so at the election – and yet the working-class electors, including a vast number of trade unionists and their wives, preferred the Coalition candidate and ... accepted the policy of the government, however reactionary we may consider it.

Many supporters of Coalition government made it clear that they felt that the general election result gave Lloyd George a mandate to deal firmly with trade union demands. Thus W. C. Bridgeman, the Parliamentary Secretary to the Board of Trade, wrote to his wife in late January 1919, 'I hope to goodness we are going to be firm and not give in at all to the colliers. The public would support us solidly – and if we give in now, it will be a miserable start for the new government.'[42]

The new Coalition government began to take the firmer line with the railway unions from mid-January. On 16 January Bromley wrote to Stanley demanding that negotiations over railway pay should be delayed no longer. The government was then trying to stall on any further concessions to the railwaymen until it was clear as to its post-war programme for transport. Sir Eric Geddes, Lloyd George's 'transport czar', pressed on Lloyd George that it was impossible to wait until a new Ministry of Ways and Communications was set up, possibly in May, to deal with ASLEF and the NUR. He warned on 18 January 1919,

> Stanley has very grave doubts as to whether the men will remain quiet for so long, and it appears to me that we are living in a fool's paradise and on the verge of a volcano.
> ... If we want a general strike of the railwaymen in the next month or two, I think we are going the right way to get it.... A strike may or may not be a good thing. It is dangerous if it does come now, but let us have it if it is to come on good grounds, and not on 'delay' and 'Dilly Dally'.[43]

The *New Statesman* cited anger over this as one of the causes of labour being in revolt at the failure of the government 'to cope with any promptitude with the very urgent needs of the situation'. It commented, 'The railwaymen find themselves referred from the Board of Trade to the Railway Executive Committee, and back again, without discovering anyone able (or, as they imagine, willing) to put effectively in operation the Eight-Hours Day that has already been conceded to them.'[44]

Irritation with the delays was mounting in both the NUR and ASLEF. On 21 January the London District Council of the NUR agreed that 'drastic action' would be taken unless the 8-hour day was introduced 'without equivocation'. Not surprisingly, there was anger when, on 1 February as the 8-hour day came into operation, it was accompanied by the posting of notices announcing the abolition of the 40-year old practice of allowing men a 5-minute break to wash their hands. Not surprisingly this caused great anger. Even more problems stemmed from varying practices as to meal breaks. The 8-hour day agreement had included recognition that 'the men's conditions should remain unchanged pending negotiations'. Engine drivers, some signalmen and some shunters worked ten to twelve hours and meals were taken whenever convenient. Under the 8-hours agreement this would continue. However other grades took their meals outside the hours counted as work. Stanley warned the War Cabinet that these men now demanded meal time to be included in the eight hours or 'they would only work eight hours (meal time inclusive) and then cease work'. He added that he had instructed the Railway Executive to dismiss any man who carried out the threat. Stanley advised the war Cabinet that 'the railwaymen were ... in some measure out of hand, and although they had been instructed by their leaders to observe this interpretation of the agreement it could not be guaranteed that they would do so.'

However on the London underground the manager of the network excluded meals in the eight-hour day, even though the drivers had had good conditions of service which had included a meal break in their nine-hour day. Stanley, who had been a director of the London underground, advised the War Cabinet on 31 January that the men's demand to include their meal time as before 'struck at the very principle of the eight-hours working day, and if their point was conceded it would become the source of further general concessions'. In the ensuing discussion others expressed concern 'as to whether, by insisting that the meal-times of these men should not be included in the eight-hours' day, the government were not, in fact, breaking their promise that the conditions of service should continue unchanged'.[45]

On 3 February the London tube drivers went on strike. The next morning the War Cabinet appointed the Industrial Unrest Committee to look into measures to deal with this dispute and a threatened strike in London power stations. Its terms of reference were 'to make the necessary arrangements for dealing with any situation that might arise from industrial unrest both at the present moment and in the future'. It was given powers to make 'decisions which did not involve important questions of principle'. The Committee was initially chaired by Shortt, and included Horne, Stanley and Munro (the Secretary of State for Scotland) – the ministers who had been dealing with the recent industrial unrest. That evening it recommended to the War Cabinet that lorries driven by personnel from the armed forces should provide alternative transport in London.

This recommendation raised the issue of whether, in the light of recent unrest in the armed forces, military personnel would obey orders to strike break. At the morning meeting of the War Cabinet Churchill, as Secretary of State for War, had advised that 'so far as the trustworthiness of the troops was concerned, conditions had improved considerably during the last fortnight.' Nevertheless, at its evening meeting Chamberlain felt that there was considerably more risk in the use of service personnel than in banning strikes in power stations, the Industrial Unrest Committee's other major recommendation. He warned that 'if the attempt to use soldiers for this purpose failed it might well lead to soldiers refusing to act in support of law and order, which they had hitherto, and notably at Glasgow, never failed to do.' Churchill did support the committee's recommendation, but the War Cabinet minutes suggest that in so doing he was notably cautious:

> He gathered from his military advisers that the men would support the government action, provided that the matter was properly handled in the press. This action was undoubtedly crossing the frontier line and, if decided upon, should be carried out vigorously ... the government should only be deterred if any question arose as to the loyalty of the soldiers. ... The press should be prepared at once for the government's policy.

After lengthy discussion the War Cabinet agreed that preparations for the use of service vehicles could be started.

The Industrial Unrest Committee also suggested

> that a statement be issued to the press, pointing out that these were not *bona fide* strikes, but a Bolshevik attack upon the whole public, and therefore the government were taking steps to meet the situation, which they would not have taken in an ordinary industrial dispute.[46]

Thus by this time the humble issue of whether the tube drivers' meal break should be included within the 8-hour day, like that of the locomotive drivers, had become subsumed in ministerial paranoia over strikes.

To the embarrassment of some ministers, the Railway Executive Committee, which managed the railways while under state control, agreed to a compromise formula of words to cover the meal-time issue until the Railway Executive met the NUR and ASLEF for further negotiations on 12 February. Several ministers were notably belligerent at the dispute being defused in this way. Long condemned the compromise as 'it would only camouflage a defeat for the government' and said that 'the extremists were beginning to realise that by the firm action of the government, they were beaten.' Churchill also saw the dispute as being in an area in which there should be no compromise. He argued that,

> at a time when everyone should be working harder to make up for the waste of the war, it was monstrous that men should be demanding what

was in reality a seven-and-a-half-hours' day. An eight-hours' working day was not too much for any man, and he failed to see how the wealth of the country could be made up if interpretations such as that now proposed were put upon an agreement which had laid down an eight-hours' working day. On the other hand the whole principle of allowing men to take their meals during working hours was an objectionable one, and it was not surprising that the whole of the railways were seething with discontent.

Churchill did, however, suggest that the tube companies should be required to provide canteens for meals to be eaten out of working hours.

Sir Herbert Walker explained that the understanding the Railway Executive was willing to accept was 'some ten minutes' for a snack. Bonar Law reflected sadly

> that the government were on weaker ground than was originally thought, and had the facts as now presented been before them at an earlier stage, they would not have chosen the present ground on which to fight, especially since the Railway Executive were prepared to accept the [compromise] formula.

Tom Jones, the Assistant Cabinet Secretary, wrote to Hankey who was in Paris, of this War Cabinet meeting,

> we had the spectacle ... of about 25 people trying to draft an agreement of two sentences long which would placate the managers and men and save the face of the government who, through Bonar Law (badly advised by Stanley and Horne), had written a published letter to Bromley. If a verbatim note of this discussion had been published last week the Coalition would have collapsed and the PM would be free to start with a clean slate. The whole wrangle was over the ordinary, reasonable physical requirements of the men and the precise number of minutes required to satisfy them, the estimate varying from none upwards. I am very curious to know whether or not Curzon and Long have even been in a tube.[47]

The tube dispute was an episode which did little for Stanley's reputation. Even before the strike occurred, Lloyd George and Bonar Law had been considering replacing him. Bonar Law wrote to Lloyd George on 27 January,

> From my talk with Stanley I am sure that there would be no difficulty whatever in getting him to give up his post but I am convinced that that would be a great mistake just now. He is not very heavy metal but there is no one I am sure whom you could get to take his place now who would be

better than he, and I say this even looking upon Maclay [the Shipping Controller] as a possible successor. I do not mean that Maclay might not be in the end a more capable head of the department, but for him to plunge into all these difficulties at a time like this would . . . be pretty hopeless and would make the position worse than it is.

Lloyd George responded with characteristic brutal frankness when commenting on those whom he felt were not serving him well. He observed,

I have come to the conclusion from a long observation of Stanley's work that he is much too weak and flabby a man for the difficult task which confronts a President of the Board of Trade under present conditions. . . . Stanley is a funk, and there is no room for funks in the modern world.[48]

In contrast Sir Robert Horne, the Minister of Labour, gained in reputation during the serious conjunction of industrial unrest of late January and the first half of February 1919. Then the government faced general strikes and accompanying social turbulence in Glasgow and Belfast, disputes involving London power workers, Thames ship repairers and the Railway Clerk's Association, the presentation of the miners' post-war demands as well as the serious unrest in the army and the dispute with London tube drivers. Before these troubles broke Bonar Law saw Horne. He informed Lloyd George that he 'was greatly pleased with his attitude altogether . . . his judgement is good and he will not be afraid . . . in taking responsibility'.[49]

Like the London tube strike and much other unrest of the period, the Belfast and Glasgow engineering disputes centred on the issue of hours of work. In terms of working days lost in the first half of 1919, the engineering disputes were the most costly (even if the number of workers involved was less than in the coalmining and textiles), amounting to 36.5 per cent of the total loss. In June 1918 the engineering unions had demanded a reduction in hours from 54 to 44 per week. The Engineering Employers Federation had already decided that reduced hours were inevitable and had braced itself for a 48-hour week, but with a reduction in meal breaks from two to one. After negotiations the unions agreed to a 47-hour week, with one meal break, as from 1 January 1919, and promised to help maintain output. This deal had been deemed a great triumph by the union leadership, especially as it established a national standard week for the first time. It was endorsed by all the unions' memberships; though in the case of the ASE by 36,793 to 27,684, revealing a dissatisfied minority of 43 per cent.[50]

By early January there was considerable dissatisfaction with this agreement, especially in the large engineering plants and shipyards on the Clyde and in Belfast. In Scotland there was very widespread support for a 40-hour week. This included the Scottish Advisory Council of the Labour Party, the Scottish division of the ILP, the Scottish TUC, the Glasgow Trades Council and the district committee of the ASE. In addition, the revived Clyde Workers' Committee was campaigning for a 30-hour week. On 18 January a committee was set up to organise a strike, which was called for 27 January (a compromise date between the wishes of the shop stewards' organisation and the Scottish TUC). The attitude of the activists was well summarised in an article (by Patrick Dollan) in the *Labour Leader*:

> Since the 47-hour week came into operation on 1 January discontent has spread like wildfire, and it has required the utmost persuasive tact on the part of the shop stewards to keep the men from coming out on strike before.
> The 47-hour week is no concession. The employers granted it on condition that the output would be no less than it was for a 54-hour week. In this way the 47-hour week became a cute device for speeding up workers who had already been stretched to the maximum. Moreover piece rates were not increased to conform with the reduction.
> ... But the chief underlying urge of the movement for a 40-hour week is the menacing increase in unemployment. A few months ago, when there was a lessening in the demand for jute products, the employers met the situation by reducing the hours of all workers to make output conform to the demand.[51]

However, the national trade unions were unwilling to break the agreements reached with the employers and endorsed by ballot. Only the Electrical Trade Union (ETU) made the strike official. The ASE forbade the payment of strike pay, suspended its Glasgow district committee and ordered its radical district secretary out of his union-owned house. Hence for a while both the employers and the government saw the action primarily as a local revolt against national trade union leaderships and one which would soon subside. As late as 30 January the Clyde Shipbuilders' Association was resolving, 'The strike was against the trade union officers and the strikers' fellow workers rather than against the employers, and therefore the latter did not wish to appear in the matter.'[52] Bonar Law wrote to Lloyd George on 28 January,

The King is in a funk about the labour situation and is talking about the necessity of your being here if, as he says, there is danger of a revolution. I told him that of course it is a great disadvantage your not being here but that you must judge between varying necessities. . . . The talk about revolution shows that he is rather in a panic and Horne thinks, and as far as I can make out he is right, the position is much exaggerated by the press. The Glasgow trouble he says is fizzling out, but one of the things wanted is more publicity and I have arranged with him today that he shall take steps to make sure that the public through the press really understand what the strikes are all about.

On the next day Bonar Law gave a lead in publicising the government's view by devoting a public speech to condemning the strike.[53] But otherwise, at this stage, the government waited on events.

At the War Cabinet meeting on 28 January Horne commented that 'the position was rendered extremely difficult as the government could not actively interfere in the settlement of these strikes over the heads of the union executives, and the men so far had totally disregarded the advice of their leaders.' Horne reported, 'The workers on the Clyde had telegraphed to him yesterday asking him to go down and negotiate, but he could not deal with these people except through their union leaders.' However, when pressed as to when he would intervene, he replied that he would feel bound to do so the next day if there was still deadlock in the shipyards. The War Cabinet asked him to supply the press with 'the full facts' about the strikes, laying stress on their 'unauthorised character'.[54]

During the next two days the government came to take a more serious view as the strikes, far from collapsing, began to spread from the Upper Clyde. Mass pickets helped to bring out workers in the shipyards of the Lower Clyde and the Forth. In due course other workers came out in sympathy strikes, including 36,000 miners in the Lanarkshire and Stirlingshire coalfields and 10,000 iron moulders.[55] Commentators at the same time remarked on the spontaneity of the strike. In the War Cabinet Bonar Law denied that the strike had been marked by intimidation of non-strikers at their homes, as had happened in some pre-war strikes. It is clear that the strike was very popular, especially among skilled workers and many unemployed former soldiers. As the *New Statesman* observed,

The general movement for a reduction of the hours of labour is largely inspired by a belief that only in this way will it be possible promptly to reabsorb in industry the two hundred thousand men whom the War Office will presently be discharging every week.[56]

On 29 January Bonar Law was still hoping that the strikes on the Clyde and in Belfast would crumble. After seeing Horne, he reported to Lloyd George that 'personally I have no doubt that at this stage at least government interference would do no good' and added that Horne felt that if strike pay was not being paid 'the men will get tired soon and go back to work'.[57] The next day, in a telephone message to Lloyd George, Bonar Law warned that 'everything depends on beating the strike in the Glasgow area, as if the strikers are successful there the disorder will spread over the country.'[58] The government did keep a close watch on the danger of it spreading to the Tyne, London and Manchester. Thus on 4 February Horne informed the War Cabinet that 'a deputation, consisting of Macmanus and a few others, had left Glasgow for Manchester in order to stir up trouble in that city with regard to the 40-hour week.'[59] However, major trouble was confined to Glasgow and Belfast. In Glasgow it came to a head at the end of January.

On 29 January Emmanuel Shinwell, the chairman of the strike committee, led a deputation to the Lord Provost of Glasgow to request him to ask Lloyd George and Horne to intervene and meet their demands. The Lord Provost sent Lloyd George a telegram in which he reported that the deputation had warned that 'they had hitherto adopted constitutional methods in urging their demand, but that, failing consideration being given to their request by the Government, they would adopt any other methods which they might consider would be likely to advance their demand.' The Lord Provost reported that they would 'delay taking any such action' until the 31st, when they would return for a reply. He also gave the information that there would be no electric power for industry as the electricity workers had joined the strike.[60] Bonar Law made a draft reply which observed that the government would only deal with the trade union leaders as to do otherwise 'would destroy the co-operation between employers and employed on which the hope of industrial peace depends'. Bonar Law felt that the fact that the deputation saw the Lord Provost was a sign of weakness. In his telephone message of 30 January to Lloyd George he observed, 'If the strike had been doing well they would not have resorted to this method.' At Bonar Law's request Lloyd George telephoned him back, and in this conversation Lloyd George approved

Bonar Law's reply and said that he would return to London if necessary.[61]

The War Cabinet, after a long discussion on 30 January, determined that 'firm but not provocative action should be taken to put down disorder and prevent intimidation.' The discussion was notable for the considerable unease expressed as to using troops and the police to maintain order and to keep the electric power stations and other municipal services going. The military men present were disparaging as to the quality of the troops. General Robertson observed that those in Scotland at that time 'consisted of all sorts of men, old, young, convalescents, and men with wounds', while their officers 'were not very efficient'. General Childs even warned that while soldiers had been used against strikers in the past, then 'we had a well-disciplined and ignorant army, whereas now we had an army educated and ill-disciplined.' As for the police, Robert Munro, the Secretary for Scotland, reassured his colleagues that they could now be relied on. Though he observed that 'there had been a little trouble' a week or two earlier when the police had demanded a pay increase; but he had settled this in the men's favour 'on the recommendation of the municipal authorities'. Munro also urged that Glasgow's 2,000 special constables should be used to maintain services as he felt that they 'might be more reliable and suitable than soldiers'.

Churchill and most of the Cabinet clearly were not fearful of a revolutionary insurrection taking place in Glasgow. Indeed Churchill urged that the dangers of the strike should not be exaggerated and referred to what he deemed to be equally serious ones before the war. He took a characteristically tough line, observing,

> The disaffected were in a minority and . . . there would have to be conflict in order to clear the air. We should be careful to have plenty of provocation before taking strong measures. By going gently at first we should get the support we wanted from the nation, and then troops could be used more effectively.

Horne similarly urged that 'if there were any possibility of seizing the leaders during the strike they should do so. These leaders were not representative of the trades unions at all, and most of them were well-known extremists.'

The War Cabinet agreed to set up a small committee chaired by Munro 'for the purposes of consultation during the continuance of disorder'. It included J. Clyde, the Lord Advocate, who was instructed to 'examine the legal grounds for the arrest of the ringleaders of the strike, should it be found desirable to do so'. Bonar Law sent Lloyd George an outline of the War Cabinet discussion and its proposed action. The latter replied, 'I am glad you are taking a firm hand'.[62]

The next morning Bonar Law telephoned Lloyd George and left a message that he still felt it necessary to be 'ready to take firm action'. He asserted that 'one of the things which would be most effective would be the arrest of some of the ringleaders' but he would discuss the matter further at the Cabinet to ensure that there were good grounds for doing so. Lloyd George was very wary of prosecutions. He had a message telephoned back that he

> wishes to make it clear that he considers that action should be taken against the strike leaders only if there is evidence which seems adequate to secure a conviction in a Court of Law. He wants Mr Bonar Law to be careful not to give the impression that the government is taking proceedings against them for striking only. It must be on a charge of sedition, e.g. an attempt to use force.[63]

However that same morning mounted police charged a massive demonstration in George Square, which had accompanied Shinwell and his deputation to receive the Lord Provost's reply. News of this – without details – was announced to the Cabinet when it met at 3.00 p.m.[64] Munro observed, 'it was more clear than ever that it was a misnomer to call the situation in Glasgow a strike – it was a Bolshevist rising.' However he felt that the number of 'malcontents' was 10,000 at the most, and reported police views that the strike looked as though it would break up soon. This view was supported by information from the Naval Intelligence Department. Army representatives advised them that 12,000 troops could be put into Glasgow at short notice, and that 6 tanks and 100 motor lorries were going north by rail that night. In view of this information the Cabinet decided that 'for the moment no further action was necessary by the government'. Bonar Law told Lloyd George of the situation, observing that 'all the information is that public opinion is dead against the strikers'. He said that Clyde shared his views on arrests, 'but the case is too flagrant and two of them – Gallacher and Kirkwood – have been already arrested, and another, Shinwell, will be arrested as soon as he can be found'. He added that Clyde was going to Scotland 'to try quietly to set the people in Glasgow to work to get a voluntary organisation of citizens to form themselves against this movement'.

Bonar Law was disposed to blame the Lord Provost of Glasgow. He informed Lloyd George,

> This trouble could not . . . be dealt with in its early stages by the government and I am afraid it has become worse than it might have been because the Lord Provost, although a capable man, has not much force and is inclined . . . to be timid.[65]

After the George Square incident there was a show of military force in the city, and the strike gradually collapsed. Bonar Law wrote to Lloyd George on 1 February that things were going as well as they could hope in Glasgow and observed that 'there seems no doubt that the rioting in Glasgow yesterday has helped towards a solution.'[66] That the unrest in Glasgow was dying down was confirmed by a report from Clyde on 3 February.[67]

The unrest in Belfast was equally worrying for the government. Before the George Square incident the Belfast situation had given the government more fear of serious unrest. On 29 January Bonar Law wrote to Lloyd George that the position in Belfast was becoming worse and that he was sending Lord French, the Viceroy, back that night.[68] Two days later Shortt (Chief Secretary for Ireland) informed the War Cabinet, 'The workmen had formed a "Soviet" Committee, and this committee had received forty-seven applications from small trades for permission to use light', but added that there were signs that the strike was weakening. Milner, however, noted in his diary, 'Things are still pretty bad at Glasgow and worse at Belfast.'[69] On 4 February French asked Bonar Law for permission to see the strike committee and warn them that on the morning of 6 February the government would take over the municipal gas works if the supply remained stopped. French added that if the government did not want him to intervene in such a way he was 'prepared to use force if the government will authorise'. Bonar Law replied that he felt these proposals were not wise and the strike should be left to fizzle out.[70] However, the strike continued and on 10 February Ian MacPherson (who had just succeeded Shortt) reported that the Commander-in-Chief was resisting local proposals for the use of troops to run the gas and electric works. MacPherson suggested they should meet the problem by enrolling volunteers as they had done in Glasgow. The Cabinet decided that a joint strike committee of members of the Belfast Corporation and the government officials should be formed to meet the situation.[71] Thus both the Glasgow and Belfast strikes contributed to the government evolving strike breaking organisations.

The key feature of the industrial unrest of late January and early February 1919 was the conjunction of so many challenges in a very short period. The threatened power strikes reinforced the impact of the widespread unrest in Glasgow and Belfast, and uncertainty as to the loyalty of soldiers in such situations made these and the underground dispute less easily manageable for the government. When Bonar Law had called an interdepartmental meeting on the Glasgow strike on 30 January, he had put forward two priorities: to prevent disorder and to maintain the supply of light.

Almost immediately the government was faced with the threat of more power strikes, but this time in London. This threat, along with the actual underground strike, led to the setting up of the Industrial Unrest Committee on 4 February. As well as being asked to make proposals with regard to transport in London, the committee had also been given as an immediate task the 'making [of] any arrangements that might be necessary for dealing with the threatened electrical strike . . . and should . . . examine and report to the War Cabinet the possibility of applying the Act of 1875 to the present situation'. Bonar Law, when reporting the setting up of the Industrial Unrest Committee to Lloyd George observed,

> I am sure the public would stand any strong action for the irritation is growing against the strikers, but I hardly see as yet what we can propose until the position has become more desperate. One of the suggestions which is being considered today, in addition to getting volunteers to run the electric works, is whether or not an old Act of 1875, which makes giving up work on the part of those engaged in gas or water undertakings a penal offence should not be extended by a Defence of the Realm Act regulation to electrical public utility undertakings.[72]

When the War Cabinet reconvened at 6.30 p.m. that evening to consider the Industrial Unrest Committee's recommendations on both the threatened electrical strike and the tube strike, it spent much time weighing up the advantages and disadvantages of resorting to the 1875 Act. Bonar Law felt that it 'should be used with caution as it might frighten every form of organised labour, and it had never been used in previous strikes'. Shortt, Munro and Curzon warmly supported its use. The War Cabinet agreed that 'the 1875 Act regarding the arrest of persons employed on gas and water services leaving their posts without permission should be adapted by Order in Council to meet the present circumstances.'[73]

As with the proposed use of service motor lorries in the tube strike, the War Cabinet laid much emphasis on the presentation of policy through the medium of the press. Bonar Law, echoing the Industrial Unrest Committee, called for a press statement which

> should say that the government could not countenance sudden strikes of this kind, which were organised by a minority for the purpose of penalising the innocent, and not for the purpose of influencing the employers, and that these were not proper strikes but a deliberate anti-social movement.

The War Cabinet agreed to issue an unofficial communiqué to that effect.

The Industrial Unrest Committee went on to lay the foundations of a permanent emergency strike-breaking organisation.[74] It formed five interdepartmental sub-committees which were to ensure the provision of the 'necessities of life'. These dealt with transport, public utilities, electric power stations, communications and the umbrella category 'protection'. The Industrial Unrest Committee received Admiralty agreement to provide 650 naval ratings as stokers. But in view of the unrest in the armed forces and the example of Russia, increasing emphasis was given to organising civilians. On the 7 February Sir Hamar Greenwood, Under Secretary in the Home Office, informed the War Cabinet that that evening there would be '1,000 extra skilled mechanics ready to take over the lighting stations'. Horne then suggested that the government should 'make definite plans for establishing a permanent organisation to meet civil emergencies in the future'. Greenwood informed them that his committee 'had registered the names and addresses of large numbers of outside skilled men who would form the nucleus' of such an organisation. The War Cabinet decided that such an organisation should be established.[75]

The feared strikes in the electric power stations did not occur. Nevertheless the Industrial Unrest Committee continued to plan to defeat major strikes. It turned its attention to the miners and railwaymen. Lloyd George, writing after the 1926 general strike, emphasised that in this planning in early 1919 his government had had unusual advantages. It was still in control of food supplies and there was a sizeable supply of lorries and trained drivers, neither of which then had returned to industry.

In commenting on his role as 'father of the original scheme of 1919', Lloyd George in 1926 wrote,

> Strikes and lock-outs as means of settling industrial disputes are methods of barbarism. But until more civilised methods have been found and accepted the 'non-combatants' in the community must be safeguarded against privation. In organising such protection governments express no opinion on the merits of a dispute. They are simply performing the elementary functions of good government.[76]

In this claim to impartiality, Lloyd George was being disingenuous. The War Cabinet discussions of February 1919 were very explicit as to the organisation being a means to defeat the workers, and above all the miners and railwaymen. But he ably expressed the problem which was to face Labour governments, that of offering the general public some degree of protection against privation arising from major industrial disputes.

Alongside the threatened electricity strike was a further threat of a rail strike. The Railway Clerks' Association demanded recognition, so as to be on a par with the other two major railway unions, the NUR and ASLEF. As the railways were still under government control, managed by the Railway Executive Committee under the Board of Trade, the union sent a deputation to the Board of Trade in late January. Stanley followed the line of the Railway Executive which was that it

> would not object to recognising a union consisting only of station-masters and other supervisory grades, but they maintained that the Railway Clerks' Association, in including station-masters and similar grades as well as the ordinary clerks, undermined the discipline on the railway.

Stanley and Eric Geddes strongly supported this view. Stanley, whilst writing in a memorandum that he recognised 'that in these times one must take a very broad view of these matters in view of the grave state of unrest and the government's decision to support the official trades unions as against those who bring about unauthorised strikes', still argued the old case that 'the railway service is a thing apart' and needed special discipline to ensure safety. Geddes argued in the War Cabinet that if recognition were granted 'it would result in the trade union running the railways'. Given their backgrounds, Stanley a director of the London underground railway and Geddes head of the North Eastern Railway, their attitude was not surprising.

From Armistice to February 1919   115

Their view, which Tom Jones dubbed 'prehistoric', was opposed by Horne and Addison, as well as by Shackleton on behalf of the Ministry of Labour. Bonar Law agreed with Shackleton's opinion that 'the government could not face a strike on the cry that it refused to acknowledge a union'. He repeated this view in a letter to Lloyd George later that day, observing that he would not wish to fight on either the issue of recognition for the railway staff or over interpretations of the 8-hour day for underground railway drivers. Not surprisingly, there was a strong feeling among many ministers that 'the Glasgow trouble should subside before entering upon a new conflict with labour'.[77]

In the hope of ending the division of opinion in the government Bonar Law set up a ministerial committee to consider the Railway Executive's case. He informed Lloyd George,

> those whom I am asking to join in addition to Stanley and Horne are Roberts, Illingworth (because of the analogy of the Post Office), Herbert Fisher, Maclay and Milner. With the possible exception of Milner, who on such questions has a very open mind, this committee will start in favour of recognition. So if they are converted to the Board of Trade point of view it will give me greater confidence that the decision of the government will be right. The trouble about this is that we cannot get out of it by any question of non-interference as the railways are under government control and the decision is, in effect, a decision of the government.[78]

The other ministers were not converted to the Board of Trade view. They persuaded Stanley to ask G. J. Wardle, the Coalition Labour MP who was Parliamentary Secretary to the Minister of Labour, to find out from A. G. Walkden, the Secretary of the Railway Clerks' Association, if a compromise was possible. Walkden, who did not want a strike, indicated that he would settle for an arrangement whereby the higher grades would join a separate section of the Association and their claims would be negotiated separately. Milner joined all but Stanley in recommending acceptance of this solution.[79]

Bonar Law, however, remained indecisive. He repeatedly warned Lloyd George that there was 'a real danger of political trouble'. He observed,

> If it were only the railways I would not be afraid of that, but there is a distinct danger that the Federation of Employers, when they hear that this has been done, will raise a great outcry saying that we have given away a

principle which has never been yielded until now, and will mean that it will be impossible for the employers to maintain the discipline which will enable them to run their business.

Bonar Law felt that whichever way the decision went would be likely to put major strain on the coalition:

If we do not recognise the union, many of the members of the government, and particularly Liberals will, if a strike comes, go against us; and if we agree to the compromise and the employers make a great fuss, there is a bigger danger of the break-away of the Conservative members.

Plaintively, Bonar Law passed the buck to Lloyd George with the comment, 'You are so resourceful that you must find a way out.'[80]

Lloyd George favoured recognition, and made this clear to Bonar Law before the War Cabinet met in the morning on 4 February. Though Bonar Law told Lloyd George later that day that 'the message you gave this morning agreed with my own views', at the time of the meeting he remained very anxious about the response of industrialists if the War Cabinet accepted the compromise. 'Employers would regard it as giving away the pass and making it impossible for them to fight in the future a similar demand in other industries', he warned; and added that 'they would be accused of the same weakness of which they were accused during the war'. But he recognised that on balance recognition of the union would be the lesser evil as otherwise 'the whole of the trade union movement would be against the government'.

It was in the context of this discussion that various ministers made their often quoted remarks as to the importance of trade union leaders to the maintenance of social stability. Horne was well aware of the worries of employers. He told his colleagues,

in certain industries the foremen fixed the amount of piece-rate on the spot, and if the foremen and the men belonged to the same union and the men were dissatisfied with the piece-rate and decided to deal with the foreman in a disciplinary way, an impossible position would result. He knew of cases where foremen had been fined by their union for reporting some of the men under them.

But, as Bonar Law, Chamberlain and Horne himself pointed out, a good 60 per cent of the supervisory grade staff were already in the Railway Clerks Association so, as Bonar Law put it, 'this evil would exist whether the Association were recognised or not'. Horne, in spite of his usual devotion to representing the viewpoint of industrial employers, argued that

> The government could not hope to win through present and future labour battles unless they had the support of the trade union executives and if the government took up the line which the Railway Executive wanted them to take up there was no doubt that the sympathy of the trade unions would be alienated. . . . In the following week there was probably to be a Trade Union Congress, and if the government refused the suggested compromise there was no doubt that the discussions at that Congress would go against the government, and the men taking part in the Congress were those upon whom the government relied.

Now, as in the First World War, when faced with a strike on such an issue as trade union recognition, the government was forced to respond more readily to trade union opinion then employer opinion. Bonar Law, who appears to have been very nervous about giving a lead in these weeks, told his colleagues that the issue was 'by far the most difficult labour problem they had yet to solve', because unlike the other labour disputes whatever was done could antagonise some of the government's supporters. Yet he also told the War Cabinet that 'the trade union organisation was the only thing between us and anarchy, and if the trade union organisation was against us the position would be hopeless.'

Churchill went further than most. He gave the opinion

> that the trade union organisation was very imperfect, and the more moderate its officials were the less representative it was, but it was the only organisation with which the government could deal. The curse of trade unionism was that there was not enough of it, and it was not highly enough developed to make its branch secretaries fall into line with the head office. With a powerful union either peace or war could be made.

Consequently the War Cabinet agreed 'to recognise the Railway Clerks' Association as representing the supervisory and supervised grades, provided that the Association would give the necessary safeguards with regard to the maintenance of discipline and public safety within the Association'.[81]

Those on the Left of the Labour movement greeted the government's concern for orthodox trade union leaders with scorn. George Lansbury, in an editorial in the *Herald* on 8 February commented,

'The tenderness of the government for official trade unionism always becomes singularly demonstrative in times of acute unrest, only to sink into oblivion as soon as order and quiet are restored.' He echoed Churchill in asserting that the trade union leaders were out of touch, and urged that 'Before order can be restored in the world of Labour the whole structure of trade unionism will have to be rebuilt from bottom to top.' Lansbury also expressed the then widespread hope on the Left that in some undetermined way trade union action would cause the transformation of society. He regretted that there was no body co-ordinating trade union action, observing that 'the greatest opportunity trade unionism has ever had may be frittered away in a series of ineffective local upheavals'.

On the government's part there was a determination to carry public opinion as well as moderate trade unionism. This had been the key consideration in recognising the Railway Clerks' Association. As Bonar Law put it, 'The only chance of coming through this was to have public opinion on our side.' The War Cabinet at this time authorised the Minister of Labour to spend 'such sums as might be necessary to defray the cost of propaganda by his Department during the present industrial unrest'.[82] A major element in the government's propaganda efforts to carry public opinion was to paint a lurid picture of Bolshevik forces at work, which were threatening to engulf moderate trade unionism and civilised society as a whole.

Not surprisingly, combating Bolshevism and 'educating' the public about the evils of Bolshevism (and indeed socialism) through propaganda paid for out of public finances was a particular concern of some members of the Cabinet. At the War Cabinet on 22 January Lord Curzon urged that a Minister without Portfolio should be appointed to co-ordinate the various government departments' efforts to work against the spread of Bolshevism in Britain.

In similar vein Shortt, as Home Secretary, recommended the prosecution of those making seditious speeches. He and his colleagues had in mind domestic activists such as Arthur Macmanus, a leading figure in the wartime shop stewards' movement and later first chairman of the Communist Party of Great Britain, David Ramsay, another prominent member of the shop stewards' movement, and John Maclean, the Clydeside socialist whom Maxim Litvinov had appointed in 1918 as the Soviet Consul for Scotland, as well as other socialists of continental European origin. Shortt informed his colleagues that subject to being given political approval, the Attorney

General recommended prosecution of Ramsay on the basis of police notes of a speech he made at the Croydon branch of the Herald League on 26 January. Shortt posed the question, 'whether the deterrent effect of successful prosecutions will or will not be so great as to counterbalance the advertisement they will give to revolutionary views, and the sympathy they will excite for labour leaders who, it will be alleged, are imprisoned for exercising the right of free speech?'[83]

The War Cabinet discussion on Shortt's recommendations was notable for ministers declaring that in such times of social unrest speeches deemed to be seditious could no longer be ignored. They were also explicit that their motivation in considering staging trials for sedition was to impress public opinion. The view was also expressed that those selected for prosecution should be 'persons who were not directly associated with the trade unions'. Shortt himself urged that examples should be made of foreign agitators and certain militant shop stewards. He stated that

> There were Bolsheviks in the country with German money.... He pointed out that the leaders of the agitation in Glasgow had been prosecuted, and he had been prepared, had it been necessary, to arrest those responsible for the unrest amongst the electrical engineers. The alien violinist, Soermus, who had been going about the country making violent speeches, had also been arrested. The Home Office had fairly reliable information about two Swedes who had come into this country with German money. He thought that if some persons of this description were arrested, and at the same time a few men of the type of David Ramsay ... it would do a great deal to show the country the kind of men who were making the mischief. He would single out the most influential and prominent for prosecution.

Bonar Law warmly agreed with Shortt, observing that 'in ordinary times prosecutions did more harm than good, but the present circumstances were exceptional'. He also commented that 'anything that would impress public opinion with the revolutionary nature of the present agitation would be an advantage'.

As with the student unrest of the 1960s in Britain when some politicians chose to argue that it was stirred up by 'foreign scum', so at this time the notion of selecting foreigners as particular targets for retribution was especially attractive to members of the War Cabinet. Sir Auckland Geddes, Minister of Reconstruction, urged that the government should take the power 'to prosecute aliens coming to this country and indulging in propaganda, and even would go the length of taking power to inflict the death penalty'. In such a drastic curtailment of free speech, Geddes urged 'that a sharp distinction should be drawn between British subjects and aliens'. He reminded his colleagues that during the 1918 general election 'the country was very excited on the subject of aliens'. Although Shortt warned his colleagues of the legal difficulties involved, nevertheless the appeal of such a chauvinist policy resulted in the War Cabinet instructing Shortt to draw up for its consideration 'proposals on the lines suggested by Sir Auckland Geddes'.[84] These attitudes were very popular among many supporters of the Coalition government. MPs like A. C. Edwards (who had defeated Henderson in the general election) were not backward in blaming 'the alien Bolshevik, who is in our midst', especially 'the foreign Jew', as fomenters of industrial unrest.

When Parliament met, Labour was quick to condemn these attitudes. In the debate on the King's Address on 11 February 1919, Willie Adamson, the Labour Party leader, deplored the recent government propaganda. He complained,

> During the past few weeks I have observed that serious attempts have been made in the Press and on the platform to create the idea that there were two factors mainly responsible for the serious industrial situation that exists ... firstly the presence in the ranks of the working classes of the country of a small band of revolutionaries who are out to upset the existing order of things, and, secondly, the presence in the trade union movement of a small band of men who are out to upset the officials of that movement, if not to undermine and destroy the movement itself.

Adamson, whilst being careful to condemn revolution or 'unofficial action', argued that the real causes of unrest were wages, hours of work, unemployment, fear of unemployment, and concern that the government was fostering monopolies.[85]

For Lloyd George the magnification of revolutionary activity was a valuable stick with which to beat the Labour movement generally. Adamson, for all his talk of being 'a constitutionalist and leader ... of a party constitutionalist', was put on the defensive. Coalition politicians did not hesitate to keep on demanding such declarations, while blaming Adamson, Henderson, Clynes and their like for associating with more fiery socialists who used class war rhetoric. Moreover, the government took great pains to smear all manner of trade union action as unconstitutional and Bolshevik in nature. Lloyd

George and his colleagues made great efforts to get public opinion to accept their view as to what constituted acceptable trade union action.

Lloyd George left the Preliminary Peace Conference in Paris on 8 February, and returned to London both to be present for the first major debates of the new Parliament and to be directly in charge of the government's response to labour unrest. He remained in London until 6 March. During that time the government called the National Industrial Conference and set up the Sankey Commission to enquire into miners' pay and working conditions and also into the organisation of the coal industry.

Notes and references

1. In this Keynes was in line with financial orthodoxy, though his reasons were somewhat different. S. Howson, '"A dear money man?" Keynes on monetary policy, 1920', *Economic Journal*, 83 (1973), pp. 456–64.
2. P. B. Johnson, *Land Fit for Heroes* (Chicago: Chicago University Press, 1968), pp. 198–9.
3. P. J. Grigg, *Prejudice and Judgment* (London: Cape, 1948), p. 183.
4. R. W. D. Boyce, *British Capitalism at the Crossroads 1919–1932* (Cambridge: Cambridge University Press, 1987), p. 6.
5. *History of the Ministry of Munitions*, vol. 3, 1, p. 2. Also Lord Riddell's diary for 13 October 1914; *Lord Riddell's War Diary* (London: Nicholson and Watson, 1933), p. 36.
6. Churchill to Lloyd George, 19 November 1918; printed in M. Gilbert, *Winston S. Churchill, Vol. 4: Companion*, part 1 (London: Heinemann, 1977), p. 416. Jones to Hankey, 27 February 1919, printed in *Thomas Jones: Whitehall Diary*, vol. 1 (ed. K. Middlemas) (London: Oxford University Press, 1969), p. 80. He made similar comments on 3 March and 11 April 1919; War Cabinet Minutes (WC 539), 3 March 1919; CAB 23–9–94/6 and *Lord Riddell's Intimate Diary of the Peace Conference and After* (London: Gollancz, 1933), p. 50.
7. 'Sunday, April 1918', *Lord Riddell's War Diary*, p. 324.
8. Lord Riddell, *Peace Conference*, p. 13.
9. *The Times*, 15 November 1918.
10. For this case, see P. K. Cline's important essay, 'Winding down the war economy: British plans for peacetime recovery, 1916–19' in K. Burk (ed.), *War and the State* (London: Allen & Unwin, 1982), pp. 157–81.
11. Shorthand notes of a Conference of Ministers on Unemployment and the State of Trade, (GT 6887), 25 February 1919; CAB 24–75–367/75. Both comments are quoted in P. K. Cline's 'Reopening the case of the Lloyd George Coalition and the postwar economic transition 1918–1919', *Journal of British Studies*, 10 (1970), pp. 162–75.

12. *The Times*, 6 December 1918.
13. War Cabinet Minutes (WC 487 and 491), 16 and 24 October 1918; CAB 23–8–34/5 and 48.
14. *The Times*, 7 March 1917. Notes for 3 March 1918; MUN 5–91–344/3. For a list of fifteen pledges for full restoration of pre-war trade union practices given by the government in the twelve months from March 1915 (drawn up on 12 June 1917) see MUN 5–91–344/1.
15. C. Addison, *Four and a Half Years*, vol. 2 (London: Hutchinson, 1934), pp. 584 and 587. Johnson, *op. cit.*, pp. 263–70, 281–5 and 288.
16. *The Times*, 15 November 1918.
17. WC (491), 24 October 1918; CAB 23–8–48. Roberts to Lloyd George, December 1918; LG F/44/1/5.
18. G. D. H. Cole, *Trade Unionism and Munitions* (Oxford: Oxford University Press, 1923), pp. 188–96 and 241–7. H. Clegg, *A History of British Trade Unions since 1889. Vol. 2: 1911–1933* (Oxford: Clarendon Press, 1985), p. 242.
19. *Report on Conciliation and Arbitration 1919* (1921), pp. 13–16 and 44. Lord Askwith, *Industrial Problems and Disputes* (London: Murray, 1920), pp. 463–4.
20. B. B. Gilbert, *British Social Policy 1914–1939* (London: Batsford, 1970), pp. 59–63.
21. 13 and 14 August 1918; *Lord Riddell's War Diary*, p. 346. 11 April 1919; Riddell, *Peace Conference*, p. 50.
22. Journal, dictated 17 November 1918; Addison, *op. cit.*, p. 583.
23. M. A. Bienefeld, *Working Hours in British Industry* (London: London School of Economics, 1972), pp. 149–50.
24. B. McCormick, 'Hours of work in British industry', *Industrial and Labour Relations Review*, 1959, pp. 423–33. J. A. Dowie, '1919–20 is in need of attention', *Economic History Review*, 1975, pp. 429–50. R. C. O. Matthews, C. H. Feinstein and J. C. Odling-Smee, *British Economic Growth 1856–1973* (Oxford: Clarendon Press, 1982), p. 71.
25. C. Feinstein, *National Income, Expenditure and Output of the United Kingdom 1855–1965* (Cambridge: Cambridge University Press, 1972), table 140. For a discussion of his figures, see Dowie, pp. 448–50.
26. Sir E. Geddes's 'Memorandum on demobilisation' forwarded to Lloyd George, 29 December 1918; LG F/18/2/36. N. B. Dearle, *An Economic Chronicle of the Great War for Britain and Ireland 1914–1919* (Oxford: Oxford University Press, 1929), pp. 263–4. Clegg, *op. cit.*, p. 241.
27. C. Nyland, *Reduced Worktime and the Management of Production* (Cambridge: Cambridge University Press, 1989), pp. 46–59. N. von Tunzelmann, 'Britain 1900–45: a survey' in R. Floud and D. McLoskey (eds), *The Economic History of Britain Since 1700*, vol. 2 (Cambridge: Cambridge University Press, 1981), p. 243. My own impression, based on non-quantitative material, is that the reduction in hours was not soon compensated for by greater intensity of work.
28. M. Gilbert, *Winston S. Churchill*, Vol. 4 (London: Heinemann, 1975),

pp. 193–6. Dearle, p. 246. A. W. Kirkaldy, *British Labour: Replacement and Conciliation 1914–1921* (London: Pitman, 1921), table 13 and pp. 109–10.
29. WC (521), 28 January 1919; CAB 23–9–30.
30. C. Wrigley (ed.), *A History of British Industrial Relations*, vol. 2 (Brighton: Harvester, 1986), p. 13. Table of disputes forwarded to Lloyd George by Hankey, 12 August 1919; LG F/24/1/8.
31. *Report on Conciliation and Arbitration 1919*, p. 6.
32. Stanley to Lloyd George, 2 and 8 December 1918; LG F/2/6/5 and 7. H. D. Henderson, *The Cotton Control Board* (Oxford: Oxford University Press, 1922), pp. 42, 62–3 and 73. Askwith, *op. cit.*, pp. 460–3. *The Times*, 12 December 1918.
33. Henderson, *op. cit.*, p. 73. Clegg, *op. cit.*, p. 267.
34. Askwith, *op. cit.*, p. 460. 'The Labour situation', week ending 12 March 1919 (GT 6974); CAB 24–76–366.
35. P. Bagwell, *The Railwaymen* (London: Allen & Unwin, 1963), pp. 365 and 370–3. N. McKillop, *The Lighted Flame* (London: Nelson, 1950), pp. 113–17. Stanley to Lloyd George, 2 December 1918; F/2/6/5.
36. McKillop, *op. cit.*, p. 118.
37. Stanley to Lloyd George, 2 December 1918; LG F/2/6/5.
38. WC (510), 6 December 1918; CAB 23–8–101.
39. Beatrice Webb's diary, 10 January 1919; Passfield Papers, 1, f. 35.
40. Hankey's diary, 5 December 1918; quoted in S. Roskill, *Hankey: Man of Secrets*, vol. 2 (London: Collins, 1972), p. 31. WC (510), 6 December 1918; CAB 23–8–101. *The Times*, 7 December 1918.
41. Riddell, *Peace Conference*, p. 4. Hankey's diary 16 December 1918; Roskill, *op. cit.*, p. 35.
42. Henderson in the Ironfounders' journal; quoted *The Times*, 14 July 1919. William to Caroline Bridgeman, 21 January 1919; Bridgeman Papers.
43. E. Geddes to Lloyd George, 18 January 1919; LG F/18/3/4.
44. 'The revolt of Labour', *New Statesman*, 25 January 1919, pp. 339–41.
45. WC (523), 31 January 1919; CAB 23–9–36/7.
46. WC (525, 526 and 527), 4 and 5 February 1919; CAB 23–9–44, 48/49, and 52/4.
47. WC (528), 6 February 1919; CAB 23–9–54/5. Jones to Hankey, 10 February 1919; printed in *Whitehall Diary*, p. 75.
48. Bonar Law to Lloyd George, 27 January 1919 and Lloyd George to Bonar Law, 29 January 1919; LG F/30/3/6 and 10. K. O. Morgan, *Consensus and Disunity* (Oxford: Clarendon Press, 1979), pp. 50–1.
49. Bonar Law to Lloyd George, 24 January 1919; LG F/30/3/4.
50. J. B. Jefferys, *The Story of the Engineers* (London: Amalgamated Engineering Union, 1945), p. 187. Clegg, *op. cit.*, p. 253.
51. 'Scotland's general strike: the forty hour movement', *Labour Leader*, 23 January 1919, p. 3.
52. Quoted in J. Foster's 'Strike action and working class politics on Clydeside 1914–1919' (paper at international colloquium, Graz, June 1989). This is the best analysis of the strike movement in the area. Also

valuable for the complex background of the local Labour movement and the strike is I. McLean, *The Legend of Red Clydeside*, (Edinburgh: Donald, 1983), pp. 112–20.
53. Bonar Law to Lloyd George, 28 January 1919; LG F/30/3/9.
54. WC (521), 28 January 1919; CAB 23–9–30.
55. Foster, *op. cit.*, pp. 19–20. Clegg, *op. cit.*, p. 270.
56. 'The revolt of Labour', *New Statesman*, 25 January 1919, p. 339. 'Myner Collier' [P. J. Dollan], 'Scotland's strike: 70,000 men out', *Labour Leader*, 30 January 1919. 'Trade union and labour notes', *Daily Herald*, 1 February 1919, p. 6.
57. Bonar Law to Lloyd George, 30 January 1919; LG F/30/3/16.
58. An undated message, in fact 30 January; LG F/30/3/13. Bonar Law made the same observation in the War Cabinet on the 30th, WC (522); CAB 23–9–33/4.
59. WC (524); CAB 23–9–40.
60. The telegram was addressed to Lloyd George but given to Bonar Law as the former was in Paris; LG F/30/3/14. From WC (522), where it is printed, it is clear that it was sent on the morning of the 30 January 1919.
61. WC (522); CAB 23–9–33/4.
62. Bonar Law to Lloyd George, 30 January 1919, and Lloyd George's reply; LG F/30/3/16.
63. These messages of 31 January 1919 are in LG F/30/3/17.
64. WC (523), 31 January 1919; CAB 23–9–36.
65. Bonar Law to Lloyd George, 31 January 1919; LG F/30/3/19.
66. Bonar Law to Lloyd George, 1 February 1919; LG F/30/3/20.
67. WC (524), 3 February 1919; CAB 23–9–40.
68. Letter and telephone message, 31 January 1919; LG F/30/3/11 and 15.
69. WC (523); CAB 23–9–36. Milner's diary, 31 January 1919; Milner Papers, vol. 90.
70. WC (525), 4 February 1919; CAB 23–9–45/6.
71. WC (530), 10 February 1919; CAB 23–9–62.
72. Bonar Law to Lloyd George, 4 February 1919; LG F/30/3/23.
73. WC (525), 4 February 1919; CAB 23–9–44. WC (526), 6.30 p.m., 4 February 1919; CAB 23–9–48/9. When there had been the threat of such a strike during the war the War Cabinet had resolved to use men from the forces if it occurred. WC (346), 14 February 1918; CAB 23–5–105.
74. The Industrial Unrest Committee records are in CAB 27/59. The best account of it and its successor, the Strike Committee, is R. Desmarais, 'Lloyd George and the development of the British government's strike-breaking organisation', *International Review of Social History*, 20 (1975), pp. 1–15.
75. WC (529), 7 February 1919; CAB 23–9–59.
76. Lloyd George's Foreword to G. Glasgow, *General Strikes and Road Transport* (London: Bles, n.d. [1926]), pp. 9–15. Also pp. 20 and 24.
77. WC (523), 31 January 1919; CAB 23–9–37/8. Bonar Law sent Lloyd George an outline of the problem in a letter of the same day; LG F/30/

3/19. He also sent a memorandum on the subject by Stanley. Eddison to Davies, 31 January 1919; *ibid.*, F/2/6/15. Tom Jones to Hankey, 10 February 1919; *Whitehall Diary*, vol. 1, p. 75.
78. Bonar Law to Lloyd George, 1 February 1919; LG F/30/3/20.
79. Bonar Law to Lloyd George, 2 February 1919; LG F/30/3/22. WC (525), 4 February; CAB 23–9–42. Bridgeman's diaries, 30 January to 3 February 1919, printed in P. Williamson (ed.), *The Modernisation of Conservative Politics* (London: Historian's Press, 1988), pp. 138–9.
80. Bonar Law's telephone message to Lloyd George of later on 2 February; LG F/30/3/21.
81. Bonar Law to Lloyd George, 4 February 1919; LG F/30/3/23. Milner's diary 2, 3 and 4 February 1919; Milner Papers, 90. WC (525), 4 February 1919; CAB 23–9–42/3.
82. WC (528), 6 February 1919; CAB 23–9–55.
83. WC (518), 22 January 1919; CAB 23–9–19. 'Prosecution of seditious speakers' (GT 6755), 5 February 1919; CAB 24–74–233/4.
84. WC (529), 7 February 1919; CAB 23–9–60.
85. 112 *HC Deb. 5s*, c. 60–1 and 83; 11 February 1919.

6
Holding on through the period of economic transition: appealing to public opinion February to March 1919

In the period from the opening of the new Parliament on 4 February 1919 the government's policy towards organised labour was marked by firmness on what it deemed to be excessive demands combined with a concern to appeal to public opinion as to the reasonableness of its responses. The government was certainly not in a panic at the challenge from the miners, but their challenge did overshadow much of the government's policies for a few months.

Lloyd George played the key role in the developments of the last three weeks of February. Many close observers of the government felt that his presence ensured greater decisiveness in government policy. In mid-February Esher observed to Hankey, 'I see no firmness of purpose or prevision in the government when you and L.G. are away.'[1] In deciding to keep his small War Cabinet until the main peace treaty was signed (and, in fact, maintaining it until 27 October 1919), Lloyd George kept much power in his own hands.[2] Indeed, on at least one occasion Lloyd George's sudden change of plans, resulting in him not being able to chair a meeting of the War Cabinet, forced Hankey to cancel all previous arrangements and to substitute 'a brand new agenda of lesser matters for a meeting with Bonar Law in the chair'. On such an occasion in October 1918, Hankey noted, 'The important discussion, on which Lord Curzon and others had laid such stress, as a question of immediate urgency, was postponed!' There was some justification in the complaint made at times, especially in 1919, that the government was coming close to resembling a one-man band.[3]

Yet in terms of policy towards industrial unrest, Lloyd George's attitudes were very much in line with most of his colleagues. For all the later talk of him being 'the father' of the emergency strikebreaking organisation, Lloyd George's part had been to approve the setting up of the Industrial Unrest Committee and then approve its recommendation to set up such an emergency organisation. Similarly, while several ministers (notably Bonar Law and Stanley) did not distinguish themselves by decisive responses to the serious outbreak of industrial discontent of late January to early February 1919, Lloyd George's main role had been to oversee policy from Paris, occasionally to strike a note of caution, and to determine to replace Stanley before long. With his return from Paris on 8 February, Lloyd George basically 'beefed up' the policy which was then evolving.

Lloyd George used the debates on the King's Speech as a major public platform for the government's attitudes towards industrial unrest and the demands of the Triple Alliance unions in particular. In his major speech in the House of Commons on 11 February 1919 Lloyd George spelt out what he felt to be the 'legitimate causes of unrest'. He recognised war weariness, fear of unemployment, bad housing and long hours of work as being in this category. He went on to state bluntly that the government should remove 'the legitimate causes of unrest . . . so as to give no justification for unrest, and so as not to give material for those who are exploiting that unrest'. As evidence of the government's good intentions, he pointed to the Bills on housing, health and rural issues that were soon to be introduced into Parliament. As for working hours, he referred to the recent agreements which had brought reductions for some 3 million workers, and to the negotiations that were in progress which would affect a further 2 million. However, when he referred to unemployment, housing and public works, he delivered a homily asserting that high wage settlements or the reduction of hours below what was 'legitimate and . . . fair and possible' (terms he did not define) were the major ways of aggravating the problem of unemployment. In so doing he was explicit that he had the demands of the coal miners and railway workers in mind.[4]

Lloyd George's attitude in February 1919 was similar to that which he had held after the serious engineering strikes of May 1917. As then, the government was concerned to remedy many of the social causes of industrial unrest. In speaking to leading ministers later in February 1919, Lloyd George was insistent on social reform:

> It is not merely to be pledged. I want to look ahead and see how we can guarantee the peace of this country. Nothing struck me more in the

conversations I had with the miners than the part this plays in the general irritation which has made them unreasonable.

Hence he asserted that he wanted reforms of substance to stem from government legislation. He observed that previous legislation which had resulted in little tangible benefit had done harm. 'That kind of thing has made them feel, "Well, it is no good going to Parliament, we must trust to our own power", and they strike, and a strike may end in revolution.'[5] For Lloyd George social reform was essential to re-establish social stability. But he clearly felt that it could, and should, be accompanied by a firm response to what he deemed to be unreasonable industrial demands.

As in 1917, housing was seen to be a, or even the, major danger area. The industrial unrest after the Armistice ensured that the government kept it at the top of its priorities for social reform. The government was already pledged to 'Homes fit for heroes', after the 1918 general election. And the link between bad housing and industrial unrest had been highlighted in the reports of the 1917 inquiries following the engineering strikes of that May.[6]

In February 1919 the main differences within the government over housing were to do with the impact it would have in hastening the successful reconversion of British industry from war to peace production, and not over whether the earlier pledges should be honoured. Sir Eric Geddes was one of those who saw housing not only as a matter of providing decent housing but also as a means of reflating the economy. Thus in late December 1918 he advised Lloyd George, 'The government with its scheme for half a million houses is in a position to stimulate a great field of direct and indirect industrial activity.' Austen Chamberlain, the leading spokesman of orthodox finance, observed of social reform measures,

> They may help the problem of unemployment temporarily, as any relief would do. The really important thing for the safety of our position is to get our trade going, and above all, to get our export trade going, and it is no real compensation for that if we are spending an enormous amount of money on housing or anything like that.

Nevertheless, in February 1919 Chamberlain was willing to be unequivocal as to housing reform being necessary in itself. He told his colleagues,

I agree that our housing problem has got into such a condition that it is a source of danger to the stability of the state, and that we have to deal with the problem in accordance with the programme which we took to the electors, on broad and generous lines, and go ahead with it as fast as we can, with due regard to carrying it out properly. I think that ought to be first charge on the public resources which we have.[7]

There was also concern to secure adequate supplies of beer and food at reasonable prices. In early 1919 the shortage of beer and its weakness were often mentioned in official circles as a cause of industrial unrest. Though unlike housing, it was not a matter that Lloyd George and certain of his colleagues wished to foster as a public issue, given their past and present relationships with temperance and Nonconformist bodies. But it was discussed in the War Cabinet both at the height of the unrest in early 1919 and during that summer. On 24 January Bonar Law informed the War Cabinet that he favoured an increase in the quantity of beer and a price reduction. He observed that 'there was no doubt that many people attributed the present industrial unrest to the lack or poor quality of beer'. Other ministers readily concurred, including Sir Robert Horne who commented that 'a good deal of irritation on the Clyde was due to the lack of beer and the bad quality of that available.' The War Cabinet decided to increase the amount available by 25 per cent, to increase the average specific gravity by 2 per cent and to reduce its price. In early February it further agreed to increase the tax on beer by 10s rather than by £1, as the higher amount 'would have the effect of reducing the quality of the beer to a very low level, and this would cause a great deal of unrest'.

As for food prices, Lloyd George had urged G. H. Roberts, when appointing him as Food Controller on 10 January 1919, to do all he could to reduce them. On 18 February the Prime Minister took the matter up again, instructing the Ministry of Food to make greater efforts to cut prices. The Ministry immediately tried to enforce greater observation of existing regulations on maximum food prices. On 20 February Roberts announced a food policy in which the control or decontrol of products would be determined by the probable effect on prices. Two days later, responding to the popular belief that there was profiteering in meat, the government announced it would investigate the impact on prices of American and other meat cartels.[8]

Such activity, especially that in February, paved the way for Lloyd

George to declare at the National Industrial Conference, held at the end of the month, that food prices for the average working-class family would fall by 4s by the summer. To be able to point to falling food prices was important for Lloyd George in combating what he deemed to be excessively high wage demands. In March 1919 the government could point to the fall in price of some commodities, notably margarine and meat. By early May government estimates of the working-class cost of living showed it to have fallen from 115 to 105 per cent above the July 1914 levels in two months. The government also continued to support the national kitchens to help the poorest of the population, even going so far as to announce, on 6 May 1919, that the kitchens would be made permanent. Until May 1919 world food prices overall were going the right way for the government, but thereafter prices began to rise again.[9]

In February 1919, as after the May 1917 strikes, the government was willing to consider industrial issues as well as more general social reforms. In his speech in the Commons on 11 February Lloyd George had declared, 'There is . . . a good deal to be said about a more general investigation into the whole causes of industrial unrest' and had stated that the government would welcome 'any method of investigation . . . which will be satisfactory to employed, to employers and to the community at large'. He added that the government had 'certain suggestions' which it would put forward during the debates on the King's Speech. In this Lloyd George was probably making the first public intimation that the government was considering calling a national industrial conference.

The Ministry of Labour prepared a file of papers on 'A proposed industrial conference', 'wages' and 'hours of labour' for Lloyd George and for Bonar Law, who deputised for the Prime Minister on 13 February in a debate on a Labour amendment to the King's Address which regretted 'the absence of any mention of definite proposals for dealing with the present unrest'. The memorandum on an industrial conference proposed that it be called 'at once', and suggested that it should 'be able to put before the government any views which it may have as to the causes of the present unrest and as to any remedies which [it] may have to offer'.[10] However it is clear that for several days leading ministers still remained undecided as to whether to call a conference. In the Commons debate on 13 February Bonar Law did not announce a national industrial conference, and during the day a backbencher was even told that the government did not intend to call such a conference.[11] However, within four days Lloyd George decided to summon a conference, and invitations were sent out for it to meet on 27 February.

The conference appears to have represented all things to all people. It revived the flagging spirit of Whitleyism. For many, joint councils represented a moderate solution to particular industries' problems. Employers and unions would resolve the sources of conflict in their industry without the often distrusted interference of outsiders from Whitehall. Indeed F. W. Gibbins, the chairman of the Tinplate Conciliation Board, wrote to Tom Jones before the conference met, pointing to his trade as being largely strike-free since the Board had been established whereas before 'hardly a day passed without some strike or lock-out in the trade'. He suggested that similar schemes for the industries covered by the Triple Alliance unions might achieve such results. Linked to this, there were many who saw such a conference as a means of emphasising that strife in private industries was primarily a problem for those in the industries to resolve. The Ministry of Labour, commenting on the National Industrial Conference, observed of industrial disputes,

> except of course where the industry is state owned or controlled, it rests, and in the first instance can rest only, on the representative organisation of employers and workpeople directly concerned. Government intervention must wait on their action; however urgent the need, it is difficult for the government to go behind them; yet their failure to effect a settlement very seriously prejudices the prospect of successful government action.[12]

For others the National Industrial Conference represented much more. It was seen as a Parliament for industry in which certain major issues would be examined and the government would respond with legislation. Those of this viewpoint, including Arthur Henderson and Sir Allan Smith of the Engineering Employers' Federation, who were willing to compromise to achieve an accommodation with the other side of industry on at least some major issues were to feel betrayed when the government failed to act on the recommendations of the National Industrial Conference's provisional joint committee.

The demand for a major industrial conference had come from a wide range of bodies and individuals. During the war Roberts, as Minister for Labour, had pressed for such a conference as complementary, though separate from, the Whitley councils. From the autumn of 1918 it had been requested by various employers' organisations and prominent individuals, notably the Federation of British Industry (FBI) and the National Alliance of Employers and Employed (a body formed in December 1916 and funded by the Engineering Employers' Federation and other business groups). Given the serious industrial unrest of early February 1919 and the threat of action by the Triple Alliance unions, the idea became timely again. In the debates on the King's Speech in the House of Commons on 12 February Horatio Bottomley pressed for such an industrial gathering and on 13 February the FBI resolved to 'take immediate action in conjunction if possible with the Engineeering Employers' Federation and the national organisations representing labour with a view to summoning a joint conference ... for dealing with the present grave conditions of industrial unrest'.[13] Sir George Riddell, who saw Lloyd George on the 16 February, came away with the clear impression that Lloyd George 'feels acutely the serious nature of the labour problems'.[14] Probably the short delay after 11 February in announcing the calling of the conference was to allow the War Cabinet to discuss the matter on 14 February.

The Cabinet considered proposals put forward by Auckland Geddes, the Minister of Reconstruction, for an enquiry into the state of British industry. He suggested that its terms of reference should be to examine first, conditions of employment of the workers, secondly the means by which the workers could be assured of an adequate return for their work and thirdly the basis on which the workers should participate in controlling the conditions governing industrial life. Strangely, Geddes suggested that this enquiry should be carried out by three committees, one 'representing all sections of labour opinion', a second representing employers and a third consisting of technical experts in economics and finance. Geddes argued that 'the immediate effect on public opinion will be good' as well as the results being valuable to the government 'in working out the programme of social and industrial reconstruction'. His ministerial colleagues were quick to respond that having three committees was unrealistic as capital and labour would inflate their suggestions to use them as 'the jumping-off point for negotiations' and 'the economists would be despised as academic'. Though Geddes argued that 'even extreme proposals from the proposed labour committee would be useful as they would probably be condemned by public opinion', the preference of those at the War Cabinet meeting was for a national conference.

The actual form of the National Industrial Council largely followed Horne's suggestions to the War Cabinet. He urged that the government should call 'a representative gathering of capital and labour, such as that held at the Caxton Hall two days after the Armistice'. Horne added,

> The Prime Minister might make a speech and then suggest that the employers and the workmen appoint twenty-five members each, to sit upon a Joint Committee. This committee might appoint sub-committees to go into the questions of wages and hours and be asked to make definite suggestions. If unanimous proposals were obtained, the government could legislate upon them.

Horne also commented on the widespread demand for such an enquiry, and mentioned that he had talked to Clynes, who hoped that from such a meeting 'might evolve a permanent Industrial Council'. Horne's recommendations were substantially followed in due course.[15]

That the government acted through such a conference has been seen as 'a betrayal ... of Whitleyism' because it breached earlier suggestions that the Whitley Councils would be 'the sole avenue of communication with the government'.[16] In that respect it was a breach. But at the time no one appears to have seen it as breaking faith with the Whitley Councils. In the War Cabinet discussion Addison suggested that the Whitley Councils and the fifty or sixty Joint Interim Reconstruction Committees could be used for the enquiry, though he himself readily admitted that in the past they had not come up with many constructive ideas. The fact was that both of these groups covered only part of British industry, and not the areas where the present and imminent industrial unrest was most menacing; so, few can have been surprised that the government consulted more widely. In broad terms the calling of the National Industrial Conference was seen very much in terms of upholding the spirit of Whitleyism, and in particular of forming a joint industrial council at the national level. Though 'Whitehall sources' were careful to put out that it was not intended to be some kind of 'a super Whitley council which will have the power to adjudicate on any dispute which might arise in any trade'.[17]

At the War Cabinet on 14 February the decision to summon the National Industrial Conference was postponed until the government had 'more information as to the probable action of the mining and transport unions'. In the discussion it had been suggested that if the miners went on strike it would be difficult to hold such a conference, though Horne had felt that even then it might still be possible if the other Triple Alliance unions did not also come out on strike. As the miners reluctantly accepted the Sankey Commission, the National Industrial Conference went ahead.

On 27 February 1919 some 500 trade unionists and 300 employers gathered in Central Hall, Westminster for the first meeting.[18] Horne, who chaired the meeting, referred to the recent industrial unrest, observing that 'strikes have been threatened which, if they succeeded, could bring nothing but disaster to the state'. He stated that as a result of the government's need 'to get at the root causes of these troubles' they had called those present together to give 'their advice and assistance'. Horne made it clear that the government favoured some concessions to labour, including reductions in working hours and the establishment of statutory minimum wages providing these did not harm British industry's competitiveness. He also promised an extension of the unemployment donation, but at a reduced rate. Horne made much of the Whitley Councils, saying

> The great positive reform to which one looks with the most hope for the prevention of industrial disputes in the future is the scheme which Mr Whitley's committee submitted to the country not long ago. There can be no question at all that the whole movement of modern life is in favour of workmen being allowed some share in the control of industry in future.

However, he went on to make it clear that he hoped these Councils would encourage working people to moderate their demands:

> When that joint control begins and we give the operatives in any industry a responsible share in determining the conditions under which the industry is to work and the rates of pay that can be afforded, we shall have advanced a long way to preventing disputes in the future.

Sir Allan Smith, speaking for the employers, was sceptical about the value of the government's initiative. He observed, 'the whole experience of the last twenty years has proved that if only the government will leave us alone we are far better able to settle our differences than any agencies outside.' Nevertheless, he formally proposed the setting up of a committee made up of twenty representatives from both the employers' side and the trade union side plus an unspecified number of representatives from the government to report back to the Conference 'on the causes of the present unrest and the steps necessary to safeguard and promote the best interests of employers, workpeople and the state'. When Lloyd George spoke towards the end of the session he referred back to Smith's speech and emphasised his observation 'that employers are prepared to go much further than the workmen imagine'. This point clearly caught Lloyd George's attention, for he repeated it in conversation with Riddell on 2 March.

While many Labour speakers were very critical of Horne's address, especially his announcement of the government's intention to cut the level of unemployment donation, Henderson and Clynes welcomed the government's initiative in calling the conference. Henderson disagreed with Smith's view that the unrest was temporary. He warned, 'Unless we do something permanently to put this industrial unrest out of the way I see no hope for the country meeting its financial liabilities.' He moved as an amendment to Smith's proposal a resolution to set up a joint committee which would consider questions relating to wages, hours and general conditions of work; unemployment and its prevention; and the best methods of promoting cooperation between capital and labour.

When Lloyd George did speak, he took up Henderson's resolution as preferable to Smith's on the grounds that it was 'more comprehensive'. Lloyd George in his frequently employed method of flattering those with whom he was dealing, made much of the importance of the Conference's views. He set aside people's reservations as to whether those present were truly representative or had a mandate to decide anything by arguing that the committee would be entitled 'provisional' until mandates had been secured. He urged, 'but I do beg you to make a beginning. It is very vital. I know the dangers, and I am a little afraid of stagnation.' These were hardly words to suggest that after the provisional joint committee had laboured the government would disregard its recommendations. Lloyd Geoge clinched the support of the majority by a stirring peroration as to how Britain had saved the world in the war. He concluded, 'I appealed to the people of this country to hold fast. Today I am making an appeal to all sections: "Hold together."' Speaking about his Conference speech to Riddell on 1 March he said, 'I got them with me during the last five minutes', and he concluded 'that notwithstanding much wild talk, the Conference displayed the sterling common sense of the British people'.[19]

The first meeting of the provisional joint committee took place on 4 March 1919 at Central Hall, Westminster. There were thirty representatives from industry, led by Sir Allan Smith, and thirty from the trade unions, led by Arthur Henderson and having G. D. H. Cole as their secretary. The government appointed only two persons, Sir Thomas Munro to take the chair and C. S. Hurst to act as the committee's secretary. Having successfully flattered the full Conference by emphasising its importance, Lloyd George exceeded even his norms of flattery when he addressed the provisional joint committee on 4 March. After pointing to social disintegration in Russia and Germany, he told those present,

> You are really a Peace Congress; you are settling the future of this country, but you may be doing more than that. You may be settling the future of civilisation. You may be making the model for civilisation which all lands will turn to and say: 'Let us follow Britain'.

After such blandishment Lloyd George pitched his appeal to a vigorous condemnation of unemployment as a blight on working people's lives and to the need for increasing British industry's productivity. He warned workers to avoid what he deemed to be the anarchy taking place in Russia and Germany. He warned employers,

> If you want the whole fabric... of society to be secure you must see that the foundations are secure. They are not. There is a good deal of what is rotten beneath them. You have got to underpin the foundations of the state.

The provisional joint committee then agreed to set up three working parties. The first was to investigate methods of trade union–employer co-operation, how to deal with war advances, and how to regulate wages. The second was to consider the desirability of legislation for maximum working hours and minimum wages. The third was to examine issues concerning unemployment.[20] These groups worked hard to produce reports in time for the second meeting of the full National Industrial Conference on 4 April. They achieved substantial agreement on most issues, the only major divisions of opinion being over some aspects of unemployment, and the provisional joint committee's report commented that the meetings had been conducted in an amicable and positive fashion. Overall there was reason to feel that they had followed Lloyd George's exhortation to 'Hold together'.

Lloyd George remained supportive and gave every impression that the government would act on many, even most, of the National Industrial Conference's recommendations. From Paris he sent Horne a letter to read out at the second full meeting of the Conference on 4 April. In this he praised the report as 'an excellent piece of work considering the short time at the disposal of the committee' and concluded with the pledge, 'If the recommendations of the committee receive the approval of the Conference the government will give them their immediate and sympathetic consideration.'[21]

However, less than a month later, when the provisional joint committee met on 1 May, he was less forthcoming in promising early action on the main proposals in the report, though he was as fulsome as before with praise. He said with flattery, 'Foreign countries are looking to Great Britain to give them a lead in the foundation of a new and better industrial order, and this report marks the beginning of such foundations.' He then stated, 'I fully accept in principle your recommendations as to the fixing of maximum hours and minimum rates of wages.' He also accepted the principle that minimum wage rates in all industries should be legally binding; though, on maximum hours, in line with the provisional joint committee's recommendation, he said that there would be categories of workers, such as agricultural labourers, merchant seamen and domestic servants, who would be excluded from any legislation as it would be impossible to enforce it in their cases. As for fixing minimum wages, he reversed the committee's proposal that there should be legislation first, with an enquiry set up afterwards to fix the details. Lloyd George's use of words also indicated to labour members of the Conference and to Ministry of Labour officials that he meant to accept the principle of trade minimum wages, not the principle of a national minimum wage that the Labour movement sought. Lloyd George concluded his letter with what appeared to be an unequivocal statement,

> I cordially welcome your proposal to set up a National Council, and hope that you will take steps to bring it into being as quickly as possible, and I am sure that it will be of great value in assisting the government to improve industrial conditions.

Lloyd George's response pleased neither moderate Labour men nor Sir Allan Smith, who publicly appeared willing to go much further than the Engineering Employers' Federation or the National

Confederation of Employers' Organisations (NCEO), the bodies which he represented. Smith, like the Labour representatives at the Conference, demanded legislation not procrastination. The *Daily Herald* commented, 'Labour wants legislation on the principle of the minimum wage forthwith, and the settlement of the individual minimum afterwards – not a Commission first (which may take years) and then possible legislation.' As for the delay on unemployment, it observed, 'It will be remembered that the Minority Report of the Poor Law Commission dealt at length with the matter in 1909!'[22]

Given the degree of agreement in the report and the demands from both sides for action by the government, Lloyd George's good faith was seriously questioned. An editorial in the *New Statesman* entitled 'Sitting on the safety valve' bluntly argued – as many members of the Labour movement and its sympathisers were to do thereafter – that Lloyd George had cynically used the National Industrial Conference as a short-term expedient. It suggested that the members of the Conference might well be saying to themselves

> that the government had been anxious enough to set them to work and to throw responsibility upon them when an industrial catastrophe seemed to be threatening. But in the meantime a temporary calm has descended upon the waters of industry, and the industrial question has therefore lost some of its urgency in the eyes of the government. It is, unfortunately, the fact that the experience of the workers has taught them again and again that the remedial measures secured from governments are as a rule strictly in proportion to the pressure applied.[23]

The question that arises is why did Lloyd George call the National Industrial Conference? This has never been satisfactorily answered – though, with some degree of plausibility, the answer that there was a lack of consensus in industry has been given to the question, why did it fail?[24] A key point is that it was a response to the recent and to the threatened industrial unrest. Tom Jones, writing to Hankey in Paris, observed when referring to its first meeting, that it had been favourable, on the whole, to the government's desire to set up a committee to examine industrial unrest'.[25] In particular, it was called at the time when Lloyd George was fearful that the miners would trigger off a strike of the Triple Alliance unions. A further important point is that Lloyd George, having returned from Paris to face the new House of Commons, had promised government action to resolve the causes of industrial unrest. As in 1911 with the Industrial Council, the summoning of the National Industrial Conference indicated that *something* was being done. This was indeed in line with one of the characteristics that Riddell noted of Lloyd George – 'Fondness for a grandiose scheme in preference to an attempt to improve existing machinery.'[26]

That Lloyd George hoped that the Conference would ease the government's passage through the difficult period of post-war economic transition does not imply that he also thought that it was incapable of offering constructive advice. In his speech to the first meeting of the Conference on 27 February, when he eventually got to the main issues, Lloyd George put much emphasis on there being 'an atmosphere of suspicion which must be removed'. From his thirteen or fourteen years' experience of trying to resolve industrial disputes he said he had learnt the lesson that

> The inherent difficulties of a dispute were not great as long as you could remove the suspicion out of the mind of the worker and out of the employer that the other was trying to get the better of him. . . . I am sorry to observe that the atmosphere of suspicion, instead of clearing, is thickening. Something has got to be done to clear the air, and clear the atmosphere and get rid of this feeling of suspicion.

It is significant that the one example he gave of how this might be achieved was to suggest that the coal owners might give their workers more information as to the costs of their enterprises.

It has been suggested that one of several reasons for the failure of the National Industrial Conference was lack of unity on the labour side.[27] Yet in assessing Lloyd George's role in the calling of it, this may have been an attraction. Lloyd George showed no anxiety as to whether the Conference was fully representative of all shades of opinion of both sides of industry. To see Labour as moving too fast as a cause of the Conference's failure is to overlook that this was precisely the cause of it being called. As with such gatherings during the war, there was every likelihood that it would highlight the divisions within the Labour movement, and, indeed, exacerbate them. Robert Williams, Secretary of the National Transport Workers' Federation, had a point when he warned ahead of the first meeting, 'I have been present at most . . . of the government conferences held during the war, and I say unhesitatingly that they are all worse than useless, except for sowing dissension among the various sections of the organised workers.'[28]

Another reason suggested for the Conference's failure was that it was unrepresentative of both sides of industry. This certainly was not seen by Lloyd George as a problem at its first meeting. Then, he brusquely brushed aside arguments that those present had no mandate, and in so doing insisted that a speedy start to the deliberations was of the greatest importance.

This concern for speed was to do with the threat of further serious industrial unrest. Hence to argue that a cause of the Conference's failure was that Labour's demands were too great is to overlook the fact that this was the major reason for the conference being called in the first place. Lloyd George was appealing to employers and union in general when his main concerns were, first, with the threatened Triple Alliance strike and, secondly, more generally with the underlying causes of the recent strikes involving groups such as engineers and power workers. If he had a subsidiary aim, it was that advocated by the Ministry of Labour in particular, of publicly shifting some responsibility for resolving serious industrial unrest back, after the war, from the government to both sides of industry.

By summoning a broad based conference, including representatives from the industries covered by Whitley Councils, Lloyd George could muster together trade union and Labour Party leaders such as Henderson, Clynes and Ben Turner who believed in constitutional methods and, in particular, in negotiating via joint councils. The attraction of a national joint industrial council, just like those existing for individual industries, was that it would help workers who did not have the industrial might of powerful unions such as those of the Triple Alliance. At the first meeting of the Conference on 27 February Henderson explicitly made his point. *The Times* account reported,

> Mr. Henderson laid emphasis on the fact that he did not want to suspend any of the efforts being carried on between the government and the railway workers, between the government and the transport workers and between the government and the setting up of the Royal Commission to deal with the mines. He, however, reminded the conference that there was just the danger of forgetting the vast body of workers outside the Triple Alliance.

For workers without the 'industrial muscle' of the Triple Alliance, national negotiations with the expectation of concessions underwritten by statute were very attractive. In a way this is reminiscent of the divisions between the powerful skilled unions, such as the ASE and the unskilled unions during the First World War. Whether or not there was an element of 'divide and rule' intended when the Conference was called, its activities did have this effect.

Lloyd George's interest in the National Industrial Conference appears to have diminished with the waning of the threat of the Triple Alliance. When he wrote a message from Paris for the second meeting on 4 April 1919, he was still stressing that 'the industrial question is perhaps the greatest of all the problems with which we are faced', and though he commented that 'there is no cut and dried or rough and ready method of solving it', he was still giving every indication that the government was eager to adopt recommendations coming from the National Industrial Conference. However, as the press noted at the time, the second meeting of the Conference was notable for the presence of J. H. Thomas, representing the railwaymen, while the miners and transport workers boycotted this meeting. By the time of the meeting on 1 May, when Lloyd George's message promised very little in the way of immediate government action, there was a lull in industrial unrest, with the Triple Alliance pressure temporarily removed, and the growth in take-up of unemployment donation was slowing down (indeed, the take-up reached its peak that week). While the government still showed interest in the Conference in September 1919, it no longer did by November. The explanation for this may lie in part in the government reassessing its industrial policy; but in large part it lies in the fact that the long-threatened railway strike started on 26 September and was settled on 5 October 1919.

The surprising thing about the National Industrial Conference between February and April 1919 was not its failure to achieve consensus but the extent to which it achieved it in the report drawn up by the provisional joint commitee and later approved by the full Conference. In these months many employers were indeed willing to make concessions to labour and to negotiate with moderate Labour leaders such as Henderson and Clynes. Indeed, at the first conference Clynes expressed his own concern as to 'whether in a short time Labour in its own interest was going to ask for too much at one time'. However, the period in which such employers as Sir Allan Smith felt that way and can have hoped to carry their organisations with them was fairly brief. As the threat of serious social unrest receded and as the economy recovered from wartime abnormalities, they, like the government, became more concerned with the productivity of British industry in competing for markets in a world economy recovered from the war and became resistant to further concessions to labour beyond those extracted in late 1918 and early 1919.

If the political will had been there, then the government could have acted on the main recommendations of the Conference. They could have accepted the 48-hour week, minimum wages and the establishment of a national industrial council even if industry was split on the issues and even if the agreement would need to be modified to be in line with the international proposals made at the Washington Hours Convention of October 1919. But there was not the political will. Lloyd George was experiencing enough difficulties with his right-wing supporters in the House of Commons over the treatment of Germany at the Peace Conference without antagonising them by proposing industrial reforms, even if apparently approved by a national joint industrial council.

Very soon in the life of the new Parliament the backbench Tories made clear their aversion to state intervention in industry. This was displayed not only in their opposition to nationalisation but in the way that Sir Eric Geddes' Bill for a new Ministry of Ways and Communications was drastically altered and reduced in scope during its passage through the House of Commons from 26 February 1919. Geddes' belief in a form of business collectivism, at least for the exceptional period of post-war economic transition, like Milner's state paternalism, lost out quickly to the soon predominant non-interventionist spirit in the Commons.[29] To rephrase Keynes famous remark, the 1919 House of Commons was full of hard-faced men who had done well out of the 1918 Coupon election. Lloyd George was always quick to sense a political mood – and that of the Tory backbenchers was quite clear by April 1919.

Moreover he himself was increasingly out of sympathy with Labour, be it the trade unions or the Labour Party, which was now the major political opposition to his government. After Lloyd George had discussed the first meeting of the Conference with him, Riddell noted in his diary,

> Notwithstanding his progressive mind and his constant readiness to receive and adopt new ideas, his point of view in this respect is essentially bourgeois. In his philosophy the world is composed of two classes – the clever and the ordinary. The former was entitled to a share of profits based on their traditional and prescriptive rights. The latter must be maintained

in comfort, but they must not be exacting, and must improve their position mostly through state aid. The working capitalist must have his whack; the state must compel him to pay a heavy toll which will in due course be doled out by the government to the grateful working classes. At the same time *he* [L.G.] is greatly in advance of most politicians and has a genuine desire to improve the position of the poorer classes; but he cannot bring himself to attack the capitalist, for whom, when all is said, he has a lawyer-like respect.[30]

For Lloyd George, in early 1919, the prime example of a section of the labour force which was trying to exact too much was the miners. Taking a tough line with overmighty trade unionists was on the other side of his political coin to the promise of social reforms.

In his major House of Commons speech of 11 February 1919 Lloyd George not only promised that the government would 'devote the whole of our strength to setting right and redressing all legitimate grievances' but made it equally clear that the government would deal firmly with the causes of labour unrest which it deemed to be illegitimate. He denounced at length those who worked 'to undermine confidence in trade union leadership', and obliquely suggested that these were akin to the Bolsheviks as depicted in the right-wing press: 'Anarchy is their aim, and anarchy is the purpose of some of those men who are seeking to destroy not merely trade unionism but the state.' His other comments suggested that the Triple Alliance unions were those in the labour movement with illegitimate aspirations.

Lloyd George pointed explicitly towards the coal mines and railways as areas where high wage demands would affect British competitiveness abroad and thereby employment at home. He told the Commons, 'Four shillings a ton on coal, and shillings added for some other ingredients, whether shipping or other transports . . . may deprive us of hundreds of millions of trade in all parts of the world.' Lloyd George's peroration implicitly referred to the Triple Alliance unions as well as to the anarchic forces that he had conjured up. Lloyd George warned,

> any demand which is pressed forward with a view not to obtaining fair conditions, but with ulterior motives – to hold up and to overthrow the existing order and to destroy government, relying not upon the justice of the claim, but the brute force which is behind it, then may I say in all solemnity on behalf of the government, we are determined to fight Prussianism in the industrial world as we fought it on the continent of Europe with the whole might of the nation.[31]

Though he did not explicitly mention the Miners' Federation of Great Britain (MFGB), its leaders took his words as a threat aimed at them.

The speech was reminiscent of Lloyd George's apparent threats of industrial conscription in the summer of 1915, when he was pressing the unions to accept the lesser, but still severe, restraints of the Munitions of War Bill. It was also characteristic in the way it deliberately conflated two different groups – first, those allegedly anarchic individuals wishing to overthrow trade union leaderships, the government and society generally and secondly, those unions with 'industrial muscle'. However, in the case of the Triple Alliance unions they were organisations where (with the exception of J. H. Thomas) the leaders were in line with the bulk of the membership when pressing for the realisation of democratically arrived at programmes.

If it was an attack on the Triple Alliance unions, it was also a promise of firm government to the right-wing Conservative backbenchers in the House of Commons. Lloyd George's peroration was almost an echo of one that Lord Claud Hamilton, the chairman of the Great Eastern Railway, had delivered to a meeting of that company on 7 February. Hamilton, in roundly denouncing the government for being weak in its stance on labour, had declared,

> One concession followed upon another on the part of the government not to reasoned arguments, not in reply to proved grievances, not in the interests of justice and fair play, but to the threats of brute force. Brute force in any shape was contrary to the instincts of the British nation, and having disposed of it on the continent, we were surely not going to allow it, fostered by those who had not risked their lives or suffered the unspeakable miseries of trench life, to raise its noxious head in our midst. The time was arriving when the government must take off the velvet gloves it had worn too long.

Lloyd George's expression of similar sentiments won him even the warm approval of the right-wing *Morning Post* and of Brigadier-General Page Croft, the leading light of the breakaway National Party, who declared that he had 'rarely listened to a speech from him with greater pleasure'.[32]

That the MFGB saw Lloyd George's speech as a threat is not surprising given the then state of negotiations over its post-war programme of demands. The day before, 10 February, the government had responded to the MFGB's demands with the offer of a

February to March 1919 145

wage increase of 1s a day and a committee of enquiry into its other demands and the state of the coal trade. Robert Smillie, the president of the MFGB, had made it clear that this was not enough but that the government's proposals would be submitted to a MFGB Special Conference on 12 and 13 February.

The miners' post-war programme was radical. It had been formulated at successive annual conferences of the union. The miners called for a six-hour day, an increase of 30 per cent on total earnings exclusive of war bonuses and 'full maintenance at trade union rates of wages for mineworkers unemployed through demobilisation'. They also demanded nationalisation of the mines which, though it had been first adopted by the MFGB in 1894, had not been accompanied before the 1918 Annual Conference with a demand for a measure of workers' control.

That conference, held at Southport in July 1918, agreed unanimously to a South Wales resolution which declared that it was 'clearly in the national interest to transfer the entire industry from private ownership and control to state ownership with joint control by the workmen and the state'. In speaking to the resolution Frank Hodges, then miners' agent for the Garw Valley (but from January 1919 secretary of the MFGB), argued 'you can have nationalisation but still be in no better position than you are now under private ownership'. Hence he suggested,

> Now, is it any good to have these mines **nationalised** unless we are going to exercise some form of control as producers? If not, the whole tendency will be towards the power of bureaucracy. We shall be given no status at all in the industry, except to be the mere producers, as we have been in the past years.

As for the overall package of demands, Hodges argued that hours could be reduced and wages raised 'without inflicting a terrible burden on the community' provided 'the coal-owner passes automatically out of the industry', thereby removing 'the burden of maintaining the rate of profit to the owners'.[33]

Though the delegates at the MFGB 1918 Annual Conference had called for their programme to be presented 'not . . . more than four weeks after the declaration of peace', the leadership had delayed beyond the December 1918 general election. This was a mistake that the railway unions, eagerly in competition with one another, had not made. Perhaps a wish to await the arrival of the newly elected secretary, Frank Hodges, who succeeded the elderly Thomas Ashton on the 9 January 1919, helps to explain the delay in putting forward their claims on wages and conditions of employment until that date. Shortly thereafter, following a Special Conference held between the 14 and 16 January, the MFGB supplemented its demands of 9 January by formally calling for the nationalisation of the mines. The leadership of the MFGB saw Horne, Shortt, Stanley and Sir Evan Jones, the Coal Controller on Friday, 31 January 1919 to demand a response to their claims. Horne reported to the War Cabinet that afternoon that the delegation had threatened 'that unless a reply on the wages issue was received by Monday trouble would ensue'. However, Horne and his colleagues 'pointed out . . . that the whole wage question was closely connected with the six hour day' and had put the miners off with a promise that the government would try to reply by the end of the following week.[34]

When the War Cabinet did discuss the miners' demands on 7 February, their opposition centred on the scale of the wage claim. Horne briskly dismissed the miners' request for preferential treatment in demobilisation as impossible to concede, especially as there had been less dislocation in coal mining than in any other industry except shipbuilding. As for the miners' call for a 30 per cent increase in wages, he warned that it would have 'a crippling effect on industry'. 'The wage demand alone', he told them 'would amount to about £40 million per annum; probably 3s 6d to 4s per ton would have to be added to the present price of coal, and . . . about 15s per ton to be added to the price of steel.' Horne did, however, point out that the miners had not had a pay rise since June 1918 and that Lloyd George had then promised to reconsider wage levels if the cost of living rose. Hence, given that pledge and the level of pay awards in other industries he recommended a wage offer of 1s per day. He suggested that alternatively the miners should be offered 'a full and impartial enquiry' which would first look into wages and hours and would issue an early interim report before considering 'the further and wider question of joint control, or nationalisation of the mines'. In recommending an enquiry, Horne observed that 'the coalowners themselves had asked for a full enquiry into the whole mechanism of the coal industry and into the question of profits.'

The War Cabinet was divided as to whether the miners wanted a show-down then or in the future. Horne felt that 'these present claims might only be regarded as an "affair of the outposts"; the big battle would be joined later.' He claimed that 'those responsible for the present industrial unrest now regarded ... the recent sporadic outbursts as a mistake.' As a result he concluded that the government should 'take immediate steps to develop their plans in order to meet a much more serious situation later'. The Coal Controller, however, observed that 'the Minister of Labour might be correct in stating that the big battle was to come later, but his own information was to the effect that the miners on South Wales, at any rate, were out for a fight now.'

Bonar Law felt that 'possibly the present would be a favourable time for the government to meet a strike.' He then argued that,

> The essence of the present problem was ... the case the government would be able to present to the country. The miners were claiming to fix their own rates of pay, irrespective of the effect that this might have on other trades, and they were taking up a very selfish position.

Hence he called on the Ministry of Labour to prepare carefully the government's case for presentation to the public, placing particular emphasis on 'the effect of a rise in miners' wages upon other wage earners in the kingdom'.[35]

Thus the War Cabinet was already determined to take a firm line with the miners before Lloyd George's return from Paris on 8 February. But with his return Lloyd George took the lead. Tom Jones informed Hankey that the Prime Minister was 'extraordinarily cheerful ... and full of schemes of dealing with the miners and railwaymen should they come out during the next week or two'.[36] At the War Cabinet held on 10 February, Lloyd George heard the proposals of the Industrial Unrest Committee to meet a coal strike and approved its suggestions to conserve coal stocks at home. However, he took a tougher line:

> He had given a good deal of consideration to the possibility of the miners attempting to hold up the life of the community, and if they chose starvation as a weapon they must not complain if society made use of the same weapon. We could control the bread and foreign supplies, and we had sufficient troops to guard the main centres, but he was a little anxious as to the protection of herds of cattle in the country.

He also gained approval from the War Cabinet for the Industrial Unrest Committee to examine a list of possible actions which he had drawn up. His proposals included looking into ways to maintain the supply of coal and where possible substitute other fuels, and also planning the protection of the various coal, food and petrol supply centres and of herds of cattle in the countryside. His list also called for an examination of the extent to which electric trains and motor transport could be used for the distribution of food supplies, and for consideration to be given to the use of the navy and of general reserve volunteers.[37]

Hence there is every appearance that the government in mid-February not only expected but was ready to take on the miners in the near future. Both Lloyd George and Bonar Law appear to have viewed such a confrontation with equanimity. If so, then Lloyd George's fighting talk in the House of Commons on 11 February was no bluff. The government's offer of 1s plus an enquiry was the only alternative on offer to an immediate showdown with the miners.

It is also very clear that the inquiry was seen by the War Cabinet as one of the ways in which the government would secure the support of public opinion in its resistance to the miners' whole programme. Bonar Law, at the meeting on the 7 February, observed

> The whole matter required the most careful handling, and it was essential that public opinion should be on the side of the government. The Committee, besides comprising members who would represent both the coalmasters and miners, should also include others not directly interested in, or connected with, mines, e.g. judges and economists; and, further, other members who would regard it from the point of view of other industries. He agreed with the Minister of Labour that the proposed Committee should envisage the problem from the point of view of the general trade of the country.

Sir Adam Nimmo, a leading Scottish coal owner who was then an adviser to the Coal Controller, was present at that War Cabinet meeting. Speaking for the coal owners, he said there was no objection 'to the terms of reference for the Committee including the nationalisation of the mines' but he urged that its membership 'must include men of undoubted experience and ability, as their enquiries would not be confined to the coal industry alone'.[38]

Given the manifest discontent already visible on the coalfields, most notably exhibited in Yorkshire where in January 150,000 men went on strike for thirteen days to secure a 20-minute per shift interval for surfacemen's meals, the government can hardly have been surprised when a Miners' Special Conference at Southport on

12 and 13 February rejected its offer and issued a national strike ballot to be returned by 22 February. Indeed, even without the expected big national mining strike, mining disputes would account for the largest number of workers on strike in the first half of 1919. There were strikes in various areas in late March and again in Yorkshire in June through to July in support of the MFGB's national programme.

The government responded to the national strike ballot by vigorously appealing to public opinion. Horne issued to the press a letter he wrote to Smillie on 15 February in which he objected to the phrase 'the government have failed to grant' being on the strike ballot with regard to the main items in the miners' post-war programme. Horne argued that the government had not rejected the miners' demands but wanted an inquiry, observing in particular of nationalisation that the government had 'not expressed any view in opposition'. The government also spent considerable sums on newspaper advertisements urging miners to vote against strike action, advertisements which appeared to be as much aimed at the general public as at actual miners. Whitehall departments also fed to newspapers government 'facts' as to the effects of the miners' proposals on industry generally.[39]

With it becoming very apparent that the miners would vote overwhelmingly in favour of strike action, Lloyd George summoned the MFGB executive to see him in Downing Street on the morning of 20 February 1919. Lloyd George urged Smillie and his colleagues to postpone the dates of strike notices (which were due to expire on 15 March) and participate in a committee of enquiry which would present an interim report, at the latest, by 31 March. Smillie replied that the miners might be willing to wait on the issue of nationalisation but, given that the government had full information at hand on the wages and hours claim and that these had been before ministers since 9 January, the miners expected action on these immediately, without the delay of an enquiry. Lloyd George refused to budge on wages and hours.

It was at this meeting that Lloyd George made his famous comments on the constitutional position of a government faced with a major industrial challenge. Lloyd George's actual words to Smillie were,

> Now the government is directly responsible for this industry. The negotiations will be with the government, the answer will be given by the

government and not by the mineowners. The responsibility will be with a government; and if there is a conflict it will not be a conflict between the mineowners and the miners, it will be a conflict between one industry and the whole of the state. I cannot conceive anything graver than that. The state could not surrender if it began, without abdicating its functions. It is not a question of this government or that government, but of government – every government. The community before we enter into this conflict will be either for us or against. If the community is against us, then another government must undertake the task. If the community is with us, it is a conflict with the community.

These comments have gone down to posterity via Aneurin Bevan's *In Place of Fear*, but in a much more dramatic version. Bevan recalled that Smillie told him that Lloyd George said,

I feel bound to tell you that in our opinion we are at your mercy . . . if you carry out your threat and strike you will defeat us.

But if you do so . . . have you weighed the consequences? The strike will be in defiance of the government of the country and by its very success will precipitate a constitutional crisis of the first importance. For, if a force arises in the state which is stronger than the state itself, then it must be ready to take on the functions of the state, or withdraw and accept the authority of the state.

Smillie rounded off his description to Bevan with '"Gentlemen", asked the Prime Minister quietly, "have you considered, and if you have, are you ready?" From that moment on . . . we were beaten and we knew we were.'

The Bevan account is interesting in that it contains Smillie's belief that the MFGB (and the Triple Alliance) challenge was defeated then. It represents a calling of the bluff of 'direct action' by trade unions – or at least of direct action with no clear plan of what should follow a strike which paralysed the country. Bevan observed, after recounting Smillie's recollections, 'After this the General Strike of 1926 was really an anti-climax.'[40] But this account is quite wrong in suggesting that Lloyd George said that the government was beaten. Lloyd George was certainly willing to face a fight if necessary.

After this meeting on 20 February 1919 Lloyd George kept the pressure on the MFGB executive to compromise and accept an enquiry and he himself also made efforts to gain Smillie's support for the participation of the MFGB in such an enquiry. The day after the meeting with the MFGB executive he released a full transcript of the meeting. This was deemed by *The Times*'s Labour correspondent to be an 'unprecedented step', and was another part of Lloyd George's offensive to win the support of public opinion for an enquiry.

Lloyd George also used Sidney and Beatrice Webb as a route to Smillie. Given Beatrice Webb's role on the Royal Commission on the Poor Laws before the First World War, he rightly expected that they would not be hostile to the very notion of a Royal Commission. Lloyd George dined with them at Lord Haldane's house on 20 February (the same day that he saw the MFGB). An interesting feature of this meeting is that he had asked Haldane to sound out the Webbs as to whether they would meet him for dinner as early as 14 February (the day after the MFGB decided to call a strike ballot), and the actual date of 20 February was fixed by Lloyd George on 16 February. Lloyd George exercised his charm to the full on the Webbs and, while ostensibly pressing them for suggestions as to names for the Royal Commission, he made – as Beatrice Webb noted – a series of 'calculated indiscretions' from which they were expected to gather 'that the PM meant the Commission to report in favour of nationalising the mines'. Lloyd George also arranged that the Webbs should find out from Tom Jones that his proposed list of names 'were all hostile to nationalisation'. As Lloyd George must have expected, the result was that Sidney Webb pressed Smillie to demand that the Commission should include members in whom the miners had confidence.

When Webb saw Smillie on 22 February he found him 'depressed with a cold and the feeling of responsibility'. Smillie indeed appears to have been demoralised by Lloyd George's analysis of the consequences of an out-and-out struggle between the MFGB and a determined government which had recently been returned with a huge majority in a general election. He may also have shared Sidney Webb's view that the bulk of the miners cared much for reduced hours and increased earnings but would not enter into a major conflict for nationalisation of the mines. In that case participating in the enquiry might win the miners' programme without industrial conflict, and it would avoid alienating public opinion by outrightly rejecting the premier's appeal to accept a speedy enquiry.[41]

Lloyd George pressed ahead with the appointment of a Royal Commission. He was well pleased with the tone of the speech that Smillie had made to the Miners' Conference after the Downing Street conference. He deemed it to be 'dignified and not provocative'. On 24 February, following War Cabinet approval, Lloyd George moved in the House of Commons the introduction of the Bill to establish a Royal Commission on the Coal Industry. The day before he had told Riddell that his speech 'required very careful preparation' as 'every word would be of importance'.[42]

In his speech Lloyd George made an appeal to public opinion. While reiterating his readiness to remedy poor housing conditions in mining areas, he emphasised – even exaggerated – the impact of an increase of 8s to 10s a ton, arising from the miners' wage demands, on employment in shipping and major export industries. Given the then considerable public outrage at wartime profiteers, Lloyd George made much of arguing that the MFGB could not use 'profiteering as if it explained everything, and as if you got the extra 8s or 10s per ton out of the colossal profits that some were making'. However, the thrust of his speech was to depict the difference between the government and the MFGB as being not the major matter of whether a Royal Commission should investigate the industry and come up with the truth as to the 'facts' of prices, profits, wages and organisation but the lesser one of whether that Commission should make an interim report by 31 March (as the government wished) or 15 March (as the MFGB demanded).

Thus Lloyd George had switched the issue before the public from whether an enquiry should take place to how fast it should produce an interim report. As usual he did not understate the consequences if the miners' refused to agree to the government's timetable. He told the House of Commons,

> Sixteen days' strike under present conditions would see the majority of the industries of this country closed down, and the government would have to feed the community with such food as was at its disposal. If there were distress, it would fall upon every branch of the community. It would not be a question of whether you could pay. The food would be entirely in the hands of the government, and they would have to distribute it. The miners would have to depend, like every other branch of the community, upon such food as we should be able to distribute with the exhausted fuel resources at our disposal.

In addition to making this public warning of starving the miners and their families into submission Lloyd George held out a promise, which was characteristically large and unspecific, of the good things that would flow if the MFGB accepted the government's proposals. He said of the miners 'that as a result of this Inquiry, in my judgement, they will get a Miners' Charter which will be the beginning of greater and better things for them, and if they . . . throw themselves into the Inquiry and present their case . . . they will achieve great things for their industry.'[43] During the debates the government went even further in its efforts to appear conciliatory, and conceded that the interim report should be published on 20 (not 31) March.

Lloyd George's appeal to public opinion from Parliament was reinforced by his attempts to secure good press coverage. About that time he contacted the Webbs, he invited C. P. Scott of the *Manchester Guardian* to travel to London to breakfast with him on 21 (though postponing it until 22) February. Though Lloyd George's motive may have been to try to gain a more sympathetic attitude both to himself and his government following recent criticism, nevertheless it is very likely that the timing of his approaches was at least partly connected to the crisis in dealing with the miners.[44]

In preparing his speech of 24 February Lloyd George was concerned not only about the reaction of the general public and the miners but also about that of the Tory Right in Parliament. He had taken similar care of Tory sensibilities in his two major speeches in the debates on 11 and 12 February (on Prussianism in industrial relations and on Peace Conference issues, including Russia). Even so, as early as 15 February Lord Esher was warning Hankey not to be 'over confident of L.G. retaining his hold on the H. of C . . . ; as I listened to the Debate on the Address it seemed to me that there were already signs of cleavage in the unwieldy majority.' And Frances Stevenson noted in her diary, when she and Lloyd George returned to Paris on 5 March, 'The Tories – at least the more difficult of them, such as Long and Curzon – have got their tails up as a result of their success in the election.'[45]

The day after he had introduced the Bill to set up the Sankey Commission Lloyd George was still expressing his readiness for an immediate confrontation with the miners if necessary. During the course of his discussion with Austen Chamberlain and other colleagues as to the need to give housing a very high priority in the government's policies he observed,

> We will try and settle these immediate disputes, and if we cannot, we shall have to fight the thing through. It may be a good thing, because Labour is getting unreasonable in some respects. I thought they were very unreasonable yesterday when they refused to give an extra fourteen days for investigation. It may be necessary to take a firm and strong line to bring them to reason.

However, he added a comment which suggests that he hoped that the miners would gain some benefits from the Royal Commission: 'Take Smillie and the miners. We all know what has happened in the past, but it is no good telling that it is ancient history. It is in their bones, and you have to win back their confidence.'[46]

On 25 February, the day when the result of the miners' ballot – with 85 per cent of those who voted in support of strike action – was publicly announced, Smillie and the MFGB decided to recommend conditional support for the Sankey Commission. They put to the Miners' Conference on 26 February the motion 'that if we secure the right to nominate one half of the members of the proposed Commission we do form part thereof.' Smillie successfully argued in favour of participation on these terms and put them to Lloyd George at a brief meeting the following day when the latter was at the National Industrial Conference. Smillie came away convinced that Lloyd George had not only conceded that the miners could nominate half the members of the Commission but also had promised 'that if the inquiry of the coal commission produced facts to justify the majority in recommending nationalisation of the mines, the government would consider it their duty to carry out the findings of the Commission.' Lloyd George later denied that he had ever made this promise, but, as Susan Armitage has observed, it is clear that he made some ambiguous comment giving that impression.[47]

Some historians have viewed the agreement that the miners should nominate half the members of the Commission to be a great victory for Smillie. Thus Robin Page Arnot wrote that Lloyd George, given ten minutes to agree by Smillie, 'yielded to the ultimatum'.[48] However, it may well be that Smillie was pushing at an open door. For if Lloyd George had presumed that Tom Jones would raise the importance of gaining a favourable composition of half the Commission with the Webbs, then it would seem Lloyd George's machinations were aimed at achieving acceptance of the Commission. Why else would he have made such a point of urging the Webbs to contact Tom Jones?

Even after the Miners' Conference had accepted participation in the Sankey Commission the government continued to make contingency plans for a future major coal dispute. At the War Cabinet on 28 February Lloyd George commented that in that event there would need to be a scheme whereby those unemployed received their benefit in the form of food rather than in cash. He urged, 'Arrangements would have to be made so that it would be possible, in the distribution of food, to differentiate between those men on strike and persons out of work through no fault of their own.' The Industrial Unrest Committee was given the task of devising a system of food coupons. At the same meeting, when considering the Home Affairs Committee's recommendations on cutting unemployment benefit, Lloyd George and Bonar Law pressed Horne to propose a less drastic reduction for men that recommended – from £1 9s to £1, not to 18s a week. But they accepted the suggested reduction in weekly benefit for women from £1 5s to 15s.[49]

It is difficult to be certain as to Lloyd George's motives in working so hard – and probably deviously – to secure MFGB participation in the Sankey inquiry. Contrary to the standard interpretation in many history books, it does seem that Lloyd George and many of his colleagues were willing to take on the miners in spring 1919; though most preferred to find a peaceful solution to the miners' claims. In this light the setting up of the Sankey Commission had much to do with winning over public opinion, especially working-class voters, to the reasonableness of the government's stance. Furthermore, as the economy was recovering from the war, there was also a desire to avoid the economic dislocation that would be brought about by a major coal dispute. As for Lloyd George himself, he was eager to reinforce his reputation as a skilled negotiator in the eyes of his Conservative backbenchers, yet he was not averse to the miners making some gains from taking their case to the Royal Commission.

However, as was too often the case, Lloyd George promised more than he could deliver. Given the composition of the House of Commons, his intimations that the miners might achieve nationalisation via participation in the Royal Commission were rash, if not outrightly dishonest. But the miners did achieve substantial concessions on wages and hours of work that way. As on other occasions it seems that Lloyd George put all his considerable powers of persuasion into achieving his short-term goal, the setting up of the Commission, with little or no thought to the long term consequences of his actions.

At the time many people in public life felt that Lloyd George had done well. Frances Stevenson, when she returned to Paris with Lloyd George on 5 March 1919, noted in her diary

> Everyone congratulates him most heartily on the way in which he seems to have brought comparative peace into the industrial world. On our arrival

in London at the beginning of February there was an atmosphere of gloom and pessimism. But the P.M. soon dispelled this by his clever negotiations, and also by his speeches on the industrial situation.[50]

Lloyd George's 'clever negotiations' also had the effect of separating the miners from their Triple Alliance allies, the railwaymen, who were again making threatening noises towards the government. But, for all his efforts, the threat of an imminent major industrial stoppage remained present until the second half of March.

In late February the negotiations over the railway workers' programme again came to a head. After meetings between the Railway Executive, the NUR and ASLEF on 12 and 21 February, Stanley advised the War Cabinet that negotiations had reached a stage which required a decision as to what offer should be made. He warned them that 'if the men's demands were conceded in full, it would mean that the government would be faced with the permanent cost of operating the railways plus £120 million which addition was equivalent to the gross earnings of the railways prior to the war.' Stanley recommended that the government should offer part of the war bonus – £1 13s – to the men as a 50 per cent advance on their pre-war wage rates, while the remainder – about £1 – should be continued as a bonus which would decrease with the decline in the cost of living. He concluded that the additional cost of this concession plus the introduction of the 8-hour day would be £35 million. Lloyd George doubted if these proposals made sufficient concessions to the railwaymen on pay, observing that 'a very considerable percentage of railway workers was drawn from the agricultural classes, whose wages before the war were between 15s and 18s, but had now gone up from 30s to 40s.' Several ministers, including Lloyd George, were impressed by the gains in real standards of living that would be made if prices fell, even if the railway workers gained little immediately; but Chamberlain warned that world currency problems could lead to food prices rising again. In the end the War Cabinet authorised Stanley to negotiate on the basis that he had suggested.[51]

Earlier, when the Transport Bill had been discussed, Lloyd George and others had considered nationalisation to be a possible answer to steeply rising costs of running the railways. The discussion had focused on whether or not a clause giving the state power to buy the railways should be included in the Bill. Lloyd George pointed out,

The railways were now working at a deficiency of £90,000,000, and the Railway Companies would not take them over in two years' time unless the government were prepared to make up that deficiency, or else allow them to raise their charges. The trading community might be prepared to submit to increased charges in the form of general taxation, but they would not agree to it if it were for the purpose of increasing the dividends of railway shareholders, and there would be a combined trade and labour opposition to any proposal to increase the rates. He was also of the opinion that if the government could say that they had in mind a proposal to make the railways State property it would be much easier to deal with the menacing industrial trouble. They would be in a position to say to the men that they were imposing a burden on the community if they persisted in their demands, which would have to be met either by increased taxation or an increase in the price of commodities.

However, he realised that this policy could run into trouble in the Commons as 'a determined minority [could] hold up the matter for months'. He was soon to find that backbench Tories and the pressure of outside interests would effectively block the nationalisation of any major industry. But on this occasion decisions were deferred until Sir Eric Geddes had had time as Minister of Transport to judge the issue and the Select Committee had reported. Lloyd George still believed that 'owing to the fierce competition among railways the majority of railway managers held nationalisation to be inevitable.'[52]

The negotiations over wages and conditions continued into mid-March with the rank and file growing increasingly restless. The railwaymen's leaders remained conciliatory. Early on they had indicated to Stanley that 'they did not wish to present an ultimatum to the government as the miners had done, but desired to reach agreement by discussion.'[53] Thomas himself had been publicly deploring the use of strikes to achieve trade union aims. On 9 February, when he had been dampening down unrest over the railway companies' interpretations of the 8-hour day, he had declared,

> The NUR was the strongest union in the country . . . they could, at any time they chose, place a demand at the head of state and say, 'Unless you do this we will paralyse the community'. That was their power, but they had to consider what was their duty. However strong, however powerful they as a union might be, the state was more powerful and more important. Citizenship had a stronger claim than any sectional interest. As railwaymen and trade unionists they had always to make their sectional claim consistent with their duty as citizens.

After Thomas had had an audience with the King at Buckingham

Palace that same day George V noted in his dairy, 'He is a good and loyal man.' Thomas had also kept in close contact with Lloyd George, having two discussions with him about 'the whole labour situation' in late January, and travelling back from Paris to London with the premier and his entourage on 8 February. However, for all the willingness of Thomas and the other trade union leaders to compromise, when Thomas took the government's proposals to a NUR special general meeting on 14 March the delegates made it very clear that they rejected compromises and viewed their national programme as 'the irreducible minimum'. However, while the NUR rejected the offer outright, ASLEF wished negotiations to continue on the offer as it was more favourable to its members, who were generally higher grade workers.[54]

On 18 March, in a dramatic move to prevent a Triple Alliance strike, Thomas flew in an open two-seater RAF plane to Paris to see Lloyd George. Lloyd George turned on his considerable charm for Thomas, entertaining him with talk of Welsh history and even with a Welsh ballad singer. But he declined to enter into detailed negotiations over the railway dispute, saying that he was not sufficiently well-informed to do so and that the matter was being conducted by others. But Lloyd George did discuss with Thomas his main concern, whether Triple Alliance action was likely. He reported to Bonar Law the next day, 'He gave me the impression of a man who was very anxious not to have a strike.' Frances Stevenson observed of Thomas in her diary, 'he is an amusing creature, not very reliable and very open to flattery and coaxing. However he is playing our game at the moment.'[55]

Stanley again raised the issue of what to offer the rail unions at the War Cabinet meeting held on the morning of 19 March 1919. He told his colleagues that Thomas was consulting his union's Special General Meeting the next day and meeting with the other Triple Alliance unions on 21 March. Stanley warned them

> that, assuming arrangements could be made with Mr. J. H. Thomas that would stand the final test of the Triple Alliance, there might still be a railway strike owing to the fact that ... [ASLEF] was powerful enough to hold up the whole railway system.

Stanley, like Horne, felt that it was essential to mobilise public opinion behind the government and so urged that the offer should be as generous as possible and should go a little further than in ordinary circumstances. There was a limit, but it was worthwhile paying something to avoid the threatening catastrophe. In addition, there had been a forecast that the Coal Commission enquiry would give something more to the miners, which in its turn would affect the railwaymen and the prestige of the railway leaders who were trying to bring the railway question to the front, and to prevent its being overclouded by the coal enquiry.

As for the size of the offer, Stanley said, 'There was nothing to guide them and it was mainly a matter of instinct. It was in no way a commercial proposition, because in any event a burden would be placed on the railways bigger than they were able to support.' The War Cabinet decided that Stanley, Horne and Sir Eric Geddes should draw up a properly costed offer that afternoon and that the War Cabinet should reconvene that evening to consider their proposals.[56]

That evening Sir Eric Geddes informed the War Cabinet that Thomas was offering to 'make the strongest recommendations to his union' for the acceptance of a package of concessions. These consisted of the war wage continuing until the end of the year, additional payments (at time-and-a-quarter) for night work, the application of uniform district rates for similar grades, time-and-a-half for Sunday duty and time-and-a-quarter for overtime to apply to all areas, and a guarantee that railwaymen had the right to make representations on questions of management.

In the War Cabinet the main concern was that the night duty concession would cost between £5 and £8 million. Chamberlain deemed the cost of such concessions to be 'appalling', observing that 'there was no prospect of the railways paying' and he did not know 'where the money to pay these extra wages was to come from'. Long, as always the defender of the agricultural interest, claimed that if the concession resulted in higher freight rates then 'the effect would be to damage home industry and especially to cripple agriculture'. Nevertheless, given the tense industrial situation, other ministers urged that concessions should be made. Bonar Law argued that as the miners would get an increase on their current wages it would not be possible to offer the railwaymen a lower wage than they were getting already. Horne expressed the key argument of the need to reinforce the railway leadership and split the Triple Alliance. He said,

> it was worth while to pay the extra cost of the railwaymen's demands in order to secure their support at the present time. If the miners came out on

strike, the railwaymen might come out, but with this difference, that if the above concessions were now granted, they would be striking without a grievance. In addition, the transport workers had no ground for a strike, although they would probably come out if the miners did so.[57]

After earlier prolonged negotiations with the railway unions, the War Cabinet, on the eve of the publication of the Sankey Commission's Interim Report, now quickly granted concessions to the railwaymen. Indeed the conjunction of the railway unions' claims and the publication of the report worried not only the War Cabinet but also the King. He argued that Lloyd George should return from Paris to deal with the crisis in person, and wanted to know if Bonar Law was 'in a position to act as head of the state in an emergency'. Bonar Law, in passing on George V's views, observed that the King had more justification at this time than in February, when he had previously urged Lloyd George to return, 'for this is more serious'. He informed Lloyd George that he had replied to the King that he had Lloyd George's 'full authority' for assuming full responsibility in an emergency, but asked Lloyd George for written confirmation. Lloyd George readily agreed to that but declined to return to London then on the grounds that Wilson, Clemenceau and Orlando had signed a letter appealing to him to stay and that his absence from the Peace Conference would have the result that 'the Peace of Europe would be postponed'. He observed, 'it is not my duty to risk the progress which has been made with the Peace Conference in order to avert serious trouble in England.' He did, however, suggest that in the event of an imminent mining strike Horne and Shortt should travel to Paris to assist him.[58]

Though in Paris, Lloyd George kept in close touch with the preparations that the government was making as a precaution in case the miners went on strike immediately after the publication of the Sankey Commission's Interim Report on 20 March 1919. The day before, he wrote to Bonar Law urging that 'it is urgently important that the method to be adopted . . . for safeguarding law and order for feeding the population should be thoroughly prepared.' He warned,

> The miners I happen to know, are relying upon the Co-operative stores to feed them. The great co-operative supplies are outside the mining areas. They ought not to be removed. Once the strike begins it is imperative that the state should win. Failure to do so would inevitably lead to a Soviet Republic.[59]

In this Lloyd George was expecting the point of conflict to be on nationalisation. He was very willing for the government to make sizeable concessions on wages and hours, and other such matters as housing. But, politically, Lloyd George did not feel able – and at this time was unwilling – to concede nationalisation.

Edwin Montagu, one of Lloyd George's most senior Coalition Liberal colleagues, had warned him of the political impracticality of conceding nationalisation at the time of the Interim Report. Montagu commented that Sir Arthur Duckham

> is prepared to say that national ownership, but not national management, is inevitable. . . . Duckham says nationalisation should be faced now if nationalisation is inevitable. Horne seems to me to be the stiffest of the lot and says that the House of Commons would never stand anything that looked like being based on fear of a strike.

Montagu reported that the second of Horne's arguments against conceding nationalisation at the time of the Interim Report was that to do so then would be premature. In setting up the Commission the miners had been told that the issue of nationalisation would be dealt with after the first report; and that by the time of the first report the Commission had not had time to consider fully the issue of ownership.[60]

Lloyd George appears to have adopted these points as a guide to his action. There is evidence that after the hearings of the Sankey Commission he himself felt that major change in the ownership and structure of the industry was inevitable. Lord Derby, who had become ambassador to France, reported to Balfour that Lloyd George, when dining with Briand (the French Prime Minister) on 17 March,

> said he had been quite horrified at the reports he had heard since the Commission had opened of the enormous profits made by certain coal companies. He admitted, in answer to something I had said, that there were certain mines which had made little or no profit during the war but on the other hand it has been clearly proved that a very large number of miners belong to companies [which had] made practically the whole of their capital together with good dividend during the four years of the war.[61]

Hence, whilst taking a tough pose on the issue when dealing with Bonar Law and his other Conservative colleagues, Lloyd George was careful to see that the government was not outrightly hostile to the miners' aspirations. He tried to ensure that the government took a stand against the miners on the issue of the need for further time for the Sankey Commission to consider nationalisation and the alternative changes in the running of the industry – not against improvements in pay or hours of work, or even on outright opposition to nationalisation. In his letter of 19 March to Bonar Law he reiterated the argument put by Horne that the government had stated very clearly from the outset that nationalisation would not be dealt with in the Commission's first report. But he also suggested that Bonar Law should make it clear that the Commission would be 'free to examine the important question [of nationalisation] without any pressure or direction either way from the government'.

Lloyd George emphasised to Bonar Law that the government needed to win over public opinion. He warned him, 'For the moment the facts brought out before the Commission as to bad housing conditions, as to the enormous profits made by the coal owners etc. have swung public opinion rather heavily on the miners' side.' To this he added, as if to reassure the Conservatives that he was 'sound' on this issue, 'and, as you know, in these matters public opinion is very indiscriminate'. For the government to gain public support, he advised,

> This cannot be done by challenging the merits of the miners' case. It must be put solely on the ground that the miners have thrown over the appeal to reason in favour of a resort to brute force; that no well ordered community could possibly permit such procedure. *The Times* and the *Daily Mail* show indications of supporting the miners. It is essential that the press should be on the side of the government and steps should be taken to secure this.

Lloyd George's observations to Bonar Law can bear two interpretations. One is that he was determined to stand up to the miners and was choosing with care the most promising ground on which to fight. Alternatively these remarks can be seen as his way of reassuring Bonar Law and yet trying to ensure that the Conservatives did not take an immediate stance of outright opposition to nationalisation. Instead Lloyd George was working to postpone decisions on that issue until the Sankey Commission came up with proposals which might well go further than his Conservative colleagues would wish, yet probably would not go as far as the miners were demanding. This latter interpretation seems more likely. If Lloyd George's motives were of this kind, then his references to public opinion were, in part, his way of reminding his Tory colleagues of the reality of public expectations of change in the coal industry and of public sympathy for the miners' case. Yet, in part, they also represented his determination to get public opinion behind the government should the miners decide to demand what he felt to be too much too quickly.

The War Cabinet busied itself in taking precautions against a major coal strike taking place. In preparing to deal with consequences of such a strike for other industries, it agreed to suspend all existing insurance benefits and instead pay a flat rate weekly benefit to those thrown out of work. The rate was to be 10s for adults and 5s for youths (15 to 18 years) and for each child up to a maximum of four per family.[62] As for the strikers, the War Cabinet drafted a Strikes (Exceptional Measures) Bill, which included the power to arrest trade union leaders and to confiscate trade union funds.

Lloyd George expressed his opposition to moves which could alienate public opinion. He observed that he and Balfour (who as Foreign Secretary was also in Paris) 'have absolutely no doubt that the strike, if it comes off, must be fought with all the resources at our command'. But they urged that the government needed to be careful as to its strategy. 'The party that secures on its side either general opinion or the opinion of the working classes of the Kingdom must win.'

Lloyd George felt that much of the working class would be opposed to a lengthy mining dispute which would disrupt other industries. In fact, only the previous day, Long had written to him, 'I gather from our SS [Secret Service] reports, and from other sources, that there is a growing feeling amongst workers who are not in this movement, against anything in the nature of a strike and that the feeling among women is very strong.' Hence Lloyd George urged that the government should do nothing that would endanger much working-class opinion remaining opposed to the miners,

> It is essential to social order that it should continue [to be] alienated. This strike would be different in character from any hitherto challenged by trade unions. It would be a menace to the whole foundation of democratic government. It would be an attempt to force great changes on the state and a threat of anarchy and economic disaster. As so much depends on victory in such a conflict we feel it is overwhelmingly important that we should secure the support of every section of the community in this struggle.

Lloyd George went on to warn, 'If the trade union leaders are arrested, trade unionism would consider its existence threatened and might rally, and probably would rally, to the miners' cause. That would be a catastrophe.' He continued,

> if trade unionism is struck at, if the right to strike (to which the working classes attach such traditional importance) is taken away, then the chances are that the indignation of the operatives will be turned against the government and not against the strikers. This would be fatal. No government was prepared to withdraw the right of striking altogether during the war and to do it now the war is over would be regarded as taking advantage of the miners' mistake, in order to deprive unions of the only weapon which the workmen believe has ever secured them fair conditions of housing and wages. And what would be gained? The strike would pass into the hands of the wilder and more irresponsible spirits. Smillie is an extreme man but the fight he put up against the extremists induced them to accept the Commission and proves that he has some measure of responsible statemanship in his equipment. If the leaders are under lock and key the movement will pass into the hands of hot heads and feather brains of the Noah Ablett type.

As for the confiscation of strike funds, he felt that would be without purpose. 'If the Co-operative Societies are prepared to feed the miners they will do it on credit.'

Instead Lloyd George urged his colleagues 'to once more consider the food weapon'. He argued,

> Under the Defence of the Realm Act all motor lorries, including those of the co-operative stores would have to be seized and food sent where, in the opinion of the government, it was most needed. No Act of Parliament would be required to stop beer in mining or other districts. All you would have to do would be to see that the transport was not burdened with the carriage of beer or any other luxuries to the mining areas. The government might find that it could not supply the mining districts at all with food owing to lack of transport, or that supplies in those areas were just barely adequate and did not include anything beyond bread. This would bring the miners to their knees in a very short time.[63]

Bonar Law's response was more decisive than it had been to the strikes of early February. He outlined what he intended to say in the House of Commons, which included on nationalisation 'that nobody expected it to be decided now' and the warning that generally a strike by the miners or railwaymen 'would be against the state, and that the state must win and use all its power for that purpose'. However, as to Lloyd George's letter of earlier that day, while declaring himself largely in sympathy with it, he went on to declare,

February to March 1919 165

I do not agree about attaching strike funds. This I shall propose to do by Order in Council under the Defence of the Realm regulations, which can be passed on Saturday if we know that there is a strike. As regards arresting the leaders, and so on, I agreed with you in thinking that that would not be wise procedure to take now, but I think it is quite possible that after the strike has broken out and we have public opinion, as I believe, entirely on our side, it would be the right thing to introduce such a Bill.[64]

Lloyd George agreed to Bonar Law's proposals and to his draft statement for the House of Commons. As a strike did not occur at this time, no major conflict of opinion developed between Lloyd George and Bonar Law as to how to deal with the unions in a major industrial dispute.

On the evening of 20 March the War Cabinet considered the Sankey Commission's Interim Report. The Commission had divided three ways, with one report made by Sankey and the three non-coal owner employers, a second by the miners and Labour movement representatives and a third by the coal owners. Bonar Law read out to his ministerial colleagues a statement, drafted in Sankey's presence, that he proposed to give in the Commons. In it he stated that the government had no alternative but to accept the recommendations made by Mr Justice Sankey and the three employers. These recommedations involved a 2s an hour increase in wages; a cut in daily hours from eight to seven from 16 July 1919, and a further reduction to six from 13 July 1921 'subject to the economic position of the industry at the end of 1920'; and for a further report to be made by 20 May 1919 on 'whether nationalisation or a method of unification by national purchase and/or by joint control is best in the interests of the country and its export trade, the workers and the owners'. Bonar Law's proposed statement to the Commons included a declaration that on nationalisation the government 'have a perfectly open mind' and that 'The government are prepared . . . to adopt this recommendation in the spirit as well as in the letter.' However, in delivering his statement in the Commons, Bonar Law balanced this offer with the threat that the state would take strong action if it was rejected and a strike took place. The War Cabinet, like Lloyd George, readily approved his statement. Indeed, Austen Chamberlain was quick to declare that to reject Sankey's proposals 'would put the government completely in the wrong and make it impossible for them to fight a strike'.[65]

However, Bonar Law's commitment to accepting a recommendation 'in the spirit as well as the letter' was to embarrass the government. Indeed, there was initially even an ambiguity as to exactly what was being accepted so firmly. Moreover, the proposals entailed 'the continuance of coal control for at least a year' and involved the presumption that profits would remain high, as 'in effect . . . the bulk of the amount which now went to the Treasury in excess profits would be transferred to the miners'. In March, ministers were most concerned about the short term, about the likelihood of imminent major industrial disputes in the coal mines and on the railways. Nevertheless it was notable that at that War Cabinet meeting doubts were expressed by two Coalition Liberal ministers. Churchill observed that he 'doubted whether the government had gained anything by appointing the Coal Commission' and H. A. L. Fisher (the President of the Board of Education) complained 'that the country would hold that the Sankey Report had given away the case against nationalisation'.

The Miners' National Conference met in London the next day to discuss whether to call off the strike. The miners immediately asked Bonar Law for clarification of his offer. He replied, 'I have pleasure in confirming . . . my statement that the government are prepared to carry out in the spirit and in the letter the recommendations of Mr Justice Sankey's Report.' The Conference welcomed this assurance and adjourned until 26 March, giving the Executive Committee the task in the interim to negotiate with the government.[66] The following day, 22 March, Smillie and Hodges, along with other representatives of the Triple Alliance unions, saw Bonar Law, Horne and Stanley. The early part of the meeting dealt with the railwaymen's programme, and was notable for Bonar Law making the most of divisions between the railway unions. When the meeting turned to the miners' demands Bonar Law made an appeal to the miners on similar lines to Lloyd George's appeal of 20 February, stressing that a strike would be a strike against the state itself and that if the MFGB won 'it would be a splendid thing for those who wished to upset the decision of these matters by constitutional means'. Smillie responded, 'None of us have any desire to provoke a strike for the purpose of upsetting industry in this country. It requires stability rather than chaos if we are to go on.' But he made it very clear that the MFGB delegates had been outraged by Bonar Law's threat of the state taking tough action if the miners did go on strike. Smillie said of Bonar Law's threatening words,

Whatever your own view on the matter may be, I feel that there is no doubt at all as to what view the capitalists in the House of Commons took of it. They could see before them armed forces shooting down the men, women and children of the working classes . . . (Bonar Law: I hope not) and finally wiping out any attempt of the workers to improve their condition.[67]

After this conference with the Triple Alliance leaders, Bonar Law reported to Lloyd George that 'the crux of the situation' would come on 25 March when he saw the MFGB Executive Committee on its own:

They will certainly press for making the six hours statutory and unless they are bluffing it looks as if there might be a strike authorised at their meeting on Wednesday [26 March] because of this. I hope they are bluffing and am half inclined to think so but in the present temper of the miners and everyone else it is impossible to feel sure.

Bonar Law went on to say that he would resist further concessions. He commented,

I do not think we could agree to this, or indeed go beyond Sankey's Report. If we stick to it we are on safe ground. If we make further concessions I am afraid it will be not only regarded as an extreme weakness, but that immediately we shall be overwhelmed with demands from the trade side to modify in the other direction.

Finally, he observed, 'I think it just possible that if you were here you might be inclined to risk some concessions beyond what I shall be prepared to agree in your absence. That is one of the inevitable risks involved in the necessity of your being away.'[68]

The key figure was Robert Smillie. He alone had the prestige to agree to Sankey's proposals as the middle way between what the mine owners were willing to offer and the full programme of the MFGB. Smillie kept his cards close to his chest. After a conversation with Vernon Hartshorn, a South Wales member of the MFGB Executive Committee and an MP, Tom Jones observed to Hankey, 'Smillie preserves, even to his intimates on the Executive, the most cryptic silence as to the line he will take.' After an earlier conversation with Hartshorn, Jones was left in no doubt that if Smillie and the committee recommended a strike, they would receive overwhelming support from their members. He warned Lloyd George on 24 March that Hartshorn is certain in his own mind that unless the government meets the miners' demands on the question of the statutory Six Hours Day to come into force in July 1920 there will be no peace. He said that the miners in South Wales would come out to a man on that issue. He . . . thinks the government would be wise to concede the miners' demand on this head right away. If it is kept in suspense for two years and made subject to the economic situation at that time, the whole coalfield will be kept in a state of agitation about it and such uncertainty and unrest will be bad for the increased output and settled conditions which all desire to see.[69]

The government remained nervous as to the miners' decision until the Miners' Conference met on 26 March. The day before, Bonar Law told the leaders of the MFGB that the government would go no further than Sankey himself had recommended, but in so doing he was careful not to appear intransigent. He told them that the government would be willing to submit any points requiring interpretation to Sankey and it would accept his ruling. Smillie decided to accept what was on offer. He carried the Executive, and then the Conference, in supporting a recommendation to MFGB members that they should accept the terms offered, including agreeing to the Sankey Commission making a further report by 20 May 1919 on the question of nationalisation.

With both the MFGB Executive and Conference recommending acceptance, the government at last felt that the threat of an imminent major strike had been removed. In fact, when the result of the miners' ballot was declared on 15 April, 90 per cent of those voting were in favour of accepting Sankey's interim proposals.[70] With the miners and railwaymen pacified for the present, Lloyd George sent Bonar Law congratulations on his role in preventing an immediate major strike. Bonar Law responded by observing of industrial trouble, 'I think it is over for the present – but only for the present. We have lots of trouble ahead of us here – you see I am not unduly optimistic – but your difficulties at Paris are . . . far worse.' To this, Lloyd George responded by reinterating his admiration for 'the extreme skill and success' with which Bonar Law had handled the industrial situation. He also agreed, 'I have no doubt there are plenty of troubles ahead of us, but it is very satisfactory to know that you have overcome the worst of them in England, and I should be very happy were I able to do as well with my troubles here.'[71]

However, the nature of the interim settlement with the miners was always likely to cause major trouble later. Sankey's report had raised expectations among the miners. The part of the miners' ballot paper which dealt with nationalisation had quoted the key words from two paragraphs (9 and 15) of his report:

> Even upon the evidence already given, the present system of ownership and working in the coal industry stands condemned, and some other system must be substituted for it, either nationalisation or a measure of unification by national purchase and/or by joint control.
>
> We are prepared . . . to report now that it is in the interests of the country that the colliery worker shall in the future have an effective voice in the direction of the mines.

Bonar Law, when discussing in advance with the War Cabinet his meeting with the miners on 25 March, raised the issue of what he could say then if the miners asked 'whether the government would guarantee to carry out the recommendations' of the Sankey Commission's report when delivered on 20 May. War Cabinet minutes record, 'He did not himself see how he could give such a promise, and he thought he should tell the miners that the question must first be considered by the House of Commons.'[72] Thus Bonar Law and the War Cabinet were clear from the outset that there would be no automatic approval given should the Commission make a recommendation that the mines should be nationalised.

Lloyd George's role in all this was not quite as deceitful as is usually thought. There is every sign that he did hope that the miners would gain a generous settlement, and that this might eventually even include nationalisation. But his prime concerns in this matter were with achieving a resumption of industrial normality after the war and with the political problem of leading a Conservative dominated Coalition government, not with taking political risks to assist the miners achieve their full programme. Nevertheless his part in setting up the Sankey Commission and thereafter keeping up the miners' expectations was an aspect of his 'live now, pay later' style of politics. With consummate skill and cunning Lloyd George often reconciled the apparently irreconcilable – but only in the short term. The real conflicts of interest frequently did not evaporate with time. So problems were often stored up for later. Moreover, by raising expectations which in due course were disappointed, he created disillusionment and often distrust.

In the case of the Sankey Commission, Lloyd George's motivation in setting it up stemmed, at least in part, from his tendency to expect that something would turn up later if immediate clashes were postponed. While in February it was a bad time to have a major clash with the miners, given the current economic dislocation and the very important role of coal in the economy, Lloyd George's aim in setting up the Commission was not simply to buy time in order to smash the miners later. Indeed, while the government preferred not to face a major industrial clash at that time, nevertheless it does appear that it was willing and ready, if necessary, to take on the miners then if they demanded too much. However, what the government was unwilling to cede in March – nationalisation – it became even less willing to cede by the summer. Hence in building up the miners' expectations of nationalisation in February and March, Lloyd George did himself much political harm in the long run when the political situation in the House of Commons ensured that these hopes were later dashed.

Notes and references

1. Esher to Hankey, 15 February 1919; Hankey Papers, HNKY 4/11.
2. P. Rowland, *Lloyd George* (London: Barrie and Jenkins, 1975), pp. 515. S. Roskill, *Hankey: Man of Secrets*, vol. 2 (London: Collins, 1972), pp. 127–9.
3. Hankey's diary, 17 October 1918; Hankey Papers, HNKY 1/5/34. For an example of a lengthy comment on the growth of prime ministerial power, A. Elliot to A. V. Dicey, 22 January 1919; Elliot Papers, 19500, ff. 71–2.
4. 112 *HC Deb. 5s*, c. 67–81; 11 February 1919.
5. 'Shorthand notes of a conference of ministers on unemployment and the state of trade' held on 25 February 1919 (GT 6887); CAB 24–75–371.
6. P. B. Johnson, *Land Fit for Heroes* (Chicago: Chicago University Press, 1968), pp. 87–95, 107–17 and 336–47. L. Orbach, *Homes for Heroes* (London: Seeley, Service, 1977), pp. 43–76. M. Swenarton, *Homes Fit for Heroes* (London: Heinemann, 1981), pp. 71–8. K. O. and J. Morgan, *Portrait of a Progressive* (Oxford: Clarendon Press, 1980), pp. 73–5 and 96–100.
7. Geddes to Lloyd George, 29 December 1918; LG F/18/2/86. 'Shorthand notes', 25 February 1919; CAB 24–75–370 and 372.
8. WC (519 and 525), 24 January and 4 February 1919; CAB 23–9–21 and 46. N. B. Dearle, *An Economic Chronicle of the Great War for Britain and Ireland 1914–1919* (Oxford: Oxford University Press, 1929), pp. 249–50. The resulting reports on meat cartels were critical of the American meat companies and of the Ministry of Food's purchase of American bacon in the autumn of 1919; 1920, Cmd. 1057 and 1921, Cmd. 1356.

9. Sir W. Beveridge, *British Food Control* (Oxford: Oxford University Press, 1928), pp. 282–4. Dearle, *op. cit.*, pp. 252–3 and 263–4.
10. 112 *HC Deb.* 5s, c. 73; 11 February 1919. Horne to Bonar Law, enclosing a file of papers for the debate on industrial unrest, 12 February 1919; Bonar Law Papers, 94/18.
11. 112 *HC Deb.* 5s, c. 374–84; 13 February 1919.
12. F. W. Gibbins to T. Jones, 22 February 1919; LG F/23/4/21. Ministry of Labour, 'The labour situation, week ending 12 March 1919' (GT 6974); CAB 24–76–366.
13. *The Times*, 14 February 1919. R. Charles, *The Development of Industrial Relations in Britain 1911–1939* (London: Hutchinson, 1973), pp. 232–3, K. Middlemas, *Politics in Industrial Society* (London: Deutsch, 1979), p. 139. For Bottomley, 112 *HC Deb.* 5s, c. 129; 12 February 1919.
14. Riddell's diary, 16 February 1919; Riddell Papers, Add. Ms. 62983, f. 48.
15. 'Proposed industrial enquiry' by A. C. Geddes (GT 6779), 11 February 1919; CAB 24–74–323. WC (533), 14 February 1919; CAB 23–9–70/71.
16. R. Lowe, *Adjusting to Democracy* (Oxford: Clarendon Press, 1986), p. 95.
17. *The Times*, 18 February 1919.
18. *The Times*, 28 February 1919. *Report on Conciliation and Arbitration 1919*, pp. 35–6. Charles, *op. cit.*, pp. 236–8. A. Gleason, *What the Workers Want* (New York: Harcourt, Brace and Howe, 1920), pp. 70–3. E. Halevé, *The Era of Tyrannies* (London: Allen Lane, 1965), pp. 116–22.
19. *Lord Riddell's Intimate Diary of the Peace Conference and After* (London: Gollancz, 1933), pp. 27–8.
20. *Daily News*, 5 March 1919. Lloyd George was present at the War Cabinet meeting which approved the policy outlined in his letter – see W.C. (557), 16 April 1919; CAB 23–10–13. The War Cabinet was still willing to take some action on the Conference's recommendations in late May – W.C. (573), 29 May 1919; CAB 23–10–67.
21. Charles, *op. cit.*, pp. 240–4. Industrial Conference, Provisional Joint Committee Report, 1919 Cmd. 501, xxiv, 21. *The Daily Telegraph*, 5 April 1919.
22. *Daily Herald*, 2 May 1919.
23. *New Statesman*, 10 May 1919, pp. 135–6.
24. R. Lowe, 'The failure of consensus in Britain: the National Industrial Conference, 1919–1921', *Historical Journal*, 21 (1978), pp. 649–75.
25. Jones to Hankey, 27 February 1919; K. Middlemas (ed.), *Thomas Jones: Whitehall Diary*, vol. 1 (London: Oxford University Press, 1969), p. 79.
26. Entry for 12 August 1917; *Lord Riddell's War Diary* (London: Nicholson and Watson, 1933), p. 265, and cited by Lowe, *op. cit.*, pp. 659 and 672.
27. Lowe, *op. cit.*, pp. 665–7.
28. 'Another "faked" conference', *Daily Herald*, 22 February 1919.

29. P. S. Bagwell, *The Transport Revolution* (London: Batsford, 1974), pp. 241–5. K. Grieves, *Sir Eric Geddes* (Manchester: Manchester University Press, 1989), pp. 78–82.
30. Riddell's diary, 2 March 1919; Riddell Papers, Add. Ms. 62983, f. 63.
31. 112 *HC Deb*. 5s, c. 76–81; 11 February 1919.
32. *Ibid*., c. 84. *Morning Post*, 8 and 12 February 1919.
33. The miner's demands are reprinted in G. D. H. Cole, *Labour in the Coal Mining Industry 1914–1921* (Oxford: Oxford University Press, 1923), pp. 70–2. R. Page Arnot, *The Miners: Years of Struggle* (London: Allen & Unwin, 1953), pp. 184–5 and his *South Wales Miners*, vol. 2 (Cardiff: Cymric Federation Press, 1975), pp. 153–4. J. R. Raynes, *Coal and its Conflicts* (London: Benn, 1928), pp. 159–60. B. Bribicevic, *The Demand for Workers' Control in the Railway, Mining and Engineering Industries 1910–1922*, unpublished Oxford D.Phil., 1957, p. 334.
34. WC (523), 31 January 1919; CAB 23–9–36.
35. WC (529), 7 February 1919; CAB 23–9–57/9.
36. Jones to Hankey, 10 February 1919; *Whitehall Diary*, vol. 1, p. 76.
37. WC (530), 10 February 1919; CAB 23–9–62.
38. WC (529), 7 February 1919; CAB 23–9–58.
39. *The Times*, 17 February 1919. Arnot, *Years of Struggle*, pp. 185–6. *Report on Conciliation and Arbitration 1919*, pp. 10–11.
40. *The Times*, 21 and 22 February 1919. A Bevan, *In Place of Fear* (London: Heinemann, 1952), pp. 20–1.
41. Beatrice Webb's diary, 22 February 1919; M. Cole (ed.), *Beatrice Webb's Diaries 1912–1924* (London: Longmans, Green, 1952), pp. 146–51. The dinner took place on 20 not 22 February as suggested in S. Armitage's otherwise shrewd account of the Sankey Commission in *The Politics of Decontrol: Britain and the United States* (London: Weidenfeld and Nicolson, 1969), pp. 116–28. With the Webbs, Lloyd George again mixed threats with his vague promises, warning, 'We shall beat them – we control the food.'
42. *Lord Riddell's Intimate Diary*, p. 24.
43. 24 February 1919; 112 *HC Deb*. 5s, c. 1441–51.
44. T. Wilson (ed.), *The Political Diaries of C. P. Scott 1911–1928* (London: Collins, 1970), pp. 369–72.
45. Esher to Hankey, 15 February 1919; Hankey Papers, HNKY 4/11. A. J. P. Taylor (ed.), *Lloyd George: A Diary by Frances Stevenson* (London: Hutchinson, 1971), p. 169.
46. 'Shorthand notes', 25 February 1919 (GT 6887); CAB 24–75–371.
47. Arnot, *Years of Struggle*, p. 188 and *South Wales Miners*, vol. 2 (Cardiff: Cymric Federation Press, 1975), pp. 166–7. Armitage, *op. cit*., pp. 117–18.
48. Arnot, *South Wales Miners*, vol. 2, p. 167.
49. WC (538), 28 February 1919; CAB 23–9–91.
50. Taylor (ed.), *op. cit*., p. 169.
51. WC (536), 25 February 1919; CAB 23–9–83/4. Lloyd George had been kept fully informed of the railway negotiations. Eddison (Board of Trade) to Davies, 13 February 1919; LG F/2/6/7.

52. WC (534), 19 February 1919; CAB 23–9–75.
53. WC (536), 25 February 1919; CAB 23–9–84.
54. Lloyd George to Bonar Law, 29 January 1919; LG F/30/3/10. *The Times*, 9 February 1919. *Morning Post*, 10 February 1919. P. S. Bagwell, *The Railwaymen* (London: Allen & Unwin, 1963), p. 378. G. Blaxland, *J. H. Thomas: A Life for Unity* (London: Muller, 1964), pp. 121–2. N. McKillop, *The Lighted Flame* (London: Nelson, 1950), pp. 122–4.
55. Lloyd George to Bonar Law, 19 March 1919; LG F/30/3/31. Blaxland, *op. cit.*, p. 123. Stevenson diary, 18 March 1919; Taylor (ed.), *op. cit.*, p. 173.
56. WC (546 and 546A), 19 March 1919; CAB 23–9–112/13 and CAB 23–15–53/7.
57. WC (547 and 547A), 9 p.m., 19 March 1919; CAB 23–9–114/15 and CAB 23–15–58/9.
58. Bonar Law to Lloyd George, and Lloyd George to Bonar Law, 19 March 1919; LG F/30/3/30 and 31.
59. *Ibid.*
60. Message from Montagu to Lloyd George, 18 March 1919; LG F/40/2/46.
61. *Ibid.*, Derby to Balfour, 18 March 1919; Balfour Papers Add. Ms. 49744, f. 259. Lloyd George made his views on this clear once he saw the report. Lloyd George to Bonar Law, 20 March 1919; LG F/30/3/33 (and printed in the Cabinet minutes).
62. WC (547), 9 p.m. 19 March 1919; CAB 23–9–116.
63. Lloyd George to Bonar Law, 20 March 1919; LG F/30/3/32. Long to Lloyd George, 19 March 1919; LG F/33/2/28.
64. Bonar Law to Lloyd George, 20 March 1919; Bonar Law Papers, 101/3/31 and WC (548), 20 March 1919; CAB 23–9–117.
65. *Coal Industry Commission, Interim Report* (1919 Cmd., 359). WC (548), 6 p.m., 20 March 1919; CAB 23–9–116/19. Lloyd George urged even stronger condemnation of the current system of ownership and working in Bonar Law's statement. Lloyd George to Bonar Law, 20 March 1919; LG F/30/3/33 and CAB 23–9–118.
66. Cole, *op. cit.*, pp. 87–8.
67. Official Report of the Conference with the Triple Alliance at 10 Downing Street, 22 March 1919; copy in Tom Jones Papers, C/5/61.
68. Bonar Law to Lloyd George, 22 March 1919; LG F/30/3/34.
69. Tom Jones to Lloyd George, 24 March 1919; LG F/23/4/42. Jones to Hankey, 26 March 1919; *Whitehall Diary*, vol. 1, p. 82.
70. WC (551), 25 March 1919; CAB 23–9–126/7. Arnot, *Years of Struggle*, pp. 201–2.
71. Bonar Law to Lloyd George, 27 March 1919; LG F/30/3/37.
72. *Coal Industry Commission, Interim Report*. WC (551), 25 March 1919; CAB 23–9–127.

7
Adopting a tougher stance towards Labour, April–October 1919

Although the threat of an imminent Triple Alliance strike receded with the settlements of late March 1919, the likelihood of a major clash in the future remained. Indeed, such a clash appeared probable when the Sankey Commission produced its second report on 20 May. But it was in the railways rather than coal where a major dispute with a Triple Alliance union came with the railway strike of late September–early October 1919. The government chose to take this as a serious challenge to its authority, even though it was a one-industry dispute which was not marked by co-ordinated action across several economically strategic industries. But by autumn 1919 the government had become markedly less willing to make concessions to labour.

Lloyd George's prime concern during the spring and early summer of 1919 was negotiating the peace treaty. When resisting pressure to return to England at the time of Sankey's Interim Report, he commented to Riddell, 'The Peace Conference will re-act on Labour.' Riddell, more dramatically, observed, 'It looks as if it is going to be a race between peace and anarchy. Until peace is signed the world will not settle down to work.'[1] The problem of serious social unrest in the defeated countries in part was of the Allies' devising, as the blockade caused extreme privation. Lloyd George was anxious that the blockade should be lifted as quickly as possible. He had warned the Supreme War Council on 8 March that by allowing starvation 'the Allies were sowing hatred for the future' and 'were simply encouraging elements of disruption and anarchism. It was like stirring up an influenza puddle, just next door to one's self.' He had argued,

> As long as order was maintained in Germany, a breakwater would exist between the countries of the Allies and the waters of revolution beyond. But once that breakwater was swept away, he could not speak for France, but trembled for his own country.

While he was probably overstating his concern for Britain in order to impress the French with the need for moderation, nevertheless he was airing a widespread concern among the Allies. Thus on 27 March the Italian General Armando Diaz observed to the 'big four' (Clemenceau, Lloyd George, Orlando and Wilson) 'Bolshevism is a popular movement which appears wherever food is scarce and central authority is weak.'[2]

From late March Lloyd George argued the case for a moderate and speedy settlement with Germany. The timing of his move was linked to fears arising from the coming to power of Bela Kun in Hungary and from the possibility that similar regimes would take over in Germany and Austria. The mood among the peacemakers was captured well by Ray Stannard Baker of the American delegation, who noted in his diary on 23 March,

> Great anxiety here lest the peace be delayed until the whole world is aflame with anarchy. Yesterday we had news of the Hungarian revolution, with the accession to power of the Bolsheviks; Egypt is in rebellion and the British industrial situation is acute. . . .[3]

It is quite likely that Lloyd George gauged this to be the right time to try to secure less punitive peace terms for Germany. As Arno J. Mayer has commented, 'at one time or another most delegations at the Paris Peace Conference wielded the spectre of Bolshevism as a weapon and a threat'.[4]

Generally Lloyd George was not over alarmed by the spread of Bolshevism among the defeated countries. Indeed, he told his colleagues on the Council of Four that he could see no reason to suppress the Hungarian regime. In his opinion, 'few countries need a revolution so badly.' For he had been informed 'that its system of land tenure is the worst in all Europe. The peasants are oppressed as they were in the Middle Ages and the *droit du seigneur* still exists.' In contrast Lloyd George pointed to the efficacy of reform in Britain. He bragged,

> I know something of the Bolshevik peril in our countries; for several weeks I have been combating it myself . . . I am fighting Bolshevism, not by force, but by seeking a way to satisfy the legitimate aspirations which may have given it birth.
>
> As a result, trades unionists such as Smillie . . . , who might have become

formidable, have in the end helped us to avoid a conflict. The English capitalists, thank God!, are frightened; this makes them reasonable.[5]

Lloyd George's natural sympathies were for a moderate peace settlement which would not embitter the defeated countries. He resisted demands to make Germany pay the whole cost of the war, instead urging that the sum finally determined must be within Germany's capacity to pay. But, when faced with a strong political wind blowing in favour of tougher demands during the 1918 general election, he had trimmed. On 11 December 1918 he had observed, 'she is wealthier ... she has a greater capacity, than we have given her credit for. . . . If that is so, you may find that the capacity will go a pretty long way.'[6] This was but one of many instances of Lloyd George operating on the dictum that politics is the art of the possible. During the post-war years, as at other times, Lloyd George tilted one way then another according to the nuances of domestic political circumstances. After December 1918 he had to work with his large coalition majority, but on peace issues occasionally he tried to redress the balance by appealing to the constituency that was committed to President Wilson's ideals of a democratic peace settlement, one which included Labour, Nonconformist and other church circles. In such moves he was also asserting his personal political standing and emphasising that the Conservatives were not the only part of the coalition.

Lloyd George's views as to the basic elements of a post-war settlement were set out in a memorandum of 25 March 1919, drafted during a weekend retreat in the Forest of Fontainebleau with Hankey, Henry Wilson, Montagu and Philip Kerr. The memorandum rebutted French demands for massive reparations and for removing parts of Germany by border changes. On reparations, Lloyd George urged that Germany should pay what she was capable of paying, rather than the total cost of the war, and that 'the duration for the payments ... ought to disappear if possible with the generation which made the war.' Rather than divide Germany, Lloyd George suggested that France's fears should be met by the British Empire and the United States giving her 'a guarantee against the possibility of a new German aggression' above and beyond any security afforded by the creation of the League of Nations. He warned, 'I cannot conceive any greater cause of future war than that the German people ... should be surrounded by a number of small states ..., each of them containing large masses of Germans clamouring for reunion with their native land.'[7]

In pressing for a less punitive settlement with Germany Lloyd George was aware that he was putting political strain on his coalition government. Earlier he had clashed with Bonar Law over Russia. On 17 January, Bonar Law had warned him of the strength of Conservative Party feeling on any official dealing with Lenin's government and that to persist in such action would 'break your government'. According to Sir William Wiseman, who had been Head of British Intelligence in the United States during the war, Lloyd George flared up at once and said that 'if that is the case the government had better be broken'. Now, in late March 1919, on reparations Lloyd George was just as willing to assert his independence. He commented in the Council of Four on 26 March,

> It will be just as difficult for me as for M. Clemenceau to dissipate the illusions which are prevalent in the matter of reparations. Four hundred members of the British Parliament have sworn to extract from Germany up to the last penny of what is due; I shall have to face them.[8]

Perhaps the response of his Conservative backbenchers was more vehement than Lloyd George expected. Perhaps not. For Lloyd George gave an off-the-record interview on his policy towards Germany to a journalist working for the Asquithian *Westminster Gazette* which was published on 31 March. However, it was a briefing which transparently came from him. In urging 'a sane peace' in such a way, Lloyd George was appealing to the supporters of Woodrow Wilson, the Labour Party and non-Coalition Liberals. Moreover, two by-election results showed Lloyd George the way the political wind was blowing. At West Derby (Liverpool) on 26 February, the Labour candidate reduced a Coalition majority from 6,004 to 1,392 (on a swing to Labour of 10.9 per cent), and at West Leyton (Essex), when the result of the poll was announced on 14 March an Asquithian Liberal overturned a 5,668 majority in a straight fight, and won by 2,019 (on a swing to Liberal of 24.7 per cent). According to Wickham Steed, the new editor of *The Times*, 'On March 17th, . . . Lloyd George was so upset by . . . West Leyton that he proposed to return to London at once and leave the Peace Conference to look after itself.'[9]

He did return to London on 14 April 1919 to face Conservative MPs in revolt over his policy to both Germany and Russia. William

Kennedy Jones, a Coalition Conservative MP, had secured the signature of 200, and eventually 370, MPs to a telegram to Lloyd George urging him to stick to his election pledge 'to present the bill in full' to Germany. As Kennedy Jones had long been an associate of Northcliffe, helping him in Northcliffe's early ownership of the *Evening News*, *Daily Mirror* and *Daily Mail* and briefly editing the first, Lloyd George judged that this was another attempt by Northcliffe to destabilise his premiership. The two men had fallen out over Northcliffe's desire to play a major role at the Peace Conference and his claims to have a say in the appointment of ministers. Thereafter the Northcliffe press's campaigns to maximise Germany's reparations and vilify any peaceable dealings with the Bolsheviks had limited his room for manoeuvre at the Peace Conference.[10]

Lloyd George drafted a reply to Kennedy Jones's telegram in which he asserted that the government would 'stand faithfully by all the pledges . . . in respect of the whole peace terms and of the social programme'. Perhaps that draft was intended to impress upon Bonar Law that he, Lloyd George, was not simply an appendage of the Coalition Unionists. The reply which was sent omitted the details as to the election pledges; for, as Lloyd George later recalled, 'Bonar Law thought that would be unnecessarily provocative in the state of the party's mind at that moment.'[11]

However it is quite likely that Lloyd George or his immediate entourage fed the *Evening News* a story ahead of the debate which in effect warned the Conservatives not to take for granted his co-operation with them. Under the heading 'A general election this year' the paper's political correspondent wrote, 'I am not prophesying without knowledge. Mr. Lloyd George will leave the Coalition as at present constituted.' The writer asserted, 'His heart is bound up with Liberalism. Of that there is no doubt'. The writer then predicted, in a style very like Lloyd George's own, the appeal that Lloyd George would make in such a general election:

> I am tired of these reactionary elements, these vested prejudices. They trim and prune my social programme until the tree of promise looks unlikely to yield fruit in due season.
>
> I stick by my programme. I ask you to endorse it. I will choose the men who will carry it out and that quickly.
>
> He will make a bid for Labour. He will say that the principle of nationalisation is accepted by him so far as mines and railroads, and possibly shipping, are concerned. Labour (he will say) must join forces with him in order to make a success of nationalisation against the enemies of it.

A Centre Party, under the leadership of Mr. Lloyd George, is quite possible.[12]

It is difficult to avoid the conclusion that this was Lloyd George's warning to the Conservatives, even to Bonar Law (given he was a ship-owner), that they needed him as an electoral asset as much as he needed them. Indeed, commenting on Lloyd George's manoeuvres before facing Parliament J. H. Thomas praised him for the way he 'had given the wild Jingoes of the House the offer of an appeal to the country'.[13]

In facing his parliamentary critics on 16 April Lloyd George was giving himself considerable freedom of action for the remainder of the Peace Conference, because a challenge of the Kennedy Jones kind could only be mounted once. Perhaps the Maurice Debate of 1918 had taught Lloyd George the benefits of defeating serious criticism in what amounted to a House of Commons vote of confidence in his premiership. As on the earlier occasion, he could be secure in thinking there was no obvious acceptable alternative to himself. Indeed, he asked the Council of Four, who was there other than Lord Northcliffe or Horatio Bottomley to take his place? As for Lloyd George's attitude to criticism at this time, Riddell noted on 9 April, 'Lloyd George is eager to do his best for his country but he wants to act in secret without criticism or interference from the public – a sort of mild dictatorship.'[14]

On 16 April Lloyd George made one of his most successful parliamentary speeches. In it he defended his policy at the Paris Peace Conference, evaded the truth as to his knowledge of a peace mission to the Bolsheviks undertaken by the American diplomat William Bullitt, avoided any detailed mention of reparations and ridiculed Lord Northcliffe. He took almost malicious delight in attacking Northcliffe, making a calculated and determined effort to discredit the persistent criticism that he had suffered from *The Times* and Northcliffe's other newspapers.[15]

Lloyd George drew on his considerable political prestige, evidenced in both his general election triumph and his role as a major world statesman, to round on his critics. And these critics were in the ranks of his supporters. In so doing, his hand was strengthened by another by-election result. On 10 April, at Hull Central, an Asquithian Liberal had won by 917 votes (on a swing to Liberal of 32.9 per cent) a seat which had been Conservative since its creation in 1885, and one which the Coalition candidate had held only four months earlier with a majority of 10,371. The opposition parties in Parliament did not attack Lloyd George's statement of 16 April. Indeed, Colonel Josiah Wedgwood, who finally left the Asquithian Liberals for the Independent Labour Party later that week, said,

> The Prime Minister, in spite of all the yapping of the Press and the telegraphing of his supporters, has maintained an even course absolutely in accordance with his Liberal past in backing up the Liberal ideas of President Wilson, and doing his best to re-establish the world on the basis of justice and self-determination.[16]

When he made efforts to achieve such a settlement Lloyd George had the support of Henderson, MacDonald, Lansbury and other leading Labour Party figures. A just reconstruction of international relations was one of the major priorities of the Labour Party after the disappointments of the 1918 general election results. Those such as Arthur Henderson, who were concerned to construct a powerful democratic Labour challenge for power, devoted much time both to the cause of a democratic peace and to rebuilding the Second International. The two were very much linked.

Before the First World War had ended, an inter-Allied Labour and socialist conference held in February 1918 had set up a small commission (initially of three, including Henderson) 'to secure from all the governments a promise that at least one representative of Labour and Socialism will be included in the official representation' at the Peace Conference and to organise a Labour and socialist conference 'to sit concurrently with the official'. In the event Lloyd George took George Barnes, his major Coalition Labour colleague, with him to Paris as his gesture to a Labour presence. However, he did agree that passports would be issued for the separate Labour and socialist conference if it were held in a neutral country. Subsequently, on 1 January 1919, Henderson announced that the conference would meet in Switzerland and its chief task 'would be to formulate a charter of international labour legislation which the Peace Conference would be invited to incorporate in the treaty'. At the end of January Balfour did invite Henderson to stop off in Paris *en route* to this conference in Berne, to advise the British members of the Allied Commission which was formulating the International Labour Charter.[17]

From the start of 1919 the British Labour movement campaigned for a League of Nations as an integral part of the peace settlement. The first of a series of rallies was held at the Albert Hall on 2 January, with Henderson and MacDonald as the major speakers. Henderson declared in his speech,

> Labour in this country, and . . . throughout the world, realises that the only path to security and enduring peace lies through the setting up immediately . . . a League of Free Peoples. Labour desires to be done with the past and all its evils.[18]

This was to be a theme echoed at the Berne Conference and at a special TUC and Labour Party Conference held on 3 April to consider the Covenant of the League of Nations. Thus the Labour Party came to be very clearly identified with the cause of a moderate peace settlement. So much so that in early June Lloyd George had to deny that either Henderson or MacDonald had pressurised him successfully to modify the Peace Treaty to be more favourable to Germany.[19]

In reality there were substantial differences between the approach of the Labour Party leadership and Lloyd George to other aspects of peacemaking. The British delegation at the Berne Conference declared its support for Home Rule not only for Ireland but also for India, Egypt and Cyprus. The Berne Conference's Committee of Action, which included Henderson, later specifically observed that 'the disposal of the German Colonies and the denial of a mandate by the League of Nations will be universally regarded as nothing more nor less than Imperialism satisfying itself with the spoils of war.' The Parliamentary Labour Party and the National Executive of the Labour Party issued a manifesto on 1 June 1919 in which they condemned the proposed preliminary peace treaty, observing that it 'is defective not so much because of this or that detail of wrong done, but fundamentally, in that it accepts and, indeed, is based upon the very political principles which were the ultimate cause of the war.' They also argued that a League of Nations 'to be effective should be . . . inclusive of all free peoples, and not . . . a restricted instrument of the victorious coalition'.[20]

In contrast Lloyd George had few, if any scruples, in acquiring extra territory for the British Empire from Germany and Turkey. Thus in conversation with Auckland Geddes and Riddell on 23 April, he remarked that it was said of Britain that in wars she 'always comes out of it with a nice fat profit'. He commented, 'surely we have nothing to complain of in this war. We shall get Mesopotamia, Palestine, the German colonies in South Africa and the islands in the Pacific, including one containing mineral deposits of great value.' When Geddes objected that to develop them those territories would require much capital, Lloyd George observed, 'I am told that Mesopotamia contains some of the richest oil fields in the world. As to trade, there are plenty of orders and if our merchants and manufacturers know their business, they will get them.'[21]

While the Labour Party was successful in making itself the most significant political force in Britain committed to a democratic and idealistic peace, in other respects it was not performing well. Henderson aired some of its problems in an uncharacteristically despondent letter he wrote to Sidney Webb on 17 May,

> The divisions in our ranks which show themselves not only nationally but internationally are very trying. Then the Party in the House is doing so badly I sometimes think that the measure of solidarity necessary for success will never be forthcoming. What with the prospect of a revival of Asquithian Liberalism and so many of the Right of our own Party changing to the Coalition the prospects of the next election which may be less than a year [away] are not good. We appear to be leaderless in the House and no better in the country, and nobody in the Executive or out of it seems to care....[22]

Most of the old Labour leadership had lost their seats in the 1918 general election. The Parliamentary Party continued to be led by Willie Adamson, who had succeeded Henderson in 1917. Adamson owed this position to his being a trade union figure and, more particularly, a miner. In the 1918 general election forty-nine of the fifty-seven elected Labour candidates were trade union sponsored, and twenty-five of these were backed by the Miners' Federation. Beatrice Webb deemed Adamson to be 'respectable but dull-witted' and G. D. H. Cole commented that he was 'innocuous'.[23] The most effective Labour speakers in the House were Jimmy Clynes, the Deputy Leader, and J. H. Thomas.

The divisions which caused Henderson such anguish, both nationally and internationally, were over whether socialism should be achieved by parliamentary means or by revolution. This issue was debated by supporters of the Second International at the Berne Conference as the choice between 'democracy and dictatorship'. Henderson had made the unequivocal exclusion of Bolshevism a condition of the Labour Party's support for the reconstruction of the Second International. At Berne on 10 February he was reported as stating, 'the Bolsheviks were substituting a tyranny of anarchism for the tyranny of capitalism. He objected to oppression, suppression and repression whether from above or below. Bolshevism was a practical negation of constructive socialism.'[24] While the British Labour Party came to be a major influence on the revived Second International, the Bolsheviks in March 1919 founded the Third International. This was to gain much support, especially as European labour movements became sickened by the Allied intervention in Russia.

Such international divisions were replicated within Britain. There were substantial disagreements within the British Labour movement as to the importance to be attached to parliamentary action and to trade union action for non-industrial as well as industrial matters. After the 1918 general election the Labour Party leadership was quick off the mark to condemn 'direct action' and to reaffirm its commitment to social change through parliamentary means. Thus J. H. Thomas, prominent as the leader of a Triple Alliance union as well as a member of the Parliamentary Labour Party, was described at the end of 1918 as 'using some very plain language' about 'the tendency in certain quarters to support industrial action because the number of Labour MPs is not larger'. Thomas then observed that, 'The total vote against the Coalition is the clearest possible indication that in the very near future we shall have a different result – indeed that we may easily, at the next election, govern.' Three days later, at Labour's Albert Hall rally in support of the League of Nations, Henderson said, 'if we had contested 600 seats under normal conditions, instead of 362, and if all the soldiers had been home to vote, I am not sure that we should not have been the largest party.' Such hopes helped to ensure that the Labour Party leadership distanced itself from extra-parliamentary action. There was some truth in Beatrice Webb's observation of the parliamentary leadership, that 'they were intensely irritated at the labour unrest in the country – took it as a personal insult to themselves.'[25]

In the first major debates of the new Parliament the Labour leadership went to considerable lengths to emphasise that it was moderate and was fit to be considered the alternative government. Thus this strategy, often ascribed to MacDonald, was adopted by the Parliamentary Labour Party leadership well before his return to

Parliament in 1922. Willie Adamson stated, 'As a constitutionalist, I speak for a party that will not give encouragement either to revolution or to unofficial action in the Labour Movement.' He went on to say that 'the small band of revolutionaries' who were 'in the ranks of the working classes' and the 'small band of men who are out to upset the officials' of the trade union movement 'represent a very small proportion of the Labour Movement'. Clynes even declared, 'I agree fully with the Prime Minister that workingmen can make extravagant claims . . . I have personally resisted those claims . . . and I say to organised Labour that it can make the great mistake of asking and pressing for too much at one time.' He went on to praise Whitley councils, saying

> Hundreds of these industrial councils have been established, and I want to see them followed by corresponding councils in the districts and eventually to see in the workshops committees of men who will act with the management in a spirit of co-operation, who will act not in any frame of mind of revolt against the firm or the heads of it, but with a desire jointly to create harmony and produce the best fruits that can be brought from the joint efforts of those who may be concerned in the shop.[26]

Such Labour Party leadership hardly deserved to be confused with Bolshevik agitators.

Henderson, in his complaints of mid-July 1919, had expressed worry about the haemorrhaging of trade union support to the Coalition. In the early months of 1919 the National Democratic Party, which had gained ten seats in the general election, could still be seen as a challenger for working-class votes. Its parliamentary membership included three miners – C. B. Stanton (Aberdare), James Walton (Don Valley) and Matt Simm (Wallsend) – as well as such other trade union figures as James Seddon, a former president of both the TUC and the Union of Shop Assistants, Charles Jesson, a former organiser of the Musicians' Union and Eldred Hallas, a leading figure in general unions in Birmingham. In February the National Democratic Party condemned the MFGB's threat of a mining strike and issued an appeal to miners which included such sentiments as, 'A stoppage of work now would help Germany and partly undo the work and sacrifices of your men on the battlefield.'[27]

While the National Democratic Party was the most successful 'patriotic labour' body in action in early 1919, it was not the only one. Indeed, at the AGM of a body calling itself the Constitutional

Labour Party it was observed 'that there are several Labour Parties in existence.' That one summed up its position as 'urging the working classes to present their demands in a constitutional manner, to maintain national unity, to reject the advice of fanatics, internationalists and revolutionaries, to remove alien agitators and punish trade union defaulters.' Alongside mushroom bodies of this variety, there were Coalition Liberal attempts to hold on to working-class loyalties. On 25 January Sir Edgar Jones, Merthyr's Coalition Liberal MP, chaired a meeting to set up the Welsh Democratic League which had the object 'to fight Bolshevists and Syndicalists in their headquarters'. Curiously, this inaugural meeting was held in Paddington, even though 'the very heart of South Wales Bolshevist activity' was identified as being at Tonypandy where Jones and his associates proposed to locate their head office. When Jones did not stand again in the 1922 general election a Liberal describing himself as an 'Independent and Anti-Socialist' candidate failed to hold the seat against Labour.

Moreover, within the Parliamentary Labour Party, members of the National Socialist Party (which had splintered away from the British Socialist Party and was affiliated to the Labour Party) campaigned against Bolshevism with the same 'patriotic' fervour with which they had denounced the Hun during the war. In mid-February five MPs – Arthur Hayday, Dan Irving, Jack Jones, James O'Grady and Ben Tillett – wrote to the editor of the right-wing *Morning Post* stating 'that the antidote to Bolshevism must and should come not from the government or from the employing class but from the workers themselves' and adding that 'the National Socialist Party is again called upon to take the lead.'[28]

In early 1919 Adamson, Henderson, Clynes, Thomas and the other Labour Party leaders were not far apart from the various groups of super-patriots on many issues which worried the propertied classes. They all condemned Bolshevism abroad and militant unofficial strike action at home. They all pressed for social reconstruction and for harmony between employers and employed in industry. Indeed, with regard to industrial harmony, Clynes, Henderson and others went a very considerable way, not only in participating in the National Industrial Conference but in the National Alliance of Employers and Employed, which had been formed in December 1916.

The prime mover in setting up the National Alliance had been the

Federation of British Industries (FBI). In so doing the FBI was promoting one of its aims, expressed in its rules as:

> The promotion and encouragement of free and unrestricted communication between masters and workmen with a view to the establishment of amicable arrangements . . . and to the avoidance and settlement of strikes and all other forms of industrial warfare between masters and workmen.

The employers' side of the National Alliance's Executive Committee included many of the FBI's leading figures such as Huth Jackson, Dudley Docker and Sir Vincent Caillard. On the Labour side there were W. A. Appleton, the leading figure of the General Federation of Trade Unions, Charles Duncan MP, of the Workers' Union, and the ultra-patriot, Havelock Wilson, the leading figure of the Sailors' and Firemen's Union.[29] If at first the Labour side had seemed largely like 'a gathering of the executive council of the General Federation of Trade Unions', after the end of the war the Alliance appears to have attracted support from many of the Labour Party's leaders.[30] Presumably Clynes, Henderson and Thomas were attracted by the support men such as Dudley Docker gave to Whitley councils and by the hostility they expressed to Lloyd George's government. They were either not aware of, or were not put off by, the fact that these same industrialists gave financial backing to anti-Labour bodies such as the British Commonwealth Union, the British Workers' League and the National Democratic Party. In late January 1919 Clynes contributed a piece entitled 'The folly of Ca' Canny' and Henderson one entitled 'Industrial strife fatal' to the first issue of the National Alliance's journal *Unity*. Henderson, in his article, reasserted his lifelong belief in co-operation in industrial relations. He commented, 'we cannot stand for the substitution of reason and goodwill for force in international relations and use the weapons of force in the reconstruction of our own social and economic life.' He concluded, 'What we have all to recognise is that this war has sounded the death-knell of class rule in politics and industry.'[31]

Henderson's views were shared by many employers in the early part of 1919. They recognised that there was a great popular groundswell of support for major social and industrial change and also for heavy taxation of excessive profits made during the war. But there was also some alarm at the support for militant trade unionism. This mood was reflected in the comments of Leo Amery, a Conservative MP, in April

1919 after Whitley had addressed a meeting on the subject of his councils. Amery noted in his diary,

> I spoke . . . pointing out that industry had become more immoral and inhuman before the end of the war and that his councils pointed the way to something that made industry based in justice and also humanly interesting to those concerned. I also hinted at a council of all the Whitley councils being the true Second Chamber of the future and the way of meeting the element of real need which underlies Bolshevism.[32]

For a while, there was an inclination among leading figures on both sides of industry towards co-operation, and this was reflected by the wide areas over which agreement was reached among the participants of the National Industrial Conference.

However, on the employers side there was increasing concern to improve British industry's competitiveness as their European rivals returned to normality. Right-wing exponents of industrial co-operation warned in *Industrial Peace* that 'Germany, in spite of sporadic outbreaks of Bolshevism will soon be straining every nerve to rebuild her economic prosperity' and so there was 'the danger of Germany ultimately turning military defeat into commercial conquest'.[33] Many employers felt that with the sizeable concessions on hours and wages made in 1919 enough had been ceded to labour. Indeed, in some industries the unions' strength was already weakening by mid-1919.[34]

In the immediate aftermath of war many employers were also keen to benefit from state aid. 'Home Rule for industry' was a good slogan against state intervention on behalf of their labour forces. But there was often little hesitation to call on the public purse to assist re-equipping and restructuring of their industries. Thus, for example, in January 1919 the heavy steel trade pressed to see either Lloyd George or Bonar Law. The Prime Minister's Office reported to Law,

> Their main point was that owing to the operations of the financial clauses of the Munitions Act and the Excess Profits Act the Heavy Steel Trade in Britain had been unable during the war to re-equip their plant in a manner comparable with America, France and Germany. Their existing plants . . . were quite unable to compete properly . . . and they said it would be difficult to find the money for the essential improvements entirely by raising British capital without burdening their industries in a manner which would make effective competition in the future with those countries difficult for British manufactures. The point really was whether it would

not be possible in some way to allow them to have greater concessions in respect of their capital developments.

They pointed out that they had suffered more than the shipowners or coalowners in being included in the Munitions Act and so subjected to its financial provisions prior to the passing of the Excess Profits Act.[35]

Similarly, while industrialists were vociferous in their complaints about the special wartime taxes, some were not slow to make clear their desire to reap any benefits as might be squeezed from the taxes. Thus one Ministry of Munitions official, while noting condemnation of the excess profits tax as 'unfair in its incidence, leads to extravagance and carelessness in management and has been an important factor in increasing prices', observed that there were several trades which expected to make losses in the next year or two, and that these trades wished the tax to remain so that they could write off such losses.[36]

Yet there was a growing reaction among many of the propertied classes against high taxes. This was especially aimed at public spending to meet the demands of the working class, whether on improved pay and working hours or social reconstruction. One irate colonel expressed such concern vividly to Austen Chamberlain, asserting that the levels of taxation of early 1919 were 'the first step in legalising Bolshevism'.[37] Concern at what was deemed to be inordinately high levels of taxation was also shared by many Coalition MPs. For many, it was far more palatable to insist that Germany pay the whole cost of the war than to agree to the popular clamour for more action against domestic war profiteers. As for Germany's ability to pay, Northcliffe bluntly put a common view among right-wing circles when he wrote, 'I, personally, have no intention of spending the rest of my life swotting to pay excess profits tax and supertax for the benefit of Germany, if I can help it. I do not believe the tales of German hard-up-ness.'[38] As the threat of revolution spreading from the continent of Europe receded, there was less inclination on the part of many of the beneficiaries of the 1918 general election to make social concessions of any kind. This was the case with regard to nationalisation, be it the mines or anywhere else.

Lloyd George's attitude to nationalisation of the coal mines hardened between April and his public rejection of the policy on 18 August 1919. Earlier he had given the leaders of the Miners' Federation the clear impression that a verdict in favour of nationalisation from the Sankey Commission would not be disagreeable to him. From April he was sphinx-like on the issue. This was not an unreasonable posture to adopt while a public enquiry was in progress. But it seems likely that Lloyd George had his nose to the political wind on this issue, as on some other matters, and kept his options open as long as he could.

In April 1919 Lloyd George appears to have felt that it was only a matter of time before the mines were nationalised. When Bonar Law complained on 11 April, 'The miners are raising troublesome points on the Sankey report. The owners will probably decline to agree to what is asked. That may force us into nationalisation before we are ready', Lloyd George replied, 'Well, if it does, that will not be very serious. It has to come. The state will have to shoulder the burden sooner or later.'[39] In May he was still reassuring Henderson as to his intentions. Henderson wrote to Sidney Webb, 'I came away from Paris with the feeling that there is one politician extremely anxious for the Report to be in our direction. It would be a great misfortune if we failed owing to our over-reaching ourselves and giving the impression that we are ready to act unjustly to any class of property.'[40]

At the end of the war Lloyd George and several of his ministerial colleagues had felt that some form of nationalisation for at least the railways was desirable. This was seen to be a matter of national efficiency. Churchill had observed to the Dundee Chamber of Commerce during the 1918 general election campaign, 'You cannot organise the great questions of land settlement, new industries and the extension of production unless the state has control of the means of transportation.' Lloyd George had expressed similar sentiments when the government's transport policies were discussed in the War Cabinet on 19 February.[41] In July, when the issue of nationalisation was especially sensitive, Churchill commented on his Dundee speech to Bonar Law,

> when I said it I understood that the matter had been so decided, for I had seen in the manifesto signed by you and the Prime Minister the expression 'Nationalisation of Railways' and I was not aware (as I had already gone North) that this expression was cut in the final revise. . . .
>
> I may add that I believe it to be a thoroughly sound policy and one which is inevitable in view of the control which the government has assumed over the property of the railway shareholders and the impossibility of relaxing that control. I believe that for practical purposes in the present position we should say, 'We are going to nationalise the railways, but we are not going to nationalise the mines.' We only lose by appearing ashamed of what we really are going to do.[42]

Within the government there was always more support for nationalising the railways. But the prospects of this were killed off by backbench hostility in the House of Commons, where there were forty-five MPs who were railway directors.

As for nationalising the coal mines, Lloyd George's attitude changed in line with public opinion – or at least the prevailing wisdom in political circles as to public opinion. In the early months of 1919 Conservative MPs were forced to admit 'the very great political pressure in favour of nationalisation'.[43] In March, during the Sankey Commission's daily sittings in the House of Lords, Smillie and the MFGB had little difficulty in making a powerful case against the coalowners. Lloyd George observed to Tom Jones that the hearings were 'arousing the social conscience in a way that no inquiry of modern times has succeeded in doing'.

Then, he believed that not only did public opinion feel that the existing system of ownership had been discredited but, as he told his War Cabinet colleagues, he 'understood privately that the coal owners agree with this view, but as they will have to be parties to bargaining with the government, they do not wish to handicap themselves by any statement at present'. Certainly there were some coal owners who resigned themselves to seeking generous compensation. The Earl of Crawford noted, after a board meeting of the Wigan Coal and Iron Company which discussed nationalisation, 'that bad as nationalisation would be for the country, expropriation on just terms would be a relief to the industry, for the conduct of business is made intolerable by the constant strife and bickering which prevails.'[44]

However, after the publication of the Commission's Interim Report on 20 March the tide began to turn against the MFGB. For one thing, the miners had secured substantial concessions. For another, the Mining Association of Great Britain (MAGB), which had appeared to be nonplussed at being expected to defend publicly its economic and social role during the first stage of the Sankey Commission, thereafter began to co-ordinate its responses to the issue of how the industry should be owned and run. It also began to counter the MFGB's appeal to public opinion.[45] Furthermore, the coal owners looked to other industrialists to support them. As one wrote on their behalf to Lord Weir,

> The principle at stake is the principle of private property which has hitherto been accepted in this country and against which the electorate has

not as yet pronounced. It has fallen to the coalowners to bear the brunt of the combined attack [by 'theorists' and 'revolutionaries'] on the principle of private property and they feel it to be their duty to enlighten the public as to the real issue which has become obscured by irrelevant matters as introduced into the proceedings at the Coal Commission and elsewhere.[46]

The Federation of British Industries (FBI) reviewed the issue of nationalisation and stated that it was 'averse to state management' but recognised 'that the public is entitled to some protection against possible exploitation by monopolies'. Hence it condemned state ownership but accepted the state providing 'only the amount of regulation necessary to prevent waste'. When government acceptance of the principle of nationalisation seemed to be imminent, industrialists put pressure on Coalition Conservative and Coalition Liberal MPs. Thus Dudley Docker, a leading figure in the FBI, complained to Sir Arthur Steel-Maitland, a junior minister, 'We feel very strongly that the Report from Justice Sankey with reference to the nationalisation of coal is most mischievous' and urged him to sign a House of Commons resolution that was going to be sent to Lloyd George and Bonar Law.[47]

Within the House of Commons many on the Right prepared to do battle to preserve the rights of private property. Sir Edward Carson reported to Lord Selborne in late June,

> The great difficulty has been to get members of this House of Commons to see that nothing effective can be done if each section affected only opposes when its own interest is concerned. I have been impressing upon them that you must get to the bed rock of principle and unite forces whenever the principle is assailed. I think they have begun to see this – and coal owners, dock trusts, roads, wagon owners are now uniting on the broad question of nationalisation or individual effort.[48]

From early in the Sankey Commission's proceedings, Bonar Law was having to reassure vested interests. In April he told a Conservative MP who represented the coal royalty owners that 'there is nothing in Sankey's Report which even suggests the idea of confiscation of royalties.' By June Bonar Law was distancing himself from Sankey, on the grounds that 'a very great amount of feeling has arisen against him on the part of those opposed to nationalisation.'[49]

Many of the middle class also abhorred the prospect of the nationalisation of the mines, regarding it as yet another concession to the power of organised labour. In May their insecurity was expressed in the formation of the Middle Class Union. Its constitution declared, 'We are being taxed out of existence. We are being exploited for the benefit of the lower classes or for the benefit of the financial groups and profiteers of the upper classes.' The miners were among the chief bogeymen of such groups and individuals, and remained so for the next seventy years. The Duke of Northumberland, a major coal owner who campaigned vigorously against the Sankey Commission, observed to Lord Esher,

> I feel there is a great mass of sound middle-class opinion to be appealed to if one only knew how. In reality Smillie and his friends are purely destructive. It is Bolshevism 'anglicised' and we are going into it gradually instead of at one bound like Russia. But the result will be the same.[50]

The MFGB's cause suffered not only because of the hostile reaction of vested interests and much of the middle class to nationalisation, but also because its opponents pointed both to low productivity in the mines and the loss of coal output through a major regional strike in Yorkshire. Much was made of low output. The government had hoped that output would rise once the March concessions on wages and hours had come into effect. This apparently did not occur. Lloyd George on 18 August, before announcing the government's rejection of nationalisation, made pronouncements on the economy on the theme, 'The cardinal feature of the moment . . . is that we are not paying our way. . . . We shall never pay our way until we increase production in this country.' He argued that coal was the key to the British economy's success: 'There could be no more serious blow at the business, the trade and the industry of this country than a diminution of output of coal.' He went on to assert that the reduction in coal output from the pre-war quantity was 'the oustanding feature of the moment'. Earlier, when he had discussed his proposed speech with his colleagues, he had identified diminution of output as being even more serious than strikes as an obstacle to national economic recovery.

This was a concern shared by many of his colleagues. In June Sir Joseph Maclay, the Shipping Controller, bluntly advised that the time had come 'when the government should intimate an immediate reduction in colliers' wages unless the colliers give an output of at least equal to pre-war conditions.' He added, 'They want something to bring them to their bearings. I incline to think a crisis would do good.' The War Cabinet's information in June suggested that output had dropped from 287 million tons in 1913 to 242 million tons in 1919, with exports falling from 77 to 28 million tons.[51]

Lloyd George also expressed great concern at the price of coal as it affected other industries' costs. He observed, 'A ton of coal raised in 1913 cost 10s at the pit head, on 16 July last it cost 26s.' While the government made more and more of the labour costs element in such price rises, it made less and less of the profits element. Initially, it had seemed that the government would be firm in restricting profits levels. In the House of Commons on 20 March Bonar Law had stated that the coal owners' profits would be limited to 1s 2d per ton, as had been recommended in Sankey's First Report. When the War Cabinet considered Sankey's Second Report on 8 July, Sir Auckland Geddes, President of the Board of Trade, pointed out that his department 'possessed no statutory powers to limit the coal-owners' profits and that the Treasury was bearing the cost of extra wages which the miners received'. He warned that the longer the government delayed in passing its planned Coal Mines (Control) Bill 'the more difficult would it be to recoup from the coal-owners the profits they were making over and above the 1s 2d per ton'. Profits per ton rose from an average 11½d for 1909–13 to 2s 8d in 1919.[52]

However, levels of profitability were distorted by state control and complicated by the abnormal demand overseas. At the War Cabinet meeting on 8 July the Coal Controller, Sir Evan Jones (Coalition Liberal MP for Pembrokeshire), advised ministers,

> It had been assumed that our profits on exported coal would be maintained, but unfortunately it had been found that the owners, who had now little interest in making good bargains, owing to the limitation of their profits, had been making advance agreements, as regards exported coal, at a price less than the market prices which had been formerly quoted. The effect of this was to reduce our average export profits. In some instances ... they had been able to nullify such action on the part of the owners by withholding export licences.

Notwithstanding Bonar Law's pledge on profit limitation, the Coal Controller also warned that such limitation

> involved such a degree of control as to be practically tantamount to nationalisation. It had all the vices and none of the advantages of nationalisation. The result of limiting profits was that the owners had no further interest in the cost of production or in the prices obtained for their coal, and threw back all the problems of management on the Coal

Controller. If there was a three years probationary period of this limitation of profit control, the owners would do all in their power to make it unworkable. It was all to their advantage to do this as the purchase of the mines by the state after three years depended on the success of this scheme, and such purchase they wish to hinder in every possible way.[53]

The coalowners campaigned vigorously against the profit limitation as well as against nationalisation. One owner urged a MAGB meeting that it should 'fight it out in Parliament' where 'the owning classes are more largely represented than they were in the last Parliament'. They put pressure on Lloyd George and other ministers, arguing that it was unfair that they alone of employers should in effect pay for social peace in this way. Lord Gainford, chief spokesperson for the MAGB and a former Liberal Cabinet minister, observed, 'We have strong arguments in the fact that the government themselves took a higher average figure under the Coal Agreement Act and that since then the rate per cent on all securities has considerably risen.' They thus took some satisfaction from Lloyd George's Commons statement of 18 August. In early September Sir Thomas Ratcliffe-Ellis, secretary and law-clerk to the MAGB, congratulated Gainford, 'so far as one can judge from what Mr Lloyd George said in his speech, he seems to have very largely adopted the suggestions you made to him.' Nevertheless in November 1919 the government did introduce legislation to limit coal profits, but took the opportunity to drop it when the MFGB opposed the measure as it would fail adequately to regulate the industry. On 14 November, ahead of the Bill being dropped, Lloyd George told a deputation from the owners that they would do well not to insist on public statements on profit limitation: 'I think the less said about it the better . . . the less you say the more you will get.'[54]

However, the government was very willing to make the most of the labour costs element in the price of coal. During the severe labour unrest at the start of the year all manner of people had suggested that the government might win over public opinion against trade unionists' wage and hours demands by emphasising the cost of such concessions to the consumer. Such advice flowed again against the MFGB in the early summer of 1919. The government had reason to be concerned, as Sir Adam Nimmo, on behalf of the coal owners, had successfully argued that the Treasury should pay Sankey's wages award.[55] At the War Cabinet meeting on 8 July much of the discussion centred on whether the anticipated annual deficit of £47 million arising from the reduction in hours and the pay settlement should be paid by the Exchequer or by the consumer. According to Tom Jones, Austen Chamberlain 'drew a most lurid picture of the country's financial position'. He urged that the consumer should pay, arguing

> It was impossible for the nation to live by the various sections of the community subsidising each other. The government had made a series of concessions to various industries, with the result that the normal course of production and distribution had been entirely upset. The solution was . . . to allow the public to realise what the increased costs of production meant to the state and therefore to themselves. He could not be a party to starting a further circle of subsidies.

Sir Eric Geddes expressed the view of most of his colleagues when he stated that 'he favoured putting up the price of coal to the full amount to the consumer immediately, as the sooner the country knew what they were up against the better.' His brother was even blunter: 'By administering such drastic medicine we might bring the community to a state of sanity.' The War Cabinet readily agreed to an announcement the next day of the government's intention of increasing the domestic price of a ton of coal by 6s. Lloyd George, who was unwell and at Criccieth, sent his approval.[56]

The MFGB and the Labour Party vigorously condemned what they felt was a crude measure to play off consumers against producers and one which would postpone a financial need for nationalisation. Moreover, the rapid announcement of the increase was deemed to be an attempt to influence the voters in a by-election at Swansea, East on 10 July.[57] Whether or not it did is hard to judge, but, in spite of a swing to Labour of 10.5 per cent, the Coalition Liberal candidate held the seat with a majority of 1,092 instead of the 4,730 of the 1918 general election. However, at a further by-election the following week at Bothwell (Lanark), on a swing to Labour of 19.7 per cent, Labour converted a Coalition Unionist majority of 332 into a Labour one of 7,168. But that was a mining seat where the government's coal-pricing policy was unlikely to be received favourably.

The Parliamentary Labour Party secured a debate on the forthcoming price rise in the Commons on 14 July. Before it, Lloyd George wrote to Bonar Law, 'I earnestly hope that you and Geddes will rub in the reduction of output. If the miners gave honest work for their pay this addition would not be necessary.' This Bonar Law did. Anticipating Labour protests that the miners must be given time to increase output, he offered to postpone the coal price rise for three months if the MFGB agreed to help secure both an increase in output and a no-strike guarantee for that period.[58]

The MFGB's Annual Conference, which met the following day, rejected his offer. It urged instead that production would be increased 'if the economies set forth in the First Sankey Report are effected and the recommendations of the majority of the Commissioners as to an immediate change of ownership and control in the mining industry be passed into law.' The following day the conference sent Bonar Law a resolution in which it noted 'the political and industrial pressure now being brought to bear upon the government' as to nationalisation and declared that 'whilst the miners are not fully satisfied with the report of Mr Justice Sankey' they would 'give the government their fullest support to carry out the recommendations of the majority report'. Having made a public display of willingness to consider options other than the 6s price rise, the War Cabinet of 18 July authorised Bonar Law to announce immediately that the increased price would come in with effect from 21 July.[59]

This rise in the domestic price of coal did much to help the government in undermining public support for the miners, but it did so at the cost of harming another government objective – helping British industry to compete overseas. Within a month Lloyd Goerge was being advised that the domestic coal price rise had been an economic mistake. The writer of one memorandum argued that in spite of the fall in output the 6s price rise was excessive, and observed,

> Every penny put on coal unnecessarily is an additional tax and restriction on our exports. Each ton of manufactured steel exported represents two to six tons of coal, and in a varying degree all manufactures exported are affected, and our competitive power in foreign markets aided or reduced according to the cost of coal.
>
> In an ordinary way, the safe course is to put on a figure which is certain to cover cost. But in the case of coal, particularly at this moment, when increasing exports and power of competition in foreign markets are life and death to the nation's future, the safe course is to keep the price of coal to our manufacturers at the lowest figure, even at the risk of some deficit to be borne out of national revenues.[60]

The rise in the price of domestic coal also cut across the government's efforts to foster a domestic spelter industry. During the war and immediately after it the Ministry of Munitions paid £56 to £60 per ton to maintain the industry, rather than to buy US spelter at £45 per ton. Ministers recognised that a sizeable rise in coal prices put the domestic smelting of zinc in jeopardy.[61]

In time it was clear that there had never been a need for the sharp 6s rise in the price of coal. By the autumn the government could no longer resist arguments to reduce the price of domestic coal – and this it did by 10s a ton. This was sufficiently astonishing a turnaround for Parliament to appoint independent accountants to investigate the figures on which both decisions were taken. Their report, sent to Lloyd George on 9 February 1920, was very damaging for Sir Evan Jones (who had resigned the previous autumn) and his department. It showed that the 6s price rise was based on an estimate of a selling price of 31s 9d per ton, whereas 'a safe estimate to have made at the time the calculations . . . were framed' would have been 48s 7d per ton. The prime error was a £30 million 'undervaluation of the proceeds to be obtained from exports and bunkers'.[62] These findings, combined with the government's rejection of the Sankey Commission majority report on nationalisation, did much to increase the Labour movement's distrust of the government.

The sharp rise in coal prices was not alone in alienating public opinion in July. A lengthy and major coal strike in Yorkshire also created hostility. It arose from arguments over the implementation of the Sankey Interim Report recommendations. Then the government and the MFGB had agreed that miners should not face reduced wages as a result of the reduction in hours from eight to seven. However, a serious situation arose after the Coal Controller, acting under orders from Sir Auckland Geddes, issued instructions that piece rates should be raised by no more than 10 per cent, not 14.3 per cent (i.e. one seventh). The MFGB therefore demanded to see Lloyd George. As he was ill, Bonar Law saw Smillie and his colleagues on 5 July. Bonar Law argued, 'We have a right to expect that if the working day be seven hours instead of eight hours there will not be the same amount of energy, but a little more energy per hour.' However, after hearing the MFGB's case the government agreed that a maximum of 12.5 per cent might be paid providing the national average remained at 10 per cent. However, in South Yorkshire the miners had already negotiated a 14.3 per cent advance with the owners, and in the county as a whole miners were pressing for a further concession because their hewing time was already shorter as allowance had been made at many pits for long walks to work. The Yorkshire

Miners' Association called a strike on 17 July.[63] The situation was made more serious by the safety-men withdrawing on 19 July, with subsequent flooding of mines until the government sent in 2,500 naval personnel to get the pumps working again. The government was angered by this local attempt to coerce better terms from them, especially as the MFGB was still in negotiaions over these issues. It was also faced with a major strike of miners in Derbyshire and lesser ones in parts of Scotland, Lancashire, Nottinghamshire, Northumberland, Kent and South Wales, though most of these were caused by other issues, and an imminent police strike. Lloyd George told the War Cabinet on 21 July,

> The present situation was practical, and not theoretical, Bolshevism, and must be dealt with a firm hand. He was rather inclined to agree that the mine owners were right, and that a fight had got to come; but if the government chose the present moment they must be certain that they were on firm ground and had public opinion behind them. . . . It would be unwise to rush into this trouble without being sure. The whole of the future of the country might be at stake, and if the government were beaten and the miners won, it would result in soviet government. A similar situation might result to that of the first days of the [February 1917] Revolution in Russia, and, although Parliament might remain, the real Parliament would be at the headquarters of the Miners' Federation in Russell Square. There must be no division in the public mind. . . . If a fight was to come, it must be certain beyond a doubt that the miners were in the wrong.[64]

By this time Cabinet ministers had clearly lost their patience with the miners. Lloyd George complained to his colleagues the next day that 'the miners seemed determined to strike, and seized on any excuse to "down tools".' Bonar Law responded by commenting that 'the reason for this was that the miners imagined that they could get satisfaction of any demands they liked to make by striking.'

Lloyd George and the War Cabinet set about making preparations so as to be ready if the 'big strike' in the coal industry took place. The War Cabinet agreed to his suggestion that all British ships carrying coal, which were then at sea, should be diverted to home ports. It also instructed the Food Controller not to distribute food in the Barnsley area, where co-op workers were on strike to get their war bonus transferred into their permanent wage rates. It further gave Sir Eric Geddes authority to announce a restriction of railway services in the strike areas and also to call together mayors in those areas in order to enforce restrictions on supplies of electric lighting, gas and water. The previous day Churchill had reported that he had ordered two divisions of the army on the Rhine to return to Britain, that a further two could be brought back if needed and that there were sixteen mobile columns within Britain which could be used.[65] Troops were sent to Leeds, Pontefract and Wakefield.

In view of their preparations and tough stance, the War Cabinet was embarrassed to learn that the Yorkshire coalowners wanted to end the strike by conceding the 14.3 per cent rise for piece rates. Sir Eric Geddes, whom Lloyd George had sent to Yorkshire to take control of the government's organisation against the strike, telegrammed the Prime Minister and urged him to see the leaders of the South and West Yorkshire Coal Owners' Associations. Lloyd George told the War Cabinet that if the owners did advise the government to concede 14.3 per cent 'it would create a serious situation . . . as the fact that such advice had been given was bound, sooner, or later, to be made public'. Chamberlain warned that for the government 'to go back on its decision . . . would condemn the government utterly and destroy its power to deal with further troubles'. By this time the government was less alarmed. Horne reported that Herbert Smith and many of the older Yorkshire miners were in a pacific mood and wanted the safety men to return and, furthermore, the Yorkshire dispute was not receiving support from the other coalfields. Sir Auckland Geddes, on the basis of information gained from Hartshorn, told his colleagues that other than those in South Wales, most miners would settle for 10 per cent, and those in Yorkshire, Lancashire and Cheshire would settle for 12.1 or 12.2 per cent.[66]

Lloyd George saw the MFGB leaders the next day, 24 July, and tried to get their support against the Yorkshire miners. With the War Cabinet's approval, he told them that the government would make a statement on their policy on nationalisation before Parliament went into recess for the summer. Lloyd George also made it very clear that he would not argue over which formula was used to arrive at piecerates as long as the hewer got the same wages as before the reduction in hours and there was no discrimination between the time-worker and the piece-worker. But he insisted to the MFGB 'that the government must have a definite proposal from them and they must stand by it.' Lloyd George told the War Cabinet, 'If the government had the Miners' Federation behind them in fighting the Yorkshire Association, it would be a very great advantage.' At the same time, Geddes reassured his colleagues with the view that 'the Yorkshire Association would not be able to continue the fight very long alone, as they were only paying 9s a week strike pay.'[67]

On the next day the government did agree with the MFGB a complicated formula for piece-rates which – according to G. D. H. Cole – 'granted practically what the Federation had asked for ... an increase of 14.2 per cent in piece-work prices as the equivalent of an hour's reduction, with proportionate increases for fractions of an hour where the reduction was actually less'. Having made such concessions and apparently settled the piece-rate issue, Lloyd George was very annoyed that the Yorkshire miners remained on strike demanding a settlement of other outstanding issues. After unsuccessfully pressing Smillie to intercede, the government then waited for the strike to collapse, making it clear that it would grant nothing more. After considerable disruption had been caused to other local industries, the South Yorkshire and West Yorkshire miners ended their strikes on 14 and 21 August respectively.[68]

While the Yorkshire dispute exasperated Lloyd George and did nothing to boost the miners' cause with public opinion, it was not a major factor in determining Lloyd George's decision on nationalisation of the mines. For Lloyd George had come to at least a provisional decision against nationalisation on 17 July, the day the Yorkshire strike began. That same day he held a small conference on the issue at Criccieth with two ministers, Sir Auckland Geddes and Sir Robert Horne and three advisers, Sir Maurice Hankey, Sir Hubert Llewellyn Smith (Chief Economic Adviser) and Professor Sydney Chapman (Assistant Secretary, Board of Trade). Lloyd George had summoned them to Criccieth to discuss trade policy as well as nationalisation. Ahead of the arrival of the others, Hankey had written to Tom Jones, 'the settlement of the nationalisation question is the root question of all our trade and labour difficulties.' After their discussion on nationalisation they came to the provisional decisions,

1. No nationalisation of the coal industry on a Post Office basis.
2. Nationalisation of mining royalties.
3. Social amelioration in mining districts as a charge on royalties of ungotten minerals.
4. Consultation with mining owners re. possibilities of combination by districts, and, if so, what arrangements to be made: e.g. division of profits after wages, charges, and dividends on capital.[69]

During his period of recuperation in Criccieth between 5 and 18

July Lloyd George reassessed several major political issues, not least his own political future now that the main peace treaty was signed. After his assertion of his own political stance against the Coalition Right over the peace negotiations in April there had been continued speculation as to his intentions. *The Spectator*, which was hostile to Lloyd George and the Coalition, predicted that as he was 'as tired of working with the Unionists as he was of working with the Liberals' he would make a bid to lead the Labour Party. This was fanciful or, indeed, malevolent.

Lloyd George, in his efforts to assert his independence from Conservative control, was more interested in appealing to that public opinion which had supported the Liberals in the past in order to strengthen his wing of the Coalition. With Asquith out of Parliament, he hoped to secure those people's backing for such policies as a moderate peace settlement, the resolution of Home Rule and social reconstruction. He was very willing to court leading Liberals who were outside Asquith's circle. Thus Haldane was drawn close to the government, was consulted by Sankey and received praise via Hankey from Lloyd George for his pre-war work as Secretary of State for War.[70] In looking to the residual strength in liberalism Lloyd George was further encouraged by a by-election result which suggested that a Liberal revival was underway. At Central Aberdeenshire on 16 April a Coalition Conservative majority of 6,004 was overturned when a Liberal defeated the Unionist candidate by 186 votes and held a Labour candidate to third place. Arthur Murray, a Coalition Liberal MP, observed of Lloyd George in late July,

> He does not himself desire a dissolution and an election this year; and I do not see any reason why there should be an election assuming that the government is not brought toppling by the coal strike lasting several months. But Lloyd George . . . already sees that the Coalition cannot go on for ever, and he will have to make up his mind in which direction he is going to swing. I have always felt that he would turn to the Left and endeavour to rush the Liberal situation in the country. . . . There has been some talk lately of a Centre Party, and on a recent occasion Winston [Churchill] met the party and delivered to it a long address.[71]

Churchill's initiative followed directly from discussions he had had with Lloyd George at Criccieth between 10 and 12 July. Churchill and Sir Henry Wilson had visited the Prime Minister to discuss policy towards Russia and the reorganisation of the Service Department.

Lloyd George appears to have diverted a little of Churchill's energies from intervention in Russia or planning to create the post of Secretary for Defence, which would be responsible for the navy, army, air force and supplies, by talking of consolidating a centre grouping which would embrace moderate Conservatives and amenable Asquithian Liberals. He had indicated his approval for moves to form such a Centre Party a few days earlier to Freddie Guest, the Coalition Liberal Whip.

Churchill aired this political possibility at the Criterion Restaurant on 15 July. He spoke of the need for 'a kind of bond of union' between the government's supporters, and argued that there was a need to maintain the unity of purpose engendered by the war and to avoid a relapse into sterile party conflict. In so doing he praised such cross-party moves of the past as those between his father and Joseph Chamberlain in the 1880s and the hitherto secret coalition talks initiated by Lloyd George in the summer of 1910. He condemned Asquith and Carson alike as men still stuck in pre-1914 politics, whereas he deemed Lloyd George to be 'the most necessary man this country has had for many years'. Churchill was soon urging Lloyd George to bring into the government the Conservative Lord Hugh Cecil and the Asquithian Liberal William Wedgwood Benn.[72] Churchill's talk of the desirability of 'national politics' rather than 'the violent partisan extravagances' of party politics amounted to a call for the consolidation of the Coalition government's supporters into a permanent body, which should act as a broad church offering a home to all but Bolsheviks and reactionaries.

Churchill clearly echoed Lloyd George in this. During his recuperative sojourn in Criccieth, Lloyd George reassessed both his government's policies and his own political prospects. By the time he left Criccieth he was committed to actions which would maintain the existing coalition. He saw it as having the political strength to deal with any serious challenges from organised labour, be it the miners or railwaymen separately, the Triple Alliance unions collectively or the police. He was willing to balance liberal approaches to the peace settlement, Ireland, housing and profiteering with public expenditure reductions and some measures of protection for British industry. He made clear his renewed commitment to a coalition of Liberal and Unionist policies to his War Cabinet colleagues in policy review discussions from 5 August onwards and to the general public on 18 August, in a three-hour speech at the end of the parliamentary session.

In his major House of Commons speech Lloyd George responded to middle-class anxieties concerning taxation by backing Austen Chamberlain's demands for economy. He urged, 'We must ruthlessly cut down all needless expenditure, public and private. . . .' Four weeks earlier he had been warned by Guest, when the latter had been reporting on discontent in the country, of the need for public economy, and in particular that 'business circles in Yorkshire (and the North generally) are peculiarly touchy on this point'. Lloyd George was clearly surprised when the Parliamentary Labour Party leader, Willie Adamson, urged reductions not only in the army and navy but in the civil service as well, thereby suggesting that there was a broader consensus for 'economy' in Parliament than he had expected.

Lloyd George followed up his speech by writing to all ministers, advising them,

> The time has come when each minister ought to make it clear to those under his control that if they cannot reduce expenditure, they must make room for somebody who can. That is the public temper, and it is right. . . . The numbers still employed in the public services have, in the aggregate, hardly decreased perceptibly since the war. That cannot be defended. The state of the National Finances is such that only what is indispensable to sound administration ought to be maintained. . . .

He required all his colleagues to report back on the matter by mid-September.[73]

Lloyd George ended his major House of Commons speech of 18 August with other pledges that pleased his Conservative supporters. He reaffirmed the government's intentions to carry out a series of trade measures which had been included in the Coalition's 1918 general election manifesto. That had specified that 'a preference will be given to our Colonies upon existing duties and upon any duties which, for our own purpose, may be subsequently imposed'; that the government intended 'to preserve and maintain where necessary . . . key industries'; and that it would provide 'security . . . against the unfair competition to which our industries may be subjected by the dumping of goods produced abroad and sold on our market below the cost of production'. When trade policy came before the War Cabinet on 8 August Barnes fruitlessly argued 'that the policy recommended by the President of the Board of Trade launched the government straight into Protection as against Free Trade.' But the move towards tariffs was already underway not only with the wartime measures but also with Austen Chamberlain's April 1919 budget. Of that budget, Chamberlain had commented, 'It *was* such a satisfaction to stand where Father had so often stood and to propose a definite preferential policy.'[74]

Lloyd George, who had always been a less than fervent advocate of Free Trade, at this time told friends that he was open-minded on the issue. Sir George Riddell, who talked to Lloyd George on the subject just before Geddes, Horne and the others visited him in Criccieth, noted in his diary.

> Evidently he has no policy. He is examining the question and feeling his way to a solution. He is impressed by the fact that certain trades may be ruined by the import of cheap foreign commodities, but on the other hand thinks that certain other trades will be ruined if the importation of these commodities is impeded. He instanced the steel trade on the one hand, and the tin plate trade on the other.
>
> He said that the steel and iron trades are making a strong effort to secure protection and have subscribed to a large fighting fund. He added, 'I do not like that. It makes me suspicious. I don't like being forced or influenced by such means.'[75]

But to many of his Coalition Liberal supporters such measures were anathema. Predictably the proposals outraged the Asquithian Liberals, and provided one of several occasions when Lord Gladstone indignantly observed, 'that almost any man would be preferable to L.G. as Prime Minister'.[76]

Lloyd George's declaration against the nationalisation of the mines was the major feature of the centre of his long speech in the Commons on 18 August, and it took its place beside these other policies which would appeal to Conservatives. Given the way that the Ways and Communications Bill was savaged in Parliament by representatives of the various vested interests in transport before it emerged in a much diminished and mild form as the Ministry of Transport Act on 15 August, Lloyd George could have had few illusions as to the likelihood of his government's ostensible supporters backing a Bill to nationalise the coal mines. Indeed, the Parliamentary situation was, as one Coalition Liberal MP observed in late July, that 'The Coalition is showing more and more symptoms of breaking up into independent groups, and of ceasing to care very much whether or not the government suffers defeat in the Division Lobby.' He added, 'On many occasions recently the government has been defeated in Standing

Committee, and on two occasions in the House itself.'[77] Thus the realities of the post-1918 House of Commons and Lloyd George's need to win his ostensible supporters' continuing loyalty made outright endorsement of Sankey's recommendations politically unfeasible.

By late July his own assessments of the swing of public opinion away from the miners and of the mood of the House of Commons was reinforced by his finding that most of his Coalition Liberal colleagues shared their Conservative colleague's distaste for nationalising the mines. This was revealed when he conferred with seventeen or eighteen Coalition Liberals at a private dinner in London on 22 July. A majority of them opposed the nationalisation of the mines 'but had less objection to the nationalisation of the railways'. Their prime objection was 'the fear that it would lead to inefficiency'. After much discussion they agreed

> that it was highly desirable to bring the men in closer touch with the business side of the coal industry and that they should be given a certain amount of voice in its management. This would be brought about by placing men on the Boards of Directors and by putting into practice a system of collective bonus, based on output.

Lloyd George's Liberal supporters were also in favour of nationalising coal royalties and minerals.[78]

Other government supporters also suggested to Lloyd George in this period that public opinion would prefer a policy short of immediate outright nationalisation. Thus the Conservative Waldorf Astor, while warning that the Triple Alliance unions had 'detailed plans for a complete stoppage ... which must affect millions of men', commented that as for the railways the unions 'wanted greater control by the government but not necessarily national operation', and as for the mines 'they ask for complete nationalisation but many might accept gradual acquisition'. Even such colleagues as George Barnes, Minister without Portfolio, and Robert Munro, the Scottish Secretary, who advocated nationalisation nevertheless urged that it should be tried as an experiment in one area first. Munro wrote to Lloyd George,

> I greatly fear that to turn down the principle of nationalisation absolutely would inflame working-class opinion to a dangerous degree: while on the other hand, to adopt it immediately would not only imperil the Coalition itself but might prove to be a national disaster.

So by late July it was clear to Lloyd George that nationalisation of the mines was politically unviable given the composition of the House of Commons. The War Cabinet collectively pronounced against it after two meetings on 7 August.[79]

In announcing the government's decision against nationalisation Lloyd George could not resist casting aspersions on the Sankey Commission and taunting Labour. In turning to the subject of the control of the coal industry, he commented, 'there were one or two incidents in the proceedings which I am bound to say detract a good deal from confidence in the findings of the Commission' and went on to specify one aspect which he deemed to be without precedent. That was, as he portentously put it, 'Two of its members left the seat of judgement to go into the witness box.' In this he referred to two of the miners' nominees, Sidney Webb and Sir Leo Chiozza Money, who in fact followed the precedent of the Poor Law Commission of 1806–9. Nevertheless, his own faith in some of the findings of the Sankey Commission were not so shaken as to prevent him accepting the policy of state purchase of mineral rights on coal and the evidence of unsatisfactory social conditions in mining areas.

In dealing with Sankey's recommendation of nationalisation he claimed unfairly it was based only on a belief that that would lead to good industrial relations. While this was a weak case, and one which then could be queried with evidence from experiences elsewhere, such as New Zealand, Lloyd George characteristically used debating rhetoric in effect to jeer at Labour. He carefully confused state control with state ownership (i.e. where any profits go to the state and not to private individuals):

> The Yorkshire miners struck against the state. Where is the promotion of harmony if you have state control and state ownership so long as that is the case? . . . There is no doubt at all that the railways at the present moment are run at the expense of the state. Thus increases in wages and the cost of the diminution in hours come straight from the taxpayers' pockets. The control is the state. I have not seen the harmony.

Using the Yorkshire miners' strike, unrest on the railways, plus a choice speech made by a militant trade unionist on strikes against the state, Lloyd George concluded 'therefore . . . the whole reason which induced Mr Justice Sankey to make that recommendation [nationalisation] is one which has been falsified by the events of the last few weeks.'[80] While pleasing the Coalition's right wing this approach to explaining the rejection of nationalisation only further enraged Labour.

The Sankey Commission was one of the more controversial episodes in Lloyd George's political career. Historians have tended to divide between those who see the setting up of the Commission and then the rejection of the majority report on nationalisation as a cynical manoeuvre by Lloyd George, and those who argue that nationalisation was unrealistic, that the case had not been made to the public and that the miners – by refusing to compromise – had themselves to blame for not gaining more. The two viewpoints are not mutually exclusive, and there is something to be said for both. Three key issues in assessing Lloyd George's response to the second Sankey Report are whether nationalisation would have improved the performance of the coal industry; whether the enactment of nationalisation was politically viable; and whether the miners had been led to expect that the government would act on a majority report.

In the Interim Report Sankey and the three non-mining businessmen had asserted that the 'present system of ownership and working in the coal industry stands condemned'. Lloyd George had been impressed by that, but until early July he was too busy with the Peace Conference to consider the matter in any depth. Such glimpses of his own thinking as are evident seemed to suggest that while he disliked the old system he never had any great enthusiasm for nationalisation, and by July his attitude to nationalisation in part was coloured by anger at the general intransigency of the MFGB. While he did express considerable concern about levels of coal output, he did not state clearly which form of control would be most likely to boost output. What he did advocate eagerly was his old radical policy of putting part of mineral royalties to social uses, such as housing and health care. Thus he told his War Cabinet colleagues, 'if the minerals were to be nationalised it would be a serious thing to compensate the owners of the land without reference to the social obligation towards the community which raised the minerals.'

By August Lloyd George was pointing his ministerial colleagues towards nationalisation of minerals, some measure of worker participation in management and some degree of amalgamation in the coal industry as the best available solution for the coal industry. On 5 August he had summed up the options as

1. Complete nationalisation of the mines as suggested by Mr Justice Sankey.
2. The Port of London scheme, by which would be set up a management board which would represent the producer, the worker and the consumer. This would be a sort of conglomerate board which would manage the mines district by district. This was really nationalisation, for it entailed buying out the owners.
3. The nationalisation of minerals would be coupled with a process of amalgamation of mining interests. There were two or three schemes put forward for effecting this, by Sir Arthur Duckham, by Lord Gainford and Sir Thomas Ratcliffe-Ellis.[81]

By this time some version of the third option was the solution he felt was politically viable. He made the point bluntly two days later, when he told the War Cabinet that 'it was impossible to carry nationalisation in the present Parliament'. Moreover, he observed, 'even if it were admitted that the present Parliament was reactionary, he was doubtful if, on an appeal to the country, a majority would be returned in favour of nationalisation.'[82]

This is another indicator of just how important the 1918 general election result was in determining the post-war settlement. Furthermore, that electoral verdict did much to nullify popular sentiments demanding action against profiteers and to lessen the scope of the social reconstruction. Vested interests were politically powerful enough to block state purchase of the coal industry just as they were able to pull apart the government's plans for the reorganisation of transport. Bonar Law, as Conservative Party leader, was repeatedly made aware of the sensitivities of propertied interests to any incursions into what they deemed to be their prerogatives. In July, when Tom Jones spoke to him about using the co-ops in regard to clothing, he replied to the effect that 'it was useless for the government to recognize co-ops in any way' as 'there would be such a howl from the private traders'.[83] The vested interests, also, saw the potential effectiveness of operating as pressure groups on Parliament and as propagandists among the public at large.

The MAGB learnt its lesson from the Sankey Commission. Wallace Thorneycroft, chairman of the Coal Association and president of the Institute of Mining Engineers, wrote to Gainford in September,

> It seems certain that nationalisation will be a political question for a good many years and I therefore think that the Mining Association should be organised to contend with that position, the first step in that direction

being the appointment of an official resident in London who would take over control of the propaganda organisation. At any rate we know that there will be some discussion in Parliament and possibly some new Act of Parliament and that the old Parliamentary Committee of the Mining Association should be so reconstituted as to take full advantage of the work done by the propaganda committee in Parliament. I do not think that it is generally recognised that the signature to the Memorial against Nationalisation by 305 Members of Parliament considerably influenced Lloyd George and the government, and that the interest that has been created among Members of Parliament should not be allowed to lapse.[84]

The restructuring of the MAGB had begun with the shock of Sankey's Interim Report. From the autumn of 1919 steps were taken to make the MAGB much more effective. Powers were extended under a new constitution (adopted in April 1920), a new committee structure was set up and a full-time secretariat was based in London.[85]

As to whether Lloyd George or the government deliberately misled the miners, the evidence suggests that 'in spirit' if not 'in word' they did. Much was made of Bonar Law's words at the time of the Interim Report. Bonar Law later vigorously protested that his use of the words accepting the Report 'in the spirit as well as in the letter' had been misconstrued. In the Commons, in defending himself, he argued, 'I am supposed to have given some kind of pledge to do something which a Scotsman never does – that is, buy a pig in a poke.' Bonar Law used words unwisely, but it is unlikely that he then intended to deceive.[86] Lloyd George, however, used words very carefully and, as we have seen, did intend to lead the miners in the direction he wished them to go. As with so much of his guile, there is a thin line between an intention to deceive and a rather reckless encouragement of expectations which may not be fulfilled. For Lloyd George a week was a long time in politics. Many of his political positions were temporary, subject to change according to the political flux.

Lloyd George, from the initiation of the Sankey Commission onwards until July 1919, did not hesitate to raise the expectations of the miners and their allies. This was the impression given well beyond the Labour movement. Sir Arthur Steel-Maitland, who as an Under-Secretary of State in his capacity as head of the Department of Overseas Trade had access to government papers, had an analysis of the nationalisation controversy prepared. This concluded.

> Examination of the statements made by members of the government and by trade union leaders, and of the general course of events during the

controversy, has given me the impression that Mr Lloyd George *intended* the miners to believe that the government would adopt the recommendations of the Commission, and without delay present to Parliament draft legislation embodying them. He himself carefully avoided saying anything which could, on careful analysis by a legal mind, be constructed as a definite pledge to this effect, but the circumstances and the manner of his statements were certainly such as to convey the impression that a pledge was given.

The writer even speculated,

> The Yorkshire strike did more harm still to the miners, but it is not clear whether Sir Auckland Geddes' action here was malicious or merely stupid. Whichever it was, it helped to clear the way for Mr Lloyd George's repudiation of pledges on August 18 – or rather, his denial of having made or authorised any pledges; and the coal output table of 3 September (Board of Trade again) was also favourable to the government.[87]

Whether or not the government provoked the Yorkshire dispute, Lloyd George clearly saw it as an opportunity to divide the Miners' Federation. The government exerted considerable pressure on Smillie to disown the Yorkshire miners' action and to intervene. Lloyd George observed on 5 August,

> He thought it just possible that the Yorkshire strike might collapse, in which case the Yorkshire miners might be so indignant with Mr Smillie for his attitude towards them that they would desert him. The government would then be in a more advantageous position. It might be preferable to wait and see whether the Yorkshire strike did not fizzle out, before we risked provoking a general strike by declaring against nationalisation.[88]

Similarly, the War Cabinet's ready agreement to the 6s a ton rise in the price of coal owed much to a desire to cause the miners maximum political discomfiture. Thus, for all the talk of the crucial need to settle the coal mines issue as quickly as possible in the economic interests of the country, the evidence of the Cabinet and other records makes it hard not to conclude that dishing the miners and other political considerations were the prime concerns of Lloyd George by the summer of 1919.

The claims of the miners were just part of what Lloyd George saw as a challenge to the government by trade unionists. As well as the Yorkshire miners and the police strikes and the possibility of a general mining strike over the rejection of nationalisation, ministers in August 1919 were anticipating a strike by the Triple Alliance as a whole over Russia and other issues and also one on the railways. In the late summer of 1919 Lloyd George was as eager as ever to divide not only the miners but also the Triple Alliance unions.

The collective threat from the Triple Alliance unions in the summer was primarily over Russia. After the Armistice had been signed in November 1918, the continued presence of British forces in Russia outraged many in the British Labour movement. During 1919 Allied intervention against the Bolsheviks overshadowed arguments about the undemocratic nature of Lenin's government. There was near universal condemnation of intervention. The Labour Party's 1918 general election manifesto had bluntly declared, 'Labour demands the immediate withdrawal of the Allied Forces from Russia.' Where there was division on Russia, it was over whether pressure on the government to withdraw should be confined to parliamentary means. Demands for withdrawal backed by threats of strikes were made repeatedly during the second quarter of 1919 – by the Miners' Federation at its annual conference in March, by a joint conference of the Labour Party and the TUC in April and by the Labour Party Conference in June.[89]

Lloyd George and the government were as well aware of the divisions in the Labour movement over what action should be taken against British intervention in Russia as they were of the very widespread trade union hostility to that policy. Such division was well illustrated after a joint Labour Party and TUC conference, held in London on 3 April to support the League of Nations, had passed as an emergency resolution,

> That this conference calls on the government to take immediate steps to withdraw all British troops from Russia, and to take such action as may be necessary to induce the Allied governments to do likewise; to raise the blockade; to withdraw the Bill now before Parliament for conscription of men for further military service; and to release forthwith all conscientious objectors

When neither body took any significant action, the Triple Alliance unions demanded that the TUC should call a special conference to decide what action should be taken to compel the government to respond positively to these policies.

Clynes and the TUC leadership realised that the calling of such a conference would lead to the threat of a general strike. Hence, instead they determined to see Lloyd George or Bonar Law to try to secure assurance which would enable them to avoid a special conference, arranging to see Bonar Law (as Lloyd George was in Paris). Bowerman explained to J. C. Davidson, Bonar Law's Private Secretary,

> that his Committee were in a difficulty because they were inclined to be against the summoning of a conference to consider the four points raised in the resolution and before coming to a decision they wanted to hear the views of the government.

Thus, when the meeting took place, the TUC leadership safely used strong language and made implicit threats while Bonar Law provided soothing answers. Afterwards he reported to Lloyd George that 'they were very well satisfied', and for his part he was very pleased that they had not raised 'the question of what is now being done in the advance on Petrograd'. To the wrath of militant trade unionists the TUC leadership then deemed enough had been done. Similarly, the Labour Party's National Executive Committee was happy to leave the handling of the issue to the industrial wing of the Labour movement. Henderson observed in his annual report,

> that if the Labour Movement is to institute a new precedent in our industrial history by initiating a general strike for the purpose of achieving not industrial but political objects, it is imperative that the trade unions, whose members are to fulfil the obligations implied in the new policy and whose finances it is presumed are to be involved, should realise the responsibilities such a strike movement would entail and should themselves determine the plan of any such new campaign.[90]

While the government realised that it had little to fear in the way of support for direct action from the TUC and Labour Party leaderships, it was still faced with potential trouble from the Triple Alliance. On 27 June this was discussed by the War Cabinet, in the context of its policy towards intervention in Russia. When Austen Chamberlain referred to the range of grievances involved (substituting 'the application of income tax to the labouring classes' for lifting the blockade), Sir David Shackleton, the Permanent Secretary at the Ministry of Labour, advised that 'the principal factor of the agitation was undoubtedly our intervention in Russia.' He warned,

> The moderate section of the Labour Party was doing its best to restrain the more ardent spirits, but it was doubtful whether they would be able to

restrain them for a longer period than the next few weeks. . . . It appeared likely that the Triple Alliance proposed shortly to declare a general strike with a view to compelling the government to withdraw at once all our troops in Russia and to refrain in future from all interference in the affairs of that country.

Though the TUC leadership had avoided a special conference, the annual conference was only weeks away. Hence, Shackleton further warned that 'there was bound to be trouble if in September at or about the meeting of the TUC a casualty list were published of British soldiers killed in Russia while fighting to suppress a soviet government.'[91]

But the question remained, would workers *en masse* strike over intervention in Russia? The scepticism felt by Henderson had been expressed earlier in a report by Basil Thomson. In late April he had commented,

> Every section of the workers appears to be against conscription and intervention in Russia. Even mild trade unionists are said to be strongly moved over these two matters because they think it is the 'thin end of the wedge' towards making compulsory military service a permanent institution. They have no sympathy for the Russian Bolsheviks, and their objection to intervention is that they do not see any necessity for it. . . . On the other hand, it is not at all likely that anything drastic will be done to stop conscription and intervention, for drastic action means the loss of wages for themselves. If their Executives choose to call a strike they will come out, but their feeling is not strong enough to force the hand of their Executives.[92]

The Triple Alliance unions appeared to be the implement which might lever others into action. In the early summer there was a groundswell of working-class opinion which might be mobilised. This was clear both from the support for the continuing campaigns by large numbers of local 'Hands off Russia' committees and the fact that intervention in Russia was cited as a contributory grievance behind several strikes.

The government acted to defuse the situation in late July, after the Triple Alliance unions agreed on 23 July that each union would ballot its members to see if they would strike in order to enforce an end of intervention in Russia and their other objectives. Churchill told the House of Commons that in the first week in March the War Cabinet had made the decision to withdraw British troops from

Northern Russia 'before another winter set in'. The announcement of that decision not only dampened down trade union unrest and caused the Triple Alliance to abandon its plan for a ballot, but also curbed Churchill, who during the process of withdrawal had planned and executed a further offensive in north Russia using volunteers who had gone to Russia on the understanding that theirs was to be a defensive role. That the decision had been taken on 4 March before the Triple Alliance pressure had become substantial, showed that withdrawal from Russia was not a direct outcome of the threat of 'direct action', though many then and later claimed it was.

In reality, the pace of British withdrawal owed most to the military problems and the cost of intervention as well as to weaknesses of the Whites. It also owed much to Lloyd George's attitudes and, again, to what he felt he could do, within the political constraints of the large Coalition majority. Lloyd George was happy to give limited backing to Russian opponents of the Bolsheviks, which he justified by arguing it gave the Russian people the chance to free themselves from Bolshevik tyranny. But from relatively early on he grasped that the Whites were a lost cause (and not a pleasant cause at that), and so judged Churchill's efforts to be futile. He realised that it would take a huge Allied army to conquer and then hold down Russia, and he shared the view well expressed in January 1919 by Colonel House, President Wilson's adviser, that 'Intervention . . . would be impossible to realise even if it were advisable and just. There is not a western country that could safely send troops into Russia without creating labor troubles at home.' The vigorous protests made by many in the British Labour movement were another major reason for Lloyd George not wishing to send a major army into Russia.

Lloyd George, anyway, was more interested in there being a weakened, even divided, Russia, with Western access to at least some of its resources, than crusading in Russia. Thus he soon saw a peace settlement with the Bolsheviks as a better bet than dogged, limited intervention. Nevertheless, Lloyd George had to proceed cautiously on Russia, given the inevitable wrath of Churchill and many Conservative backbenchers, and possibly some Conservative ministers, if he ended the existing relatively small-scale intervention (relative to the force needed to conquer Russia) and abandoned the Whites too quickly.[93]

At the time of his return to domestic politics after his lengthy spell in Paris, Lloyd George's use of 'Bolshevism' was frequently designed to alarm his Conservative colleagues and to tilt policy-making within the War Cabinet his way. Thus in early August, at the time of the police strike and when concern over possible Triple Alliance action over Russia and MFGB action over nationalisation was at its height, Lloyd George came out with some extraordinary comments. He prefaced his review of desirable government measures with a lurid account of a conspiracy to undermine democracy and capitalism. According to the minutes of the meeting, he told colleagues that there was well-co-ordinated dangerous propaganda being spread among the working classes:

> Responsible labour leaders had told him that there was in existence a formidable body of young men whose aim was to destroy the present industrial and Parliamentary system, whose method to accomplish this was diminution of output, and who would then take the reins of government. . . .
> The only people now who used the Press were the Bolsheviks, and they held meetings on Sundays which were attended by thousands. . . . They had also captured the trade union organisation.

However, such Lloyd Georgian versions of Basil Thomson's nightmares derived from his determination to ensure that measures to deal with profiteering, to secure the regeneration of rural areas and to carry out major housebuilding came high on the government's list of priorities.

It is notable that he used similar tactics to press for action to resolve Ireland. Carson had not only been organising opposition to nationalisation but in Belfast, on 12 July, he had declared that if there was any attempt to implement dominion Home Rule 'I will call out the Ulster Volunteers.' Carson made very clear his opposition to compromise, calling for the repeal of the Home Rule Act and stating that the only alternatives were 'maintenance of the Union and loyalty to the King' or 'an Irish Republic with your hats off to the President, Mr de Valera'. Lloyd George, well aware of Bonar Law and other Conservatives' deep commitment to Unionism, repeated some of Sir Nevil Macready's worst prejudices in his efforts to ensure that the government did carry out its 1918 general election manifesto promise 'to explore all practical paths towards the settlement of this grave and difficult question on the basis of self-government' other than those involving either complete severance from the British Empire or the 'forcible submission of the six counties of Ulster to a

Home Rule Parliament'. The War Cabinet minutes record him telling his colleagues,

> The Irish question... had more to do with the existing industrial unrest than the great majority of people imagined. The policemen on strike, the many agitators who were actively engaged in various parts of the country in stirring up trouble and fomenting unrest, were generally of Irish extraction, and they were creating a vicious atmosphere. He had been told by the Commissioner of the Metropolitan Police that none of his Irish officers were really to be trusted. A satisfactory settlement of the Irish question was most important... not only as regards the industrial world, but also our relations with the Dominions and the United States.[94]

For all Lloyd George's colourful talk of the Bolshevism in Britain at this time the events of March to August 1919 showed that the bark of the advocates of 'direct action' was worse than their bite. The miners did not strike over the rejection of nationalisation and the Triple Alliance leaders hit problems in mobilising their own members over Russia. The annual conference of the MFGB in July refused to allow strikes to be called without ballots, a move which had been aimed to benefit the Triple Alliance. In the case of the NUR, whose executive had the power to call a strike ballot, of 218 branches sending in resolutions over Russia, 100 supported the call for strike action, 44 objected to a strike for political purposes and a further 4 refused to take any action, and 68 demanded a ballot. This mixed response from the Triple Alliance unions' membership was known to the government.[95] Moreover, there had been a poor response to a call to hold demonstrations across Britain on Sunday 20 July, as part of co-ordinated action in France, Italy and Britain against intervention in Russia.[96] These events did much to suggest that Henderson, Clynes and other moderate trade unionists were right to doubt whether enough working men and women who had voted for the Coalition in December would strike the next summer to enforce their political views. Before July 1914 they had been similarly dismissive of expectations that trade unionists would strike to force a British government to stop a newly declared war on Germany.

The hesitations of the summer of 1919 further encouraged J. H. Thomas to take the NUR its own way in its dispute with the government. After tough words on Russia and the other issues, the Triple Alliance had delayed taking action and finally had agreed on 4 September to postpone indefinitely the ballots of the unions' members.

At the 4 September meeting Thomas declared that should the NUR need to take action it would do so without a ballot, for it could not win 'if it gave the other side notice of its intentions'. He went on to observe, 'You cannot blackleg the mines, it is an entirely different thing. But with a transport service, if you give them an opportunity of having a depleted service in order to run certain public services . . . it would be merely giving an invitation to the other side to prepare in order to defeat us.'[97]

However, when the NUR did call its members out on strike with effect from midnight on Friday, 26 September 1919, the government was ready to operate its strike-breaking organisation and to make maximum use of its internal propaganda facilities. From 17 February the strike-breaking organisation had been developed specifically to meet any future challenge from the Triple Alliance. Planning had continued after the dangers of an immediate coal or rail stoppage had receded in March. The government had the advantages of still having available the wartime food rationing machinery and controlling shipping. By early April the Ministry of Food had made emergency arrangements to ensure that milk reached London in the event of a rail strike. Farmers would deliver milk to railway stations and road transport would take it on to the London terminals, where it would be collected by the wholesale dairy firms. Similarly, contingency plans were drawn up for ensuring the distribution of coal supplies with priority being given to the food industry.[98]

The government also made careful plans to deal with any unrest associated with a major strike. It was stated in a Home Office memorandum of July that

> The first consideration is the prevention of actual riot or revolutionary violence. A mobile reserve should always be maintained for this purpose if there is any danger.
> Assuming such a reserve is provided, the first claim for protection is that of the Food Supply.

It was felt that in the event of major trouble the police and special constables would not be sufficient. There were too few police for such a role and while many special constables would come forward in London and middle-class areas, there would be few in mining and industrial districts, since working men willing to serve as constables during the war would not serve in industrial disputes. Instead the government looked to the army and the navy.

The army and navy had mobile forces ready to deal with 'actual riot or revolutionary violence'. The former had available:

Infantry, 10 brigades, say 32,000 men.
10 Guards battalions, 8,000 men.
3 Machine Gun Companies, 48 guns.
2 Reserve Cavalry Brigades and 3 Regiments of Household Cavalry, about 3,000 in all.
Tanks, 6 sections of 6 each, say 36 tanks.
Armoured cars, 14.

The navy had a mobile force of 1,200 which would be moved by sea to wherever necessary. In addition, 'suitable men-of-war could be sent on short notice for the protection of any of the ports selected for the landing of food.' The Royal Air Force could assist with reconnaissance and communications.[99]

By this time, the government was more confident of the loyalty of service personnel and the police. In mid-February Churchill had sent a 'Secret and Urgent' communication to all army commanders requiring a weekly report on the reliability and political views of their troops. He specifically asked for information on such matters as:

Will the troops ... respond to orders for assistance to preserve the public peace?
Will they assist in strike breaking?
Will they parade for draft overseas, especially to Russia?
Is there any growth in trade unionism?
Have any soldier's councils been formed?[100]

Then there had been serious doubts, especially over Russia and strike-breaking. By July, Sir Douglas Haig, the British Commander-in-Chief, could report that on the basis of the information coming from his commanders that

there is every justification for the government to be confident that the troops, with small local exceptions, will loyally carry out any duty which they may be asked to perform for the maintenance of law and order....

In regard to the replacement of civilians who are on strike it is further considered that the troops will not hesitate to carry out any duty in connection with those public works and industries which are vital to the existence of the community provided the duty is fully explained to them before they perform it.

The recent occurrences clearly demonstrate the urgent necessity of unifying the various societies formed in connection with ex-soldiers and sailors into one common and loyal Union, thereby ensuring that a large body of men will assist the government in case of a national emergency and that this body will be denied to the revolutionary elements.[101]

In early September Haig called a meeting of his senior area commanders 'to discuss our plans for dealing with a General Strike'. At the meeting he outlined the 'protection' role which had been set out in the Home Office memorandum of July.[102]

The government's preparedness to deal with a major strike contributed to Lloyd George taking a tougher line with the railwaymen in September than the government had done in March. In the interim, negotiations between the government, the railway companies and the NUR had proceeded at a snail's pace even though they met forty times. In early May Sir Auckland Geddes had complained to Bonar Law that 'we have been having a deal of trouble with the railwaymen's negotiations.' The biggest area of dispute was standardising the 512 grades in the various railway companies and reducing the number of grades very substantially, and then agreeing rates of pay and conditions of work for them.[103]

The government appears to have decided to divide the railway unions. At about the time the government decided to announce its rejection of nationalisation of the mines, it made major concessions to ASLEF, after very protracted negotiations. These did provide the skilled workers with wage rates based on the highest previous levels – 'standardisation upwards'. But this was not offered to other grades of railway workers. As J. H. Thomas observed in a press statement of 21 September,

> This means that the basis of standardisation makes no allowance for the position of those who have higher pay than the others, and if the existing agreement for the war wage to terminate in December came into operation, this would mean an actual reduction of varying amounts up to as much as 14s per week in some grades.[104]

By late September the NUR leadership was exasperated. Their members were becoming increasingly restless at the failure to secure similar terms to ASLEF. After Thomas had demanded on 16 September a clear offer from Sir Auckland Geddes, he had received three days later a take-it-or-leave-it response which involved substantial pay cuts. Geddes informed Thomas that 'the proposals contained in the attached memoranda are not put forward as a basis for negotiation, but as a definitive offer of government.' The proposals were a clear breach of one of the reassurances that Bonar Law had given on 22 March when the government had made considerable concessions to the railwaymen. Then, Bonar Law had stated that standardisation of wages 'would mean more money'. Faced with unacceptable and apparently final terms, the NUR leadership advised branch secretaries on 24 September to organise a strike from midnight on 26 September.[105]

Several accounts of this strike have quoted with approval Beatrice Webb's opinion that the strike had been

> desired, if not engineered, by the Geddes brothers, and subconsciously desired by the P.M. The Geddes brothers represent the universal determination of the capitalists to reduce wages to pre-war level – if possible, pre-war money level, but in any case pre-war commodity-value level.

There is much to be said for this view, though Lloyd George's attitude appears to have been ambivalent. The Geddes brothers, indeed, appear to have been determined to insist that pay cuts should take place. In the final negotiations on 26 September Lloyd George observed,

> Whatever we lay down with regard to the railwaymen, you may depend upon it is going to be claimed throughout the country, and, therefore, we have to consider not merely your case, but the case of all the other trades in the kingdom.[106]

Yet at this final meeting Lloyd George made suggestions which gave many present the impression that he was trying to be conciliatory. He spoke of the government being willing 'to consider and discuss anomalies and cases of hardship' and later he proposed that wage cuts would only operate after 31 December and if the cost of living fell below its September 1919 level of 115 per cent over July 1914.[107]

Lloyd George may have been genuinely seeking to avert the strike or he may have been wishing either to prolong negotiations or to wrong-foot the NUR in the eyes of the public. Certainly it seems that the government did not expect a big strike so quickly. Lloyd George observed to his wife that it had come 'quite unexpectedly – as a thief in the night'. Barnes emphasised in a letter to Henderson that the government had expected the negotiations to continue. Hankey felt that Lloyd George and Thomas had been thwarted by NUR intransigence. In his diary he commented,

> on Tuesday the Railwaymen's Union pointed a pistol at the government, and after two days most hectic discussions, suddenly broke off negotiations and declared a strike. J. H. Thomas . . . tried his utmost to effect a settlement but, since his trip to America, he has been losing ground to his deputy, a man named Cramp, a sinister looking fellow reputed to be a Bolshevist.
> I was present at all the negotiations, which took the form of a duel between the PM and J. H. Thomas, both Welshmen and full of cunning, and in private life good friends. Thomas had a terribly difficult role to play, as, in his official position, he had to advocate a policy that he did not believe in. He carried it out with skill and dignity.
> When the PM at the end made a final concession and offered to leave the room for the men's representatives to consider it, some of the men at the back called out, 'We have made up our minds' or words to that effect. It was clear that most of them merely wished to pick a quarrel.

In contrast, Beatrice Webb felt,

> The railwaymen seem to have been tricked into a false position which no sane person can defend. Lloyd George's offer made on Friday completely transformed Geddes' ultimatum and does not differ substantially from the men's demand. But the offer was made in vague terms across the table and not one of the NUR Executive . . . understood it, and refused to follow Thomas's advice and put off the strike and take time to reconsider the whole business.[108]

Whether or not Lloyd George's move was genuine, he was soon leading the government's propaganda offensive against the NUR. In a telegram, which was issued as a public statement, he deemed the strike to be an 'anarchist conspiracy' and declared that, 'In a long and varied experience I can recall no strike entered into so lightly, with so little justification, and with such entire disregard for the public interest.' The government tried to win public support through advertisements in newspapers and on the screen in cinemas. Lloyd George's claims that the strike 'had been engineered for some time by a small but active body of men who wrought tirelessly and insidiously to exploit the labour organisations of this country for subversive aims' were echoed by the Conservative press.[109]

The NUR, aided by a hastily improvised group of socialist intellectuals linked with the Labour Research Department, effectively countered the government's propaganda by getting over the message that the dispute was purely over wages and conditions, indeed over safeguarding them. Thus one NUR advertisement quoted Lloyd George's remarks on railwaymen's wages not being treated in isolation under the heading 'Lloyd George speaks the truth', and followed it with:

> The government proposals mean a reduction of thirteen shillings a week to the worst paid. Mr Lloyd George has told you he means to treat all other workers in the same way. YOUR TURN NEXT IF THE RAILWAYMEN LOSE. THEIR FIGHT IS YOUR FIGHT. SEE TO IT THAT THEY WIN.

Soon even some of the hitherto hostile press was admitting that the railwaymen had a case.[110]

While Thomas was delighted that ASLEF came out on strike with the NUR, he declined other offers of sympathetic strike action. Indeed, soon afterwards, he wrote of the situation in terms not far from Lloyd George's telegram. Thomas commented,

> I set myself resolutely both against any proposed extension of the strike and any attempt to shift the issue from the question of a wages dispute to something else. There were people quite prepared to use a railway upheaval . . . for the purpose of ending the existing social order. I felt that to allow anyone else to step in and control the strike would have been as disastrous to the railwaymen as it would to the country.[111]

At the time there can have been no doubt that Thomas was always eager to negotiate a compromise settlement.

As for Lloyd George, he soon swung towards compromise when it became apparent that public opinion was moving against the government. Initially he had been belligerent, even urging the Cabinet Strike Committee that the strike leaders should be prosecuted. The government's strike-breaking organisation worked smoothly, though the government was disappointed at the number of volunteers who came forward. After the strike ended, Hankey observed,

> The spectacle of the superb working of the government machine has been very impressive. For some days, for example, we have been putting surplus milk into cold storage in London and in some parts of the country stocks of food have actually increased.

However, the government's intelligence reports soon recorded public sympathy for the railwaymen and warned that the strike might spread.[112]

On 1 October Lloyd George received a deputation of moderate trade union leaders, including Henderson and Clynes, under the auspices of the Transport Workers' Federation. This attempt at mediation was instigated by Ernest Bevin, who was well aware of growing pressure in his and other unions for sympathetic strikes. He was to warn his union's executive against such action on 4 October, saying

> I think it must be civil war, for I cannot see how it is possible, once all the trade unions are brought in, for the government to avoid fighting for the supremacy and power, and I do not believe that our people, if they knew what it meant, would be prepared to plunge into it.[113]

Thus Bevin's response to the prospect of an all-out confrontation with the government was similar to Smillie's. Lloyd George, though stating to the deputation that it would be 'quite impracticable to continue negotiations until work was resumed', did talk with the executives of the NUR and ASLEF later that day. Beforehand, he sent the Geddes brothers and Horne notes asking whether he could tell the NUR that future negotiations would consider their 'alternative proposals for standardisation', or would they 'insist on confining negotiations merely to redressing anomalies affecting individual groups'?[114] In these discussions on 1 October Lloyd George reiterated the offer to look at any anomalies but declined to negotiate on standardisation until the strike was called off.

At the War Cabinet on 3 October his colleagues expressed 'their desire that the Prime Minister should feel he had a perfectly free hand in conducting the government's case'. More specifically, Lloyd George received their approval to use a compromise formula advocated by Whitley and Seebohm Rowntree 'if and when the right moment should come'. This was to readjust the basic rate of pay and offer a minimum 'equivalent to 25s a week reckoned at pre-war prices'. However, when Lloyd George saw the executives of the two unions that evening they made no concessions and neither did he. Lloyd George left London for the country, leaving the trade union mediators to see Bonar Law on 4 October. They arranged with the Deputy Prime Minister for further negotiations with Lloyd George the next day. At this meeting a compromise settlement was formulated, which was approved by the Geddes brothers, Horne, Churchill and Bonar Law. It laid down that negotiations would be started immediately after the strike was called off; that the negotiations would be completed before the end of the year; that wages would be stabilised at their current level until 30 September 1920, but could be reviewed after 1 August 1920; and that 'no adult railwaymen in Great Britain shall receive less than 51s so long as the cost of living is not less than 110 per cent above pre-war level.'[115]

From the outset of the strike Lloyd George and Thomas were in private contact. Hankey noted in his diary, 'There was a continuous liaison between the Prime Minister and Thomas throughout the whole strike. This was conducted partly through Tom Jones . . . who was in daily touch with him.' Seebohm Rowntree probably played an even greater role. The Astors also were involved, with Thomas even staying in their London house. Hankey further recorded in his diary, 'Late on Friday night, after negotiations were supposed to have been broken off, Thomas actually came to see Lloyd George at 10 Downing Street.' Hankey also suggested that Thomas even arranged that the negotiations on 5 October should be protracted so that he could announce the settlement that evening at a railwaymen's rally at the Albert Hall without it being published earlier in the evening newspapers.[116] To what extent Thomas's collusion with Lloyd George affected the outcome one can only speculate. However, something was known of Thomas's activities at the time. Beatrice Webb noted in her diary,

> There is considerable bitterness about the action of Thomas in carrying on private negotiations with the PM and with the Northcliffe and other newspapers behind the backs of his colleagues, alike of the NUR executive and of the mediatory neutral unions. Also 'the fourteen' are offended that in his speech at the Albert Hall he went out of his way to give Lloyd George the credit for the settlement – in conjunction with himself – and omitted all mention of the t.u. leaders . . . 'Another Welshman in his devious ways' was the remark of one t.u. official.[117]

Nevertheless, the NUR executive, like the union's members, was pleased with the settlement and organised a collection (which raised £2,598) for Thomas.[118]

As for Lloyd George, he had further enhanced his reputation for settling major industrial disputes. Moreover, on the evening of the settlement, he could observe with considerable satisfaction to Riddell,

The railwaymen have agreed not to strike until September 1920. That breaks up the Triple Alliance. The strike came too soon for the colliers and transport workers. They were not ready. Now we have detached the railwaymen. I think the result of the strike will have a most salutary influence.[119]

Notes and references

1. Diary entries 19 and 21 March 1919; *Lord Riddell's Intimate Diary of the Peace Conference and After* (London: Gollancz, 1933), pp. 36–7.
2. Supreme War Council Minutes, 8 March 1919; reprinted in S. L. Bane and R. H. Lutz, *The Blockade of Germany after the Armistice 1918–19* (Stanford: Stanford University Press, 1942), pp. 200–21. 27 March 1919. P. Mantoux, *Paris Peace Conference 1919: Proceedings of the Council of Four*, transl. J. B. Whitton (Geneva: Droz, 1964), p. 34.
3. Quoted in A. J. Mayer, *Politics and Diplomacy of Peacemaking* (London: Weidenfeld and Nicolson, 1968), p. 571.
4. ibid., pp. 10–11.
5. 26 and 27 March; Mantoux, *op. cit.*, pp. 36 and 27.
6. D. Lloyd George, *The Truth about the Peace Treaties*, vol. 1 (London: Gollancz, 1938), pp. 461–5.
7. ibid., pp. 401–16. Mayer, *op. cit.*, pp. 579–83. S. Roskill, *Hankey: Man of Secrets*, vol. 2 (London: Collins, 1972), pp. 70–3. H. W. V. Temperley (ed.), *A History of the Peace Conference of Paris*, vol. 6 (Oxford: Oxford University Press, 1924), pp. 544–51.
8. Wiseman's diary, quoted in Mayer, *op. cit.*, p. 419. Mantoux, *op. cit.*, p. 14.
9. H. Wickham Steed, *Through Thirty Years*, vol. 2 (London: Heinemann, 1924), p. 296.
10. H. Fyfe, *Sixty Years of Fleet Street* (London: W. H. Allen, 1949), pp. 49–50, 62–6 and 115–16. *The Times, The History of* The Times, vol. 4 (London: The Times, 1952), pp. 384–401 and 465–9. R. Pound and G. Harmsworth, *Northcliffe* (London: Cassell, 1959), pp. 171–4, 661–2, 676–83 and 698–712. Wickham Steed, *op. cit.*, pp. 301–7. S. Koss, *The Rise and Fall of the Political Press in Britain*, vol. 2 (London: Hamish Hamilton, 1984), pp. 346–59.
11. Lloyd George, *op. cit.*, pp. 558–64. Mayer, *op. cit.*, pp. 627–31.
12. *Evening News*, 15 April 1919. This explanation seems to me more credible than just an attempt by the paper to further enrage the Conservative backbenchers.
13. Tom Jones to Lloyd George, 11 April 1919; LG F/23/4/52.
14. 11 April 1919; Mantoux, p. 175. Riddell's diary, 9 April 1919; Riddell Papers, 62983, f. 124.
15. The strength of Lloyd George's animosity to Northcliffe is clear from Riddell's diary, for example, 9 April 1919; Riddell Papers 62983, f. 119; and from Frances Stevenson's diary; 17 April 1919; A. J. P.

Taylor, (ed.) *Lloyd George: A Diary by Frances Stevenson* (London: Hutchinson, 1971), p. 180.
16. 114 *HC Deb*. 5s, c. 2936–56 and 2971–2. Lloyd George, *op. cit.*, pp. 576–7. Temperley, *op. cit.*, pp. 314–16.
17. *The Times*, 2 January 1919. C. J. Wrigley, *Arthur Henderson* (Cardiff: University of Wales Press, 1990), pp. 128–32.
18. *The Times*, 3 January 1919.
19. *The Times*, 6 June 1919.
20. The Labour Party, *Report of the Nineteenth Annual Conference, 1919*, pp. 196–8, 205, 212–13 and 217.
21. Riddell's diary, 23 April 1919; Riddell Papers 62983, ff. 146–7. For Lloyd George and the British delegation's negotiations regarding those areas, H. Elcock, *Portrait of a Decision* (London: Eyre Methuen, 1972), pp. 72–9 and M. L. Dockrill and J. D. Goold, *Peace Without Promise* (London: Batsford, 1981), pp. 64–8 and 131–79. Lloyd George's attitude to the German colonies had scandalised Wickham Steed as early as October 1918; Wickham Steed, *op. cit.*, pp. 244–6. On oil, see M. Kent, *Oil and Empire* (London: Macmillan, 1976).
22. Henderson to Webb, 17 May 1919; Passfield Papers, II, g 133 a and b.
23. G. D. H. Cole, *A History of the Labour Party From 1914* (London: Routledge and Kegan Paul, 1948), pp. 37 and 85. N. and J. MacKenzie (eds), *The Diary of Beatrice Webb*, vol. 3 (London: Virago, 1984), p. 329.
24. *The Times*, 12 February 1919.
25. *Morning Post*, 1 January 1919. *The Times*, 3 January 1919. The *New Statesman*, 4 January 1919, p. 271, made similar comments. Beatrice Webb's diary, 10 February 1919; Passfield Papers, I, f. 35.
26. 11 and 12 February 1919; 112 *HC Deb*. 5s, c. 60–1 and 166–70.
27. *Morning Post*, 17 February and 10 March 1919.
28. *Morning Post*, 28 January, 14 and 20 February 1919. On Merthyr politics, K. O. Morgan, 'The Merthyr of Keir Hardie' in G. Williams (ed.), *Merthyr Politics: The Making of a Working-Class tradition* (Cardiff: University of Wales Press, 1966), pp. 58–81.
29. The Labour Research Department, *The Federation of British Industries* (London: Labour Publishing, 1923), pp. 42–7.
30. The view of the *Yorkshire Factory Times* in 1917; H. A. Clegg, *A History of British Trade Unions since 1889*, vol. 2 (Oxford: Clarendon Press, 1985), p. 231.
31. R. P. T. Davenport-Hines, *Dudley Docker* (Cambridge: Cambridge University Press, 1984), pp. 119–32. *Morning Post*, 29 and 30 January 1919.
32. Diary, 2 April 1919; J. Barnes and D. Nicholson (ed.), *The Leo Amery Diaries*, vol. 1 (London: Hutchinson, 1980), p. 259.
33. *Industrial Peace*, 4, 21 (May 1919), p. 89.
34. S. Tolliday has argued that in the motor industry the tide had turned against the unions as early as 1918 and that the unions' position 'was sliding' in 1919; 'Mass production unionism's failure in the motor

industry' in C. Wrigley (ed.), *A History of British Industrial Relations*, vol. 2 (Brighton: Harvester, 1986), p. 312.
35. The Prime Minister's Office to Bonar Law, 29 January 1919; LG F/30/3/12.
36. Memorandum by B. Ellingus, 25 February 1919; Ministry of Munitions Papers, MUN 4–6673.
37. B. Waites, *A Class Society at War* (Leamington Spa: Berg, 1987), pp. 84–5.
38. Northcliffe to Rothermere, 10 April 1919; Pound and Harmsworth, *op. cit.*, p. 712. Similar points were made by Conservative MPs in the Commons, 2 April 1919; 114 HC Deb. 5s, c. 1315–33.
39. Riddell, *Peace Conference*, p. 49.
40. Henderson to Webb, 17 May 1919; Passfield Papers, 2g, 133ab.
41. Churchill at Dundee, 10 December 1918 (and similarly on 4 December); R. Rhodes James (ed.), *Winston S. Churchill: His Complete Speeches 1897–1963*, vol. 3 (New York: Chelsea House, 1974), pp. 2647–8. WC (534), 19 February 1919; CAB 23–9–75. Lloyd George had earlier made very sympathetic comments of a similar nature to a TUC delegation, 20 March 1918; copy of TUC memorandum, Thomas Jones Papers, C/5/69.
42. W. Churchill to Bonar Law, 5 July 1919; Bonar Law Papers, 95/5/4. In December 1918 Stanley had cautioned Eric Geddes to say no more than 'the exact form of government control is a matter which is receiving the consideration of the government.' T. Hill (Board of Trade) to Davies, 9 December 1918; LG F/2/6/8.
43. P. S. Bagwell, *The Railwaymen* (London: Allen and Unwin, 1963) pp. 406–7.
44. Lloyd George to Jones, 17 March 1919; LG F/23/4/37. Lloyd George to Bonar Law, 20 March 1919; LG F/30/3/33. J. Vincent (ed.), *The Crawford Papers* (Manchester: Manchester University Press, 1984), p. 401.
45. On the MAGB see B. Supple, '"No bloody revolutions but for obstinate reactions"? British coalowners in their context, 1919–20' in D. C. Coleman and P. Mathias (eds), *Enterprise and History* (Cambridge: Cambridge University Press, 1984), pp. 212–36 and B. Supple, *The History of the British Coal Industry*, vol. 4 (Oxford: Clarendon Press, 1987), pp. 126–37.
46. Letter of May 1919; Weir Papers 4/1/13–14. For a similar letter warning of 'This killing of private enterprise, commencing with the coal trade, which is at the base of all manufacturing production', see T. H. Coggins (of Birmingham colliery agents) to A. Steel-Maitland, 1 July 1919; Steel Maitland Papers GD 193/87/5.
47. Report from the FBI's nationalisation committee; copy of pamphlet, 30 July 1919; Steel-Maitland Papers GD 193/80/1. Docker to Steel-Maitland, 1 July 1919; Steel-Maitland Papers GD 193/87/5. On Docker's press support for the Duke of Northumberland's attacks on the Sankey Commission see Davenport-Hines, *op. cit.*, p. 125.
48. E. Carson to Selborne, 29 June 1919; Selborne Papers, 87/59.

49. Bonar Law to Colonel G. C. Wheler, the Coalition Conservative MP for Faversham, 2 April 1919; Bonar Law Papers, 101/3/39 (and 45, also 97/1/15, 97/2/4 and 7). Bonar Law to E. Geddes, 20 June 1919; Bonar Law Papers, 101/3/107 (and 97/4/15).
50. The Duke of Northumberland to Esher, 23 June 1919; Esher Papers, 5/57. Waites, *op. cit.*, pp. 53–4. An anxious Birmingham magistrate, James Blackwell, thundered similarly to Steel-Maitland, 'We are now having a taste of godless and savage democracy, which is anarchy. May God save our land from Bolshevism.' 10 August 1919; Steel-Maitland Papers, GD 193/87/1/2.
51. 119, *HC Deb*, 5s, c. 1979–2022; 18 August 1919. WC (606A), 5 August 1919; CAB 23–15–148. Maclay to Lloyd George, 13 June 1919; LG F/35/3/23. War Cabinet Papers GT 7905, 16 June 1919; CAB 24–86. The figures were later revised to an output still of 287 million tons, but with exports at 73 million, with total 1919 figures of 230 million tons and exports of 35 million. Supple, *Coal Industry*, p. 174.
52. WC (589), 8 June 1919; CAB 23–11–13/14. For the profits, see Supple, *Coal Industry*, p. 174.
53. WC (589), 8 July 1919; CAB 23–11–14/15.
54. Supple, 'No bloody revolutions', pp. 227–8. Supple, *Coal Industry*, pp. 141–2. Gainford to C. Carlow, 8 August 1919. Gainford to Sir Thomas Ratcliffe-Ellis, 20 August 1919. Sir Thomas Ratcliffe-Ellis to Gainford, 3 September 1919. Gainford Papers, 98.
55. In the event, the government only paid the back-pay from 9 January to 1 April. This cost £7 million. Supple, 'No bloody revolutions', pp. 228–9.
56. WC (589), 8 July 1919; CAB 23–11–14/15. Jones to Hankey, 8 July 1919; K. Middlemas (ed.), *Thomas Jones: Whitehall Diary*, vol. 1 (London: Oxford University Press, 1969), p. 89.
57. G. D. H. Cole, *Labour in the Coal-Mining Industry 1914–1921* (Oxford: Clarendon Press, 1923), pp. 102–3.
58. Lloyd George to Bonar Law, 14 July 1919; LG F/95/5/16. Horne to Bonar Law, 12 July 1919; Bonar Law Papers, 105/3/1.
59. WC (595), 18 July 1919; CAB 25–11–46/7. Cole, *Labour in Coal-mining*, pp. 104–5. Telegram from Hodges to Bonar Law, 16 July 1919; Bonar Law Papers, 103/9/2. WC (595), 18 July 1919; CAB 23–11–46/7.
60. J. T. Davies (a member of Lloyd George's secretariat), 14 August 1919; Thomas Jones Papers, C/5/65.
61. WC (558), 17 April 1919; CAB 23–10–16. WC (589), 8 July 1919; CAB 23–11–14.
62. *Report of Messrs Alfred Tongue and Co. on the Coal Industry*, Cmd. 555, 1920.
63. Davidson to Hodges, 4 July 1919. Report of a conference between Bonar Law and the MFGB, 5 July 1919. Bonar Law Papers, 103/9/1 and 6. For the Yorkshire dispute, see Cole, *Labour in Coal-mining*, pp. 106–11.

64. WC (596A), 21 July 1919; CAB 23-15-136/7. S. Armitage's shorter selection from this source gives a somewhat different slant to Lloyd George's words. S. Armitage, *The Politics of Decontrol of Industry* (London: Weidenfeld and Nicolson, 1969), p. 124.
65. WC (596A), 21 July 1919; CAB 23-15-139. WC (597), 22 July 1919; CAB 23-11-51.
66. WC (598), 23 July 1919; CAB 23-9-57. Geddes to Lloyd George, 23 July 1919; LG F/18/3/13.
67. Press notice of Coal Conference, 10 Downing Street, 24 July 1919; Thomas Jones Papers, C/5/64. WC (599), 25 July 1919; CAB 23-9-63.
68. WC (601), 29 July 1919; CAB 23-11-75. WC (602), 30 July 1919; CAB 23-11-87. WC (610), 8 August 1919; CAB 23-11-110. Cole, *Labour in Coal-mining*, pp. 109-11.
69. *Whitehall Diary*, vol. 1, p. 91. Hankey to Jones, 12 July 1919; Thomas Jones Papers, W/9/136. Riddell diary 12-15 July 1919; Riddell, *Peace Conference*, p. 104. At this time he was also eager to discuss trade and industrial issues with prominent Coalition Liberals: Lloyd George to F. Guest, 14 July 1919; LG F/21/4/4.
70. 'Political vampirism', *The Spectator*, 24 May 1919. Sankey to Haldane, 23 May and Hankey to Haldane, 14 August 1919; Haldane Papers, 5914, ff. 125 and 142-3. Also Haldane to Jones, 13 May 1919; Thomas Jones Papers, W/9/88. Beatrice Webb's diary, 20 May 1919, on Haldane acting on behalf of Tom Jones; Passfield Papers, I, 35. For Barnes's speculations whether the Coalition Labour ministers would stay in the government now peace with Germany had been signed, see G. N. Barnes's memorandum, 'The position of Labour in the government', 25 July 1919; copy, LG F/4/3/23.
71. A. Murray to Sir W. Wiseman, 28 July 1919; Elibank Papers, 8808, ff. 20-33.
72. Sir Henry Wilson's diary, 10-12 July 1919 and Churchill to Lloyd George, 14 July 1919; printed in M. Gilbert, *Winston S. Churchill, Vol. 4: Companion*, part 2, pp. 739-46. Riddell, *Peace Conference*, p. 104. F. Guest to Lloyd George, 8 July 1919; LG F/21/4/1. James (ed.), *Churchill: His Complete Speeches*, vol. 3, pp. 2814-20.
73. 119 *HC Deb. 5s*, c. 1979-2022 and 2027; 18 August 1919. F. E. Guest to Lloyd George, 23 July 1919; LG F/21/4/8. Lloyd George to Addison, 20 August 1919; Addison Papers, Box 25.
74. 119 *HC Deb. 5s*, c. 2011-15; 18 August 1919. WC (609A), 8 August 1919; CAB 23-15-216. Sir C. Petrie, *The Life and Letters of the Rt. Hon. Sir Austen Chamberlain*, vol. 2 (London: Cassell, 1940), p. 143.
75. Riddell's diary, 12-15 May 1919; Riddell Papers, Add. Ms. 62984, ff. 9-10, partly printed in *Peace Conference*, p. 104. On the prominent role of the iron and steel trade in pressing for protection at this time, see F. Capie, *Depression and Protectionism: Britain between the Wars* (London: Allen and Unwin, 1983), pp. 63-4.
76. On Coalition Liberal hostility, see K. O. Morgan, *Consensus and Disunity* (Oxford: Clarendon Press, 1979), pp. 199-200 and 333-34. Gladstone to W. Runciman, 21 August 1919; Runciman Papers, Box

2. For Gladstone's condemnation of him in the context of high public expenditure, see Sir C. Mallet, *Herbert Gladstone* (London: Hutchinson, 1932), p. 277.
77. A. Murray to Sir W. Wiseman, 28 July 1919; Elibank Papers, 8808, ff. 20–33.
78. Summary of conference at 36 Belgrave Square, 22 July 1919; Addison Papers, Box 25. WC (598), 23 July 1919; CAB 23–11–57.
79. Astor to Lloyd George, 24 July 1919; LG F/2/7/7. Munro to Lloyd George, 4 August 1919; LG F/1/7/32. WC (607A and 608A), 7 August 1919; CAB 23–15–174/204.
80. 119 *HC Deb. 5s*, c. 2001–6; 18 August 1919. J. R. Raynes, *Coal And Its Conflicts* (London: Benn, 1928), p. 166. On New Zealand, article by W. H. Triggs of the New Zealand Legislative Council, *Times Trade Supplement*, 9 August 1919; copy in Steel-Maitland Papers, GD 193/80/1.
81. WC (606A), 5 August 1919; CAB 23–15–153. The expected effect of the various options on improving the performance of the coal industry is discussed in M. Kirby, *The British Coal-mining Industry 1870–1946* (London: Macmillan, 1977), pp. 37–43.
82. WC (608A), 5.30 p.m., 7 August 1919; CAB 23–15–198.
83. Jones to E. F. Wise, 10 July 1919; *Whitehall Diary*, vol. 1, p. 89.
84. Thorneycroft to Gainford, 10 September 1919; Gainford Papers, 98.
85. Supple, 'No bloody revolutions', pp. 231–3.
86. 114 *HC Deb. 5s*, c. 2081–2; 18 August 1919. This is not to say that Bonar Law was without guile. Cole suggests he displayed this in commenting on the causes of the Yorkshire coal strike, *Labour in Coal-mining*, p. 108, and the writer of the memorandum for Steel-Maitland (see 87) suggested that many passages in Bonar Law's statements on the coal industry were so 'involved that even after a second reading their meaning is uncertain'.
87. Memorandum, 'Coal mines nationalisation controversy, 1919' (no date, probably December 1919); Steel-Maitland Papers, GD 193/80/1/206–17. The author of the memorandum may have been his private secretary. His copies of secret War Cabinet minutes on coal are also in GD 193/80/1.
88. WC (606A), 5 August 1919; CAB 23–15–158.
89. *Labour's Call to the People* (1918). S. R. Graubard, *British Labour and the Russian Revolution 1917–1924* (Cambridge, Mass.: Harvard University Press, 1956), pp. 65–82. S. White, *Britain and the Bolshevik Revolution* (London: Macmillan, 1979), pp. 27–35. M. H. Cowden, *Russian Bolshevism and British Labor 1917–1921* (New York: Columbia University Press, 1984), pp. 29–43. H. Clegg, *A History of British Trade Unions Since 1889*, vol. 2 (Oxford: Clarendon Press, 1985), pp. 284–6.
90. *Report of the Nineteenth Annual Conference of the Labour Party 1919*, pp. 26–7. *TUC Conference Report 1919*, pp. 220–8. Davidson to Horne, 17 May 1919; Bonar Law Papers, 101/3/75. Bonar Law to Lloyd George, 20 May 1919 and n.d.; LG F/30/3/64 and 65.

91. WC (585B), 27 June 1919; CAB 23–15–113/14.
92. 'Report on revolutionary organisations in the UK' (Cabinet Paper, GT 7916), 30 April 1919; CAB 24–78–387. R. H. Ullman, *Britain and the Russian Civil War* (Princeton, NJ: Princeton University Press, 1968), pp. 132–3 and 186–8.
93. As well as Chapter 2 of this book, see Ullman, *op. cit.*, especially pp. 294–304 and White, *op. cit.*, pp. 27–8. House to N. Hapgood, 16 January 1919; quoted in I. Floto, *Colonel House in Paris* (Aarhus: Universitetsforlaget, 1973), p. 105.
94. WC (606A), 5 August 1919; CAB 23–15–149/50 and 157. I. Colvin, *The Life of Lord Carson* (London: Gollancz, 1936), pp 374–6.
95. P. S. Bagwell, 'The Triple Industrial Alliance 1913–1922' in A. Briggs and J. Saville (eds), *Essays In Labour History 1886–1923* (London: Macmillan, 1971), pp. 107–8.
96. White, *op. cit.*, pp. 33–4. Cowden, *op. cit.*, pp. 51–5.
97. Bagwell, *op. cit.*, p. 401. I am much indebted to this excellent trade union history for its account of the autumn 1919 rail dispute. Other accounts include J. R. Raynes, *Engines and Men* (Leeds: Goodall and Suddick, 1921), pp. 263–74 and G. Alcock, *Fifty Years of Railway Trade Unionism* (London: NUR, 1922), pp. 549–58.
98. 'Arrangements for the supply of milk to London in the event of labour troubles', 9 April 1919; Ministry of Food, MAF 60/397. R. Desmarais, 'Lloyd George and the development of the British government's strikebreaking organisation', *International Review of Social History*, 20 (1975), pp. 7–9.
99. 'Emergency supplies in the event of coal and transport strikes' (Home Office Memorandum), 20 July 1919; Thomas Jones Papers C/5/63.
100. *Daily Herald*, 13 May 1919. Adamson in the Commons, 29 May 1919; 116 HC Deb. 5s, c. 1469–70. Bagwell, *op. cit.*, pp. 376–7. Ullman, *op. cit.*, pp. 130–1.
101. 'Emergency supplies...', memorandum, 20 July 1919 (see above, 99).
102. K. Jeffery and P. Hennessy, *States of Emergency* (London: Routledge and Kegan Paul, 1983), p. 14.
103. Geddes to Bonar Law, 5 May 1919; Bonar Law Papers, 97/3/5. Bagwell, *op. cit.*, p. 380.
104. N. McKillop, *The Lighted Flame* (London: Nelson, 1950). pp. 131–2.
105. Bagwell, *op. cit.*, pp. 382–4.
106. Diary entry, 28 September 1919; N. and J. MacKenzie (eds), *op. cit.*, p. 349. Alcock, *op. cit.*, p. 552.
107. Bagwell, *op. cit.*, pp. 385–86.
108. Barnes to Henderson, 8 October 1919; copy, LG F/4/2/28, Lloyd George to his wife, 26 September 1919; K. O. Morgan (ed.) *Lloyd George: Family Letters 1885–1936* (Cardiff: University of Wales Press, 1973), p. 190. Hankey's diary, 28 September 1919; Hankey Papers, HNKY 1/5, ff. 88–9. Beatrice Webb's diary, 2 October 1919; Passfield Papers I, 35. Baird diary, 4 October 1919. The government made the maximum propaganda use of Lloyd George's offer. See WC (623 and 625), 24 and 26 September 1919; CAB 23–12–14 and 20/1.

109. *The Times*, 29 September 1919. The statement was approved at the War Cabinet (WC 626), 26 September 1919; CAB 23–12–22.
110. Bagwell, *op. cit.*, pp. 392–5. C. Wrigley, 'The trade unions between the wars' in C. Wrigley (ed.), *op. cit.*, pp. 79–81.
111. Thomas's Foreword to Alcock, *op. cit.* (published 1922), p. xiii.
112. Armitage, *op. cit.*, p. 79. Hankey to Esher, 6 October 1919; Hankey Papers, HNKY 4/11. Barnes also warned Lloyd George of widespread trade union sympathy. Barnes to Lloyd George, 1 October 1919; LG F/4/3/25. Also, Baird diary, 13 October 1919.
113. A. Bullock, *The Life and Times of Ernest Bevin*, vol. 1 (London: Heinemann, 1960), pp. 108–9.
114. Note, n.d. (1 October 1919); LG F/18/3/28. The discussions of 10 October are detailed in an appendix to WC (627), 3 October 1919; CAB 23–12–25/6.
115. WC (627), 3 October 1919; CAB 23–12–24. Agreement signed by Lloyd George and J. H. Thomas, 5 October 1919; LG F/24/1/13. For the negotiations see Bagwell, *op. cit.*, pp. 397–8 and Hankey's diary, 12 October 1919; Hankey Papers, HNKY 1/5, f. 90–1. For Rowntree, see A. Briggs, *Social Thought and Social Action* (London: Longmans, 1961) pp. 249–52.
116. Hankey's diary, 12 October 1919; f. 91–2. Roskill, *op. cit.*, pp. 123–4.
117. Entry, 6 October 1919; Passfield Papers, I, 365.
118. Bagwell, *op. cit.*, p. 399.
119. Riddell, *Peace Conference*, pp. 130–1.

8
The Road to 'Black Friday', April 1921

The challenge of the trade unions remained potent while the economy was booming. This was the case until the summer of 1920. Wholesale prices were at their highest in April and May 1920 but fell fast from August; while the cost of living index (reflecting selected retail prices) peaked in October 1920 and fell rapidly from December 1920. The quarterly indices of production also showed a dramatic drop in the last quarter of 1920. Trade union membership in Great Britain, which had been at 4.1 million at the outbreak of the First World War and 6.5 million at the end of 1918, reached a peak of 8.3 million at the end of 1920 but fell to 6.5 million a year later and to 5.6 million by the end of 1922.[1] By late 1920 trade union action was primarily defensive in nature.

The government's attitude to the unions was affected by its increasingly deflationary economic policy. In August Lloyd George had warned, 'The war taught military men that it was easier to capture a position than to retain it. That is a lesson for Labour. They have captured much more advanced positions than they have ever held before.'[2] Thereafter, beginning with the autumn 1919 rail strike, the government appeared to be supporting, or even actively promoting, wage cuts in British industry. During that dispute Sidney Webb wrote in the *New Statesman*, 'There is, it is believed, a determination, in which the Cabinet concurs, that irrespective of current price, wages have got to be reduced throughout all industry.' He ascribed such a determination to farmers, some engineering employers and coal owners. By August 1920 a writer in the *New Statesman* expressed views commonly held in Labour circles:

> It is plain, as the inevitable reaction from the artificial prosperity of war approaches, that many politicians and employers are looking to that reaction to lower wages nearer to their old level, to create unemployment which will weaken trade union resistance, and to provide the occasion for a complete return to the pre-war economies to which they cling. The

reported determination of employers in all the leading trades, acting in more or less open collusion with the government, to resist further wage advances, even despite advancing prices, may be regarded as the first step on this path.[3]

Pushing down wages was one aspect of economic policies which were geared to decontrolling industry and returning to fiscal and monetary orthodoxy.

Even in the midst of the post-war economic boom, the competitiveness of British industry was a matter of major anxiety for the government. In August 1919 Lloyd George had told both his War Cabinet colleagues and the House of Commons that low output was the greatest economic problem for the country. In what was to be a familiar litany aired by twentieth-century British premiers, he declared, 'We are spending more, we are earning less; we are consuming more, we are producing less.'[4] Whitehall was concerned in particular with the industries under government control, where industrialists were deemed to be colluding with the trade unions, agreeing to extra pay and better conditions, maintaining high profits, and passing the cost on to consumers through higher prices. During the boom the impact on exports of low productivity and high prices was masked by the scale of overseas demand and by the falling exchange rate of sterling. Between 20 March 1919, when the wartime artificial supports for sterling were ended, and 4 February 1920 the pound fell from \$4.76½ to a low of \$3.20½.

From August 1919 Lloyd George gave a much higher priority to tackling inflation. Following his reassessment at Criccieth of government priorities and the current political scene, he was in no doubt about the seriousness of growing middle-class unrest over both the level of inflation and taxation. That month he agreed to measures which would restrict the number of bank notes in circulation (note issue had been unlimited during the war) and would remove wartime control on the movement of capital overseas, thereby ensuring higher interest rates within Britain. Subsequently, the rates on three-month and six-month Treasury bills were increased first from 3.5 to 4.5 per cent and from 4 to 5 per cent respectively on 6 October and then by a further 0.5 per cent on 7 November. The bank rate was also raised from 5 to 6 per cent on 6 November 1919. These measures played an early part in bringing about the deceleration in the rate of growth of the money supply from 17 to 5 per cent between the twelve months starting in January 1919 and the twelve months from January 1921.[5] Thus the policy of currency deflation was well under way before Austen Chamberlain, on 15 December 1919, formally announced the government's commitment to accept the Cunliffe Committee's recommendation to return to gold at the pre-war parity.

Chamberlain, the Treasury and the Bank of England attacked inflation by taking tough monetary measures advocated by the Cunliffe Committee Reports. Of central importance was the restriction of the number of bank notes in circulation. In its first report the committee had commented that the 'unlimited issue of currency notes has been both an inevitable consequence and a necessary condition of this growth of credit.' In its second report the committee laid down that 'the actual maximum fiduciary circulation [the number of currency notes available above those covered by the Bank of England's gold reserves] in any one year should become the legal maximum of the following year.' Chamberlain expressly accepted this in the Commons on 15 December. Indeed, the note limit was fixed at £320 million in 1920 (against nearly £326 million in 1919) and at £317 million in 1921, with the aim of reducing it to £248 million by 1924.

Even higher interest rates in the spring of 1920 added to the monetary squeeze. With the government firmly ruling out the alternative of an expansion of the money supply and with the economy still booming, the banks pressed for a further rise in interest rates. The government itself was pushed this way by a fall in the sales of Treasury bills at a time when it wished to sell more of them as a means of drawing surplus money from the economy. Hence, on 14 April 1920, the rate of interest on Treasury bills was raised from 5.5 to 6 per cent, and on the next day the bank rate was increased from 6 to 7 per cent. This put the bank rate at a higher level than at any time since 1873, other than to meet the panics accompanying the outbreak of the First World War and the 1907 American banking crisis. This high rate of 7 per cent was maintained until 28 April 1921, by which time Britain was in the depths of an acute economic depression.[6] The accompanying rising value of sterling, which reached an exchange rate of $4.45 in October 1922 (the month Lloyd George fell from office), contributed to the problems of British industry from mid-1920 onwards.[7] Overall, the government's dear money policy ensured that in Britain the 1921–2 slump was both more severe and more prolonged than it might otherwise have been.

These deflationary policies were one aspect of 'sound finance'. Another major financial problem which had a substantial impact on labour was Britain's war debts. At the start of the 1919–20 financial year Britain had accumulated an internal debt of £6142.1 million. The scale of the problem of servicing this debt was due to the preference of wartime governments for raising a large proportion of wartime revenue by issuing high-interest government war loans, Treasury bills and War Savings Certificates rather than by heavy direct taxation. During the First World War revenue only covered about 36 per cent of expenditure. By the end of the war the internal debt carried an average rate of interest of 4.65 per cent (compared to 3.25 before the war). Paying the interest charges on internal public debt took a very substantial proportion of the revenue of peacetime budgets, amounting to 34, 31 and 36 per cent in 1920, 1921 and 1922 respectively (as against 12.3 per cent in 1914). In the immediate aftermath of the war inflation depreciated the value of the interest payments. But as prices dropped, the real burden of the war debt was increased.[8]

By 1920 the government was backing away from radical measures to settle the war debt quickly. In this it was responding to the hostility of financial interests, much in the way it had made concessions to business pressure over its plans for the reorganisation of transport and over the Sankey Commission's Second Report. Earlier, given public opinion in the latter stages of the war and the first year of the peace, it had seemed that some major move to 'conscript capital' was inevitable. So much was this the case that for a period influential financial figures advocated a forced loan as a less objectionable policy than a capital levy.[9]

The notion of a capital levy had appealed to both Lloyd George and Bonar Law during the war. In the earlier part of the war Lloyd George had considered mobilising capital by a combination of a levy and a forced loan.[10] In November 1917 Bonar Law had publicly aired the probable need of a capital levy after the war – and for his pains had received exceedingly indignant responses from many of the Conservative Party's most influential supporters. After the war Bonar Law distanced himself from the need for such a tax, but he still observed to one former right-wing Liberal MP in May 1919, there is ... more in it than probably you would be ready to acknowledge, if it could be looked upon simply as a fiscal measure without the prejudice involved in it by the fact that the Labour Party are putting it forward for the express purpose if not of confiscating capital at least of making it pay to finance every kind of social reform.[11]

As Bonar Law appreciated, such a financial move could have an appeal well beyond organised labour, indeed to income tax payers generally. Some form of capital levy would deal with war debt on a once-and-for-all basis, thereby removing the annual debt-servicing burden on the taxpayer. For the Labour Party it was not just seen as a matter of social justice. The move was also viewed as a way to free potential funds for social reform, rather than allocating such money annually for the payment of interest on war loans.[12]

In late 1919 there was widespread acceptance of the need to act on war fortunes. This was true both in ministerial circles and among some of the leading Asquithian Liberals. In October Austen Chamberlain informed J. L. Garvin, the editor of *The Observer*,

As to a levy on war fortunes, my instructions to the Inland Revenue were that they were to produce the best scheme that they could. I hope that they will be able to produce a practical scheme, for I think that the existence of large accretions of war wealth are not only a fair subject of taxation but that the prejudice created by them endangers all capital.[13]

In the case of the Asquithian Liberals, Herbert Samuel sent Runciman a proposal for a 75 per cent tax on wartime increases to fortunes over £10,000. In this its purpose 'to remove social discontent' was put very bluntly:

The chief purpose of the tax is not financial but social. The working class will not settle down; they will not actually increase production, or co-operate contentedly in a system of joint industrial councils, so long as they have before their eyes the evidence of great fortunes made during the war.

The contrast of riches and poverty tended to make our social system unstable before the war. The accentuation of those contrasts as a consequence of a war in which all classes were exhorted to make every sacrifice for the country, is likely to render it far more unstable. It is true that the total yield of such a tax cannot at present be foretold. But even if it were comparatively small, it is worth exacting as the only means of preventing the continuous growth of social discontent.[14]

However, there were divisions of opinion among both ministers and

Asquithian Liberals as to whether it was fair or practically possible to apply a special heavy tax just to war wealth.

During 1919 Lloyd George had appeared to be among those most eager to take decisive action on war wealth in particular and profiteering in general. In August he had been at his most colourful in warning his colleagues against delay. He went so far as to tell them that 'he would be most anxious if Parliament separated and the government was faced with ruling this country for three or four months without any powers for dealing with the profiteers.' The War Cabinet minutes record him saying on the subject of profiteering:

> The agitation was receiving the support of the professional classes and the people with small incomes: they were behind the working class. He had heard army officers talk wild Bolshevism on the subject of profiteering; when these men returned to civil life they were made to pay enormous prices for everything. Profiteering was wielding these classes together in one common persistence against the state of things, which undoubtedly constituted a great danger to the state. . . .
>
> Everyone was out for a profit. Pre-war profits, which were regarded as legitimate and reasonable, were now looked upon as trivial. . . . [there were huge profits in iron and steel] But the same thing applied everywhere: drapers, grocers, everyone was trebling his profits. The making of money had become a craze, like an alcoholic craving, which could not be resisted. The working classes would not tolerate it and . . . it was at the bottom of the trouble in this country more than any other individual cause.

In this, as with his similar warnings on housing, Lloyd George had been pressing hard to ensure a high priority for those parts of the Coalition's general election manifesto which appealed most to its Liberal members. In the case of profiteering action was quick. On the following day, 6 August, the government informed the Commons of its intention to introduce a Bill. The War Cabinet had considered a Bill on 14 July, and had it redrafted after further discussion on 7 August.[15] The resulting Profiteering Act of 18 August 1919 empowered the Board of Trade to examine the operations of trusts and combines, to investigate charges of profiteering and to take action against profiteers.

Thereafter Lloyd George maintained an interest in the progress of both the profiteering enquiries and the practicability of a levy on wartime increases in wealth.[16] But in early June 1920, when it came to a Cabinet decision on the introduction of a tax on war wealth, to the dismay of at least Churchill, Addison and H. A. L. Fisher of his

Liberal Coalition colleagues, Lloyd George came down against it. By the time that a House of Commons select committee chaired by Sir William Pearce, the Coalition Liberal MP for Limehouse, reported in May the political mood was changing. By then there were signs that the consumer boom was ending, the government had been pursuing a tougher line with organised labour for some months and the popular pressure for such action had weakened.

In June 1920 Conservatives in the Cabinet were now much less impressed by talk of ex-servicemen and others expecting that those who had come out of the war with increased wealth 'should be made to surrender some considerable part of their abnormal gains'. They were more mindful of warnings that if the tax was adopted the government 'would incur immense odium, more particularly among their principal supporters and those on whom the permanent commercial prosperity of this country largely depended, without giving satisfaction to their opponents'.[17] Moreover, there were also widespread feelings that if a special tax were introduced it would be better if it were applied to all wealth and not just that which had been gained during the war. For, as Tom Jones summarised the point, 'You cannot distinguish money made during the War from money made out of the War.'[18]

A very striking feature of the Cabinet's discussion of a war-wealth tax was its readiness to respond to the sensibilities of financial interests. Ministers took notice of the information that financiers, along with many industrialists, feared that its 'adoption might even produce a grave financial panic'. In contrast they gave short shrift to businessmen's opposition to the alternative option of maintaining the Excess Profits Duty. In the latter case, while 'all the evidence before the Cabinet showed the opinion of the business world throughout Great Britain to be unanimous against the tax', the ministers ignored it, the Cabinet minutes noting that 'Such protests were always made when a new tax was threatened, and prophecies of complete disaster had been falsified.' In the end the government did not introduce a war-wealth tax, nor a more general capital levy, nor a forced loan (the latter being a proposal which the Cabinet were advised not to consider 'particularly on the ground of the dangerous precedent which would thereby be created').[19] Financial prudence was readily equated with the interests of the savers in general and the rich in particular. The failure to ensure that they made sacrifices contrasted with the experience of other groups in society. As Kenneth

Morgan has observed, 'The demands of ex-servicemen and of millions of trade unionists, who were confronted with wage cuts while the massive war profits remained untouched, were set aside in the interests of the "centre" as identified with anti-socialism and anti-egalitarianism.'[20]

Failure to take action to remove rapidly much of the war debt adversely affected social reconstruction, just as did the dear money policies. The need to service the war debt made less funds available for social reform. On 5 August Chamberlain observed that 'it was not extravagance which was our danger so much as that we were trying to carry into effect at one moment more schemes for the benefit of the country than we were able to afford.'[21] In the case of housing, the government's major social reconstruction programme, the increases in the bank rate in November 1919 and April 1920 caused very serious problems to policies which were already in difficulty. After the second rise Addison complained to Lloyd George,

> The recent issue of £7 million stock by the London County Council mainly for housing has resulted . . . in more than 80 per cent of it being left with the underwriters, and the issues for Middlesex, Essex and Kent for the same purposes are paralysed. For some reason of uncanny contrariness the Treasury put up the rate of interest on Treasury bills to 6½ per cent in the middle of the County Council Stock Issue at 6 per cent and the whole thing dried up dead.

While most of the major problems of Addison's housing campaign stemmed from sources other than the government's tough financial policies – notably shortage of building materials, an inadequate supply of skilled labour and trade union restrictions on semi- and unskilled workers taking such work, a disorganised building industry and multitudes of local authorities all scrambling to borrow money at the same time – nevertheless, as Kenneth Morgan has observed, 'The finance of Addison's schemes had been laid in ruins.'[22]

Indeed, in some banking and business circles the fact that moves to financial orthodoxy could restrict the possibilities of social reconstruction was warmly welcomed. This was the case with the moves to convert the floating debt into long-term debt in 1921–3. The removal of many highly liquid loans was very desirable in the inflationary circumstances of 1919–20 for the Treasury bills had to be renewed quarterly. If the holders were disinclined to do so, the Treasury would have to either raise interest rates or create new credit. Thus the conversion to long-term loans strengthened the government's hand in keeping a tight constraint on credit. But in the eyes of Montagu Norman, who was the Governor of the Bank of England from 31 March 1920 until 1944, it could also constrain the government. Thus he commented, 'so long as a government has directly or indirectly a large floating debt, I wonder if any system can leave the Central Bank of that country really free to manage affairs from a purely financial standpoint.' In fact, this conversion of debt proved immensely costly, raising the total value of British internal public debt from £463 million to £693 million – a gigantic increase which may reasonably be deemed to outweigh the benefits to the Treasury of a better position on maturity dates and interest.[23]

Lloyd George may well have been slow to grasp the full implications of the government's increasingly orthodox financial policies for both social reconstruction and his own political position. In February 1920 he and Bonar Law did press Chamberlain for a cheaper money policy in order to help the housing programme and to reduce the cost of government borrowing, but they did not press sufficiently hard to overturn the decision to accept the Cunliffe Committee's Reports.[24] Politically these economic policies did much to undermine the government's social reconstruction programme, which was a major plank of Liberal Coalition politics and of wide appeal to working-class voters. Moreover, such financial orthodoxy curtailed Lloyd George's distinctive flair in domestic politics. As Riddell astutely noted in August 1919,

> His reputation has been made by his tongue and by projecting and carrying out great schemes. In the war money was no object and he was enthused by a great idea. It remains to be seen how he will shape in the management of unromantic detail involving all sorts of unpleasant decisions affecting individuals. . . . It is a different thing to be called upon to use the knife in order to carry out a humdrum policy which makes no appeal to the emotions. Today the country requires the qualities of a businessman rather than a reformer or a champion of attractive causes.[25]

In the autumn of 1919 Lloyd George was still making radical noises. He was still fighting for housing and for rural regeneration. He appealed to consumers with his promises of action against profiteers. On 17 September, surrounded by Nonconformists at the Brotherhood's Congress, Lloyd George could still draw cheers for his denunciations of 'grasping, greed, avarice, faction, timidity, indulgence' and for his denial that he had 'accepted the position of leading counsel for the old order of things'. Then he developed his speech on the theme that 'the peace of the world, the security of the world, the happiness of the world depends on the ray of fair play', which he applied to industrial relations at home as well as to international relations.[26]

By 1920 the radical strand in Lloyd George's politics was becoming very thin indeed. When he sent a message of support to the Coalition Liberal candidate in a by-election in the Norfolk South constituency its positive side was, 'The government is earnestly devoted to the task of re-establishing the peace of the world, and is determined to realise its policy of social amelioration at home, ... to reduce the burden of national expenditure which is grievously felt, and to maintain our national credit, which has always been the best in the world.'[27] By this time the programme of social amelioration was fast running out of steam and indeed was countered by the theme of economy. Indeed, Lloyd George's appeal to the middle ground of politics was increasingly negative, often made up of promises of what would not be done and what would be curtailed. The high points of his rhetoric were frequently reserved for the theme of 'Bolshevism' within Britain.

Lloyd George banged the anti-Bolshevik and anti-socialist drums repeatedly when he was appealing for a new centre party to be formed from the Coalition Liberals and Coalition Conservatives. This was the case with what Trevor Wilson has deemed to be his first public move in this direction, a speech at the Manchester Reform Club on 6 December 1919. But perhaps more striking was Lloyd George's decision to run a Coalition Liberal candidate in the Spen Valley by-election of 20 December – in spite of the local Liberals having selected the leading Asquithian Sir John Simon as their candidate to replace the deceased Coalition Liberal MP – as this marked a major public parting of the ways between him and the Independent Liberals. Lloyd George again reverted to a full-blooded denunciation of Bolshevism on 16 March 1920 when he tried unsuccessfully to convince his Coalition Liberal colleagues of the need for 'fusion' between the two wings of the government.[28]

By early 1920 Lloyd George was very anxious about the political future of the Coalition. When he had Sunday dinner with Frances Stevenson and Riddell on 1 February, he confided that he felt there was need for fusion: 'I am faced with a serious crisis ... I have told

Bonar Law that I am not going on like this. We are losing by-election after by-election. There is no proper political organisation in the country and no enthusiasm.' In this he was saying privately what Birkenhead had aired publicly. Following the Coalition candidate's defeat in the Spen Valley by-election, Birkenhead had written a series of three articles for the *Weekly Dispatch* in which he called for fusion. The articles appeared on 11 and 25 January and 1 February and caused a political sensation. Lloyd George's political concern at this time was heightened by the prospect of Asquith's return to Parliament in the Paisley by-election, an outcome which he deemed to be 'a great blow for the Coalition'. Similarly, Lloyd George had been anxious in October lest the railway dispute damage Labour's chances, and so boost those of the Asquithian Liberal, in the Manchester Rusholme by-election.[29]

Clearly, at this time Lloyd George's prime concern was not with the rise of the Labour Party but to realign politics on Centre versus Labour lines before the Asquithian Liberals revived. Presumably he did not yet fear a Tory revolt blocking his plans. The Coalition Liberal backbencher Arthur Murray noted in his diary after Lloyd George had addressed the Parliamentary Coalition Liberal Party on 18 March,

> The speech was the speech of a man fighting for his political life. It marks the beginning of a new era in the development of political parties. Personally I disagree with this attempt to divide the nation into two camps, the 'haves' and the 'have nots'. This division would inevitably lead to a bitter class war.'[30]

Lloyd George failed to carry out the fusion of the two wings of the Coalition in the spring of 1920 because many Liberal Coalitionists believed in Liberalism and disliked class-based politics. But the existence of the Coalition government and its policies were having the effect of polarising British politics between those with property and their supporters and the Labour movement and its sympathisers.[31] This was very apparent in the electoral pacts aimed at defeating Labour Party municipal candidates which were being made in many places across much of Britain. Thus one leading figure of the Washwood Heath (Birmingham) Conservatives wrote to Steel-Maitland after Labour's triumphs in gaining eleven seats on the City Council.

> There is a growing feeling amongst the Liberals in our district that they would be glad to unite with the Unionists for election purposes at least . . .

they realise that they can do nothing by themselves and yet still they form a good section of the people. . . .

There is no question but that they are afraid of 'Labour' and in my opinion there is no question but that of old time association that prevents many of them coming right over to our party.

On the other hand, as the Secretary of the Scottish Liberal Federation observed when speculating on the impact of fusion, 'If the [Liberal] camp is divided into the "haves" and "have nots" (which it really amounts to), then tens of thousands of the best type of Liberal will go with the "have nots". Of that there is no doubt.'[32]

Lloyd George's failure to carry through fusion then or later made him more dependent on the Conservatives. Though Bonar Law had been willing, albeit somewhat reluctantly, to press upon Conservative Coalitionists the need for fusion, he was not sorry that Lloyd George failed to convince the Liberal Coalitionists. Indeed, Bonar Law fully recognised, as he observed to Balfour, that 'complete fusion . . . always seemed to me more important from LG's point of view than from ours.'[33] Many of the Coalition government's by-election failures, which ostensibly had prompted Lloyd George to raise fusion, showed up the weakness of Coalition Liberalism in the country. As early as the Spen Valley by-election Sir George Younger, the Conservative Party chairman, was complaining to Bonar Law, 'We have the usual experience in this case, the Liberal organisation not being worth a rap. . . . Although this is not our seat, I have had to authorise a considerable sum to be expended in importing our own agents and workers to the constitutency.'[34] Hence, as Maurice Cowling has observed,

> the chief effect of the Labour advance was to destroy Lloyd George's credibility as a Radical, to weaken the Coalition on which his authority depended and greatly to reduce his ability to compel Conservatives to swallow Radical policies. From this point of view the events of 1920, 1921 and 1922 were an almost continuous capitulation to the wishes of the Conservative Party.[35]

Labour's electoral advance was particularly marked from the autumn of 1919. Labour had been much encouraged by many wins in the elections to Poor Law Guardians and the London County Council (LCC) elections early in the year. In England and Wales at least 1,245 Labour Guardians were elected. In the LCC elections in

March, on a very low poll (18 per cent), the Labour vote had risen from 36,690 in 1913 to 97,468 and its numbers of seats had increased from 5 to 15 (on a council of 124 seats, not 118). Much of the gain was achieved at the expense of the old Progressive group, rather than the Municipal Reform group (Conservatives and allies) – though the latter's share of the vote did fall by 15.6 per cent. At the end of August Henderson scored a notable win in a parliamentary by-election at Widnes, taking the seat on an 11.9 per cent swing from Coalition Unionist to Labour. In this he was helped by the Liberals not contesting the seat and, indeed, by the Liberals supporting his candidature.[36] These successes – and many council by-election successes – were overshadowed by the scale of Labour's triumphs in the municipal elections on 1 November 1919.

In urban areas across Britain Labour won many municipal council seats, often where earlier it had held none. In London the results were sensational, with Labour notably replacing the old Progressives (though some individuals remained as Labour councillors). Labour took outright control of Battersea (winning 43 of 54 seats), Bethnal Green (24 of 30), Camberwell (32 of 60), Deptford (21 of 36), Fulham (24 of 36), Greenwich (20 of 30), Hackney (32 of 60), Islington (44 of 60), Poplar (39 of 42), Shoreditch (32 of 42), Stepney (42 of 60) and Woolwich (25 of 36); and in each of St Pancras and Southwark it was the leading party with half the membership and a Labour mayor. In 1912 Labour had 46 councillors in the London boroughs: in 1919 the number was 572 (of a total of 1362). Herbert Morrison, the Secretary of the London Labour Party, exulted, 'London Labour has come out of the wilderness and has entered into the domain of responsible power.' In particular he pointed to Chelsea, where eight seats were won, observing 'yet there was no Labour Party there up to two months ago', and to Greenwich, where Labour took control, observing 'The Greenwich Labour Party is only a year old'. There were equally impressive Labour wins in parts of South Wales, notably in Monmouthshire and Glamorgan, and in the north of England, notably County Durham. Little wonder that on 2 November Riddell found Lloyd George 'rather perturbed at the victory of the Labour people'.[37]

In December 1919 and early 1920 Labour achieved some remarkable parliamentary by-election successes. It had done well in the autumn, achieving swings to Labour from the Coalition of 9, 17.5 and 13.5 per cent at Pontefract on 5 September, Manchester Rusholme on 7 October and Plymouth Sutton on 15 November respectively, but without winning the seats; and had held on to its Durham mining seat of Chester-le-Street on 13 November with 77 per cent of the total vote. But on 20 December it won the Spen Valley seat in spite of Sir John Simon standing as the Liberal candidate (and beating the Coalition Liberal candidate into third place).

It also scored some very high votes in seats it had not contested before and which over the years had been poor places for Labour candidates. On 10 December, in a three-way contest, Labour came within 713 votes of winning St Albans, Hertfordshire, from the Coalition Unionists, and a week later – in a straight contest with a Coalition Unionist – it took 47 per cent of the votes cast and came within 1,071 votes of winning Bromley, Kent. In two three-way contests in late January 1920 Labour came within 737 votes of winning Ashton-under-Lyne and 538 votes of winning the Wrekin (Shropshire). Labour had never stood a candidate before in St Albans, Bromley or the Wrekin. On 27 March, after coming third at Horncastle (Lincolnshire) and second in Argyllshire (with a swing to Labour from Coalition Liberal of 16.5 per cent), Labour scored its most remarkable by-election victory of 1919–20 at Dartford (Kent). There, J. E. Mills converted an 8,120 Coalition Liberal majority into a 9,048 Labour majority in spite of four opponents. In so doing he received just over half the votes. Though the scale of the triumph owed something to a Coalition Unionist being run there in place of a Coalition Liberal and there also being a Liberal candidate, it was nevertheless a major victory.[38] Taking all these results together, it is no wonder that the Labour Party was seen as a major political force, one of much more significance than the results of the 1918 general election might suggest.

In the heady atmosphere of 1919 and 1920 Labour Party organisations mushroomed up across the country, drawing strength from local trade union branches which themselves were flourishing in the post-war boom. By mid-1920 the Labour Party had over 2,000 constituency and local parties and trades councils and had set up 425 women's sections. It had appointed 112 Labour Party agents. A further 24 had been appointed by affiliated organisations (14 of whom were miners' agents).[39] While the optimism and enthusiasm of those years was bound to be tempered in time, and Labour's organisation was weakened, especially in rural areas, in the economic recession of the 1920s,[40] nevertheless in 1920 politicians of other parties were right to be impressed. Ahead of the Paisley by-election of 12 February 1920, Lloyd George privately commented to Herbert Lewis that he 'thought that the Labour organisation was so far superior to that of other parties that in all probability they would capture a considerable proportion of this [electors who did not vote in 1918] and similar elements throughout the country'. He even commented publicly in the Commons that 'the Labour Party . . . is organising well, efficiently and with great skill throughout the country. There is no doubt about that.'[41]

The Labour Party and the Labour movement generally could readily unite in opposition to the Coalition government. Even on issues on which there were very real divisions of opinion within the Labour movement, the government's actions often provided ample cause for all to act together. This was the case with Russia in 1919. Although there were major differences as to the merits of Bolshevik rule, there were very few Labour Party members or trade unionists who were not outraged by Allied intervention. Similarly, while the issue of 'direct action' caused considerable friction between many of the Labour Party and TUC leadership and socialist activists, few were not appalled by Churchill's military preparations as illustrated in his questions to commanders of February 1919 or by the advertisements linked to the government's supply and transport organisation. Hence a feature of the period was Labour Party or Labour Party and TUC deputations making representations on such matters to either Lloyd George or Bonar Law.[42]

The Labour Party also gained strength by vigorously representing consumers' interests, just as it had done during the First World War. The cost of food was a potentially explosive issue both during and after the war, even though problems concerning food in Britain never remotely reached the dire situation of Petrograd in February 1917 or in Germany and Central Europe in 1918 to 1920 following the Allied blockade. Before the war had ended, profiteering in food was already a major political issue, and one which it was noted in Whitehall was being taken up by Labour parliamentary candidates. But curiously, when in October 1918 Sir Albert Stanley wished to set up an enquiry having been prompted by a mass meeting of miners at Cannock Chase who 'felt very keenly on this question', Clynes as Food Controller had obstructed this on the grounds that it would be 'likely to cause grave misconception amongst working classes' and be likely to achieve nothing after prolonged investigations.[43] Thereafter, in spite of Clynes, Labour and the Co-operative Movement became firmly identified with the poplular demand for action or profiteering and for the continuance of the Ministry of Food.[44]

Labour had also become identified with wartime campaigns to hold down rents and to improve housing conditions. After the war it maintained its campaigning in this area. While Addison did succeed in getting considerable numbers of houses built, albeit at a high price and at a high political cost, these did little for working-class people in industrial areas who increasingly looked to municipal socialism for action on housing and related matters.[45] Labour's success in the November 1919 municipal elections was seen within the Labour movement to be a mandate to provide 'better education, better housing, better sanitation; in fact better everything that concerns our everyday life', and it was expected that there would be 'a revival of the demand for the granting of greater powers to local authorities without the cumbrous and costly procedure of Private Bill legislation'.[46] Such issues appealed to a wider electorate than just trade unionists. In a study of Clydeside politics Ian McLean has commented that 'the appalling and unchanging quality of housing formed the basis of a very popular Labour appeal.'[47] The Labour Party was well aware of the importance of housing in particular in attracting the support of women electors. In conjunction with a campaign on the issue, it published in 1919 *The Working Woman's House* by Mrs Sanderson and Dr Marion Phillips.

Labour gained still more strength by inheriting much nonconformist support which before the First World War had gone to the Liberals. Arthur Henderson in particular was one of the pre-eminent nonconformist political figures of the post-First World War period. Labour's emergence from the war as the party of democratic diplomacy and a major supporter of the League of Nations contributed, as Christopher Howard has commented, to it being 'more than ever seen as a moral crusade'.[48] It became a natural focal point not only of those who deplored the intervention in Russia but also of those who opposed the government's use of the army to suppress dissent in India, Egypt and the Middle East in the immediate post-war period. Labour's criticism of such imperial actions became all the more powerful when linked to their cost at a time of middle-class demands for cutting public expenditure and reducing taxes.[49]

Labour gained the support of many more Irish voters living in Britain as the party came to support a Republic in Ireland. But this took a while, for Henderson and other Labour Party leaders had been committed Home Rulers before the First World War. They remained so until at least early 1920. They were converted by the scale of opposition to British rule that existed outside of the northern counties and by the ever increasing use of force by the British authorities. Support for a Republic grew rapidly as many in the Labour movement were as outraged by the use of undue force there, just as they had been at the similar repressive action in India which had led to many deaths at Amritsar on 13 April 1919. In addition, after Sinn Fein had run a candidate against Labour in a by-election at Stockport on 27 March 1919, the Labour Party leadership was very aware of the need to be unequivocal on Ireland if they were to inherit the organised Irish vote in Britain. Henderson made a point of publicly taunting the Coalition Liberals with such comments as 'they have to tolerate a policy of coercion in Ireland that would have made Gladstone sick with horror; they have to tolerate a scheme of Home Rule for Ireland, which Gladstone would not have looked at for a moment.' Hence, within two or three years of the Armistice, the Irish Catholic community in Glasgow was firmly behind the Labour Party and many leading figures of the United Irish League were Labour councillors.[50]

The Labour Party also built on its pre-war reputation as the champion of the unemployed. In the immediate post-war period local parties and trades councils in many cities and larger towns took up with differing success the grievances of unemployed ex-servicemen and discharged munitions workers. But nationally the Labour Party failed to foster the National Union of Ex-Servicemen, and the hostility of some skilled trade unions to waiving apprenticeship regulations or to ease ex-servicemen's way into work by other means added further strains to relationships between ex-servicemen and the Left. A minority of veterans did remain very radical, some being involved in such 'direct action' as occupations of empty houses.[51] Later, with the downturn in the economy in mid-1920 and with growing disillusionment over the Coalition's reconstruction promises, the Labour Party did better in winning and maintaining support from unemployed people.

The solid bedrock of the Labour Party's support remained the trade unions. In 1920 trade union membership in Great Britain reached a peak of 8,253,000, a figure which it was not to attain again until 1946. Unionisation covered some 58 per cent of all male workers who could be deemed potential union members, and some 25 per cent of women workers. In sectors such as coalmining, cotton, pottery, printing, construction, gas, footwear, metals and engineering, the railways, land, sea and inland water transport, post and telecommunications, local and national government union membership covered more than half the workforce.[52] The strength and the confidence of the unions compensated for the weakness and lacklustre nature of the Parliamentary Labour Party, much as it was to do after 1931.

Just as what were seen as the misdeeds of the Coalition government helped to unite the Labour movement, so the many and varied faces of Labour gave Lloyd George many targets for his rhetoric and offered him a threat against which he could rally the disparate supporters of his government. In his attacks on the Labour Party Lloyd George was skilful at highlighting Labour's inconsistencies. Thus he could point to the Independent Labour Party's rhetoric against capitalism and ask whether Labour, if it obtained office, intended to end capitalism or make it work. Similarly, he made much of the conflict of approach between the supporters of 'direct action' and those dedicated to purely parliamentary means of achieving change. In this, he was primarily aiming to rally support for himself both among politicians and the electorate, though on some occasions he may also have sought to divide moderate Labour supporters from that Party. This tactic was expressed clearly by Sir William Sutherland, Coalition Liberal MP and a political organiser close to Lloyd George in mid-April 1920 (after Labour had come third in by-elections in Basingstoke and Edinburgh North and failed to win in Camberwell and Northampton):

> In the Labour world the moderates and the extremists are very dissatisfied with one another, and are saying so. The moderates are blaming the extremists violently for the bad show that Labour has made in the recent by-elections. Our biggest gain with them is always to drive in the wedge.[53]

Lloyd George warned against socialism and the Labour Party in his speech on 18 March 1920 to Liberal Coalition MPs, when he was arguing the case for fusion. He claimed that Labour MPs were not representative of the real movement. He also spoke darkly of the party having common ownership as its doctrine – which was known in France as communism, in German as socialism, and in Russia as Bolshevism. *The Times'* parliamentary correspondent observed that

Lloyd George had used the meeting as 'the opportunity to pick another quarrel with the Labour Party' and that in denigrating moderate Labour MPs 'he seems ... to have swung definitely to the Right'. Henderson, in a press release, replied by asserting:

> The organised Labour movement has just emphatically declared against a policy of direct action and in favour of political methods. That implies a rapid development of the political labour movement, based on a broad appeal to all classes of the community....
>
> What was there in the Labour Party document from which Mr Lloyd George quoted that justified the description of Bolshevism? It is an unscrupulous misrepresentation to suggest that we conceal subversive aims behind the definitions of our programme. When Mr Lloyd George says that Labour does not seek to redress grievances and secure the improvement of conditions because that would strengthen the existing system, he says what no man more than himself knows to be untrue....
>
> We desire to give the electors a fair opportunity of choosing between the class politics of Mr Lloyd George and the policy of public ownership and democratic administration of public enterprises for which Labour stands.[54]

While Lloyd George delighted in publicly linking Henderson and other Labour leaders to Bolshevism, he was well aware of their abhorrence of the Bolsheviks and of communism. In private, his main criticism of the Labour leadership was that it was mediocre and unfit to govern. He observed to Bonar Law, Birkenhead, Riddell and others in January 1920 that in a revolutionary situation a Labour government would not have the will to use the army and navy to re-establish order:

> They would allow themselves to be rushed and would lose control. That is the great danger of a Labour government. If Henderson and his friends were in authority and there was a strike say in Manchester, they would not be prepared to use force to preserve law and order. They would send a man down to talk to the crowd. And they would share Kerensky's fate. He was a great talker, but he let the time for action slip by.

In a way his belief in the incompetence of Labour was matched by Lenin, who observed later in the year, 'I hope Henderson comes to power with the Labour Party; it will be a lesson to the workers.'[55]

Lloyd George was fully prepared to take tough action against militant trade unionists, let alone against revolutionaries. He made much of this to Conservative politicians. On the same occasion that he doubted a Labour government's willingness to put down revolutionary disorder, he expressed similar contempt for the British upper classes' ability to act decisively. He observed, 'They are always afraid to begin [fighting] for fear of precipitating a catastrophe. Consequently they let the psychological moment pass and the change takes place before they have time to muster their forces.'

Immediately after the autumn 1919 rail strike Lloyd George made it known publicly that he was ready and willing to use the government's emergency supply organisation. On 7 October when rebutting Labour charges that the government had used a war organisation on the workers, he declared that in fact it had been set up after the war, in February, and stated, 'I want to make it clear that it was not a war organisation which will pass away the moment you demobilise completely. That is an important fact to bring home.' Two days later, when seeing a deputation from the TUC and the Miners' Federation about nationalisation of the mines, he warned,

> I am far from counselling that we should purchase the goodwill and cooperation of any section of labour at the price of concessions which would harm every other secton of the land. . . . We cannot submit to a section of the community who would hold all industry up because it cannot get its own way on one subject on which it has set its heart.[56]

Lloyd George and other ministers had been well pleased by the operation of their strike-breaking organisation during the railway strike. On 14 October the War Cabinet agreed to its continuation and placed it under a new Cabinet committee called the Supply and Transport Committee (in place of the Industrial Unrest Committee), which was chaired by Sir Eric Geddes, the Minister of Transport. During the autumn and winter of 1919–20 civil servants worked on plans to improve the organisation. The arrangements for milk supplies to London were remodelled. By mid-December 1919 the Ministry of Food's Emergency Committee was reassured that all schemes to ensure the supply, transport and distribution of food, other than that for coastal transport, were ready for operation. Steps were taken to recruit skilled volunteer labour. This included approaching the professional bodies of electrical and civil engineers and getting them to agree 'to invite their members by circular to volunteer for service during a strike'. Similarly, plans were made for local authorities to take the major role in maintaining local transport and gas and electricity supplies.[57]

However, the very act of planning against internal emergencies appears to have caused a state of panic among some ministers. Probably this was brought about by a combination of alarmist reports from Sir Henry Wilson, the Chief of the Imperial General Staff, and an awareness that in the midst of a still-booming economy Lloyd George was determined to confront any further challenge from the miners. The alarm was precipitated by negotiations with all three members of the Triple Alliance running into trouble at this time, and it appearing that a co-ordinated strike might occur in March.[58]

Wilson and Macready had been unduly anxious at the time of the railway strike. The day before it began Wilson warned Lloyd George, 'if the Triple Alliance does join them, watch Ireland' and Macready apparently told newspaper owners and their representatives on 4 October that if all the trade unions came out on strike on 8 October 'the result may be a revolution'.[59] In late December 1919 and early January 1920 Wilson was very alarmist. On 31 December he warned Bonar Law that 'the Triple Alliance would undoubtedly beat us if we had no plans.' On 7 January he wrote to Lloyd George,

> In view of the industrial unrest in England, in view of the revolutionary or separatist movements in Ireland, Egypt, Mesopotamia and India, in view of the untrained condition of our new Regular Army and of the deplorable lack of skilled and trained mechanics in all branches of the Army, I am getting increasingly anxious about the future. I would therefore urge in the strongest possible manner that the despatch of 11 battalions to the Plebiscite areas be cancelled. I realise the difficulties of such a course but I am much impressed with the necessity of looking after our own affairs and our own safety before the affairs and safety of other people.[60]

When the Supply and Transport Committee met on 15 January it was clear that several ministers shared Wilson's anxieties about the government's ability to quell a serious challenge to its authority. By this time the government had backed away from setting up a citizen guard to maintain order and to protect property. On 3 October the Home Secretary had appealed to mayors to organise such a body, but the proposal had met with opposition in some areas then and had gained very little support later, with many suggesting that special constables were quite adequate.[61] Ministers were shaken when Churchill described the inadequate supply of troops available for dealing with a major strike or serious social disorder. Wilson noted in his diary, 'One after another said there was nothing to be done, that the police were powerless, that the Citizen Guard had been forbidden by the unions, and that now the unions would not allow special constables to be sworn, and treated them as blacklegs.'[62]

Several ministers reiterated their alarm to Lloyd George in Paris the next day, when they conferred with him on aspects of the peace negotiations. On the 18 January Horne saw Lloyd George and painted a lurid picture of imminent revolution, one element of which included the information that the miners planned 'to take the country at its weakest, that is to say, in March'. Lloyd George, like Hankey, appears to have viewed their excessive concern with some degree of incredulity. Before Horne's arrival Hankey observed to Lloyd George,

> I was surprised to hear that so serious a view was taken of the outlook . . . so far as I have been able to judge, though there are many clouds on the horizon, on the whole the sky seemed to be getting clearer, the output of coal is steadily increasing, trade is getting going, I understand that bankers all over the country are not dissatisfied with the outlook, labour is a good deal divided in its own house, and so far as my opportunities for observation extend, the spirit of labour as a whole is better. The very winning of elections by labour tends to strengthen the Moderates at the expense of the Extremists.[63]

Hankey's view was buttressed by that of Basil Thomson, usually an unrestrained alarmist. He reported to the Cabinet:

> Reports appear to be circulating in London that a revolution is to be expected within the next two months. This is quite at variance with the evidence. On the contrary, there has never been a time within the last nine months when the extremists were so ill-equipped to bring about a sudden *coup d'état*.[64]

A very notable feature of ministerial fears was of a *coup d'état*. During a conversation with political colleagues over a meal on 10 January, even Lloyd George speculated that there was a strong chance that within ten years there could be a change of government in Britain through a 'forcible seizure of the instrument of government'. Such a danger was deemed to be imminent by those at the Supply and Transport Committee on 15 January. According to the minutes, 'Fears were expressed that the country would have to face in the near future an organised attempt at seizing the reins of government in some of the large cities, such as Glasgow, London and Liverpool.' In addition, they feared 'that the next strike would commence with sabotage on an extensive scale, directed towards the destruction of means of communication and transport.'[65] Lloyd George's colleagues gave vent to their every revolutionary fear at a meeting on industrial unrest that he chaired on 2 February. Roberts talked of industrial sabotage and of 'large groups preparing for Soviet government', Bonar Law spoke of organising stockbrockers ('a loyal and fighting class'), Churchill envisaged an attempt to stage a coup in central London ('a sort of Gunpowder Plot'), and Walter Long complained, 'The peaceable manpower of the country is without arms. I have not a pistol less than 200 years old.' Tom Jones, who took detailed minutes of the meeting, observed that 'throughout the discussion the PM did a lot of unsuspected leg-pulling as he does not believe in the imminence of the revolution and more than suspects the War Office of trying to increase the army on these lines.'[66] Lloyd George was happy to encourage such anxieties when he was pressing to create an anti-Labour new party. Nevertheless, ministers still seriously considered the dangers of a coup as late as the 1921 coal strike.[67]

Yet the expectation of a major confrontation with organised labour also owed something to Lloyd George's determination to take it on in a time of economic boom. Lloyd George did move to the right in the winter of 1919–20. He did aim to redraw party lines on a property versus socialism basis. As Lady Lee of Fareham noted in May 1920, 'He is impatient with the Liberal "Wee Frees" and wishes them out of the way in order that he may get to grips with the "real enemy – Labour".'[68] But his swing to the right was not just opportunism or an awareness where the centre of gravity lay in the 1918 House of Commons, rather a reflection of his views during that winter.

Part of this was an extension of his long-held belief in the need to restore industry to its peacetime state as quickly as possible. As 1919 went on he appears to have become more and more convinced of the need to decontrol industry and cut subsidies as quickly as possible. Even so, while his attitude swung that way he nevertheless remained willing to assess each case individually and pragmatically. Indeed, ministers as a whole were pushed towards flexibility given the post-war international economic dislocation and the lengthy time it took to restore industries and markets to something approaching a peacetime equilibrium. This was very much the case with controls over food and with those industries where total deregulation and decontrol would lead to high unemployment. A good illustration of this was the herring fishing industry. In mid-1919, in spite of the Chancellor of the Exchequer's protests at 'the accumulating proposals for government guaranteees in order to induce traders to carry on their industries', the War Cabinet accepted the need to share any loss of a limited barrelage of cured herrings for a year given the loss of normal export markets in Germany and Russia, the services of the fishermen in the navy during the war and the prospect of more than 12,000 people out of work. A year later, in spite now of talk of 200,000 people being unemployed and that rival industries in Norway, Holland and Denmark were being subsidised, the Cabinet announced the end of subsidies. But after the Cabinet was informed that this 'had caused dismay throughout the fishing community of Great Britain, local authorities were passing resolutions of protest, and agitators were beginning to prey on what was normally a peaceful industry', it soon decided to provide a smaller guarantee, albeit combined with consideration of 'the advisability of reducing prices and, indirectly, wages'.[69]

Although economic and political circumstances often slowed down decontrol, Lloyd George did display a growing disposition against 'big government'. Thus when on 23 December 1919 he saw a deputation from London local authorities about the price of milk he expressed sympathy for the needs of children but ruled out a milk subsidy because of 'the state of the national finance'. Significantly, he did not end the argument there. According to one press report, he went on to express the view:

> It was bad in principle, and was bound to end in disaster. It would degrade the general level of the manliness of the country; therefore the object really ought to be rather to get out of subsidies than to get into them.

He had always been an admirer of entrepreneurs. In this period he was often unrestrained in his praise. In condemning nationalisation of the mines in the House of Commons on 11 February 1920, he observed:

> You have got now the incentive of private profit, the incentive that a man may have a fortunate venture and his capital be increased considerably. He knows that he runs the risk of losing it, but there are men in the country engaged in operations of that kind who are prepared to take the risk. I do

not believe that you would get that risk by committees of this kind [i.e. for a nationalised coal industry]. There is not sufficient incentive. You impede, you retard, you freeze development.

Riddell, who was usually perceptive when commenting on Lloyd George, noted in March 1920,

> I believe LG is honestly convinced that Socialism is a mistaken policy. The war has shown him the value and strength of individual effort and the weakness of government departments. I have observed this conviction growing upon him during the past four years. His point of view has entirely changed, so both from conviction and expediency the No-Socialism cry appeals to him.[70]

There was the same mixture of conviction and expediency in the way that Lloyd George moved increasingly in harmony with many of the predominant attitudes among businessmen. By 1920 employers generally were taking a harder line with labour. In some cases this was due to dissatisfaction with trade union promises of increased production in return for the reduced working hours and higher wages. In other cases it owed much to a restored confidence in the unrevolutionary nature of the British working class and a desire to move 'the frontier of control' back somewhat in their favour. In most industries the return of European competitors to international markets further played a part. By late 1919 Lloyd George was markedly sympathetic not only to complaints about workers failing to increase output but also to the general demand of 'Home Rule for industry'. Sir Alfred Pease put this viewpoint bluntly in a private letter of July 1919:

> It is quite time that the government declared against Nationalisation, Socialism and Disorder. No one knows where they are – either in industry or in agriculture or anything else. The first thing is for the government to get back to its proper functions and leave trade, land, industries and people alone. All this regulating business is making chaos.[71]

On another major issue of concern to businessmen, that of government action against profiteering, Lloyd George, was adopting a less populist stance by 1920. In August 1919 he and other Coalition Liberals had been passionate on the subject. H. A. L. Fisher had eagerly told his colleagues that he knew of a case of profiteering 'where a small village retailer had been able to buy an estate of 600 acres out of profits made during the war'. Then Liberal Coalition ministers had been in tune with popular outrage,[72] but by early 1920

Lloyd George was trying to pour cold water on the subject. In his response to the debate on the King's Speech on 10 February he said what people as diverse as Clynes and Bonar Law had felt from the outset, namely that the profiteering enquiries would not achieve much. His speech was notably orthodox in its approach to the issues of prices and profits. He said,

> The real explanation of the high cost of living is the devaluation of money. You may put a percentage on to cost for profit, but it was only a percentage and not a considerable one . . . there is only one way which prices can be reduced and that is more production.

While few of his audiences would have disagreed as to the relatively very small role of profiteering in the post-war inflation, his remarks nevertheless were very different in tone from the previous summer and avoided the moral and social issues. Moreover, the following day, he strained the credulity of those on the Left in British politics when he gave the optimistic verdict on the coal industry: 'There has never been an increase of profit in recent times in which the miners have not shared. High profits mean higher wages.'[73] In aligning himself increasingly with the views of many in the business community Lloyd George strengthened his position with the Coalition Conservatives, but on a few issues this was even to the point of perplexing some of his Coalition Liberal colleagues.

From this political standpoint it followed that he was likely to take an increasingly firm line with organised labour. In his speeches of the winter of 1919–20 Lloyd George was eager to proclaim that he fought autocracy whether it be that of an aristocracy or a trade union organisation. This rhetoric ran parallel to his increasingly strident denunciations of 'socialism' as his own domestic reform programme was whittled down in size. In June 1919 Sir Eric Geddes had told his colleagues that the government should be more worried about 'capital unrest' than 'labour unrest'.[74] By the end of 1919 Lloyd George appeared to be going some way in that direction, being more alert to many of the concerns of businessmen and financiers than to those of labour.

He had some grounds for being less wary of the Labour movement for in early 1920 the much feared united challenge of the Triple Alliance again did not take place. Even while some ministers were in a state of near panic, the government was reaching agreement with the railwaymen and dockers. Indeed, Tom Jones observed to Hankey on 19 January 1920, 'The railway settlement is bound to weaken any united action by the Triple Alliance. One knows how furious Smillie and Bob Williams are with Thomas and in today's papers Henderson is down on him for accepting the principle of the sliding scale.'[75]

The railway settlement of January 1920 was another notable example of J. H. Thomas getting as good a deal as he could get for his members through negotiations with the government which included him dealing secretly with ministers. After the October railway strike had ended, the government and the NUR resumed negotiations on standard rates of pay. The War Cabinet took the view that in any settlement 'the railwaymen must be made to face the question of the effect of rises in wages upon the finances of the railways.' The government offered a standard rate for each grade based on giving 38s on top of the average paid in July 1914, with changes thereafter being linked to a sliding scale based on the cost of living. The government's offer was firmly rejected by the Special General Meeting of the NUR on 7 January. Thereafter both Lloyd George and Thomas worked hard again for a compromise. Lloyd George had Sir Eric Geddes and Horne visit him in Paris and gave them full authority to reach a settlement. On 13 January the Cabinet approved the terms which Geddes and Horne had negotiated. These involved making the settlement applicable to Ireland, for standardised rates to cover all grades and for a back-dated lump sum to be paid to all employees. Geddes, in a letter to Lloyd George, paid tribute to Thomas's very hard work in achieving a settlement. He also gave Lloyd George details of the NUR Special General Meeting's voting, which Thomas had privately passed on. This revealed just how close the NUR was to taking further action rather than accepting the terms:

> The first [motion] was to reply to the government's refusal to alter the basis by striking [on 16 January]. This was defeated by 9 out of 56.
> The next was to refer the proposal to the branches; that was defeated by 9.
> The next was to accept under protest; defeated by 20.
> The next was to call in the Triple Alliance and that was a tie for and against, 28 voting in each direction.
> The next was to accept the settlement. The voting at first was even, 28 and 28, and then one delegate said he had voted the wrong way, in mistake, and that made it 29 to 27.[76]

In the case of the dockers, pressure was also taken off the government when, on 30 December 1919, the Transport Workers' Federation agreed to the employers' proposal that their claims on wages and hours should go to a public court of inquiry under the

Industrial Court Act. This Act, which had become law in November 1919, had set up a standing industrial court and enabled the Minister of Labour to appoint *ad hoc* courts of inquiry into industrial disputes. In this the Act followed the fourth report of the Whitley Committee. It was in effect continuing the wartime Committee on Production, but under this legislation arbitration was voluntary – though at a fairly late stage the government removed (after conferring with Labour leaders) a clause in the draft Bill which would have made strikes taking place against the awards within four months illegal.[77]

The dockers' case was heard in public in February and March 1920 at a court of inquiry chaired by Lord Shaw of Dunfermline (a former Scottish law officer in Liberal governments). Bevin argued the dockers' case for a better quality of life with great skill. On 31 March the majority verdict of the court recommended a national daily minimum wage of 16s for a 44-hour week, the setting up of a joint industrial council and that the system of casual labour be ended. The Shaw Inquiry proved to be a triumph for Bevin and for all those who believed that Labour could achieve a fair deal through arbitration. It could be seen, like the hearings before the Sankey Commission, to have succeeded in raising bigger issues than 'bread and butter' ones. As a *New Statesman* editorial commented, 'While the coalminers were asserting their distaste for the prospect of continuing to work for private profit, the dockers were no less firmly maintaining that they would no longer submit to the old conditions of casual employment, with the degradation of status and insecurity of standards which it involves.'[78]

Thus the government was left with one dissatisfied member of the Triple Alliance, the Miners' Federation. Smillie and the other leaders of the MFGB had learnt the lesson of the need for good public relations after the government's effective propaganda on the consequences of large coal price rises for consumers and for the employment prospects of workers in coal dependent industries. They had also found, through the failure of their 'Mines for the Nation' campaign, that nationalisation was not a popular issue with the general public. Hence in 1920 the MFGB made great efforts to persuade the public that the miners could receive a better deal out of excessive profits in the industry without harming the consumer. Their attempt to do so alarmed many in the propertied classes. Thus Lord Esher wrote to his son at the time of the October coal strike,

> People laughed at the idea of revolution. What is revolution, except the transfer of political power from one set of people to another, from one set of institutions to another. Well, now you have it. These people, miners, railwaymen etc. are determined to redistribute profits in a different manner and by a different method. They are doing it.[79]

But in fact by October 1920 economic conditions were turning to the disadvantage of the miners.

As for Lloyd George, the main features of his policy towards the miners in 1920 were a desire to decontrol the industry and a willingness, if necessary, to take on the miners. Decontrol depended greatly on there being an end to the soaring world prices for coal. Once prices dropped, wages would follow. On both counts (decontrol and wage cuts), Lloyd George expected conflict with the miners. He was very willing to face such a clash providing he could carry public opinion and keep the other Triple Alliance unions out of the dispute. As trouble loomed, he made further organisational and legal preparations and paid attention to propagating the government's case against the miners.

The Cabinet reviewed its policies on the coal industry at two meetings on 27 January 1920, the day before Lloyd George was due to see a deputation from the MFGB. In December the government had abandoned a bill it had prepared based on the Duckham version of the Sankey Report. As Sir Auckland Geddes put it, 'that Bill had not pleased either the miners or the coalowners and the government therefore considered themselves released from their undertaking to carry out the recommendations of the Commission.' In the Cabinet's discussions it was felt that 'the government ... would never be free until they resigned their control over the industry.' But ministers had to recognise that they still could not decontrol the industry because of the continuing very high international prices due to world shortages of coal. Geddes warned that the results of immediate decontrol would be

> that all mine-owners would enter the export trade and would neglect the home trade; home prices would probably rise 15 shillings a ton on the first day of decontrol, and would subsequently reach the world level; export prices would tend to drop; the miners in all coalfields would at once demand an increase in wages and there would probably be a general strike, with the result that the whole industry and export trade of the country would be upset and there would be complete chaos.

So the Cabinet preferred to find 'a *via media* between a complete decontrol and complete nationalisation'. Subsequently, the government pushed through Parliament the Coal Mines (Emergency) Act of 1920 which amended the conditions of government control of the industry, dealing with finance generally and the distribution of profits in particular.

The miners' claims gave the government a major public relations problem as the miners hoped to reduce coal profits in the interests of industrial users as a means of helping to lower the cost of living. The miners felt aggrieved as much of their wages gain from the First Sankey Report had been eroded by inflation by the start of 1920. Hence they demanded that

> there should be an immediate and considerable reduction in the price of industrial coal, followed by government action to reduce the cost of commodities now produced in factories, etc. into which the cost of coal largely enters; or, alternatively, the consideration by the government of an application by this federation for an advance in wages consequent upon the high cost of living.

As the labour correspondent of *The Daily Telegraph* observed, this marked 'a new departure in trade union procedure' as 'in effect, the miners asked the Prime Minister to enter into an agreement with the organised workers in the coal mining industry as to the way in which the state shall use the income which it receives from the industry'. The writer added that as 'much the larger portion of the excess profit is now taken by the state ... the state is bracketed with the coalowners as profiteers'.

When Lloyd George, accompanied by Bonar Law and Sir Auckland Geddes, saw Smillie and his colleagues he was careful not to enlighten the MFGB deputation as to the expected profits of the industry in the first part of the next financial year. Smillie ably presented the miners' case using statistics carefully based on the official ones from the Board of Trade; but these were for the current financial year. To Smillie's case Lloyd George could truthfully reply that the Coal Controller's department had estimated that 'if there was a surplus on the year to 31 March, it would only be of a very small amount.' However, in the Cabinet the previous day Geddes had pointed to an unexpected surplus of £11 to £12 million (after the coal owners had been given their guaranteed profits) in the five months from April 1920. Geddes had even suggested that there was a good case for granting the miners a shilling a shift pay rise at the cost of £15 million in a full year. Against this it had been argued that 'the miners had already set the pace in the increase of wages and other trades had not reached their level. A further rise in miners' wages would initiate a new cycle of wage increases.' As for the price of domestic coal, the Cabinet was not at all inclined to make any further reduction as it was already deemed to be at 'an uneconomic level'. As the MFGB did not know of the Government's expectations for the early part of the next financial year, they readily agreed to Lloyd George's suggestion that they adjourn the meeting until the government had the report on the coal industry's financial position which was being prepared by an independent accountant.

The MFGB met Lloyd George again on 19 February to discuss the accountant's report which did reveal that there was a surplus in the current financial year. This amounted to £7.5 million after the owners had received £26 million as guaranteed profits. At this meeting the miners did extract agreement that this surplus would become much bigger in future months. However, Lloyd George largely stuck by the Cabinet's agreed view that the state should keep the surplus – though he did hint at the possibility of that money being used to purchase coal royalties for the state. On the issue of reducing the price of coal for domestic consumers, the government's case was that even if it were done, it would need a massive system of government controls to ensure that in all cases the benefit went to the consumer. As the government was removing controls, not adding to them, this would be unacceptable.[80]

The miners' hopes of achieving the early public ownership of the coal industry also faded in early 1920. The 'Mines for the Nation' campaign, begun on 1 December 1919 with a big public meeting in London, in effect died on 18 March. Then a Special Trades Union Congress convened at the MFGB's request overwhelmingly rejected 'trade union action, in the form of a general strike' as a means of compelling the government to nationalise the mines. This method of attempting to obtain the miners' end gained 1,050,000 votes, while the alternative of 'political action, in the form of intensive political propaganda in preparation for a general election' received 3,732,000 votes.

The very same evening that that decision was made, the MFGB leadership returned to Lloyd George to press for a straightforward increase in wages. They called for a rise of 3s per day for all workers aged 16 and over, and 1s 6d for boys. In presenting the case for this increase Frank Hodges emphasised the scale of profits in the industry. The miners' leaders also made the point to the press that 'when our wage demand is granted it will be unnecessary to put a single penny on the price of either domestic or industrial coal.' Lloyd George criticised their demand on the grounds that it implied 'that any piece of national luck in coal deposits should go, not to the colliery owners or the state, but to the workmen employed in the industry'. He also made much of the fact that the profit came from only the export part of the coal industry and that it was 'a very precarious one'. Lloyd George also criticised the MFGB for coming to him first, rather than turning to the government only if they reached deadlock with the coal owners. The union then entered into negotiations with the Coal Controller who made an offer which it rejected. The MFGB then saw Lloyd George on 25 March and received from him a slightly better offer. When this was also firmly rejected by the Miners' Conference on 26 March, the union entered into further negotiations with the Prime Minister. This resulted in him making what the Cabinet felt was to be a 'final offer' of 2s for men, 1s for those between 16 and 18, and 9d for boys. The MFGB balloted its members on this offer, and in mid-April the result showed that 56.7 per cent of those who voted found it acceptable.[81] Thus March 1920 passed without the revolution which had been feared in some quarters.

Nevertheless, throughout the early months of 1920 the government continued to make preparations in case major industrial trouble occurred. Until mid-April there remained the possibility of the miners striking for a better wages deal. Thereafter, Lloyd George and the government had few doubts that there would be trouble when the mines were decontrolled and wages were reduced. Moreover, they still felt some concern about the possibility of a Triple Alliance strike for in spite of all J. H. Thomas's exertions the NUR votes in January had been very close. In late March Sir Eric Geddes warned Lloyd George that they faced 'the three railway unions . . . all in a ferment at the one time'. He commented that the NUR and ASLEF were making further demands direct to him, thereby already disregarding recently set up negotiating machinery, and that the Railway Clerks Association was also 'throwing over the settlement which we believed had been made in their case'. In late March Lloyd George was much involved in reviewing government plans to face an emergency. When writing to invite Hamar Greenwood to be Chief Commissioner under the Supply and Transport Organisation, he observed that he had been paying attention to arrangements in view of 'the possibility of serious industrial disturbances in the near future'. From the War Office he received detailed information as to the numbers and distribution of effective troops available should there be a general coal strike. But at the same time, he was warned of 'the defective condition of Army Motor Transport and the Signal Service' (which was deemed due to Treasury parsimony) and that 'the general standard of training throughout the Army at home is low, and is far below that attained by the regular army prior to the Great War'.

Given the reluctance of the Army's senior personnel to become involved in dealing with civil disputes, the government was particularly anxious to secure reliable quasi-military support other than from the Armed Services. On 31 March, following on from the anxieties of the meeting on 2 February, a Cabinet meeting chaired by Bonar Law considered the question of arming loyalists. It accepted the recommendation of a committee which Macready had chaired 'that should it be necessary to issue arms to persons unconnected with the forces of the Crown, the organisation of the Special Constabulary should be made use of.' They were told that 'efforts were being made to enlist ex-servicemen as far as possible'.[82] Another potential source of emergency support for the government was the territorial force. In late April 1920, when pressed to state whether the Territorial Army would be used to break strikes, Churchill replied that while they could not be summoned to suppress labour disputes or civil disturbances, they could be 'in the event of a grave emergency such as an attempted revolution endangering the fundamental peace and safety of the entire country'. As Peter Dennis has commented, this left open what would constitute 'a grave emergency'. The Cabinet was to deem the coal disputes in 1921 and 1926 to be such emergencies. In 1921 members of the Territorial Army were 'specially invited' to join a special defence force and territorial drill halls were used as its recruitment centres.[83] Earlier, in February, the Cabinet had considered arrangements for the recruitment of volunteer labour and for out-of-work pay in the event of a major strike.[84]

From January 1920 the government began to prepare emergency legislation for use in place of the wartime Defence of the Realm Regulations. What was to become the Emergency Powers Act took a long time to reach the statute book, only doing so on 28 October 1920. Earlier on, ministers' ideas of what they wanted fluctuated with circumstances. In late March the Supply and Transport Committee was considering legislation in terms of it dealing with coal strikes or a Triple Alliance strike. By the summer, when the Emergency Powers Bill was ready, the government hesitated to introduce it. When the Cabinet discussed it on 12 August they agreed to delay it in view of a miners' strike ballot being in progress. In the discussion it was stated that the introduction of the Bill 'would provoke most violent opposition from Labour and would do much to precipitate the crisis'. Similarly, the Cabinet agreed not to allow the Supply and Transport Committee to 'take open measures to meet the crisis' until it authorised the Committee to do so.[85] In April ministers were also attracted to the notion of legislation to curb trade unions. Then, when considering a Private Member's Bill for providing machinery for secret ballot strikes, it was felt in the Cabinet that legislation might become necessary as 'recent labour troubles had shown the necessity for strengthening the powers of the state to deal with lightning strikes and with strikes which were not ascertained to be supported by proper majorities obtained after an approved ballot.'[86]

While much of the government's emergency preparations were geared to either a Triple Alliance or a major coal strike, the government's anxieties went beyond these unions. There was recognition that there would be general trouble once the abnormal conditions of the post-war period had gone. During the post-war boom, demand was buoyant and employers often had been able to pass on the costs of meeting labour's demands, either to the taxpayer or to the consumer. Both sides of industry had been willing to accept the stabilisation of wages under the Wages (Temporary Regulation) Act 1918 and then under the Industrial Courts Act 1919, albeit reluctantly in the case of some employers. When the latter Bill had been under consideration in October 1919 it was put to the Cabinet

> that while on the one hand workingmen were agitated at the prospect of wages being reduced and were claiming that war advances should continue in spite of a possible fall in the price of food, employers were anxious for a definite period of stable wages and did not think that food could fall by the autumn of 1920.[87]

This provision was due to expire on 30 September 1920, and by the summer it was very apparent that employers would be seeking wage cuts then.

In July Basil Thomson was predicting widespread unrest in the latter part of September. He claimed that 'according to present indications' the strikes would either begin with the miners (followed by the transport workers) or with the engineers who were 'in a very restless state'. He also stated,

> There have been many private meetings between employers during the last few weeks and they seem to be resolved not to pay higher wages and to stake everything upon being in a position to quote prices on a basis of a two years' guarantee that claims for higher wages would not be made. . . . The employers think that if the struggle must come, it had better come now and it had better come all at once rather than piecemeal. They would rather it began by strikes than lock-outs.

Thomson also referred to non-industrial unrest, including the prospect of a 'No Rent Strike' in London in September, with 'street upon street' passively refusing to pay rent. He warned, 'The steady body of Labour is so much irritated that it has lost its steadying effect.'[88]

By this time an eruption of rank and file support for direct action had occurred. This took place over government policy on Russia and Ireland, not over an industrial issue. In both cases, in May 1920, workers at a local level took unofficial action over the handling of munitions. In the case of Russia, many in the Labour movement were horrified when, on 25 April, Polish armies launched an offensive against Russia. In the East India Docks, on 10 May London dockers refused to load either what they suspected to be munitions or coal on to the *Jolly George*, a ship bound for Poland. In the case of Ireland, on 20 May 400 railway workers, who were members of the Dublin North Wall branch of the NUR, refused to unload munitions and thereby stopped rail traffic in the Dublin–Holyhead area. These were the most dramatic local actions on these issues but they were by no means the only ones.[89]

In both cases the men's actions gained much support within their unions (though the Dublin railwaymen were not given strike benefits, even with the strike lasting until 31 December). Bevin backed the London dockers. He told the Labour Party Conference that he felt the circumstances warranted direct action in that case:

> When the men came to him and asked if he would stand by them if they refused to load munitions for Poland, he felt the psychology was such that he was warranted in saying to them, 'Take the risk, and I am sure that the union will stand by you', and the authority next came from the union for them to do it. That was a circumstance in which they had the keen political feeling of the men themselves who refused to do certain actions because

they believed them wrong. . . . The trade union movement was not a military force where men had to go blindly, at the orders of the leaders, one way or another.

Thus Bevin cogently pointed to the difference between successful trade union direct action – that which represented the deep feelings of the members – and what he dubbed 'fiascos owing to orders and resolutions which could not be carried out when the time came'.[90]

In the case of the Dublin railwaymen the NUR's Special Conference instructed Thomas to have the matter discussed at a full delegate conference of the Triple Alliance. This in due course led to the summoning of a special TUC on 13 July 1920. In the interim Thomas led two NUR delegations to see Lloyd George at Downing Street on 3 and 18 June. Lloyd George replied to vigorous criticism of his use of force in Ireland by bluntly telling the second NUR delegation (made up of members from both southern and northern counties of Ireland) that he would use the whole of Britain's military strength if necessary. Thomas himself deplored the British government's repressive measures but was not sympathetic to the republican cause. In taking a delegation including both Sinn Fein and Ulster representatives Thomas demonstrated the divided views within his own union. He told the 1920 Labour Party Conference in June that his Ulster members had warned the union 'that if their other members did not carry munitions for the government they would'. At the Labour Party Conference Thomas also made the powerful point:

> if this policy in Russia is wrong, if we have got to stop this business, then it is not the duty or the responsibility of any one section of the Labour Movement. If it is wrong for the railwaymen to carry munitions, it is wrong for people to be working overtime in making munitions. If their policy with Russia was wrong then it should be the responsibility of the Labour Movement as a whole to tackle the question.[91]

Both the Labour Party Conference and the special TUC of 13 July 1920 determined to take action against government policy on both Ireland and Russia. While there were differences at the Labour Party Conference as to whether it should support an Irish Republic or an Irish Parliament 'within the British Commonwealth', there was an overwhelming determination to put an end to 'shilly-shallying' on the issue and there was also anger at the government's measures. One speaker declared of Lloyd George, 'The man was growing brazen in his crimes.'[92] The Conference agreed that 'the principles of free and absolute self-determination shall be applied immediately in ... Ireland' and called for 'the withdrawal of the British Army of Occupation'. As for Russia, the Labour Party Conference agreed (with only one delegate dissenting) to call for Allied recognition of Lenin's government, for them 'to abstain from all direct or indirect attacks' and to help Russia with economic development and trade. However, it overwhelmingly defeated a call for a special Labour Conference 'having for its object the organisation of a general strike that shall put an end once for all to the open and covert participation of the British government in attacks on the Soviet Republic'.

The special TUC on 13 July backed the NUR call for a truce in Ireland, the withdrawal of British troops and the summoning of an Irish Parliament 'with full Dominion Powers in all Irish affairs'. This was in line with Thomas's views and more moderate than the policy adopted by the Labour Party. But after it had been carried Frank Hodges successfully moved a motion which demanded 'the cessation of production of munitions of war destined to be used against Ireland and Russia, and, in case the government refuses these demands . . . a general down-tools policy' (with each union balloting its members). However, no action followed on Ireland. Thomas was against it even though the Dublin NUR branch members remained on strike. He later said at a public meeting that he had not called a sympathy strike 'not because he did not understand their position, nor because he did not approve of their opinions, but because we knew that not five per cent of the men would strike in England on that issue'.[93]

In contrast, the Labour Movement was electrified when, in early August 1920, it seemed that the British government would imminently join Poland in its war with Russia. At this time the Red Army was advancing well into Poland, having turned back the Polish invasion of Russia at Kiev. On 4 August Henderson sent telegrams to all local Labour Parties and Trades Councils calling for demonstrations against war with Russia to be organised for Sunday 8 August. Henderson was well pleased with the scale of the resulting demonstrations. He later wrote, 'The appeal met with an unparalleled response, and it was evident that Labour had mobilised public opinion rapidly and successfully.' On 9 August a joint meeting of the Parliamentary Committee of the TUC, the National Executive Committee of the Labour Party and Parliamentary Labour Party formed a Council of Action. The meeting also issued a resolution which stated that they 'feel certain that a war is being engineered between the Allied Powers and Soviet Russia on the issue of Poland ... that such a war would be an intolerable crime against humanity', that a conference of affiliated organisations would be called and that these organisations would be 'advised to instruct their members to "down-tools" on the instructions from that national conference'.[94]

In August the Council of Action was very successful in continuing to mobilise the Labour movement against government policy towards Russia. The conference of affiliated organisations, held at a Central Hall, Westminster on 13 August, was judged by Henderson to have been 'one of the most striking examples of Labour unanimity, determination and enthusiasm in the history of the Movement'. Local Councils of Action followed, eventually numbering about 350. The cores of these were made up of the regular Trades Councils and Labour activists, and in some areas this determined that they became very radical bodies (being seen by some enthusiasts as embryo local soviets). In some sixty cases they went on to call for a wider remit involving action against repression in Ireland as the Russo-Polish issue became less pressing. In August 1920 they had a considerable impact in mobilising much anti-government sentiment and boosting the morale of the Labour movement at a time when a hostile government with an overwhelming majority had not yet reached its midterm in office. Their campaign had an appeal which went well beyond the Labour movement as it touched on widespread feelings of war weariness and on fears of a return of conscription.[95]

The scale and the determination of the Council of Action campaign was one, but only one, consideration in encouraging Lloyd George to be cautious in backing the opponents of Soviet Russia. But he had been wary of public opinion well before the Council of Action had been formed. This was the case in January 1920, when he had opposed Polish action against Russia, and was so again when the Red Army advanced. Thus, on 27 July, he had told the French premier,

> The British Cabinet were of opinion that they must either fight or make peace. It was impossible to fight, as neither France nor England would stand any more fighting. On the previous Wednesday, when he himself was explaining the situation to the House of Commons, he had stated in very strong terms that in the last resort, if the armistice broke down, and Poland were invaded the British would be prepared to fight. This statement ... had excited very great uneasiness in the House, even among

the Conservative elements, and it had aroused the apprehensions of the public. Nobody wanted war, and nobody was disposed to send troops. . . . It was impossible to get any enthusiasm from an exhausted nation to incur fresh sacrifices.[96]

The pressure from the Labour movement in August served to reinforce this caution. After the earliest demonstrations of 8 August Basil Thomson passed on to the Cabinet a summary of all the reports he had received on them: 'Never have we known such excitement and antagonism to be aroused against any project as has been aroused amongst the workers by the possibility of war with Russia.'[97] The knowledge of such opposition constrained Lloyd George's room for political manoeuvre.

However, it seems very likely that Lloyd George throughout was reluctant to assist the Poles. The problem was, as Richard Ullman has commented, that 'such was the Prime Minister's reputation for deviousness, especially on the Russian question, that few of his statements were accepted at face value.' Members of the Council of Action, led by Bevin, saw Lloyd George on 10 and 12 August without getting the assurances they hoped for. Thereafter they spent much time elucidating Russian policy and reporting back to the government.[98] However, the matter was resolved by the Polish army at the battle of the Vistula when, in the third week of August, it turned the Red Army back.

The Council of Action episode served to provide another cause for alarm in this period for the propertied classes. A common viewpoint was expressed by the editor of the *Daily Graphic* to Addison on 16 August:

> The pretext for the creation of the council is that it is a protest against war with Russia. Nobody, as you know, wants a war with Russia. Therefore the pretext is false and futile.
> Personally I regard the formation of the Council of Action as the first step in the gravest movement that has ever threatened this country.[99]

But for Labour, it soon became one of the most heroic moments of the movement's past history. A year later, Henderson summed up the work of the Council of Action by stating, 'There is no doubt whatever that the action of the Labour Movement early in August prevented open war with Russia.' While such comments were wrong, nevertheless the episode did provide the Labour movement with a period of almost unparalleled unity and of apparent success before the divisions and disappointments of the 1921–2 recession. Moreover, it did lead trade unionists, including even J. H. Thomas, into wider spheres. Thus Bevin told the conference of 13 August,

> Our great work in life until now has been mainly wages, but I say in all sincerity that this question you are called upon to decide today – the willingness to take any action to win world peace – transcends any claim in connection with wages or hours of labour.[100]

However, even as the Russo-Polish conflict gained the main attention of the Labour movement, the government embarked on a pricing policy for coal which would make it easier to decontrol the industry. On 6 May the Cabinet determined to end 'the present abnormal and indefensible system of coal control'. Horne, now President of the Board of Trade, argued for a return to normal market conditions, as in the case of cotton, wool and other commodities which all sold at world prices. He advocated raising the price of household coal by 14s 2d, thereby more than reversing the price reduction of December 1919, and the price of industrial coal by 4s 2d a ton. Such prices would make all the pits profitable. Among the arguments put forward for this move was that

> the psychological effect of a rise in the price of coal would be of greater importance than the actual increase it caused in the cost of living, and that the middle class would be particularly hard hit by the withdrawal of the one concession (the reduction of 10 per cent in the price of coal) which has been given to it.

As for the cost of living, Cabinet members were reassured that it would only cause a two-points rise in the *Labour Gazette*'s index, which would be overshadowed by the rises in the cost of bread and sugar. (Subsequently the Cabinet were told that the impact on the cost of living index would be double that initially predicted.) At the same time the Cabinet agreed to relax control over coal for home consumption. Decontrol of the wholesale and retail prices of coal came on 3 June.[101]

The government followed this major change of the price structure by introducing the Ministry of Mines Bill into the House of Commons on 21 June. (This reached the statute book as the Mining Industry Act 1920.) The Act set the date of 31 August 1921 for the complete decontrol of the industry. It also established a Mines Department within the Board of Trade and a Miners' Welfare Fund, based on a levy of 1d per ton produced, and it provided for a system of joint committees stretching from individual pits to the national level. The MFGB objected to the Bill and boycotted the operation of the Act. Its opposition was strengthened by the fact that the system of joint committees would have made bargaining subject to local variations, thereby getting away from purely national bargaining.[102]

By July the miners had a good case for a further pay award. Since March, when the last pay rise had come into effect, the cost of living as measured by the *Labour Gazette*'s index had risen from 130 to 152 (1914 = 100). Robert Smillie and the MFGB executive thus argued at the union's Annual Conference on 6 July that the union should put forward as 'an indivisible demand' the combination of a reduction in the price of household coal by 14s 2d and a 2s per shift pay increase. Smillie urged that to demand the cut in the cost of coal was essential if they were to keep consumers on their side. He warned that 'as soon as our campaign . . . for this advance in wages is set on foot, you will have 99 per cent of the capitalist press ranged against you, lying like troopers; and no troopers lie like some parts of the press'. At an earlier conference, on 10 June, he had said of a substantial pay rise and the removal of the increased charge to householders for coal that, 'Either of these cuts fundamentally into the government's policy. The government cannot decontrol if we get an increase in wages.'[103] Hence it was very much more than an ordinary pay demand.

Horne, on behalf of the government, firmly rejected the miners' claim on 26 July, saying that any surplus coal profits should go to the Exchequer. On 12 August a MFGB Special Conference ordered a strike ballot. The same day the Cabinet reviewed what action it could take and Lloyd George 'undertook to consider the selection of suitable personnel for the conduct of government propaganda'. The Board of Trade also carried out extensive propaganda while Horne himself pressed ministers to write articles for the press. He told Addison, 'I am very anxious to have an article in support of our case by a member of the government in each of the Sunday papers on 29 August – just before the strike ballot is announced.' By early September Lloyd George was able to inform Bonar Law, 'The propaganda has been done uncommonly well here and it has clearly put public opinion very emphatically on our side.' But he warned that 'when the counter-propaganda begins, as undoubtedly it will, we must be prepared for a certain falling off in the unanimity and strength of the opinion behind us.'[104] Strong publicity was not the only element in the government's strategy. It also ensured that its Supply and Transport Organisation was ready, and the Treasury was instructed to treat such a major strike 'as comparable to a state of war' and to provide finance accordingly.[105]

When the miners' ballot result was announced on 31 August it showed that 72 per cent of those who voted were willing to take strike action to back the 'indivisible demand'. Horne on 2 September offered the miners arbitration by an industrial council on their wage claim, and on 8 September he spoke of linking proportionately an increase of wages to greater coal output. The government was well aware of the sizeable minority of the MFGB which had wanted a wage increase rather than the 'indivisible demand', and ministers played on that to try to divide the miners. The largest block vote against the 'indivisible demand' was that of South Wales. This was perhaps because the South Wales miners worked on export coal and could expect bigger wages under a decontrolled industry. It is notable that two of their leaders, William Brace and Vernon Hartshorn were very quick to make contact with ministers. Brace, the president of the South Wales Miners' Federation, arranged to see William Bridgeman, the Secretary for Mines, in secret and suggested to him that the miners were willing to 'give up the 14s 2d demand but adhere firmly to the 2s rise in wages which . . . they *must* have'. Hartshorn, who had often been in contact with Lloyd George in the past, appears to have used Riddell and Sutherland as intermediaries. Bridgeman took the opportunity to offer Brace the post of Labour Adviser to the Mines Department and, even though he and the other miner MPs had opposed the Mining Industry Act 1920, he accepted.[106]

Lloyd George and his colleagues were also adroit at trying to split off the Triple Alliance unions from the miners. The offer of arbitration was especially effective, as the dockers had accepted a court of inquiry and had gained much from it and J. H. Thomas was no stranger to compromise. On 23 September, shortly before the strike began, Lloyd George made (according to Bridgeman) 'a most moving and eloquent appeal to them in tragic strains not to force matters to extremes'. That afternoon Smillie himself urged a MFGB Special Conference to accept arbitration or to take a vote on the offer, but he was defeated. On 21 September the other Triple Alliance unions declared their belief in the justice of the miners' wage demand, but during Triple Alliance discussions on 23 September Thomas announced that the NUR delegates had voted against a sympathetic strike and he was joined by Harry Gosling of the transport workers in offering further mediation.[107] For a long time such ministerial tactics, combined with the MFGB's unwillingness to let Thomas act on its part, made it seem very improbable that the Triple Alliance unions would act together.

Lloyd George's role in the dispute was marked early on by an apparent determination to take a firm line with the miners, and later by concern to achieve a settlement when it seemed likely that after all the dispute would broaden into one with the Triple Alliance. On 4 September he was expressing an eagerness to confront the miners. He then wrote to Bonar Law,

> I have become more and more convinced that the time has arrived for coming to grips with the conspiracy which is seeking to utilise Labour for the purpose of overthrowing the existing organisation. . . . The opportunity will show itself over the miners' demands. . . . Now is the acceptable moment for putting everything to the test. We must show Labour that the government mean to be masters . . . but we must carry with us every phase of national sane well-ordered opinion.[108]

In mid-September, while those around him, such as Hankey, felt that 'the temper of the men does not seem to be bad and . . . they would be glad if someone could find a way out', Lloyd George continued to speak of an impending clash.[109] This was not withstanding the MFGB on 15 September dropping half the 'indivisible demand', that for a reduction in coal prices, after the government published figures showing a sharp drop in profits.

Throughout, Lloyd George was willing to press home his advantage over a union divided within itself and whose unwillingness to accept arbitration on its pay claim was threatening the existence of the Triple Alliance. In so doing, he continued to push the notion of pay rises being linked to productivity. He spelt this out in a letter to Smillie sent on the morning of the MFGB Special Conference of 23 September:

> There will be fixed certain datum lines on which rates of wages will be calculated in the following way. If output reaches:
> x tons, wages will be increased by 1s. per shift.
> x plus y tons, wages will be increased by 2s. per shift.
> x plus y tons plus 2 tons, wages will be increased by 3s. per shift.

> If, after increases have been obtained there are subsequent diminutions of output, the increases will come off.

When this approach was rebuffed, he wrote again to Smillie, regretting that the MFGB was not taking up a plan which would immediately 'give to the miners an increased rate of wages in return for an enlarged output which, as you yourself are confident, can be readily obtained' but reminding him that 'a peaceful method of settling the wage claim is still open to you by a similar means to that which is adopted by the railwaymen and the majority of your colleagues of the Triple Alliance'. This correspondence, of course, Lloyd George released to the press. The next day the miners' delegates saw him and agreed to postpone the strike for a week in order to discuss with the mine owners schemes to increase both wages and output. Afterwards Bridgeman commented, 'L.G. was wonderful, and did the emotional turn which Horne could not have played.'[110]

Following lengthy negotiations the coal owners made an offer linked to productivity. But the miners overwhelmingly rejected it. Given the 78 per cent vote against the offer of 1s a day and higher increases all linked to productivity in the ballot which was declared on 14 October, the MFGB Special Conference felt there was no alternative but to declare a strike from the end of the shifts on 16 October 1920. On 14 October Lloyd George wrote a further letter to Smillie for public consumption, in which he again outlined the two alternatives to a strike and observed that some of the miners' leaders favoured accepting arbitration while others, also including Smillie, favoured accepting a productivity deal. Smillie put the letter to a Special Conference, commenting on how it was 'cleverly written . . . in such a way as is likely to secure the greatest amount of support outside amongst the general public'. At the end of the meeting Smillie shook the delegates by announcing his resignation, as he deemed the ballot result a vote of no confidence in him as president of the MFGB since he had argued for the acceptance of either arbitration or the datum line. With some difficulty they successfully pressed him to withdraw his resignation. Thus the 'datum line' strike almost began without the miners' president.

During late September to mid-October Lloyd George still gave the appearance of a man who would be happy if the miners gave him the opportunity to teach them a lesson. On 1 October he had overruled efforts by the Coal Controller and Riddell to move the datum line for a 2s advance nearer to a point acceptable to Brace and Hartshorn (at a cost of £6.5 million), thereby leaving the ballot to go ahead on the less attractive figures. On 15 October, when he and Bonar Law had lunch with Sir Edward and Lady Carson, he observed that 'if the railways remained in we could get on all right' and gave the impression of being 'very firm and determined with the strikers'. Similarly, with Riddell the next day, he took the view 'that there was bound to be a row. It had to come.'[111] On 15 October the Cabinet had authorised the Supply and Transport Committee to operate its measures 'as and when the situation requires' but had turned down a request by Wilson to send two battalions of troops to Liverpool the next day on the grounds that that 'might be regarded as provocative'. In the House of Commons on 19 October Lloyd George and his colleagues made no sign of being willing to make concessions, Lloyd George eulogising productivity agreements ('nature herself works on these principles') and suggesting that in some cases increased wages in coal 'had something to do with' lower output.[112]

However, on 21 October it appeared probable that the railwaymen would not stay at work after all. The NUR Special General Meeting on that day agreed to warn Lloyd George 'that unless the miners' claims are granted or negotiations resumed by Saturday 23 October which result in a settlement' it would call a strike. By this time railwaymen were realising that a defeat of the miners would be followed by pressure to withdraw recently won advances to other groups of workers, including themselves, and that a prolonged coal strike would affect their members anyway. Lloyd George offered the MFGB immediate talks to reach a settlement. Negotiations resumed on 24 October and took place over four days. Meanwhile, the government carried out a Cabinet decision of 15 October that should the railwaymen join the strike the Emergency Powers Bill would be introduced. It received the Royal Assent on 27 October. The outcome of the negotiations was that the miners were given the 2s a shift, which was guaranteed by the government, in return for a temporary scheme which linked increased pay to higher output. The temporary scheme was to operate until the owners and the MFGB had negotiated a National Wages Board, which was to be done by not later than 31 March 1921. With enthusiasm Lloyd George informed the Cabinet that 'This was the first time that wages were related to output' and his colleagues praised his negotiating skills.[113]

However, as with so many of Lloyd George's negotiating triumphs, the fundamental problems were merely postponed. The real question of the determination of the level of miners' wages was put off until 31 March 1921. Moreover, Lloyd George's agreement to guarantee the 2s was based on the premise that export prices of coal would hold up. In fact, as Horne told the MFGB on 13 January 1921, 'The government took the big risk of guaranteeing the prices and they had been hopelessly wrong in their conclusions.' Indeed, on 28 January he told the Cabinet that

> the price per ton has fallen from something like 80s. to 40s. today, and of this latter sum wages took 25s. per ton ... if the present conditions were allowed to continue ... the Treasury would be called upon to make up a deficit running into many millions of pounds.

In consequence, the Cabinet took the decision to decontrol the industry as quickly as possible, even though this meant repealing the Act which guaranteed owners their pre-war profits until 31 August. The Cabinet decided that this should be done as from 31 March, though Horne was to be 'free to vary the proposed date if he found it absolutely necessary in the course of the negotiations with the coal owners'.[114] Horne informed the Miners' Federation of this decision on 23 February. With the Government determined to disengage itself from the problems of the coal industry, the owners took the opportunity to confront the men with the declaration of a return to district wage agreements and of substantial wage reductions (in some areas 40–53 per cent).[115] The miners expected some cuts, but not on this scale, and they still hoped that a national wages pool might be operated. They refused to agree to these proposals and a national lock-out commenced. As the safety men had also received notices they too stayed out.

Lloyd George did not come into this affair until the lock-out began. Horne had handled the negotiations and apparently thought the miners were bluffing. Lloyd George later told Riddell that 'he did not know the dispute was serious until it was too late to take action'. After hearing Geddes talk of 'revolutionary possibilities', Lloyd George, on 5 April, 'was much surprised to learn that the movement is not one of extremists, but that the men at the back of it are old-fashioned miners like Hartshorn, Stephen Walsh, Tom Richards etc.' and he told Riddell, 'We will do anything that can be done, except resume control and subsidise the mines.'[116] This lack of awareness on Lloyd George's part, if true, seems surprising; but it is quite possible that he was deluded into thinking that the owners would make generous terms to avoid trouble until late March when they published their proposals. That this is so is suggested by the fact that there were no reviews of the strike-breaking organisation in the weeks before the lock-out, apart from a Cabinet meeting on 10 January which determined to maintain the organisation in case of 'a great strike' in 'the next two years', and considered proposals to improve the emergency communications system which had been deemed to be weak during the previous strike.[117]

However, from 31 March the Supply and Transport Committee put its plans into operation, and the following day the government invoked the Emergency Powers Act. On the 2 April Henry Wilson once more urged Lloyd George that troops should be brought back from the Plebiscite areas, and canvassed other ministers before the Cabinet meeting two days later. Lloyd George himself felt that 'the number of troops required here was over-estimated'. But, given talk of the possibility of a small minority using the situation for a coup, he and the Cabinet agreed to Wilson's proposal. At this meeting on 4 April ministers spent much time discussing 'a loyal citizen's organisation', Lloyd George himself saying he was impressed by the need of such a force 'in the case of first class trouble'. Hankey privately blamed Wilson for again infecting ministers with panic.[118] On 7 April a conference of ministers agreed to spend £1,000 on propaganda in Scotland. Lloyd-Graeme, who was in charge of publicity, observed that 'the art of propaganda was to conceal it', and informed his colleagues that during the last strike the Government had sent 'matter out to 900 newspapers via the Coalition and Unionist organisations etc., and the local organisations were paid, and the public suspected little or nothing'.[119]

At the same time as making such preparations, Lloyd George and Horne from 1 April tried to reopen negotiations with the Miners' Federation. However, nothing came of this. The miners refused to send the pump men back unconditionally (as the owners and government wanted before negotiations resumed) and called for a national wages pool and the postponement of the reduction in wages. When Lloyd George saw the Miners' Federation Executive Committee on 7 April he found that they were in no mood to budge. On the next day the other Triple Alliance unions announced that they would take sympathetic strike action on 12 April, unless negotiations were resumed. Subsequently, the Government called out the reserves, fully mobilised the strike-breaking organisation and deployed army and navy forces. Lloyd George resumed negotiations on 11 and 12 April with no success. He rigidly maintained his opposition to a national wages pool, which he saw as 'another way of getting nationalisation'. These negotiations caused the Triple Alliance strike deadline to be postponed until 15 April. But the breakdown of these talks seemed likely to cause a conflict between the whole of the Labour movement and the government.[120]

However, on the evening of 14 April there were the two famous meetings in the House of Commons, the first addressed by the chairman of the owners' association, the second by Frank Hodges. Austen Chamberlain wrote to Long that the owners had

> produced upon the members present the worst possible impression, and before dinner the Party seemed to have been stampeded. The issue which the Prime Minister had left perfectly clear in the morning had been befogged and confused, and the House with the help of the owners was hot foot on the trail of the false issue on which the miners wished to go to the country.

That evening Frank Hodges spoke to the MPs. Chamberlain informed Robert Cecil that this meeting 'would have followed on the same lines if we had not taken some trouble to get the right questions put'.[121] Garbled reports reached the press that Hodges had been willing to make concessions; though it appears that he did nothing of the sort, only saying that he would be willing to discuss better terms.[122] The following morning Lloyd George invited the Miners' Federation to renew discussions on the basis of reports of Hodges' remarks. But by one vote the Miners' Federation executive decided to decline the invitation.[123]

This refusal resulted in the crumbling of the Triple Alliance that day, 'Black Friday' – 15 April 1921. The miners remained on strike until 1 July 1921. It proved to be a long and bitter strike, later remembered as a time of suffering comparable to, or even greater than, the 1926 dispute. In the end Lloyd George agreed to a settlement in which they were given more generous wages than the owners had first offered but on a district basis; and for three months the government did provide a subsidy to maintain a minimum level for wages.[124] It appears highly probable that without the collapse of the Triple Alliance the government would have made concessions. Not only were the MPs and business interests having doubts about forcing a final show-down with the miners, but so were several Cabinet Ministers.[125] Lloyd George's role can reasonably be considered to have been decisive. He was determined not to be drawn back into some form of control or subsidies for the coal industry. He maintained hopes throughout that Thomas and the other moderates would save the situation for him. On 4 April Lloyd George recounted to Wilson that Thomas earlier had told him that 'Jesus Christ could not now stop this revolutionary movement' but added his own judgement that 'Thomas, Bevin and Gosling would try and stop the triple strike'. Similarly, on other occasions he had observed, 'J. H. Thomas ... wants no revolution. He wants to be Prime Minister' and that Thomas was for peace, 'He does not want a row to please Hodges. I have complete confidence in Thomas's selfishness.' From early on he took the view that the railwaymen were the key to the situation, and on 8 April he felt confident that the transport workers were also 'very anxious not to come out'. As well as having this faith that the Triple Alliance would not operate, Lloyd George was a shrewder negotiator than his colleagues and it is reasonable to think that they would not have followed up Hodges' comments.[126]

'Black Friday' and the ending of the 1921 miners' strike marked, in effect, the end of the post-war trade union challenge to the government. The major engineering dispute of 1922 and the other disputes of 1921–2 were defensive, with the trade unions desperately trying to hold on to what they earlier had gained. The problem facing both the unions and the government was the increasing unemployment. With the fading of 'direct action' the remaining serious challenge of Labour to Lloyd George was the constitutional one from the Labour Party.

Notes and references

1. These are the seasonally adjusted prices. F. Capie and M. Collins, *The Inter-war British Economy: A Statistical Abstract* (Manchester: Manchester University Press, 1983), pp. 20, 32 and 38. G. S. Bain and R. Price, *Profiles of Union Growth* (Oxford: Blackwell, 1980), p. 39.
2. 114 *HC Deb. 5s*, c. 1995; 18 August 1919.
3. S. Webb, 'The facts of the strike', *New Statesman*, 4 October 1919, pp. 4–6. 'The government's industrial failure', *New Statesman*, 21 August 1920, pp. 542–3.
4. 114 *HC Deb. 5s*, c. 1986; 18 August 1919.
5. See Chapter 5, pp. 81–3. N. B. Dearle, *An Economic Chronicle of the Great War for Great Britain and Ireland 1914–1919* (Oxford: Oxford

University Press, 1929), pp. 255, 288 and 293. S. Howson, 'The origins of dear money 1919–20', *Economic History Review*, 27 (1974), pp. 88–107. The value of the currency notes not covered by gold had reached £230,412,000 by July 1918, when the grand total of legal money in circulation was £382,730,000 compared to £179,926,000 at the start of July 1914. *First Interim Report of Committee on Currency and Foreign Exchanges after the War*, Cmd. 9812 (1918).
6. Howson, *op. cit.*, pp. 100–7. Dearle *op. cit.*, pp. 297, 312 and 350. R. S. Sayers, *The Bank of England 1891–1944* (Cambridge: Cambridge University Press, 1976), pp. 115–18.
7. S. N. Broadberry, 'The emergence of mass unemployment: explaining macroeconomic trends in Britain during the trans-World War I period', *Economic History Review*, 43 (1990), pp. 271–82, especially pp. 279–81.
8. E. V. Morgan, *Studies in British Financial Policy 1914–1925* (London: Macmillan, 1952), pp. 106–15. D. P. Silverman, *Reconstructing Europe after the Great War* (Cambridge, Mass.: Harvard University Press, 1982), pp. 118–28. C. H. Feinstein, *National Income, Expenditure and Output of the United Kingdom 1855–1965* (Cambridge: Cambridge University Press, 1972), p. T31. U. K. Hicks, *The Finance of British Government 1920–1936* (London: Oxford University Press, 1938), pp. 316–23.
9. Silverman, *op. cit.*, pp. 125–6. K. Middlemas (ed.), *Thomas Jones: Whitehall Diary*, vol. 1 (London: Oxford University Press, 1969), p. 114.
10. C. J. Wrigley, *David Lloyd George and the British Labour Movement* (Hassocks: Harvester, 1976), p. 88.
11. Silverman, *op. cit.*, pp. 73–4. Bonar Law to Sir Robert Perks, MP, 31 May 1919; Bonar Law Papers, 101/3/94 and cited, ibid., p. 74. Perks also complained about the likely acceptance of the capital levy by the Asquithian Liberals in a letter to Runciman, 16 May 1919; Runciman Papers, Box 2.
12. R. C. Whiting, 'The Labour Party, capitalism and the national debt' in P. J. Waller (ed.), *Politics and Social Change in Modern Britain* (Hemel Hempstead: Harvester Wheatsheaf, 1987), pp. 140–60, especially 144–45.
13. Chamberlain to Garvin, 31 October 1919; Austen Chamberlain Papers, 24/1/35.
14. Samuel to Runciman, 13 October 1919; Runciman Papers, Box 2.
15. WC (606A), 5 August 1919; CAB 23–15–151/2. WC (592 and 607), 14 July and 7 August 1919; CAB 23–11–31/2 and 104/5. The issue had been discussed earlier on 3 June. WC (575), 3 June 1919; CAB 23–10–73.
16. Lloyd George to A. Geddes, 22 September 1919 (on Profiteering Act); LG F/17/5/55. Sir John Anderson to Lloyd George, 6 February 1920; LG F/2/3/1.
17. Cabinet 31 and 32 (1920), 2 and 4 June 1920; CAB 23–12–168/9 and 173/6. Tom Jones's diary, 4 June 1920; *Whitehall Diary*, pp. 114–15.

Addison to Lloyd George, 4 June 1920; LG F/1/69. H. A. L. Fisher to Chamberlain, 5 June 1920; Austen Chamberlain Papers 23/10/4. *Report of Select Committee on Increase of Wealth (War)* (1920); and 1920 Cmd. 594.
18. Maclay wrote to Lloyd George arguing this (though as a businessman he was keen to see the Excess Profits Duty reduced), 21 May 1920; LG F/35/3/52. Runciman felt similarly. Runciman to Samuel, 19 October 1919; Runciman Papers, Box 2. *Whitehall Diary*, p. 114.
19. Cabinet 31 and 32 (1920), 2 and 4 June 1920; CAB 23–21–169, 173 and 175.
20. K. O. Morgan, *Consensus and Disunity* (Oxford: Clarendon Press, 1979), p. 175.
21. WC (606A), 5 August 1919; CAB 23–15–170.
22. Addison to Lloyd George, 22 April 1920; LG F/1/6/7. On the problems of the housing programme see in particular Morgan *op. cit.*, pp. 88–95, and K. and J. Morgan, *Portrait of a Progressive* (Oxford: Clarendon Press, 1980), pp. 122–7.
23. Silverman *op. cit.*, pp. 129–31. Morgan, *Consensus*, pp. 140–6.
24. Sir Henry Clay, *Lord Norman* (London: Macmillan, 1957), p. 124.
25. Riddell diary, 14 August 1919; Riddell Papers, 62984, f. 46 (partly quoted in J. M. McEwen (ed.), *The Riddell Diaries 1908–1923* (London: Athlone Press, 1986), p. 287.
26. *The Times*, 18 September 1919. He made similar comments in Sheffield on 20 October and also elsewhere. *Morning Post*, 21 October 1919.
27. Lloyd George to J. H. Batty, 20 July 1920; LG H/131.
28. T. Wilson, *The Downfall of the Liberal Party 1914–1935* (London: Collins, 1966), pp. 192–3; *The Times*, 17 March 1920. On the moves for 'fusion' see in particular Wilson, *op. cit.*, pp. 194–8, and Morgan, *Consensus*, pp. 177–87.
29. *Lord Riddell's Intimate Diary of the Peace Conference and After* (London: Gollancz, 1933), p. 164. Frances Stevenson's diary, 23 January 1920; A. J. P. Taylor (ed.), *Lloyd George: A Diary by Frances Stevenson* (London: Hutchinson, 1971), p. 199. J. Campbell, *F. E. Smith* (London: Cape, 1983), pp. 530–6. Sir Donald MacLean raised the articles in his comments on the King's Speech, 10 February 1920, and Lloyd George responded by saying his Party could only hope to govern again as part of a coalition. 125 *HC Deb.* 5s, c. 35. Riddell's diary, 11 October 1919; Riddell Papers, 62984, f. 150 (partly quoted in *Peace Conference*, p. 131).
30. Arthur Murray diary, 18 March 1920; Elibank Papers, 8815, f. 42. Also memorandum 26 March 1920; Elibank Papers, 8808, f. 72.
31. On other Liberal Coalitionists' attachment to Liberalism, see Wilson *op. cit.*, pp. 197–8.
32. Miss Annie Herrick to Steel-Maitland, 24 November 1919; Steel-Maitland Papers, GD 193/87/1. W. Webster to A. Murray, 19 March 1920; Elibank Papers, 8808, f. 67–9.
33. Bonar Law to Balfour, 24 March 1920; quoted in Morgan, *Consensus*,

p. 187. Frances Stevenson's diary, 16 March 1920; Taylor (ed.), *op. cit.*, p. 205.
34. Younger to Bonar Law, 12 December 1919; Bonar Law Papers, 98/5/11.
35. M. Cowling, *The Impact of Labour 1920–1924* (Cambridge: Cambridge University Press, 1971), p. 110.
36. *Morning Post*, 6 March 1919. The Labour Party, *Report of the Twentieth Annual Conference, 1920*, p. 35. R. McKibbin, *The Evolution of the Labour Party 1910–1924* (London: Oxford University Press, 1974), pp. 116–18.
37. McKibbin, *op. cit.*, pp. 35–7. *Daily Herald*, 4 November 1919. *New Statesman*, 8 November 1919, p. 146. Riddell diary, 2 November 1919; *Peace Conference*, p. 138.
38. In the case of the Dartford by-election the swing against the Coalition was 37.4 per cent – but this is artificial given the change from Coalition Liberal to Coalition Unionist.
39. Labour Party, *Conference, 1920*, pp. 14, 19, 30 and 207–9.
40. C. Howard, 'Expectations born to death: local Labour Party expansion in the 1920s', in J. M. Winter (ed.), *The Working Class in Modern British History* (Cambridge: Cambridge University Press, 1983), pp. 65–81.
41. Lewis's diary, 25 January 1920; J. H. Lewis Papers 10/231/131. 125 HC Deb. 5s, c. 35–6; 10 February 1920. Lloyd George's remarks reflected more than just his desire to see Asquith do badly in that by-election.
42. Thus, for example, after Churchill's circular to commanding officers became known, a deputation saw Bonar Law and demanded that the practice should be stopped. Bonar Law promised to look into it, and urged Lloyd George to discuss the matter with Churchill. Bonar Law to Lloyd George, 26 May 1919; Bonar Law Papers, 101/3/86.
43. Stanley to Clynes and Clynes to Stanley (two telegrams), 3 October 1918. Syrett (Ministry of Food) to Major Astor, 9 October 1918. MAF 60/264.
44. Henderson tried to arrange that a Labour and Co-op delegation should see Lloyd George over the proposed winding-up of the Ministry. But in replying a fortnight later Lloyd George could inform him the Ministry would continue. Henderson to Lloyd George, 19 June 1919, and Lloyd George to Henderson, 4 July 1919; LG F/27/3/34 and 35.
45. K. O. Morgan, 'Post-war reconstruction in Wales, 1918 and 1945', p. 89 in Winter (ed.), *op. cit.*, pp. 82–98. J. Melling, *Rent Strikes: People's Struggles for Housing in West Scotland 1890–1916* (Edinburgh: Polygon, 1983). D. Englander, *Landlord and Tenant in Urban Britain 1838–1918* (Oxford: Clarendon Press, 1983), pp. 193–317.
46. *Daily Herald*, editorial 'Labour sacks the lot', 4 November 1919. *New Statesman*, 8 November 1919, p. 146.
47. I. McLean, *The Legend of Red Clydeside* (Edinburgh: Donald, 1983), p. 169 and generally pp. 165–73. Michael Savage argues the case that the Labour Party came 'to rely increasingly on neighbourhood bases of

48. C. J. Wrigley, *Arthur Henderson* (Swansea: University of Wales Press, 1990), pp. 140. Howard, *op. cit.*, p. 66.
    support (rather than work-based ones)' in his *The Dynamics of Working-Class Politics* (Cambridge: Cambridge University Press, 1987), p. 163.
49. J. Darwin, *Britain, Egypt and the Middle East: Imperial Policy in the Aftermath of War, 1918–1922* (London: Macmillan, 1981), pp. 26–44. P. S. Gupta, *Imperialism and the British Labour Movement 1914–1964* (London: Macmillan, 1975), pp. 40–8.
50. Wrigley, *Henderson*, pp. 134–42. McLean *op. cit.*, pp. 176–200. *The Times*, 9 January 1920. P. G. Robb, *The Government of India and Reform* (Oxford: Oxford University Press, 1976), pp. 171–80.
51. S. R. Ward, 'Great Britain: land fit for heroes lost', p. 26 in S. R. Ward (ed.), *The War Generation: Veterans of the First World War* (Port Washington: Kennikat Press, 1975), pp. 10–37. On Edinburgh, J. Holford, *Reshaping Labour* (London: Croom Helm, 1988), pp. 113–14. Englander, *op. cit.*, p. 290.
52. G. S. Bain and R. Price, *op. cit.*, pp. 39–78.
53. Sutherland to Lloyd George, 15 April 1920; LG F/22/1/29.
54. *The Times*, 19 and 20 March 1920. Henderson, to Lloyd George's irritation, was still making use of Lloyd George's March attack in speeches in June. *Evening News*, 8 June 1920.
55. Riddell's diary, 10 January 1920; Riddell Papers, 62985, f. 7–8. Dr Haden Guest on an interview with Lenin; *The Times*, 30 September 1920.
56. *The Times*, 8 October 1919. Report of Lloyd George's meeting with the TUC and MFGB deputation, 9 October 1919 (GT 8305); CAB 24–90 and *The Times*, 11 October 1919.
57. WC (630), 14 October 1919; CAB 23–12–33. K. Jeffery and P. Hennessy, *States of Emergency* (London: Routledge and Kegan Paul, 1983), pp. 20–1 and 27–9. Minutes of the Ministry of Food Emergency Committee, 5 November and 17 December 1919; MAF 60/419, f. 2–4. There were also emergency committees to relieve the problem of congestion at the docks, which worried the authorities in case there was a major strike. Minutes of Traffic Emergency (Lorry) Scheme, six meetings between 15 October and 19 December 1919; MAF 60/422. Minutes of Liverpool Local Traffic Emergency Committee, ten meetings between 15 October and 17 December (with a further five to 4 April 1920); MAF 60/423. Minutes of Manchester Port and Transit Executive Committee, eight meetings between 13 October and 15 December 1919 (with a further five to 29 March 1920); MAF 60/424. Hull Traffic Emergency (Lorry) Committee, five meetings between 10 November and 18 December (and one further meeting on 5 January 1920); MAF 60/426.
58. S. Armitage, *The Politics of Decontrol of Industry* (London: Weidenfeld and Nicolson, 1969), pp. 137–8.
59. Wilson to Lloyd George, 29 September 1919; LG F/47/8/36. Riddell's diary, 4 October 1919; Riddell Papers, 62984, f. 145.

60. Major-General Sir C. E. Callwell, *Field-Marshal Sir Henry Wilson*, vol. 2 (London: Cassell, 1927), pp. 218–19. Wilson to Lloyd George, 7 January 1920; LG F/47/8/38. Lloyd George later agreed to eight battalions staying in Britain.
61. Jeffery and Hennessy, *op. cit.*, pp. 18–19. WC (635), 27 October 1919; CAB 23–12–46.
62. The estimated number of troops in Great Britian and Ireland (including 6,000 in hospital, detention or otherwise not effective) was 158,801 for 31 March 1920 and 127,928 for 30 April 1920. T. P. Hill (Cabinet Office) to J. T. Davies, 10 January 1920; LG F/24/2/1/. Wilson diary, 15 January 1920; Callwell, *op. cit.*, p. 222.
63. Cabinet conferences, 16 and 18 January 1920; CAB 23–35–S.10 and 11. Hankey to Lloyd George, 17 January 1920 (repeating views expressed on 16); LG F/24/2/3. Also his letter to Tom Jones, 17 January 1920; *Whitehall Diary*, pp. 97–8.
64. Cabinet Report (CP 491) 22 January 1920; CAB 24–96; quoted in Armitage *op. cit.*, p. 138.
65. Riddell diary, 10 January 1920; Riddell Papers, 62985, f. 7. Jeffery and Hennessy, *op. cit.*, pp. 33–4.
66. Tom Jones's notes, 2 February 1920; *Whitehall Diary*, pp. 99–103. Cabinet meeting, 2 February 1920; CAB 23–20–136/40. The rumours may even have been fostered by Wilson not only for that purpose but in an attempt to reverse the decisions to wind up GHQ Great Britain and to cease supplying industrial intelligence.
67. Riddell diary, 3 April 1921; Riddell Papers, 62987, f. 104.
68. Ruth Lee's diary, 30 May 1920; in A. Clark (ed.), *A Good Innings* (London: Murray, 1974), p. 196 (and in the original, vol. 2 (1940), p. 795). For similar remarks, Riddell's diary, 11 October 1919; *Peace Conference*, p. 131.
69. WC (570 and 577), 22 May and 6 June 1919; CAB 23–10–54/5 and 82. CAB 33 and 35 (1920), 7 and 11 June 1920; CAB 23–21–183/5 and 241.
70. *Morning Post*, 24 December 1919. 125 *HC Deb 5s*, c. 127; 11 February 1920. Riddell diary, 27 March 1920; Riddell Papers, 62985, f. 87.
71. Sir Alfred Pease to his brother, Lord Gainford, 24 July 1919; Gainford Papers, 97. On engineering employers' dissatisfaction with the failure of the unions to deliver results at the local level see A. McKinlay and J. Zeitlin, 'The meanings of managerial prerogative: industrial relations and the organisation of work in British engineering 1880–1939', *Business History*, 31 (1989), pp. 32–47; and J. Zeitlin, 'The internal politics of employer organization', in S. Tolliday and J. Zeitlin (eds), *The Power to Manage?* (London: Routledge, 1990).
72. WC (606A), 5 August 1919; CAB 23–15–153. A similar case in Tonypandy was still part of folk memory of the First World War to my knowledge in March 1972. For working-class bitterness on the subject, see B. Waites *A Class Society at War* (Leamington Spa: Berg, 1987), p. 70. For Bonar Law's low expectations of the success of the

government's profiteering measures see his letter to Lloyd George, 13 July 1919; LG F/35/3/30.
73. 125 *HC Deb. 5s*, c. 39 and 128; 10 and 11 February 1920.
74. For an example of his 'autocracy' theme, see *The Times*, 8 October 1919 and 19 March 1920. Sir Auckland Geddes' comment was in the context of a discussion on profiteering, WC (575), 3 June 1919; CAB 23–10–73.
75. *Whitehall Diary*, p. 98.
76. WC (630), 14 October 1919; CAB 23–12–31. P. S. Bagwell, *The Railwaymen* (London: Allen & Unwin, 1963), pp. 415–16. Cabinet meeting, 13 January 1920; CAB 23–20–42/4. Tom Jones to Lloyd George, with details of the negotiations, 10 January 1920; LG F/24/2/2. E. Geddes to Lloyd George, 15 January 1920; LG F/18/4/1.
77. Cabinet meeting, 31 October 1919; CAB 23–18–17/18. C. J. Wrigley, 'The trade unions between the wars' in C. J. Wrigley (ed.), *A History of British Industrial Relations*, vol. 2 (Brighton: Harvester, 1986), p. 86.
78. A. Bullock, *The Life and Times of Ernest Bevin*, vol. 1 (London: Heineman, 1960), pp. 121–33. Lord Shaw of Dunfermline, *Letters to Isabel* (London: Cassell, 1921), pp. 55–6 and 298–303. *Transport Workers – Wages and Conditions of Employment of Dock Labour, Court of Enquiry*, 1920 Cmd. 936 and Cmd. 937. E. Taplin, *The Dockers' Union* (Leicester: Leicester University Press, 1985), pp. 141–6. H. A. Clegg, *A History of British Trade Unions Since 1889*, vol. 2 (Oxford: Clarendon Press, 1985), pp. 257–8. 'The searchlight on industry', *New Statesman*, 28 February 1920, pp. 607–8. 'The dockers' report', *New Statesman*, 10 April 1920, pp. 4–6.
79. Esher to Brett, 22 October 1920; Oliver, Viscount Esher (ed.), *Journals and Letters of Reginald Viscount Esher*, vol. 4 (London: Nicholson and Watson, 1938), p. 267.
80. Cabinet meeting at 11.30 a.m. and 5 p.m. 27 January 1920; CAB 23–20–97/102, 111 and 113/17. *The Daily Telegraph*, 29 January 1920. G. D. H. Cole, *Labour in the Coal-mining Industry 1914–1921* (Oxford: Clarendon Press, 1923), pp. 122–5. Sir R. A. S. Redmayne, *The British Coal-mining Industry During the War* (Oxford: Clarendon Press, 1923), pp. 232 and 316–26. R. Page Arnot, *The Miners: Years of Struggle* (London: Allen & Unwin), pp. 232–4.
81. Cole, *op. cit.*, pp. 118–21 and 126–28. *The Daily Telegraph*, 19 March 1920. Cabinet meeting, 28 March 1920; CAB 23–21–21.
82. Lloyd George to Hamar Greenwood, 27 March 1920; LG F/19/2/6. A. Williamson (War Office) to Hankey, 25 March 1920; LG F/24/2/21. Cabinet meeting, 31 March 1920; CAB 23–21–27.
83. P. Dennis, 'The reconstitution of the territorial force 1918–1920' in A. Preston and P. Dennis (eds), *Swords and Covenants* (London: Croom Helm, 1976), pp. 190–215, especially 208–10, and 'The territorial army in aid of the civil power in Britain', *Journal of Contemporary History*, 16 (1981), pp. 705–24.
84. Cabinet meeting, 18 February 1920; CAB 23–20–160/1.

85. Jeffery and Hennessy, *op. cit.*, pp. 50–3. Cabinet meeting, 12 August 1920; CAB 23–22–131/2.
86. Cabinet meeting, 22 April 1920; CAB 23–21–46/7.
87. Cabinet meeting, 31 October 1919; CAB 23–18–17.
88. Memorandum on the general situation, July 1920; copy in LG F/46/9/11.
89. On these events see Bagwell, *op. cit.*, pp. 445–7. Bullock, *op. cit.*, pp. 133–42. D. G. Boyce, *Englishmen and Irish Troubles* (Cambridge, Mass.: MIT Press, 1972), pp. 66–9. S. R. Graubard, *British Labour and the Russian Revolution 1917–1924* (Cambridge, Mass.: Harvard University Press, 1956), pp. 90–8. L. J. Macfarlane, 'Hands off Russia: British labour and the Russo-Polish War, 1920', *Past and Present*, 38 (1967), pp. 126–52. S. White, *Britain and the Bolshevik Revolution* (London: Macmillan, 1979), pp. 39–51 and 'Labour's Council of Action 1920', *Journal of Contemporary History*, 9 (1974), pp. 99–122.
90. On 24 June 1920, Labour Party, *Conference, 1920*, p. 144.
91. Bagwell, *op. cit.*, p. 446. G. Blaxland, *J. H. Thomas* (London: Muller, 1964), pp. 142–3. Labour Party, *Conference, 1920*, pp. 139–40 and 166–7 (23 and 24 June 1920).
92. J. H. Hudson of the ILP, in seconding the initial motion on 24 June. Labour Party, *Conference, 1920*, p. 162.
93. Thomas quoted in Boyce, *op. cit.*, pp. 70–1 (drawing on *Cardiff Western Mail*, 18 January 1921). *Report of the Special Trades Union Congress*, 13 July 1920. B. C. Roberts, *The Trades Union Congress 1868–1921* (London: Allen & Unwin, 1958), p. 341.
94. Labour Party, *Report of the Twenty-First Annual Conference, 1921*, pp. 11–18. For the background see R. H. Ullman, *The Anglo-Soviet Accord* (Princeton, NJ: Princeton University Press, 1972) and E. Mawdsley, *The Russian Civil War* (London: Allen & Unwin, 1987), pp. 250–61.
95. White, 'Council of Action', pp. 106–12. A. Clinton, *The Trade Union Rank and File* (Manchester: Manchester University Press, 1977), pp. 117–21.
96. Draft notes of a conference held at Boulogne on 27 July 1920 printed in R. Butler and J. P. T. Bury (eds), *Documents on British Foreign Policy 1919–1939*, first series, vol. 8 (London: HMSO, 1958), pp. 650–61. He made similar remarks at a further meeting with the French held at Lympne on 9 August 1920, printed in *ibid.*, pp. 731–55. See Ullman, *op. cit.*, pp. 143–4, 176–93 and 209–19 on Lloyd George's tactics in his talks with the French.
97. Report, 12 August 1920 (CP 1772); CAB 24/110, quoted in Macfarlane, *op. cit.*, p. 126, and Ullman, *op. cit.*, pp. 221–2.
98. Ullman, *op. cit.*, p. 224. Bullock, *op. cit.*, pp. 136–9. Labour Party, *Conference, 1921*, pp. 13–15. Graubard, *op. cit.*, pp. 106–14.
99. The editor of the *Daily Graphic* (or possibly Viscount Burnham) to Addison, 16 August 1920; Addison Papers, Box 123.
100. Labour Party, *Conference, 1921*, p. 18. Bullock, *op. cit.*, p. 139.

101. Cabinet meeting, 6 and 10 May, and 3 June 1920; CAB 23–12–73/6, 83 and 208/10.
102. Cole, *op. cit.*, pp. 130–6. B. Supple, *The History of the British Coal Industry*, vol. 4 (Oxford: Clarendon Press, 1987), p. 145.
103. Arnot, *op. cit.*, pp. 237–43.
104. Cabinet meeting, 12 August 1920; CAB 23–22–131/2. Horne to Addison, 20 August 1920; Addison Papers, Box 14. Lloyd George to Bonar Law, 4 September 1920; LG F/31/1/44.
105. Quoted in R. H. Desmarais, 'The British government's strike breaking organisation and Black Friday', *Journal of Contemporary History*, 6 (1971), p. 122. The Ministry of Food Emergency Committee began meeting again from 24 August 1920; MAF 60/419, f. 7–43.
106. Bridgeman's diary, 2 September 1920; P. Williamson (ed.), *The Modernisation of Conservative Politics* (London: Historians' Press, 1988), pp. 146–7. Riddell's diary, 1 October 1920; *Peace Conference*, p. 238. Sutherland to Lloyd George, n.d.; LG F/22/2/16. Armitage, *op. cit.*, p. 140. Editorial on Brace, *New Statesman*, 13 November 1920.
107. P. S. Bagwell, 'The Triple Industrial Alliance', pp. 112–14 in A. Briggs and J. Saville (eds), *Essays in Labour History 1886–1923* (London: Macmillan, 1971). Williamson (ed.), *op. cit.*, p. 148. Cole, *op. cit.*, pp. 150–2.
108. Lloyd George to Bonar Law, 4 September 1920; LG F/31/1/44.
109. Hankey to Philip Kerr, 11 and 21 September 1920; Lothian Papers, GD 46–17–210, f. 409/10 and 412/14. Riddell diary, 16 September 1920; *Peace Conference*, p. 237.
110. Arnot, *op. cit.*, pp. 256–8. Bridgeman to his wife, 25 September 1920; Williamson (ed.), *op. cit.*, p. 149.
111. Riddell diary, 1 October 1920; Riddell Papers, 62986, f. 100 (partly in *Peace Conference*, p. 238). Lady Carson's diary, 15 October 1920; Carson Papers, D.1507/6/6. Riddell diary, 16 October 1920; *Peace Conference*, p. 241.
112. Cabinet meeting, 15 October 1920; CAB 23–22–278/81. 133 HC Deb. 5s, c. 884–93; 19 October 1920.
113. Bagwell, pp. 457–9. Arnot, *op. cit.*, pp. 271–5. Cole, *op. cit.*, pp. 158–61. Cabinet meetings, 26 and 28 October 1920; CAB 23–22–288/90 and 293/4.
114. Armitage, *op. cit.*, p. 142. Cabinet meeting, 28 January 1921; CAB 23–24–35/6.
115. Arnot, *op. cit.*, pp. 291–4. The owners' proposals are printed in tabular form in Cole, *op. cit.*, p. 197.
116. Riddell diary, 22, 5 and 3 April 1921; *Peace Conference*, pp. 292 and 291 and Riddell Papers, 62987, f. 101.
117. For Horne's negotiations, see Armitage, *op. cit.*, pp. 143–7. Cabinet meeting, 10 January 1921; CAB 23–24–42/4.
118. Geddes to Lloyd George, 31 March 1921; LG F/18/4/70. The Ministry of Food Emergency Committee met regularly from 7 April; MAF 60/419, f. 45–55. Cabinet meeting, 4 April 1921; CAB 23–25–3/5. There

is a more important account of the meeting in *Whitehall Diary*, pp. 132–6. Jeffery and Hennessy, *op. cit.*, pp. 58–66.
119. *Whitehall Diary*, p. 139.
120. Arnot, *op. cit.*, pp. 302–9. *Whitehall Diary*, pp. 136–54. Desmarais, *op. cit.*, p. 125. For an example of Lloyd George's appeal to local authorities, see telegram to Crewe; Crewe Papers C/31. Cabinet meetings (two) on 12 April 1921; CAB 23–5–6/9 and 13/15. On the constitutional problems of calling out the reserves, Hankey diary, 17 April 1921; Hankey Papers, HNKY 1/5, f. 199.
121. Chamberlain to Long, 16 April 1921; Austen Chamberlain Papers, AC 24/3/69. Chamberlain to Cecil, 16 April; Cecil Papers 51078, f. 5–7.
122. Bagwell, 'Triple Industrial Alliance', pp. 118–19. At the time R. Page Arnot took the view that Hodges had been misrepresented. Letter to Beatrice Webb, 18 April 1921; Passfield Papers, 2G, f. 170–2.
123. Lloyd George's correspondence with the MFGB is printed in Arnot, *op. cit.*, pp. 314–16.
124. Perhaps a secret meeting between Stephen Walsh and Lloyd George on 20 June 1921 laid the foundation for the settlement. Walsh to Lloyd George, 26 June 1921; LG F/46/13/15.
125. Armitage, *op. cit.*, pp. 150–2. *Whitehall Diary*, pp. 145–6.
126. Callwell, *op. cit.*, vol. 1, pp. 133 and 136. *Whitehall Diary*, pp. 134 and 136. Chamberlain to Cecil, 16 April 1920; Cecil Papers, 51078, f. 5–7.

9
Lloyd George and the challenges of Labour

The central feature of the immediate post-First World War years was the problem of readjustment from war to peace. The international economy was seriously dislocated and within Britain there were major problems for British industry and finance in returning to something approaching the conditions of July 1914. The problems of determining both the pace and extent of decontrol and also of dealing with the social and political disturbances arising from the reconversion of the economy were major reasons for maintaining the Coalition government. These problems were also major sources of division within the Coalition government.

For supporters of the Coalition government it was often difficult, especially in the first eighteen months after the Armistice, to judge whether the widespread popular discontent would be expressed in a dramatic manner. The political instability in Central and Eastern Europe was seen as a grave warning – though in the aftermath of such a massive war, it did not surprise ministers that there was dissatisfaction on a very broad front. As in other former belligerent countries, there was serious discontent in urban areas, especially those which had been munitions centres. In these the mass influx of additional workers had both made bad housing conditions worse and added to the instability of industrial relations. Elsewhere, returning soldiers and sailors who became unemployed were also concentrated in the cities and larger towns. There were also pent-up industrial demands which had been postponed while the war was on because of the overwhelming working-class commitment to win the war (a commitment which had been heightened by the German offensive of March 1918). These and other resentments, were released with the Armistice.

Ministers were also faced with serious discontent arising from consumer issues. The drastic food shortages of Central and Eastern Europe – the fuse that ignited cities elsewhere – was lacking in an extreme form in Britain. But in a lesser form it was present. In June 1919 Long writing to Lloyd George specifically related these issues to 'the unrest in the country' when he stated,

> There can be no doubt whatever that this is due to the increased prices of food, the scarcity and the inferior quality of the beer and spirits in circulation. Prices are extraordinary; meat of all kinds is scarce and dear, butter and cheese cannot be obtained in many places at all, and the deprivation of these necessary articles of food is telling seriously upon the health of the people and therefore upon their spirits.[1]

There was also resentment at the scarcity of other goods at the end of the war. Many working people had worked long hours and enjoyed good take-home pay during the war but were able to buy relatively few consumer goods. When these became available, the price was often high. Discontent over the availability and the price of food and other goods played a major part in boosting Labour in 1919 and 1920. This dissatisfaction was also revealed from the second half of the war by the explicitly political role of the co-operative movement and by the support which it frequently provided for strikers in the post-war period. The impact of inflation encouraged more white collar and other hitherto thinly unionised workers to join them at a time when the unions' prestige was generally high and in particular when they had established more extensive national wage bargaining than ever before.

High prices also raised issues about the fairness of society. Sir Robertson Nicoll, the owner and editor of the *British Weekly*, pointed to this in a letter he wrote to Lloyd George in February 1920:

> The question which occupies the minds of many electors, to the exclusion of all others, is the question of profiteering. They are concerned about how they are to live, and they are dismayed as new announcements come each day of increased prices and of the great prosperity of the wholesale profiteers.[2]

The upsurge of feeling over profiteering in the immediate post-war period was very much an early twentieth-century expression of popular beliefs in 'a moral economy'. The fact that the government was deeply involved in the overseas purchase and the domestic regulation of food ensured that much of this dissatisfaction was directed at the government. In the summer of 1919 the political sensitivity of the issue led both to the government going ahead with its profiteering legislation and to it reluctantly maintaining the Ministry of Food and various controls much longer than it wished.

Politicians had also added to the social expectations of the end of the war, not least Lloyd George himself. The talk of 'the war to end wars' and 'a fit land for heroes to live in' had more than just a touch of the millenarian about it. Politicians were also quick to attach themselves to the spirit of camaraderie of the returning soldiers. By the autumn of 1919 there was a clash between such expectations and those of business and financial circles for 'back to 1914'. In due course the failure to match the popular hopes aroused at the end of the war led to considerable disillusionment. This was well expressed in *A Soldier's Diary* published in February 1923, in which a young officer noted bitterly in August 1920 that his worst predictions at the Front had by then come true – 'the sway of the old men has returned, the dead are forgotten, and betrayed.'[3] In time the government's failure to give substance to many of the high expectations it had aroused in the 1918 general election became portrayed by its most dedicated opponents as having been no more than a Tory exercise in 'how to ride the crisis, how to lie, deceive, cajole and buy time so as once more to snatch a reprieve for wealth and privilege'.[4]

The economic and social problems of the transition from Great War to peace were seen by leading politicians as inevitable and potentially dangerous. Lloyd George frequently made them a key theme in his major speeches in the House of Commons for more than eighteen months after the Armistice. They were also the reason given for the continuance of the Coalition. Balfour lucidly outlined the problems of the period in a letter to Lord Aldenham in March 1920, at the time of the talk of fusion. He wrote:

> Before the war there was a natural adjustment between the supply of raw materials and the demand. . . . This adjustment has been destroyed; and as an inevitable result great natural monopolies have grown up which cannot be left wholly to themselves. It is impossible that in such circumstances there should not be industrial unrest; it is impossible that this should not be aggravated by the rise of prices, as it may be some day by their fall; it is impossible that our task should not be complicated by the political revolutions which have changed the face of Germany, of Russia, and of all that once was Austria. We cannot feel surprised that, in such circumstances, there should be strikes and lock-outs, or that subversive elements to be found in all countries should not be eagerly on the look-out for some opportunity of furthering their disastrous projects. It is the

tragedy of the situation that, while the ills that Europe most suffers from are deficient production and shattered credit, the first of these diseases should be aggravated by industrial disputes, and the second by political instability.[5]

One of Lloyd George's major roles, as head of a government seen to be the best possible bastion of political stability, was to deal with Labour.

In the post-war period there was not one unified challenge by Labour, but two or three. One was a constitutional challenge by the Labour Party, which aimed at achieving majorities in Parliament and in local government, and whose major figures were embarrassed by talk of 'direct action' and confrontations with employers. A second challenge was industrial, with the scale and success of such action seeming to change the balance of power not only in industry but appearing to offer the prospect of changing it in society as a whole. Linked to that, in a somewhat blurred fashion, was a revolutionary challenge, in reality of no great dimension but nevertheless a matter which caused anxiety in governing circles until at least the summer of 1921.

These different challenges signified the British form of the bitter divisions within the labour and socialist movements of continental Europe. Throughout Europe, ideological differences which had been present before 1914 were widened by the issues raised by the First World War and also by the example of the Bolsheviks in Russia in October 1917 and their subsequent treatment of other socialists. In Britain the revolutionary tradition remained weak.[6] British trade unionists were long accustomed to working within the framework of the liberal semi-democratic nineteenth-century constitution and in more highly-unionised trades they had achieved collective bargaining. Even so, in the upsurge of working-class discontent in 1919 and 1920, the possibilities of widening industrial action through sympathy strikes, spearheaded by the Triple Alliance unions, greatly worried many ministers.

Lloyd George was very willing to take a firm line with serious labour unrest, just as Gustav Noske, a socialist minister, did in Germany in 1919. He seems to have been quite confident that in a modern state, with sufficient loyal forces – be they from the armed services or volunteers – minority working-class uprisings could be successfully suppressed. Perhaps he had learned lessons from the crushing of the Paris Commune in 1871 or the repression of the Moscow working class in December 1905; he certainly felt he understood Kerensky's failure in Russia in 1917 and Count Karolyi's in Hungary in 1919. In Britain in 1919 Lloyd George was decisive in stamping out dissent in the police force and was very ready to approve the setting up of the state's emergency supply organisation. He had no hesitation in agreeing to the movement of troops to areas of serious industrial unrest (notably Glasgow) or prospective trouble (such as the coalfields), but he was less impressed than most of his colleagues by the possibility of an attempt at a *coup d'état* in London.

Inflated ministerial fears of Bolshevism in Britain owed much to the level of left-wing activity in certain areas as well as to the actions of militant shop stewards, to dissent within the armed forces or to links between a few on the Left and Moscow. The Clyde, South Wales and London were three such areas. Clydeside was the major centre of strength for the Socialist Labour Party, a Marxist body, and for a large and left-wing Independent Labour Party. It was also notable for many able orators and socialist proselytisers like John Maclean, who ran socialist economics classes and who had been appointed 'Bolshevik Consul' for Glasgow; Tom Anderson, who ran Proletarian Sunday Schools; and Guy Aldred, the main figure of the Anti-Parliamentary Communist Federation (which emerged in 1921 from the Glasgow Anarchist Group). The coalfields of South Wales also worried ministers. One report sent to Lloyd George in March 1919, which referred to Merthyr Tydfil as 'a very hot centre for agitators', noted with concern meetings which were being organised by the National Council for Civil Liberties (which had begun as the National Council against Conscription), by the Liberty League ('which requires careful watching') and the ILP. In 1920 the Merthyr ILP was the centre of attempts to carry much of that party into the Communist Party of Great Britain, which was formed on 1 August of that year. London as the capital was central to all manner of groups, including various Left bodies backed by European exiles and also Sylvia Pankhurst and her Workers' Socialist Federation.[7]

Links between British Left-wingers and Russian Bolsheviks and the presence of Bolshevik representatives in Britain added fuel to early post-war alarm. Certainly 'Bolshevik gold' was sent by couriers to many groups on the revolutionary Left in the period after the end of the First World War, including Sylvia Pankhurst and the Workers'

Socialist Federation, the British Socialist Party, the Socialist Labour Party, the 'Hands off Russia' Committee (which had been initiated by James Crossley of the British Socialist Party in early 1919), the Russian Information Bureau and the Communist Unity Group. When in August 1920 in the midst of the uproar over the possibility of Britain helping Poland against Russia, it was found that Francis Meynell, a director of the *Daily Herald*, had collected a Russian subsidy of £75,000, the Labour Party leadership was most embarrassed. Beatrice Webb judged this incident to be 'a severe blow to the prospects of the Labour Party', observing in her diary, 'If Meynell had been an *agent provocateur* he could not have done his job more effectively!'.[8] In its reaction to social and political unrest, the government blew the Bolshevik connection out of all proportion. They and the press made much of the 'un-British nature' of Bolshevism, and used the term to smear all manner of Labour figures. Indeed 'Bolshevik' was used to describe almost any dissent from government policies by those on the Left of British politics, and also any unorthodox social behaviour.

Lloyd George, however, was much more impressed by the threat of a Triple Alliance strike than by the possibility of action by any of the avowedly revolutionary groups in Britain, although the two threats were often linked in ministerial minds. Thus on 2 February 1920, when the Cabinet discussed the possibility of revolutionary disturbances occurring, it was felt 'that the struggle would begin probably with transport questions and that it would very largely centre round the problem of maintaining the transport services of the country'.[9] To the government, the Triple Alliance represented 'direct action' in a very tangible form. The Triple Alliance was seen as a weapon which could be used not only to defend or improve wages and conditions of service but which might also be used to enforce public ownership of the mines and railways, or – in the case of the MFGB – to determine the price of the product for domestic consumers.

The continuation of many of the government's wartime labour problems encouraged the continuation of many of its wartime means of dealing with them, albeit sometimes in different forms. During the First World War the government had been able to rely on the Defence of the Realm Act to deal with emergencies. In 1918 Lord Shaw of Dunfermline had been sufficiently concerned at its use to complain to Herbert Samuel that 'my view of the Defence of the

Realm Act is that it did not warrant, and Parliament unless it had been tricked, could not have sanctioned, the implications that compliant governments have put upon it.'[10] In autumn 1920 Lloyd George took the opportunity of the 'datum line' strike to provide the state in peacetime with the continuance of virtually unlimited reserve powers under the Emergency Powers Act, 1920. The Act was used in the 1921 mining dispute (and on later occasions).

At other times Lloyd George's government did consider special trade union legislation. This was given very serious attention after the early 1919 wave of industrial unrest, when the War Cabinet reviewed a draft 'Strikes (Exceptional Measures) Bill' which would have given powers to declare strikes to be conspiracies against the state, to have arrested those inciting others to strike and to seize union funds. However, on this occasion and most others special legislation was not pursued. For the Defence of the Realm Act and then the Emergency Powers Act covered national emergencies, and in a period of instability the government was not eager to thwart orthodox, moderate trade unionism. Thus after the 1921 coal lockout, when the eastern division of the Conservative Party was calling for compulsory ballots before strikes, Austen Chamberlain replied that he agreed with Clynes that 'the dispute would have been settled much earlier but for the fact that the miners' organisation left the responsible leaders without any discretion or authority.' He went on to observe,

> The strike was eventually settled only by the leaders assuming a responsibility beyond their mandate and over-riding the decision of the miners' ballot. This experience gives much food for reflection and may make us doubt whether a compulsory ballot – even if it were practical to enforce it – would really have the pacifying and steadying effect which its supporters expect. My own conclusion ... is that a *voluntary* ballot before a strike is declared might often be salutory and useful, but that at a *compulsory* ballot there would be no means of getting the workmen to vote and no assurance that wise counsels would prevail, and no possibility of effectively enforcing the provisions against illegal strikes.[11]

The most notable other case of legislation was the extension of restriction on strikes in public utilities by the Electricity Supply Act, 1919. After the strike in power stations in February 1919, the government extended the provisions of 1875 legislation against strikes called without 'reasonable warning' in public utilities to cover electricity workers. Many employers in 1919 hoped that the government would go much further, and apply the anti-trade union provisions of the Police Act, 1919 to all other public service workers, including Post Office employees and even miners and railwaymen should nationalisation take place.[12]

As well as extending general emergency legal provisions into peacetime, Lloyd George's government continued – and extended – other wartime practices. During the First World War internal surveillance was developed well beyond pre-war levels, when it had been particularly concerned with anarchists and Irish nationalists. By the spring of 1917 MI5 had compiled 250,000 cards and 27,000 personal files, thereby going well beyond the estimated 70,000 adult enemy aliens resident in Britain at the outbreak of the war. During the war several ministries and sections of the armed services (as well as MI5) were involved in making reports on members of the Labour movement. Although the army ended surveillance of industrial workers in early 1920, surveillance of the Left by other official bodies was continued after the First World War.[13] In addition, big business also funded bodies such as the Economic League, which provided employers with details of persons and groups deemed to be subversive.[14]

Similarly, the government continued the practice of internal propaganda which it had developed during the First World War. In May and June 1917, following the May engineering strikes, the War Cabinet had agreed 'that the time had come to undertake an active campaign to counteract the pacifist movement, which at present had the field to itself'. Lloyd George gave vent to very similar sentiments in the summer of 1919. Then, when expressing concern about strikes and low industrial output, he declared,

> The first remedy did not involve legislation, and it was that we should use propaganda among the working classes. . . .
> The only people now who used the Press were the Bolsheviks, and they held meetings on Sundays which were attended by thousands. . . . They had also captured the trade union organisation. The question was, what steps should be taken to counter this propaganda?

After the war, the government continued to use the cinema as well as the press to get its message over to the public.[15] Both the government and the Triple Alliance unions attached the highest importance to winning the support of public opinion in major industrial disputes. This was very much the case in the autumn 1919 rail and the 1920 and 1921 coal disputes. The Coalition government had the considerable advantage of the support of much of the national press – and many newspapers unscrupulously misrepresented the unions' case.

Lloyd George also tried to deal with serious industrial and social unrest by remedying its causes. As Sir David Shackleton of the Ministry of Labour observed in the autumn of 1917, there would be no serious likelihood of revolution in Britain 'if the workers are convinced that the government is earnestly and sympathetically seeking a thorough remedy for the evils which undoubtedly exist'.[16] After the end of the war, Lloyd George genuinely wished to achieve substantial housing and other reforms. In March 1919 Lloyd George commented to Riddell of Bolsheviks,

> It may be that they are sent by Providence to keep the rich in check. It may be just as well that they should have something to fear. Now that Lenin is here, I hope that he may last for another six weeks, so as to give us an opportunity to carry out reforms which are necessary for the safety of society.

However light-hearted that remark was, he certainly acted on it when urging his ministerial colleagues to press ahead with reforms. Thus, when the War Cabinet reviewed government policy on 5 August 1919 he remarked,

> they could not take risks with Labour. If we did, we should at once create an enemy within our own borders, and one which would be better provided with dangerous weapons than Germany. We had in this country millions of men who had been trained to arms, and there were plenty of guns and ammunition available. . . . No risks could be taken in respect of the health and labour of the people.[17]

Lloyd George and his government did carry out some measures of reform which were intended to lessen conflict in industrial relations. In this context, in mid-August 1919 Lloyd George discussed with Sir Robert Horne such matters as profit sharing and an extension of unemployment insurance.[18] The Industrial Courts Act of 1919 was an especially important measure. During the most serious unrest there were other government initiatives which were in 'the spirit of Whitleyism', not least the summoning of the National Industrial Conference. Even the setting up of the Sankey Commission can be seen as a move to resolve differences through enquiry and reflection, rather than through conflict. Yet while Lloyd George preached the virtues of industrial harmony as opposed to 'direct action' and conflict in industrial relations, he failed to give strong support to Whitley councils in the public sector and soon disregarded the National Industrial Council. Such government enthusiasm as there was for corporatism soon wilted under pressure from business interests and in the face of the militancy of some sectors of labour.[19]

In confronting the expected challenge of the Triple Alliance unions Lloyd George relied heavily on the government's emergency transport organisation. Though this was set up in February 1919, it had its roots in the war. Lloyd George later recalled, 'Even before the end of the war preparations were being made by my Cabinet to meet any industrial crisis which would involve interference with the transport and food supplies of the country.'[20] Moreover, its creation in February 1919 was greatly aided by the availability of large supplies of army vehicles and other surplus resources left from the war. In turning to volunteers, especially former soldiers and also middle-class men, Lloyd George's government was responding in a similar, though less dramatic, way to several continental European governments which were also faced with labour and socialist challenges. The danger in having such an effective strike-breaking organisation was that it could be used more generally against strikes. Eric Geddes warned against this in July 1920, observing, 'No definition has ever been given of the class of strike which the Supply and Transport Committee should deal with, but I find a growing impression that all strikes are its concern.' In resisting such general use, the government was assisted by the weakening of the trade unions with the end of the economic boom.[21]

Lloyd George's most distinctive contribution to the government's response to the threat of Triple Alliance action was his extremely skilful ability to weaken the unions by creating or strengthening divisions in their midst. According to Alan Taylor, Beaverbrook once instructed his newspapers: 'Sow the seeds of discontent, sow the seeds of discontent' to the tune of 'Polly put the kettle on'.[22] Lloyd George excelled in doing this in his dealings with the trade union leadership after the war, just as he had done during it. In the period of state control of major industries, major industrial relations issues naturally gravitated to the government. Trade union leaders came to have contradictory expectations of Lloyd George's interventions, either that they would gain concessions which no other member of the government would dare grant or that he would outmanoeuvre them. Leading figures in Triple Alliance unions – not only J. H. Thomas but others such as Hartshorn, Brace, Walsh and Tillett – were very willing to deal privately with Lloyd George to try to gain concessions without major industrial conflict.

J. H. Thomas's private contacts with Lloyd George and other ministers during the major rail and coal crises of 1919 to 1921 aroused much criticism among the Left. While Thomas tried to manipulate the situations to make gains for his members, where possible without strike action, he did so at the cost of lessening the bargaining power of the Triple Alliance as a whole. Thomas was well aware of the case for the Triple Alliance. He himself stated it clearly to Bonar Law on 22 March 1919:

> if the miners stop work large numbers of railwaymen will automatically be thrown out just as large numbers of transport workers will be. Our experience of that was in 1912, when for seven weeks the miners were on strike. During those seven weeks my own union paid £94,000 in dispute pay to our own men affected by that strike. . . .
>
> Just as Capital says, 'We must organise our forces, and in the event of a struggle mobilise our forces to the best advantage', we feel that, as Labour, in a fight we must mobilise our forces to the best advantage. I say without hesitation there is undoubtedly that agreement, not in writing, but obviously there is a moral obligation one towards the other.[23]

While such approaches may be judged to be part of Thomas's various manoeuvres to outwit his union's radical executive committee and avoid 'direct action', his private relationships with leading coalowners, railway managers and wealthy Tory MPs appear to have been simply a matter of personal indulgence. In the summer of 1919 Thomas had recuperated from stress by going by sea to the United States, apparently as the guest of Henry Thornton, the general manager of the Great Eastern Railway. In March 1920 he seriously considered the offer of being taken on another trip to the United States, this time by Pomeroy Burton, the general manager of Associated Newspapers. Thomas also had the use of a cottage on Lord and Lady Astor's estate as well as being a frequent guest in their houses. Riddell observed in his diary, after he had dined with leading employers plus Thomas:

> The semi-capture of J. H. Thomas by the capitalist class is an interesting phase. I don't forget Lady Astor's vituperative observations when LG would not make her husband Minister of Agriculture. 'Look what they owe me for keeping J. H. Thomas quiet!'

It is the old story. You cannot serve God and Mammon. You cannot fight the devil with your claws dipped in eau-de-cologne. Thomas is a clever fellow, very bright and quick, and no doubt he has done good work for his people, but metaphorically and actually he is always telephoning the opposite side to say how he is getting on and whether he has succeeded in calming the ardent spirits in the movement.

Lloyd George both knew of this weakness and made use of it.

Nevertheless the Triple Alliance did not fail to achieve its ends simply because of Thomas. From early in 1919 doubts had been expressed by such left-wing figures as George Lansbury and Israel Zangwill as to whether the Triple Alliance could be effective in changing government policies. The problem of getting three different trade union memberships to take simultaneous 'trade union action' had been well illustrated by the vacillations and delays over Russia and other issues in 1919. The divided and difficult position that the miners' leadership got themselves into in the autumn of 1920 was further evidence of inherent weaknesses in the alliance as a tactic. Then Bevin, who clearly saw the problems, warned: 'I have said over and over, "When the test comes, if you do not make a real organisation it will be found to be a paper alliance." By God, it has revealed itself to be a paper alliance this week.'[24] Later, when Bevin complained during the coal dispute in April 1921 that no progress had been made to make the alliance effective, the MFGB simply replied that they had done nothing as they 'did not think that the Triple Alliance would again function'.[25] There were divisions of interest within the Triple Alliance even when the economy was booming, which Lloyd George could exploit. These became even greater when the unions were faced with economic recession.

The constitutional challenge to the Coalition from Labour was present throughout the 1918 to 1922 period albeit of varying strength. After the dramatic municipal gains of 1919, Labour continued to gain seats in some towns and cities in the autumn of 1920 but lost seats in others. The *New Statesman* observed of these results 'for Labour at the present time failure to advance is equivalent to retrogression, and there have been serious positive defeats in some of the most important centres.' After a good by-election win at Norfolk South on 27 July 1920, on a 19.9 per cent swing to Labour, Labour's momentum in parliamentary by-elections only resumed on 3 March with the defeat of Griffith-Boscawen, the Minister of Agriculture, at Dudley, on a 10.9 per cent swing to Labour from

Coalition Unionists and on 5 March 1921, with the capture of the Independent Liberal seat of Penistone on an 8.7 per cent swing to Labour from Liberal.[26] The Labour Party continued to do well in by-elections during the early summer (when the mining dispute was on), scoring 11.3 per cent swings to Labour at both Taunton and Hastings and winning the Lancashire seat of Heywood on a 17.1 per cent swing on 8 June 1921. Thereafter Labour did well where the Liberals or the Coalition parties were divided and in inner city or mining seats. Thus Labour won South-east Southwark (London) on a 39.7 per cent swing on 14 December 1921 and in 1922 won Manchester Clayton on an 18.7 per cent swing on 18 February, Camberwell (London) on a 22.4 per cent swing on 20 February, Leicester East on a 33 per cent swing on 30 March, Pontypridd on a 13.8 per cent swing on 25 July, and came within 72 votes of winning Hackney (London), which it had not contested before, on 18 August. Labour's advance, albeit patchy at times, helped Lloyd George in so far as it made many Unionists unsure of the desirability of an early general election.[27]

Moreover, even the Labour Party's constitutional challenge was in one sense mostly extra-parliamentary. It was a looming threat outside, a potential winner of many seats which had been won by Coalition supporters in the unusual circumstances of the 1918 general election. Inside Parliament, Labour's leadership was remarkably weak. J. H. Thomas, who felt he was the obvious leader, commented to Riddell and others in March 1920, 'Poor old Adamson cannot follow a complicated debate and always jumps in and does the wrong thing. He is a nice old boy, but quite useless as a leader.' Although Henderson did return to Parliament mid-way through the 1919 session, he was seriously ill at the start of the 1920 session and effectively out of things for some months thereafter. In early 1921, after just over three years as chairman of the Parliamentary Party (the designation before 'leader' was accepted), Adamson stood down and Clynes succeeded. Beatrice Webb observed of the Parliamentary Labour Party in January 1922:

> Clynes is not a great Parliamentary leader but he does not disgrace the party as Adamson did – that is about all you can say. Henderson is a good outside manager, and if the party inside the House was better material might even rise to the height of a good Front bench leader. But according to Ben Spoor . . . the Parliamentary Party is altogether deplorable, alike in membership and in its constitution. . . . The party votes solidly for

dull-witted trade unionists as Whips and speakers. Clynes takes the nominations mechanically and never asks anyone else to speak unless the subject is one that no trade unionist will accept; refusing in fact to act as leader but only serving as chairman.

In spite of such parliamentary shortcomings, Henderson, Clynes and other Labour Party leaders rightly expected the Parliamentary Labour Party to at least double, or even treble, in size at the next election.[28] In November 1922 142 Labour MPs were returned, compared to the 61 MPs who had accepted the Labour whip at the start of the 1919 Parliament; and Labour polled 4,235,457 votes in 1922, compared to the 2,244,945 of 1918.

Lloyd George made Labour's constitutional challenge a major issue in his political manoeuvring of 1919 to 1922. At various times after the Armistice he and his supporters tried to smear Labour's moderate leaders by arguing guilt by association with Ramsay MacDonald, supporters of 'direct action' or – in the case of Henderson – absolutely falsely as one who had 'hob-nobbed' with Lenin and Trotsky when he had been in Russia.[29] Lloyd George and his associates had more success in undermining Ramsay MacDonald's attempt to return to Parliament for Woolwich in March 1921.

However, between 1918 and 1922 the overwhelmingly solid, constitutional and worthy utterances of Adamson, Clynes, Henderson and Thomas, the four trade union leaders at the heart of the Parliamentary Party's leadership, clearly defied even Lloyd George's attempts to portray them as a menace to the established order. Not only did they set very restricted limits to political action outside of local and parliamentary elections, but they vigorously supported moves to establish 'cosy co-operation' (Ben Turner's later phrase) in industry between trade unions, employers and the government. The First World War had simply strengthened such views in men like Henderson. In January 1917 he had expressed the hope

> that the fellowship and comradeship which had been so marked a feature of our war experience might so continue that they would find expression in the removal of class distinctions, the lessening of glaring social and economic inequalities, the development of mutual confidence and closer co-operation between employers and employed, and the fuller and more complete recognition of community of interest and responsibility between the state and the people.

After the war, when opposing direct action, Henderson declared,

'The problem was to restore popular confidence in representative institutions and to guide the mass movement along the path of constitutional change and enable democracy to become master in its own house without violence and disorder.'[30]

Hence, Lloyd George and other ministers went on to portray the Labour leadership not as a menace in itself but as being made up of weak politicians who were puppets of the wider Labour movement and who would be unable to control any outbreak of serious civil disorder. Lloyd George frequently expressed such views. Austen Chamberlain, who succeeded Bonar Law as Conservative Party leader on 21 March 1921, was a devoted supporter of the Coalition as a means of containing Labour. Chamberlain's views of the inadequacies of the Parliamentary Labour Party leadership were confirmed during the 1921 coal dispute by the actions of Clynes as well as the Triple Alliance leaders. When reporting to the King the proceedings in the House of Commons, he warned,

> The leaders may be men of moderation – they may have attained to a greater sense of public responsibility, and a wider knowledge and broader experience than have those whom they lead. If their views prevailed with their party to the same extent as the views of the leaders of other parties control the action of their followers, the advent of a Labour government to office might indeed result in a policy very different from that of Your Majesty's present servants, but would not constitute a menace to the order and good government of the state. But when leaders have to confess that policy is directed from below instead of from above, and when leaders whose advice has been rejected upon the most vital matters of national concern feel obliged to carry out resolutions which they have opposed, and are unable to dissociate themselves publicly and directly from action which they believe to be disastrous, a new situation arises.[31]

Fears of a Labour government gave Lloyd George grounds to support reforming, and so strengthening, the House of Lords. Some restoration of the constitutional position of the House of Lords was a high priority with the die-hard wing of the Conservative Party throughout the 1920s. Chamberlain, like Lloyd George was very sympathetic to reforming rather than simply restoring the power of the Lords. He felt that, 'Everyone in the country with something to lose must wish to see a reformed Second Chamber.' Lloyd George treated the issue as another element in his efforts to scare the propertied class into support of his anti-Labour Coalition. In May 1921 he warned, 'If by chance there should be a great wave of socialism, and the House of Lords had not been reformed, the situation might be a very serious one.' His viewpoint, according to the minutes of a meeting he held then with Chamberlain was:

> A very slight turnover of voting would put the Labour Party in power. It was most important that before this happened a strong Second Chamber should be set up, but it was not enough to give that Second Chamber power, it must also be given authority, without which it would be as matchwood in a serious crisis. He would like to see the British Second Chamber regarded with much the same feelings that the Senate inspired throughout the United States of America.

Though Lloyd George pledged that the Coalition government intended to reform the House of Lords, it can be doubted if he felt that there would be agreement among supporters of some such measure as to what should be done.[32]

Lloyd George's ploy of playing up to fears of Labour at first strengthened his political position. The Coalition did receive considerable Coalition Conservative support in 1919 and into 1920, and fear of social instability and, in particular, of the Labour movement played a major part in that. By mid-1920 support for the Coalition was receding, especially in southern England. But many leading Conservative figures continued to see it as necessary. In October 1920 St Loe Strachey wrote to Carson, 'I distrust LG probably more than you do, but at the same time I am terribly afraid of anything like splitting the forces opposed to revolution whether in Ireland or here.' Coalition Conservatives, such as Walter Elliot, continued to press in public that 'co-operation was just as essential in the groundswell that was running after the storm as it was to get it through the great storm of 1914 to 1918', and to warn that the extremists in the Labour movement 'were the tail, but they were the tail that wagged the dog'.[33]

But in time Lloyd George's playing of the 'Red card' became redundant as the strength of the unions was weakened during the economic recession. Indeed, among many Conservatives, the harping on class conflict came to be seen as positively harmful, not least because of their need for working-class votes. It was also contrary to the tenets of Conservative paternalism, as exemplified by Lord Salisbury and his late nineteenth-century governments. His third son, Lord Robert Cecil, complained to Chamberlain, 'you must remember that I was brought up to think that a class war, whether the class attacked be landowners or Labour, is the most insidious form of national disintegration.' In a further letter he observed that 'if it becomes inevitable to repeat constantly to the country that the only alternative to Lloyd George is Labour, sooner or later the country will say in that case they will try Labour; and I do not know that I should blame them.'[34] By 1922 many of those who had seen the Coalition as a bastion against revolution in both Britain and Ireland were disillusioned. Thus George Dewar, the former editor of the *Saturday Review*, complained to Carson in April 1922,

> The two most disgusting things which the Coalition Conservative group have done... since 1918 have been (1) scuttling out of Ireland after swearing that they were winning against crime and disorder there; and (2) trying to work up an electioneering 'stunt' against British Labour as a form of Bolshevism.[35]

In 1921 and 1922 sentiments such as these, combined with distrust of Lloyd George's foreign policy and such matters as the sale of honours, and also the upsurge of feeling against waste (i.e. high public expenditure), were sweeping through the Conservative Party up to junior ministerial level – and publicly were most powerfully expressed in the victory of Anti-Waste candidates in hitherto safe Conservative seats at Dover in January 1921 and at Hertford and also at St George's, Westminster in June 1921.[36]

Lloyd George's determination to establish in British politics a 'general line of demarcation between the contending forces' which would be between 'reform as against revolution' involved demolishing as a separate entity the Independent Liberals.[37] For Asquithian Liberals the Spen Valley by-election revealed the Coalition 'as a purely partisan movement, factious and self-regarding, willing to use Tory organisations or indeed any other instrument in order to destroy Liberalism, containing in itself no positive aim or principle except the desire to perpetuate its own power'. By mid-1920 the divisions between Liberals were very bitter. As one Asquithian put it, 'Mr Lloyd George has done about as much for the health and unity and peace of the Liberal Party as the late Emperor of Germany did for the health and unity and peace of Europe.'[38] Moreover, many of the Coalition government's policies – from protectionist measures to repression in Ireland – were anathema to older Liberals. This was well put by the Coalition Liberal, Arthur Murray, after commenting in April 1920 to Ian

Macpherson that he would feel better now that he had left the post of Chief Secretary for Ireland:

> 'Yes thanks', he replied. 'I'm already feeling much better. The strain was tremendous and (*sotto voce*) its no job for a Liberal.'
> He is quite right – the Irish policy of the government is no job for a Liberal, and yet it is a policy framed by a government whose head is exceedingly annoyed if it is suggested that he is no longer a Liberal. He has sold the pass to the Tories.[39]

In attacking the Independent Liberals, Lloyd George was reinforcing problems that they already had. Like Labour, they were weakly led in the House of Commons, first by Sir Donald Maclean, and then, from a little way into the 1920 session, by Asquith, who by this time was well past his best. Apart from Free Trade, they had few issues of general appeal. Indeed, Elibank warned Asquith in June that along with Free Trade 'the main subject that is interesting the country at present is the future position of Labour in relation to Capital.' The general social turbulence and, in particular, the major industrial disputes of 1919 to 1921 tended to polarise voters between the Coalition and Labour. The electoral system gave the Asquithians further problems. Thus Samuel, when consoling Runciman over a by-election defeat in 1920, observed, 'With the Labour Party uncompromisingly opposed to us and with no PR (Proportional Representation) or Alternative Vote, the path of a Liberal is steep and stony.'[40]

Lloyd George continued to claim that he represented the true Liberal succession, not only because of the social reforms but because of his opposition to Labour extremism. Thus, before the 1922 general election he condemned the Independent Liberals for persisting 'in treating the Labour Party as if it were still merely the left-wing of the Liberal Party' and commented:

> It preaches doctrines that would make all the great Liberal leaders of the past shudder. What would Gladstone, Cobden, Bright, Lord John Russell say to the programme of common ownership, state protection and elimination of individual effort which is presented by Labour?[41]

In speeches such as this, as Riddell shrewdly judged, Lloyd George was trying to appeal to Labour voters as well as Liberals. Riddell observed in his diary,

With great dexterity, he has raised the battle cry against socialism. He cannot oppose the claims of Labour to higher wages, better housing, better education etc. On these heads, ostensibly at any rate, there is no difference between the policy of the Tories and the Liberals on the one hand and Labour on the other, but the cry of 'Socialism' will rally the former and split the latter. Labour gains its strength from the belief among the wage-earning classes that the Labour Party is likely to do more for them than the other parties, which are tarred with the capitalist brush, but many members of the Labour Party have no liking for socialistic experiments involving armies of officials and a bureaucratic government.[42]

Lloyd George succeeded in making deeper the class dividing lines in British politics. But the problem for the rest of his career was that he did not succeed in carrying a viable Coalition Liberalism into a fused new party. The nature of some of the policies of 1918 to 1922 and the damage he inflicted on the Asquithian Liberals created wounds in British Liberalism which did not heal in his lifetime. So much so that when Lloyd George was Liberal leader, the Asquithian Sir Charles Mallet published in 1930 *Mr Lloyd George: A study* in which he contrasted Lloyd George's qualities, much to his detriment, with 'the character which Mr Gladstone bore and the standards of conduct which he left us'. Indeed he went so far in his book as to warn that Lloyd George's return to office would be 'serious for Liberals who still place some value on principle in public life'.[43]

The major problem for Lloyd George was that he ran out of sufficient issues to keep up sufficient support for the Coalition government. His 'solving' of Ireland in December 1921 and his bringing Russia back into trading relations with Britain were major achievements; but, as with his more liberal policies at the peace conferences or in India, they did nothing to endear the Coalition to many on the Right of the Conservative Party. There were major social reforms – such as education, housing and unemployment insurance – but after the 1919 and 1920 sessions of Parliament there was little reform, and with the 'Geddes axe' falling on public expenditure in 1922 the government's social policy record took on a regressive complexion.[44] Although Lloyd George tried to alleviate unemployment through such means as public works and facilitating the recovery of Central and Eastern European trade, his government's political standing probably suffered from the rising levels of unemployment which accompanied the acute economic recession of 1921–2. Lord Crewe, a leading Asquithian, judged that in the

1922 general election 'the mass of unemployment must have meant a great addition to the Labour vote'. Indeed, he noted that he had had several reports that 'at many Liberal meetings there was a sulky crowd of unemployed in some corner of the hall, who poisoned the atmosphere for the Liberal speakers.'[45]

By 1922 Lloyd George had manoeuvred and manoeuvred so often to survive that there was very few of his Coalition Liberal principles still in position, and equally few leading Coalition Liberal ministers surviving.[46] In January 1920, when Birkenhead's first newspaper article on the Coalition had raised intense speculation as to whether or not the Coalition could survive much longer, an editorial in the *New Statesman* observed,

> If Mr Lloyd George were anyone else, if he were some Mr X, a politician of wide but not unprecedented popularity, of great but not incredible adroitness, with a keen but not infallible ear for the movements of public opinion, then there would be no obscurity at all about the present position.

The politician would be out of office.[47] Lloyd George's remarkable feat of holding the coalition together into October 1922 was bought at the price of creating immense dislike for and distrust of his methods. It is notable that both Baldwin and Henderson made much political capital out of not being 'supermen' in the mould of the leading Coalition figures (notably Lloyd George, Churchill and Birkenhead) and emphasised their own straightforward and direct qualities.

Lloyd George's admirers laid much stress on the nimbleness of his ways. After his death Sir Geoffrey Shakespeare recalled of his Coalition days,

> What impressed me most in Lloyd George was his infinite resourcefulness, his resilience of mind and his complete and utter absorption in the tasks that lay to hand. If he found the frontal attack on a problem blocked . . . he would send his armour round the flank searching for a weak spot. He was an empiricist. He was never afraid to make an experiment.[48]

The problem for Lloyd George was that what some saw as his flexibility and adroitness often appeared to many others on both the Left and the Right of British politics to be lack of principle and trickery. Thus, for example, as early as December 1919 Steel-Maitland told a Conservative Party official that he was 'not a convinced

Coalitionist' and offered as an explanation the comment, 'I think that one ought to look away and beyond the needs of the immediate present to the real problems of the future.'[49]

This point was very much at the heart of growing criticisms of Lloyd George's interventions in industrial relations, which eventually made it hard for lesser figures to achieve settlements in major disputes. It had been the basis of criticism by both Asquith and G. R. Askwith, the government's Chief Industrial Commissioner, before 1914. In September 1920 Brace told Bridgeman that if the Mines Department did not cede the miners' demand of a 2s rise in wages, then Lloyd George would. Bridgeman noted in his diary, 'This sort of thing is calamitous as it makes the strikers think they have only got to go on fighting Horne, and they will be sure to get the case before the PM and get something out of it.'[50] In many industrialists' eyes, Lloyd George's settlements bought industrial peace at the cost of higher wages – and with the recession, although wages fell substantially, it was later felt that real wage rates fell insufficiently to maintain the competitiveness of British exports.

As for Labour, Lloyd George alienated most sectors of it in 1918 to 1922, not least by his fierce verbal attacks. The setting up of the Sankey Commission and the subsequent failure to implement the majority recommendations was a major cause of Labour's distrust. But it was only part of the reason for it; the use of the strike-breaking organisation and the often savage government propaganda during strikes, the intervention in Russia and the repression in Ireland all played their part. Lloyd George also alienated the corporatist wing of the Labour movement by his disregard of the National Industrial Conference and by his government's failure to do more to foster the Whitley proposals. While Lloyd George had dented his Radical reputation in British politics during the First World War, he brought it very near to total destruction between 1918 and 1922.

The striking feature of his post-war government was the way his room for political manoeuvre narrowed as time went by. In 1919 he was very much the 'big beast' of British politics. Seldom, if ever, since the time of Pitt the Younger, can a prime minister have faced such weak opposition in the House of Commons as that led by Adamson and Maclean in the 1919 parliamentary session. Moreover, until late October 1919 he conducted business through the War Cabinet, to which small body he summoned whichever ministers or officials he chose, according to the subject under discussion. However, with the reversion to a full Cabinet from November 1919 he had less control over policy. Lord Lee noted then, 'LG's manner became markedly more formal and deferential to the Cabinet as a corporate body.' In addition, Lloyd George had his own secretariat to provide him with additional advice to that from Whitehall. This power base caused resentment, especially over foreign policy. In October 1922 Lord Derby complained, 'I cannot trust Lloyd George any longer, especially so long as he has a second Foreign Office in Downing Street.'[51] Yet for all his special advantages, Lloyd George's opportunities for policy initiatives, especially on domestic matters, became increasingly restricted.

This was because of the size and nature of the Coalition majority and because of the economic decisions that were made during the second half of 1919. There was a transformation of political attitudes during the year following the Armistice. In the last stages of the war, Chamberlain, then a member of the War Cabinet without a ministerial portfolio, could urge that with an armistice,

> Generally the principle to be borne in mind was that every legitimate effort should be made to prevent unemployment and its accompanying demoralisation. It was far better to run the risk of manufacturing commodities which would not be required ... than to have multitudes in receipt of unemployment benefit.[52]

In the immediate aftermath of war Lloyd George received much support for interventionist policies to ease British industry during the transition to peacetime production. But by the summer of 1919 Austen Chamberlain, now Chancellor of the Exchequer, urged restraint on public expenditure as part of the orthodox financial remedies proposed by the Cunliffe Committee. Yet if Lloyd George was unhappy at the constraints imposed on his government's social policies by the economic orthodoxy of the Cunliffe reports, he nevertheless shared with his Conservative colleagues a belief in the need to get the free market system fully operating as quickly as possible. He, like most of his ministerial colleagues and most Coalition MPs, was wary of state control of industry. Chamberlain expressed many non-Labour politicians' fears when, in August 1919, during a discussion on the control of wool he observed: 'The moment you began control you were inevitably driven to complete control which, if prolonged, led to nationalisation.... Control eliminated all the usual motives which induced economic production.'[53]

Lloyd George's Coalition government had to deal with the problems of the transition from war to peace and it did so in a time of major domestic political transition. The Labour movement in Britain was moving rapidly towards an independent and major role in British politics. Yet in early 1920 the TUC was still sending its deputations, almost cap-in-hand, to ministers.[54] The Labour Party did not put up candidates at many by-elections during 1919 to 1922 because it lacked any organisation in the areas. As a result, at times Coalition candidates were returned unopposed. Where the Party did put up candidates, these often divided the anti-Coalition vote with the Independent Liberals, who still had strong support in many areas (though in some cases Labour benefited from a split anti-Labour vote). While the Labour Party was seen as a threat, it was very much an impending threat in this period.

In Britain the propertied classes were not faced with the collapse of the authority of the state, as happened in Russia in 1917, Germany in November 1918 and in Austria and Hungary in 1918 and 1919. The tensions of 1917 to 1920 were contained within the parliamentary system. Most working people who demanded change wanted their 'revolution by constitutional means'. Most middle-class people, once the immediate post-war turmoil had passed, wanted stability, tranquility and economy — and as the main political beneficiaries of the 1918 general election they were in a strong position to achieve their aims. There was no need for them to turn outside the existing system as happened elsewhere in Europe during the inter-war period. They could vent their concern at the prospect of paying for 'a fit land for heroes to live in' by voting for Anti-Waste candidates or pressing for a renewed Conservative Party unsullied by contact with Lloyd George and his more colourful Coalition supporters.

During the period of maximum post-war stress Lloyd George's government did readjust, or 'recast', some aspects of the state apparatus to meet what were felt to be the dangers of the situation.[55] In the case of maintaining supplies during a major strike, the government drew on the resources of road transport and other private firms as well as individual volunteers. In so far as many of the volunteers were middle-class, such action had the flavour of class war. But for all of the bad feeling engendered by this organisation's existence and its use in 1919 to 1921, in time it was accepted by Labour Cabinet ministers. Similarly, the Parliamentary Labour Party's leadership accepted the need for a measure such as the Emergency Powers Bill and later, in office, were willing to use the Act themselves. Thus while the reserve powers of the state were strengthened in 1918 to 1920, in time the main measures secured fairly wide political acceptance.

Yet for all his efforts during these difficult years, on 19 October 1922, the day of the Carlton Club meeting which ended the Coalition government, Lloyd George had little political support left. Like Peel in 1846, while he still held the loyalty of many of the most able ministers, he was a leader without a party. He was left to draw such consolation as he could from discovering during a tour of Lancashire 'a very large section of the community who were entirely outside the party organisation', many of whom had grown up during the suspension of the party system in the previous eight years.[56] Such talk was a way of boosting his supporters' morale, and perhaps his own.

The reality was that to make an effective impact on British politics Lloyd George needed a party. He had failed to lead a majority of the Conservative Party into a new party and he was unsympathetic to pure Toryism. He had alienated Labour, and he was equally, or possibly even more, unsympathetic to socialism. He was left with the Liberal Party, a large part of which he had made every effort to destroy. Little wonder that he was to remain in the political wilderness, distrusted and out of office, for the rest of his parliamentary career.

Notes and references

1. Long to Lloyd George, 15 June 1919; LG F/33/2/54.
2. Nicoll to Lloyd George, 4 February 1920; LG F/43/7/15.
3. Diary entry, 30 August 1920. Ralph Scott, *A Soldier's Diary* (London: Collins, 1923), with a Preface by Major-General Sir Frederick Maurice, p. 193.
4. 'Celticus' (Aneurin Bevan), *Why Not Trust the Tories?* (London: Gollancz, 1944), p. 13.
5. Balfour to Aldenham, 10 March 1920; copy, LG F/3/5/4. (Aldenham had given his safe City of London seat to Balfour after the latter lost his in the 1906 general election.)
6. For a shrewd brief account of the wider European situation in 1918–22 see D. Geary, *European Labour Protest 1848–1939* (London: Croom Helm, 1981), pp. 144–52. For a discussion of the non-revolutionary nature of the British working-class movement see R. McKibbin, 'Why was there no Marxism in Britain?', reprinted in his *The Ideologies of Class* (Oxford: Clarendon Press, 1990), pp. 1–41.
7. I. McLean, *The Legend of Red Clydeside* (Edinburgh: Donald, 1983),

especially chapters 9 and 12. I. G. Hutchinson, *A Political History of Scotland 1832–1924* (Edinburgh: Donald, 1986), pp. 278–9. Report (no. 3189) on opinion in Merthyr Tydfil and the Rhondda, sent by J. R. Murray, 4 March 1919; copy, Thomas Jones Papers, C/5/55. For a far Right assessment drawing much from the *Morning Post* and possibly secret service or Economic League material, see Nesta H. Webster, *The Socialist Network* (London: Boswell, 1926), pp. 62–71.

8. W. Kendall, *The Revolutionary Movement in Britain 1900–21* (London: Weidenfeld and Nicolson, 1969), pp. 237–56. Beatrice Webb's diary, 17 September 1920; Passfield Papers, I, 36.
9. Cabinet meeting, 2 February 1920; CAB 23–20–139.
10. Lord Shaw to Samuel, 19 January 1918; Samuel Papers, A/60/22.
11. Chamberlain to Sir John Gilmour, 7 July 1921; Austen Chamberlain Papers, 24/3/45. Nor did the government back a Private Member's Bill to amend the 1913 Trade Union Act on the political levy, which passed its Second Reading on 18 May 1922.
12. R. Shackleton, 'The 1919 police strike in Birmingham,', p. 72 in A. Wright and R. Shackleton (eds), *Worlds of Labour: Essays in Birmingham Labour History* (Birmingham: University of Birmingham, 1983).
13. C. Andrew, *Secret Service* (London: Heinemann, 1985), pp. 174–5 and 192–6. N. Hiley, 'Counter-espionage and security in Great Britain during the First World War', *English Historical Review*, 101 (1986), pp. 100–26. B. Porter, *The Origins of the Vigilant State* (London: Weidenfeld and Nicolson, 1987) and *Plots and Paranoia* (London: Unwin Hyman, 1989), pp. 143–50.
14. M. Hollingsworth and R. Norton-Taylor, *Blacklist* (London: Hogarth, 1988) and A. J. McIvor, 'Political blacklisting and anti-socialist activity between the wars', Society for the Study of Labour History, *Bulletin* 53 (1988), pp. 18–26.
15. WC, 22 May and 5 June 1917; CAB 23–2–180/1 and 3/4. WC (606A), 5 August 1919; CAB 23-15-149/50. (His exaggeration was part of his effort to secure agreement from Conservative colleagues to give reforms a high priority.) N. Reeves, *Official British Film Propaganda During the First World War* (London: Routledge, 1986), pp. 27–8 and 34–5.
16. Ministry of Labour Report, 6 September 1917; CAB 24–25–302.
17. Riddell diary, 13 March 1919; Riddell Papers, 62983, f. 74. WC (606A), 5 August 1919; CAB 23–15–156.
18. WC (614), 14 August 1919; CAB 23–11–125.
19. L. G. Gerber, 'Corporatism in comparative perspective: the impact of the First World War on American and British labor relations', *Business History Review*, 62 (1988), pp. 93–127.
20. Foreword to G. Glasgow, *General Strikes and Road Transport* (London: Bles, 1926), p. 11.
21. Eric Geddes to Bonar Law (on a threatened strike of Metropolitan Water workers), 6 July 1920; copy, Addison Papers, Box 39. The government's expenditure cuts in the recession were to hit its emergency organisation hard.
22. A. J. P. Taylor, *Beaverbrook* (London: Hamilton, 1972), p. xv.

23. Official Report of Conference with the Triple Alliance and Railwaymen, 10 Downing Street, 22 March 1919; copy, Thomas Jones Papers, C/5/61.
24. Riddell diary, 8 September 1919 and 2 March 1920; Riddell Papers, 62984, f. 113 and 62985, f. 66. J. Grigg, *Nancy Astor* (London: Sidgwick and Jackson, 1980), p. 65. On J. H. Thomas and the internal politics of the NUR see A. J. Adams, 'Leadership and oligarchy: British rail unions, 1914–1922', *Studies in History and Politics*, 5 (1986), pp. 23–45. For Thomas being awarded an honorary degree at Cambridge University on 16 June 1920, in the company of Lloyd George, Bonar Law, Austen Chamberlain and other notables, see G. Blaxland, *J. H. Thomas* (London: Muller, 1964), p. 142.
25. A. Bullock, *The Life and Times of Ernest Bevin*, vol. 1 (London: Heinemann, 1960), p. 152. P. Bagwell, 'The Triple Industrial Alliance 1913–1922' in A. Briggs and J. Saville, *Essays in Labour History 1886–1923* (London: Macmillan, 1971), especially pp. 120–8.
26. The Dudley win came the day after Ramsay MacDonald lost the Labour seat at Woolwich in a remarkably bitter by-election.
27. For Bridgeman on fears of a general election, P. Williamson (ed.), *The Modernisation of Conservative Politics* (London: Historians' Press, 1988), p. 156.
28. Riddell diary, 2 March 1920; Riddell Papers 62985, f. 67. Beatrice Webb diary, 4 January 1922; Passfield Papers, I. 36. Spoor was MP for Bishop Auckland and later was Chief Whip during the first Labour government. Conservative expectations were even higher for Labour. In September 1922 Chamberlain predicted 200–50 seats for Labour. Sir C. Petrie, *The Life and Letters of Sir Austen Chamberlain*, vol. 2 (London: Cassell, 1940), p. 171.
29. *East Ham Echo*, 15 and 29 November and 6 December 1918. *Widnes Guardian*, 26 and 29 August 1919.
30. *The Times*, 16 January 1917 and 17 September 1919.
31. Chamberlain to the King, 15 April 1921. He made the same point in a letter to Robert Cecil, 26 April 1921. Austen Chamberlain Papers, AC 33/3/4 and 24/3/16. On Chamberlain's position see J. Ramsden, *The Age of Balfour and Baldwin 1902–1940* (London: Longman, 1978), pp. 149–56.
32. Minutes of a meeting following the reception of a deputation from the National Union of Conservative and Unionist Associations at 10 Downing Street, 6 May 1921; Austen Chamberlain papers, AC 24/2/38. Chamberlain later was forced to dwell on the problems of finding a widely acceptable measure of Lords reform. Chamberlain to J. Hope, 3 February 1922; Austen Chamberlain Papers, AC 24/2/16.
33. Strachey to Carson, 13 October 1920; Carson Papers, D 1507/1, 1920/41. Carson himself had earlier been advocating the need for the Coalition to avoid chaos. Carson to F. S. Oliver, 25 October 1919; F. S. Oliver Papers, 7726/87/76. *Glasgow Herald*, 19 November 1920.
34. Robert Cecil to Chamberlain, 20 and 27 April 1921; Austen Chamberlain Papers, AC 24/3/15 and 17.

35. Dewar to Carson, 15 April 1922; Carson Papers, D 1507/1, 1922/14.
36. In addition at the Wrekin the electorate returned 'Bottomley' candidates in February and November 1920. On Conservative disillusionment with the Coalition, see M. Kinnear, *The Fall of Lloyd George* (London: Macmillan, 1973), M. Cowling, *The Impact of Labour* (Cambridge: Cambridge University Press, 1971) and Ramsden, *op. cit.*, pp. 135–67.
37. He explicitly formulated it this way in a letter to Balfour, 18 February 1920; LG F/3/5/3.
38. H. Storey, *The Case Against the Lloyd George Coalition* (London: Allen & Unwin, 1920), pp. 59 and 96.
39. Arthur Murray's diary, 23 April 1920; Elibank Papers, 8815, f. 42–3.
40. Elibank to Asquith, 26 June 1919; Elibank Papers, 8804, f. 211. Haldane outraged his former colleagues by suggesting 'there being room only for two parties in the future, Labour and Protectionist'. Runciman to Arthur Murray, 6 May 1921; Elibank Papers, 8808, f. 106. Samuel to Runciman, 4 May 1920; Runciman Papers, Box 2.
41. Lloyd George's notes for a speech, 1922; Lloyd George Papers, National Library of Wales, 20446 A.
42. Riddell's diary, 27 March 1920; Riddell papers, 62985, f. 86.
43. *Lloyd George: A Study* (London: Benn, 1930), pp. 309–13.
44. On these reforms and the impact of the Geddes report see Morgan, *Consensus and Disunity*, especially pp. 80–108 and 288–95 and B. B. Gilbert, *British Social Policy 1914–1939* (London: Batsford, 1970).
45. Crewe to Lord Islington, 21 November 1922; Crewe Papers, C/28. For other similar contemporary views, see Hutchinson, p. 284, but he himself comments that Labour's support in Scotland did not fluctuate with levels of unemployment.
46. On the problems of Addison, Montagu and others, and the general weakness of Coalition Liberalism, see K. O. Morgan, 'Lloyd George's stage army: the Coalition Liberals 1918–1922' in A. J. P. Taylor (ed.), *Lloyd George: Twelve Essays* (London: Hamish Hamilton, 1971), pp. 225–54.
47. *New Statesman*, 17 January 1920, p. 421.
48. 409 HC Deb. 5s, c. 1383–4; 28 March 1945.
49. Steel-Maitland to T. Ainge, 18 December 1919; Steel-Maitland Papers, GD 193//87/2. Steel-Maitland advised Chamberlain on 21 March 1922 that he would no longer keep private his opposition to the continuance of the Coalition; Steel-Maitland Papers, GD 193/95/4/41.
50. Bridgeman's diary, 2 September 1920; Williamson (ed.), *op. cit.*, p. 147.
51. Lord Lee of Fareham, *A Good Innings*, vol. 2 (privately published, 1940), p. 777. Derby to Blumenfeld, 3 October 1922; R. D. Blumenfeld Papers, DER 31. For a shrewd assessment of Lloyd George's overall performance as prime minister see K. O. Morgan, 'Lloyd George's premiership: a study in "prime ministerial government"', *Historical Journal*, 13 (1970), pp. 130–57, as well as his *Consensus and Disunity* (Oxford: Clarendon Press, 1980). For Lloyd George's

'Garden suburb' up to the Armistice, see J. Turner, *Lloyd George's Secretariat* (Cambridge: Cambridge University Press, 1980).
52. WC (491), 24 October 1918; CAB 23–8–47.
53. WC (606A), 5 August 1919; CAB 23–15–160.
54. In an editorial, the *New Statesman* called for 'this undignified and time-wasting procedure' to be dropped; 31 January 1920, p. 483.
55. On the nature and extent of this see the discussion by C. J. Nottingham, 'Recasting bourgeois Britain?', *International Review of Social History*, 31 (1986), pp. 227–47. Also J. E. Cronin, 'Coping with Labour 1918–1926' in J. E. Cronin and J. Schneer (eds), *Social Conflict and the Political Order in Modern Britain* (London: Croom Helm, 1982) and 'Labour insurgency and class formation: comparative perspectives on the crisis of 1917–1920 in Europe' in J. E. Cronin and C. Sirianni, *Work Community and Power* (Philadelphia: Temple University Press, 1983), pp. 20–48.
56. He spoke of his 'extraordinary reception' in Lancashire to ministers on 17 October 1922 and was still considering his appeal 'to the unattached class' after the Carlton Club meeting, when he spoke to Coalition Liberals on 21 October 1922. J. H. Lewis diary, 17 October 1922; J. H. Lewis Papers, 10/231/149.

Primary Sources

Private Papers

Addison	Bodleian Library, Oxford
Asquith	Bodleian Library, Oxford
Baird	National Library of Australia (1919 transcripts by courtesy of Dr P. Williamson)
Balfour	British Library
Blumenfeld	House of Lords Record Office
Bridgeman	Shropshire Record Office (transcripts by courtesy of Dr P. Williamson)
Carson	Northern Ireland Public Record Office
Cecil	British Library
Chamberlain, Austen	Birmingham University Library
Crewe	Cambridge University Library
Croft	Churchill College Library, Cambridge
Curzon	India Office Library
Davies, W. Watkin	National Library of Wales
Elibank	National Library of Scotland
Elliot	National Library of Scotland
Emmott	Nuffield College Library, Oxford
Esher	Churchill College Library, Cambridge
Fisher, H. A. L.	Bodleian Library, Oxford
Gainford	Nuffield College Library, Oxford
Gladstone, Herbert	British Library
Haldane	National Library of Scotland
Hankey	Churchill College Library, Cambridge
Jones, Thomas	National Library of Wales
Lansbury	British Library of Political and Economic Science
Law, Bonar	House of Lords Record Office
Lee of Fareham	House of Lords Record Office
Lewis, Sir Herbert	National Library of Wales
Lloyd George	House of Lords Record Office

Lloyd George Family	National Library of Wales
Lothian	Scottish Record Office
MacDonald, J. Ramsay	Public Record Office
Milner	Bodleian Library, Oxford
Morton of Darvel	Scottish Record Office
Mottistone	Nuffield College Library, Oxford
Oliver, F. S.	National Library of Scotland
Passfield	British Library of Political and Economic Science
Ponsonby	Bodleian Library, Oxford
Riddell	British Library
Runciman	Newcastle University Library
Samuel	House of Lords Record Office
Scott, C. P.	British Library
Selborne	Bodleian Library, Oxford
Simon	Bodleian Library, Oxford
Simon of Wythenshawe	Manchester Central Library
Spender, J. A.	British Library
Steel-Maitland	Scottish Record Office
Strachey, St Loe	House of Lords Record Office
Trevelyan, C. P.	Newcastle University Library
Vickers Ltd	Millbank Tower, London
Weir	Scottish Record Office
Whiteley	Borthwick Institute, York

Government Papers (Public Record Office)

Cabinet (CAB)
Ministry of Food (MAF)
Ministry of Labour (LAB)
Ministry of Munitions (MUN)

Index

Ablett, N., 164
Adamson, W., 120, 182, 184, 185, 203, 303, 304, 311
Addison, C., 81, 86, 88, 91, 115, 133, 238, 240, 271, 273
agricultural labourers, 37, 55, 99, 137, 156
Aldenham, Lord, 293, 314
Aldred, G., 295
Allenby, General E. H. H., 48
Amalgamated Society of Engineers (ASE), 88–9, 95, 97, 105–6, 140–1
Amery, L., 186–7
Anderson, T., 295
anti-semitism, 14, 120
Appleton, W. A., 186
army unrest, 15, 24–52, 54, 69, 102, 105, 112, 113, 218, 219, 295
Ashton, T., 146
Askwith, Sir George, 90, 97, 311
Asquith, H. H., 3, 10, 11, 201, 202, 243, 308, 311
Associated Society of Locomotive Engineers and Firemen (ASLEF), 97–103, 114, 156–60, 219, 222, 264
Astor, W. and N., 205, 224, 301
Austria, 15, 25, 175, 247, 293, 313

Baker, R. S., 175
Baldwin, S. 39, 310
Balfour, A. J., 3, 21, 26, 161, 163, 244, 293
Barnes, G. N., 7, 41, 98, 180, 203, 205, 220, 232
Baruch, B., 84
beer, 129, 164, 292
Belfast strikes, 19, 31, 97, 105–6, 111–12
Belgium, 13
Benn, W. Wedgwood, 202
Bevan, A., 150

Bevin, E., 223, 260, 267–8, 271, 272, 281, 302
Billing, P., 71
Birkenhead, Lord, 3, 243, 251, 310
Black and Tans, 47,
Board of Trade, 101, 105, 114, 115, 193, 262, 272–3
Bolsheviks
  British, 8, 14, 16, 19, 35, 45, 76, 82, 83, 103, 110, 118, 119, 175, 185, 192, 198, 202, 295–6, 298
  Russian and European, 14, 15, 17, 19–21, 33, 46, 175, 178, 187, 211–14, 247, 250, 294, 296
Bolshevism, as term of political abuse, 8–9, 118, 120, 143, 188, 214–15, 238, 242, 296
Bondfield, M., 22
Borden, Sir Robert, 20
Bottomley, H., 28, 132, 179
Brace, W., 274, 277, 301, 311
Bradbury, Sir John, 81
Briand, A., 161
Bridgeman, W. C., 100, 274, 311
British Commonwealth Union, 16, 186
British Empire Union, 16, 22
British Legion, 46, 219
British Socialist Party, 31
British Workers' League, 4, 7, 186
Bromley, J., 87–101, 104
Buckmaster, Lord, 6, 11
building workers, 90
Bullitt, W. C., 20, 179
by-elections, 38, 177, 179–80, 195, 201, 242, 243, 245–6, 249, 250, 302–3, 307, 313
Byng, Sir Julian, 31

Caillard Sir Vincent, 16, 22, 186
Calthrop, Sir Guy, 25
capital levy, 236–9
Carson, Sir Edward, 3, 40–1, 84, 191, 202, 215, 277, 306, 307
Cave, Sir George, 55, 56, 58, 60, 65

322 Index

Caxton Hall conference 1918, 86–91, 133
Cecil, Lord Hugh, 202
Cecil, Lord Robert, 280, 306
centre politics, 83, 176–9, 201–2, 242–4, 255
Chamberlain, A., 3, 19, 33, 42, 81, 82, 83, 85, 86, 94, 102, 116, 128, 153, 156, 165, 188, 195, 199, 203, 204, 233, 237, 240, 241, 256, 280, 297, 305, 312
Chapman, S., 200
Childs, B. E. W., 35, 40, 109
China, 14
Churchill, W. S., 1, 18–22, 29–33, 42, 49, 65, 76, 83, 86, 102, 103–4, 109, 117, 166, 189, 199, 201–2, 213–14, 223, 238, 247, 253, 255, 265, 310
Clemenceau, G., 160, 175, 177
Clyde, J., 109–11
Clyde strikes 1919, 19, 31, 97, 105–12, 115, 129
Clynes, J. R., 36, 74, 120, 133, 135, 140, 141, 182, 184–6, 211, 216, 223, 247, 258, 297, 303–5
coal shortages, 25–6
Cole, G. D. H., 22, 136, 182, 200
Colne Valley, 2
Comrades of the Great War, 35, 39, 46
conscription, 29–33
co-operative movement, 160, 164, 198, 208, 248, 284, 292
Council of Action, 269–72
Cramp, C. T., 221
Crawford, earl of, 190
Crewe, Lord, 310
Cunliffe Committee, 81, 235, 241, 312
Curzon, Lord, 14, 21, 112, 118, 126, 153
Cyprus, 181

Daily Express, 25
Daily Graphic, 271
Daily Herald, 34, 35, 72, 117, 138, 296
Daily Mail, 25, 162, 178
Daily Mirror, 178
Daily Telegraph, 262
Daly, J., 47
Davidson, J. C., 212
Davies, D, 39
demobilisation, 24–37, 63, 90, 93–4, 145, 146
Denikin, A. I., 20

Derby, Lord, 33, 38, 39, 161, 312
Desborough Committee, 66, 75
Dewar, G., 307
Diaz, A., 175
direct action, 15, 76, 100, 150, 183, 211–14, 216, 250, 251, 268, 281, 294, 296, 300, 301, 304
Docker, D., 16, 186, 191, 227
dockers, 75, 258–60, 267, 274
Dollan, P., 106, 124
Duckham, Sir Arthur, 161, 208, 261
Duncan, C., 186
Duty and Discipline Movement, 16

Eady, Sir Wilfred, 5, 11
Economic League, 298
Edwards, A. C., 120
Egypt, 15, 47–8, 175, 181, 248, 253
Electrical Trade Union (ETU), 106
Elibank, Master of, 9, 308
Elliot, W., 306
Emergency Powers Act 1920, 265–6, 279, 297, 313
Engineering Employers' Federation, 89, 105, 131, 132, 137
Esher, Lord, 17, 126, 153, 192, 260–1
Evening News (London), 178

Federation of British Industries (FBI), 5, 115, 132, 186, 191
Fisher, H. A. L., 115, 166, 238, 257
Fisher, V., 6, 11
food prices, 36, 37, 81, 89, 129–30, 156, 247, 266, 273, 292
France, 13, 19, 26, 28, 30–1, 32, 174, 176, 216
French, Lord, 111

Gainford, Lord, 194, 208
Gallacher, W., 110
Garvin, J. L., 237
Geddes, Sir Auckland, 83, 119–20, 132, 181–2, 193, 195, 199, 200, 203, 204, 210, 219, 221, 223, 261
Geddes, Sir Eric, 26, 41–2, 85, 92, 99, 101, 114, 128, 142, 157, 159, 195, 198, 223, 227, 252, 258, 259, 264, 278, 300, 309
general elections
  1900, 1
  1906, 100
  1918, 1, 62, 80, 96, 100, 153, 180, 183, 208, 303
  1922, 304, 310

Index

General Federation of Trade Unions (GFTU), 40, 186
German colonies, 18, 182
Germany, 2, 13, 15, 17, 18, 20, 28, 32, 136, 142, 174–6, 178, 181, 184, 187, 188, 247, 293, 313
Gibbins, F. W., 131
Gladstone, Lord, 204, 230
Gosling, H., 275, 281
Gough, General Sir Hubert, 5, 11
Greenwood, H., 264
Guest, F., 202, 203

Haig, Earl, 30, 31, 46, 48
Haig, Sir Douglas *see* Haig, Earl
Haldane, Lord, 151, 201, 229, 317
Hamilton, Lord Claud, 144
Hankey, Sir Maurice, 11, 17, 18, 25, 63, 64, 82, 104, 126, 138, 153, 167, 176, 200, 201, 221, 222, 224, 254, 258, 275, 279
Hartshorn, V., 167, 199, 274, 277, 278, 301
Havelock Wilson, J., 186
Hayes, J. H., 67, 68–71
Henderson, A., 4, 9, 73, 88–9, 120, 131, 135, 136, 140, 141, 180–1, 182–6, 189, 212, 213, 216, 223, 245, 248, 249, 251, 259, 269–71, 284, 303–5, 310
Henry, Sir Edward, 54, 58
Herald League, 34, 119
Hodges, F., 145, 166, 264, 280, 281
Hogge, J., 38
Horne, Sir Robert, 45, 66, 72, 102, 104–5, 107, 108, 115, 116–17, 129, 133, 134, 137, 146–9, 158–62, 166, 199, 200, 204, 223, 254, 259, 272–4, 276, 278, 299, 311
House, Colonel E. M., 214
housing, 90, 127–9, 152, 153, 202, 207, 215, 238, 240, 241, 248, 291, 299, 308–9
Hungary, 20, 25, 175, 313

Illingworth, A., 69, 115
India, 9, 15, 28, 47, 181, 248, 249, 253, 309
Industrial Unrest Committee, 102–3, 112–13, 124, 127, 147, 155, 222
Ireland, 4, 15, 29, 44, 47, 69, 100, 181, 201, 202, 215–16, 248–9, 253, 259, 267–9, 270, 298, 306–8, 309, 311
Irving, D., 185
Italy, 19, 216

Jackson, H., 186
Jerram Committee, 42, 43
John Bull, 28
Jolly George, 267
Jones, Sir Edgar, 185
Jones, Sir Evan, 146, 193–4, 197
Jones, J., 185
Jones, T., 13, 82, 104, 115, 131, 147, 154, 167, 190, 195, 200, 208, 224, 239, 255, 258
Jones, W. Kennedy, 178, 179

Kerr, P., 83, 176
Keynes, J. M., 81, 121, 142
Kinmel Park Camp, 32–3
Kirkwood, D., 110
Kolchak, A. V., 20, 21
Kun, Bela, 20, 175

Labour Party, 33, 91, 106, 237, 295–6
 conferences, 73, 209, 211, 267–8
 divisions in, 4, 182, 184–5, 250
 in elections, 2, 182, 195, 244–6, 302–4, 313
 growing support for, 44, 62, 244–50, 313
 Parliamentary, 73–4, 120, 180–4, 186, 195, 211–12, 216, 269–72, 303–4, 313–14
Lansbury, G., 34, 35, 117–18, 180, 302
Lansdowne, Lord, 13
Law, Andrew Bonar, 2–4, 7, 20, 43, 64, 66, 82, 126, 129, 130, 155, 161, 177–9, 187, 208, 212, 237, 241, 247, 255, 256, 275, 287
 on broadening Conservative appeal, 7, 39
 on industrial unrest, 33, 55–6, 71–2, 104–19, 127, 158, 220, 223–4, 301
 on Lloyd George, 1, 17, 244
 on miners, 147–8, 159–60, 162–4, 166–9, 189–98, 209, 230, 262, 265, 273–4
League of Nations, 176, 180–1, 248
Lee of Fareham, Lord and Lady, 255, 312

Lenin, V. I., 18, 20, 21, 177, 211, 251, 269, 299, 304
Lewis, Sir Herbert, 247
Litvinov, M., 118
Lloyd George, D.
  admires free enterprise, 142–3, 181–2, 256–7
  and Bonar Law, 82, 104–19, 160, 161–2, 164, 168, 177–8, 195
  characteristics, 1, 5, 126, 169–70, 179, 255, 300, 310–11
  and Churchill, 19, 29–30, 201–2, 238
  and Conservative Party, 3, 5, 9, 144, 153, 161–3, 169, 176–80, 201–4, 214–15, 241–4, 251–2, 255, 258, 294, 305–7, 314
  dislikes socialism and industrial disputes, 6, 83, 250–1, 255, 308–9, 314
    cotton, 95–7, 100
    mining, 25–6, 114, 133–4, 138, 143–56, 175–6, 188–201, 204–11, 253, 261–4, 272–81, 296–7
    police, 53–76
    railway, 98–105, 114–17, 133–4, 143, 156–60, 219–25, 252, 258–9, 277
    other, 94–5, 105–8
  and Ireland, 3, 215–16, 268–9, 307–9
  and Labour Party, 8–9, 14, 86–90, 131–42, 180, 189, 203, 206, 250–1, 304–6, 311–12
  political manoeuvres, 1, 3, 8, 83, 153, 178–9, 300, 306–8, 310, 314
  and reform, 17, 41, 82–4, 127–30, 178, 203, 240–2, 293, 299, 309, 312
  and Russia, 18–21, 177, 202, 211–15, 270–1, 309
  views on revolution, 14, 17, 22, 83, 91, 175–6, 254–5, 296
Lloyd-Graeme, P., 279
Long, W., 14, 15, 42, 43, 55, 69, 71, 103, 153, 159, 163, 255, 280, 292
Luton, 44

Macarthur, M., 22
MacDonald, J. Ramsay, 4, 8–9, 11–12, 180, 181, 183, 304, 316
Macdonogh, Sir George, 25
Maclay, Sir Joseph, 105, 115, 192
Maclean, J., 118, 295, 311
MacManus, A., 108, 118
MacNamara, T. J., 6, 11
Macpherson, I., 111, 308
Macready, Sir Nevil, 54–71, 77, 78, 79, 215, 253, 265
Mallalieu, F. W., 2
Manchester Guardian, 153
Marston, J., 56, 59, 60, 63, 65, 67, 69, 73, 74
Middle Class Union, 16, 192
Milner, Lord, 4, 5, 6, 11, 13, 24–27, 29, 54, 55, 58, 115
miners, demobilisation of, 25–6, 145, 146
Miners' Federation of Great Britain (MFGB), 128, 143, 144–55, 188–200, 207, 210, 211, 215, 252, 260–4, 273–81, 296, 302
Mining Association of Great Britain (MAGB), 190–4, 208–9
Ministry of Food, 129, 217, 248, 293
Ministry of Labour, 89–90, 97, 115, 130, 131, 140, 147
Money, Sir Leo Chiozza, 206
Montagu, E., 161, 176
Morning Post, 32, 144, 185
Morrison, H., 245
Munro, R., 68, 78, 102, 109, 110, 112, 205
Murray, A., 11–12, 201, 243, 307

Nansen, F., 20
National Alliance of Employers and Employed, 132, 185–6
National Democratic Party, 7, 184, 186
National Federation of Discharged and Demobilised Soldiers and Sailors, 38, 44–5, 46
National Industrial Conference, 67, 87, 90, 121, 130–42, 154, 185, 187, 299–300, 311
National Party, 5, 16, 144
National Socialist Party, 185
National Union of Police and Prison Officers (NUPPO), 53, 56–76
National Union of Railwaymen (NUR), 75, 97–103, 114, 156–60, 216, 219–25, 259, 264, 267, 268, 277
nationalisation, 145, 148, 151, 157, 161, 164–6, 168–9, 178, 188–94, 200, 204–10, 215, 219, 252, 256, 257, 260, 263, 296, 298, 308

naval blockade, 18, 174, 211, 212, 247
naval unrest, 15, 24, 41, 69, 71, 113
New Statesman, 101, 107, 138, 233, 260, 302, 310
Nicoll, Sir William Robertson, 292
Nimmo, Sir Adam, 148, 194
Norman, M., 241
Northcliffe, Lord, 17, 30, 178, 179, 224, 225
Northumberland, Duke of, 192, 227

Observer, 237
O'Grady, J., 74, 185
Oliver, F. S., 5
Orlando, V., 13, 160, 175
out-of-work donation, 91–4, 134–5, 141

Page Arnot, R., 154
Page Croft, Sir Henry, 144
Pankhurst, S., 295–6
Paris Peace Conference 1919, 1, 8, 17, 19, 29, 83, 121, 126, 142, 153, 160, 174–6, 178, 179, 180, 207, 254, 309
Parker, J., 7
Pearce, Sir William, 239
Pease, Sir Alfred, 257
Phillips, M., 248
Poland, 267–72, 296
police unrest, 15, 24, 34, 45, 53–79, 202, 216, 217, 295
press, massaging of, 30, 103, 107, 113, 118, 147, 149, 162–3, 221, 273, 279
Post Office, 69, 115, 200
profiteering, 129, 170, 192, 215, 238, 241, 247–8, 257, 258, 262, 287, 292
Prothero, R. E., 55

Railway Clerks' Association, 69, 114–18
Railway Executive Council, 99, 101–4, 114, 115, 117, 156
Ramsay, D., 118, 119
Ratcliffe-Ellis, Sir Thomas, 194, 208
reparations, 18, 176–8, 188
Restoration of Pre-War Practices Act 1919, 87, 89, 122
Richards, T., 278
Riddell, Sir George, 19, 76, 83, 84, 132, 135, 139, 142, 152, 174, 179, 181, 204, 224, 241, 242, 245, 251, 257, 274, 277–8, 299, 301–3, 308–9
Riddell, Lord *see* Riddell, Sir George
Roberts, G. H., 7, 86, 89, 115, 129, 131, 255
Robertson, Sir William, 28, 63, 109
Romania, 20
Rowntree, S., 223, 224
Runciman, Sir W., 237, 308
Russia, 4, 13, 14, 17–21, 29, 39, 48–9, 113, 136, 153, 177, 192, 198, 201, 247, 293, 294, 304, 309
Russia, intervention with, 18, 20, 25, 26, 31, 44, 46–7, 183, 202, 211–14, 218, 247, 248, 267–72, 296, 302, 311

Salvidge, Sir Archibald, 76
Samuel, H., 237, 296, 308
Sankey Commission 1919, 121, 134, 140, 148, 150–5, 160–2, 165–70, 188–91, 201, 205–9, 260, 261, 262, 299, 311
Scott, C. P., 6, 153
Seely, J. E. B., 33
Selborne, Lord, 191
Shackleton, Sir David, 87, 88, 115, 212–13, 299
Shaw of Dunfermline, Lord, 260, 296
Shinwell, E., 108, 110
Shortt, E., 64, 65, 66, 68–70, 72–3, 76, 78, 79, 102, 111, 112, 118–20, 146, 160
Simon, Sir John, 242, 246
Sinn Fein, 15, 16, 249, 268
Smillie, R., 8, 145, 149–51, 154, 164, 166–8, 175, 190, 192, 200, 210, 223, 259, 260, 262, 273–6
Smith, Sir Allan, 131, 134–8, 141
Smith, Sir Frederick E. *see* Birkenhead, Lord
Smith, H., 199
Smith, Sir Hubert Llewellyn, 200
Smuts, J., 20, 55
Snowden, P., 8, 22
Soldiers', Sailors' and Airmen's Union (SSAU), 33–4, 43
Spackman, W., 69, 74
Spectator, 201
Spoor, B., 303, 316

Stanley, Sir Albert, 25, 96, 98–102, 104–5, 114–15, 127, 146, 156, 158–9, 166, 247
Steel-Maitland, Sir Arthur, 191, 209, 243, 310, 217
Stevenson, F., 153, 155, 242
Strachey, St Loe, 306
Strikes (Exceptional Measures) Bill 1919, 163–5
strikes and lock-outs
  coal
    October 1920, 260, 276–7
    March 1921, 16, 265, 279–81, 298–9
  coal, Yorkshire
    January 1919, 148, 149
    July 1919, 192, 297–200, 206, 210
  cotton, September and November 1918, 95–7
  engineering
    Belfast and Clyde 1919, 19, 31, 97, 105, 295
    March 1922, 281
    London Underground 1919, 102, 105
  police
    August 1918, 53–8
    July 1919, 74–6, 198, 210, 215
  railway, September 1919, 141, 174, 216–25, 298–9
Supply and Transport Committee, 252–5, 264, 265, 266, 274, 278, 279, 300, 311
Sutherland, Sir William, 250, 274

Tariff Reform League, 5, 7
Thiel, T., 53, 55, 56
Thomas, J. H., 29–30, 98–100, 141, 144, 157–8, 179, 182, 183, 185–6, 216–17, 219, 221–2, 224, 259, 264, 268, 272, 274, 281, 301–4, 316
Thomson, B., 13, 18, 34–5, 42, 213, 215, 254, 266, 271
Thorne, W., 38
Thorneycroft, W., 208
Tillett, B., 38, 185, 301
Times, The, 34, 140, 150, 162, 177, 179, 250
Trades Union Congress (TUC), 55, 73, 117, 181, 211–13, 227, 247, 252, 263, 268–71, 313

Transport Workers' Federation, 139, 223, 250
Treasury, 81, 82, 235, 265, 274, 278
Triple Alliance, 45, 87, 97, 113–14, 127, 131, 133–4, 138–41, 143–4, 156, 158–60, 166–7, 174, 183, 202, 205, 211, 216–17, 225, 253, 258–61, 274–5, 280–1, 294, 296, 300–2
Turner, B., 140, 304

unemployment, 4, 91–4, 97, 106, 107–8, 127, 128, 135, 136, 141, 145, 154–5, 163, 249, 256, 309–10, 312

Versailles, Treaty of, 17, 85, 200

Wages (Temporary Regulation) Act 1918, 89, 90, 266
Walkden, A. G., 115
Walker, Sir Herbert, 99, 104
Walsh, S., 278, 290, 301
Wardle, G. J., 7, 115
Webb, B., 10, 13, 99, 150, 154, 172, 182, 183, 220, 221, 224, 296
Webb, S., 151, 154, 172, 182, 189, 206
Wedgwood, J., 180
Weekly Dispatch, 243
Weir, Lord, 190
Wemyss, Admiral, 42
Westminster Gazette, 177
White Russian armies, 20–1, 214
Whitley councils, 90, 131, 133, 135, 140, 184, 186–7, 237, 260, 299, 300, 311
Wickham Steed, H., 177, 226
Williams R., 139, 259
Wilson, Sir Henry, 11, 27–8, 30, 48, 55–6, 176, 201–2, 253–4, 277, 279, 281, 286
Wilson, Woodrow, 18, 160, 175, 176, 177, 180
Wiseman, Sir William, 177
workers' control, 145
Workers' and Soldiers' Councils, 39, 40
Workers' Union, 41, 44, 186
Worthington-Evans, Sir Laming, 32, 45, 83

Yexley, L., 41–2, 51
Younger, Sir George, 244

www.ingramcontent.com/pod-product-compliance
Lightning Source LLC
Chambersburg PA
CBHW070012010526
44117CB00011B/1538